Long Loan

This book is due for return on or before the last date shown below

07 DEC 2007		
25 MAR 2008		

St Martins Services Ltd

The Council on Foreign Relations and American Foreign Policy in the Early Cold War

The Council on Foreign Relations and American Foreign Policy in the Early Cold War

Michael Wala

Providence • Oxford

Published in 1994 by

Berghahn Books
Editorial offices:
165 Taber Avenue, Providence, RI 02906, U.S.A.
Bush House, Merewood Avenue, Oxford OX3 8EF, UK

Library of Congress Cataloging-in-Publication Data
Wala, Michael.
[Winning the peace. English]
The Council on Foreign Relations and American foreign policy in the early Cold War / Michael Wala.
p. cm.
Includes bibliographical references and index.
ISBN 1-57181-003-X : $49.95
1. United States—Foreign relations—1945-1953. 2. Council on Foreign Relations—History—20th century. I. Title.
E813.W35 1994 94-29652
327.73—dc20 CIP

British Library Cataloguing in Publication Data
A CIP catalog record for this book is available from
the British Library.

Cover photo: The Harold Pratt House, the Council on
Foreign Relation's headquarters, 58 East 68th Street, New York, NY

Printed in the United States.

for

GERTRUD and ERNST

and for INGEBORG

Contents

Preface

One of the major concerns in the analysis of American foreign relations is the decision-making process of United States foreign policy. Historians and other scholars try to determine why particular decisions have been arrived at by policy-makers. A number of different — and often sharply differing — models are advanced, suggesting that a variety of factors and prerequisites influence this process. In an attempt to determine the most critical of these influences on the policy-making process, scholars have assigned dominant roles to the American president, Congress, the bureaucracy, the public, public interest groups, elites, and even the "establishment." One of the reasons that such studies often have more to do with educated guessing than with a systematic and analytical approach is the lack of evidence in the form of documents, the historian's main tool to support any interpretations.

The Council on Foreign Relations (CFR) has been singled out in the context of U.S. foreign policy as one of the most influential organizations. Despite the increased attention the Council has received during the last few years, however, little is known about the major aspects of its activities, and a conclusive evaluation of the Council's impact on the decision-making process of American foreign policy is still lacking.

To provide readers with a firm understanding of the Council's role during the crucial years following World War II, this study delineates the Council's activities — its study and discussion groups and its publications — and the activities of Council members in correlation with developing international political, military, and economic situations. Not all relevant events that today, with the wisdom of hindsight, may be regarded as important, received significant attention by the Council. I have tried to depict (without concentrating merely on the more interesting issues) a spectrum of Council activities in order to provide an authentic picture of its mode of operation. This entails developments within the Council as well as differences among Council members. My main emphasis, however, is on the Council's responses to events and developments unfolding in the international arena and its affiliations with the Truman administration.

The original German study, which appeared under the title *Winning the Peace: Amerikanische Außenpolitik und der Council on Foreign Relations, 1945–1950* (Stuttgart, 1990), and the extensive research necessary for the alterations and additions made to this American edition, would not have been possible without the financial support of a number of organizations. I am grateful to the Friedrich-Ebert-Stiftung, the German Academic Exchange Service (DAAD), the Harry S. Truman Library Institute, the German Marshall Fund of the United States, and to the Society for Historians of American Foreign Relations for a Stuart L. Bernath Dissertation Award.

Access to documents and archival collections was granted freely, and I am grateful to the staff of the many libraries I have consulted. Many of them went out of their way to make documents available and to point out important material I would never have found by myself. Despite all of their help, I can only agree with Warren Ohrvahl, archivist at the Harry S. Truman Library, who, after one particular unsuccessful day going through one box of documents after the other without finding anything useful, remarked: "You have to kiss a lot of frogs to find one princess!" — a most appropriate motto, I believe, for historical research.

Many friends, colleagues, and teachers — Allan G. Bogue, John Milton Cooper, Jr., William Diebold, G. William Domhoff, Thomas J. McCormick, Kurt L. Shell, and Winfried Steffani among them — have helped through inspiration, discussion, critique, and support. They may not agree with everything I conclude in my examination of the Council on Foreign Relations, but I am, nevertheless, indebted to all of them. Reinhard R. Doerries, as a teacher and as a friend, has supported this study over the years with patience and highly appreciated advice. Tomas Jaehn assisted me in the translation of chapter 7, and I gratefully acknowledge his support. Sharon Mulak helped tremendously by editing and proofreading the entire manuscript. She spent many hours at this, sustained by friendship and quite a bit of Vic's popcorn. Last but by no means least, I would like to thank Robert Riddell and Marion Berghahn of Berghahn Books; it was a pleasure working with them.

Any factual or interpretive faults in this study are, needless to say, my own responsibility.

Nürnberg and Stanford *M.W.*
June 1993

Introduction

Subversion from "the Right" or from "the Left"?

"The C.F.R.'s [Council on Foreign Relations'] passionate concern for the direction of American foreign policy," Garry Allen, the John Birch Society's expert on conspiracies, claims, "has amounted to an attempt to make certain that policy continues marching Leftwards towards World Government." This allegedly was possible because the Council had totally undermined the Department of State. To Allen, the Council is a "conspiratorial organization" and "the nexus of th[e] organized subversive effort in America."[1]

Whereas Allen maintains that not only the State Department but also the armed forces of the United States have been subverted by this conspiracy, John F. McManus, also an author affiliated with the John Birch Society, even claims that "[t]he Council on Foreign Relations[']... purpose right from its inception was to destroy the freedom and independence of the United States."[2]

While critics from the political right perceive the Council as a front for left-wing, liberal, and even communist interests, liberal left, "revisionist," and "Marxist" students of the Council, although attributing a similar importance to this organization, have deduced a strikingly different mission. This faction perceives the Council as "a central link binding American foreign policy formulation to the corporate upper class." This influence, historian Laurence H. Shoup and sociologist William Minter argue, is responsible for American foreign policies to "have been and . . . [to be] against the interests of the majority of the American people and the people of the world."[3]

1.Gary Allen, *The C.F.R.: Conspiracy to Rule the World* (Belmont, MA, 1969), 1–2 (reprinted from *American Opinion*, April 1969). Not surprisingly, Pat Robertson features a similar understanding of the CFR in his *The New World Order* (Dallas, TX, 1992).

2. John F. McManus, *The Insiders* (Belmont, MA, 1983), 7.

3. Laurence H. Shoup and William Minter, *Imperial Brain Trust: The Council on Foreign Relations and United States Foreign Policy* (New York, 1977), 6, 278–80. Political sociologist G. William Domhoff was the first scholar to study the Council briefly in his *Who Rules America?* (Englewood Cliffs, NJ, 1967), 71–73, and more extensively in his later books. See especially chapters 4 and 5 in his *The Power Elite and the State: How Policy Is Made in America* (New York, 1990), 113–44. See also Laurence H. Shoup and William

This constitutes the peculiar span of the political right and the liberal left analyses of the Council on Foreign Relations' contribution to the United States' foreign policy. Some basic data on the Council, however, can be gathered from sources without assuming an ideological stance: The Council on Foreign Relations, residing in New York City, is primarily occupied with studying and discussing issues of foreign policy and publishing the results of its deliberations. Founded in 1921, with a current membership of more than 2,900, the Council on Foreign Relations has been ascribed an important function since its incorporation. That the Council is without outside control and has refrained from publicity, remaining by choice in the background, has helped to foster the development of conspiratorial theories about its influence and function over the last three decades. These well-publicized theories, based on the assumption that the Council has worked clandestinely as an agent for foreign or domestic interests, are hardly able to provide any insight into the motivations and activities of Council members.

One of the reasons for these speculations (which have even inspired authors of science fiction thrillers[4]) is certainly the problematic situation of sources on the Council on Foreign Relations. Council members and guests invited to meetings are requested to abstain from disclosing information regarding the content of the "off-the-record" gatherings. Thus, the public receives only very scant information on Council activities. Council documents, digests of discussions as well as correspondence between members, have only been partially disclosed, and only since 1975.[5] Important additional information and access to digests of the Council's internal committee meetings, providing pertinent information about the inner workings of the Council, has to be gained through personal papers and collections of individual Council members.

Despite this lack of documentary material, a few serious studies of the Council do exist. Aside from the unscholarly and heavily biased

---

Minter, "The Council on Foreign Relations and American Policy in Southeast Asia," *The Insurgent Sociologist* 7 (Winter 1977): 19–30; and R. Ovinnikov, "U.S. Foreign Policy 'General Staff,'" *International Affairs*, Moscow (November 1979): 62–71.

4. I am referring to the *Illuminatus* trilogy written by Robert Shea and Robert A. Wilson, a mixture of political thriller, science fiction, and modern "acid" fairy tale. The authors pick up the threat cultivated by the Birchers and unfold a tale connecting the 11th century "Order of the Assassins," the "Illuminati" created by professor Adam Weishaupt of Ingolstadt, Germany, in 1776, to the cannabis George Washington is supposed to have grown. See *Illuminatus!: The Eye in the Pyramid* (New York, 1975).

5. The Council on Foreign Relations' Archive is located at the Harold Pratt House, 58 East 68th Street, New York City. Documents are divided in Records of Groups, Records of Meetings, Records of Conferences, Scrapbooks, and War and Peace Studies.

pamphlets and booklets published by the John Birch Society and its disciples, such accounts have occasionally appeared in the form of magazine and newspaper articles.[6] Only a few scholarly studies of the Council are available. Most of these provide brief, unsystematic glimpses of the Council's role in American society and in the decision-making process of U.S. foreign policy. The important period of the early Cold War, which — even after the Cold War has been declared over — determines the current political situation of the world, has not been investigated thoroughly in these accounts, as published studies pay only marginal attention to the decisive years from 1945 to 1950.[7]

The end of World War II, the termination of the War and Peace Studies (the close cooperation between the Council and the State Department which was inaugurated in 1939), and the launching of the Korean War, mark the beginning and end of this period. These events were significant to American and Council history alike.

From the Council's founding until the end of World War II, the organization developed from an elitist men's club to a renowned forum for high-level discussions of experts on international affairs. During World War II, the Council grew into the role of respected advisor and listening post for the attitude of elites throughout the nation.

Based on these experiences, the Council after 1945 continued to participate in a network of public agencies and private organizations bound together through formal and informal ties. In its study and discussion groups the Council could assemble elites drawn from these groups. They collaborated to devise foreign policy by attempting to mediate a consensus (often even before a decision on a specific foreign policy had been reached), which the Council itself could then sustain and support. In addition to playing a pivotal role in this corporatist strategy, the

---

6. John Franklin Campbell, "The Death Rattle of the Eastern Establishment," *New York*, 20 September 1971, 47–51; Carl Gershman, "The Rise and Fall of the New Foreign Policy Establishment," *Commentary* 70 (July 1980): 13–24; Joseph Kraft, "School for Statesmen," *Harper's* (July 1958): 64–68; and J. Anthony Lukas, "The Council on Foreign Relations — Is It a Club? Seminar? Presidium? 'Invisible Government'?," *New York Times Magazine*, 21 November 1971, 34, 123–31, 138, 142.

7. Scholarly accounts by historians include: Robert D. Schulzinger, *The Wise Men of Foreign Affairs: The History of the Council on Foreign Relations* (New York, 1984), providing a good overview of the Council's history from 1921 to the present but rather sketchy and unsubstantial for the early Cold War years and the Council's role in American society; and the aforementioned *Imperial Brain Trust* by Shoup and Minter, with an emphasis on the World War II period. See also Schulzinger, "Whatever Happened to the Council on Foreign Relations?," *Diplomatic History* 5 (Winter 1981): 277–90, for an argument that the Council has lost its momentum and aim since the 1960s.

Council served as a pool for recruitment for high-level posts in State Department and other governmental agencies, and it attempted to educate the American public to support internationalist foreign policy.

1
The Founding of the Council on Foreign Relations:
"To Create and Stimulate International Thought."[1]

The Peace Conference in Paris had been in progress some months when, on 30 May 1919, more than thirty members of the American and British delegations to the Conference met at the Hotel Majestic to discuss the founding of an "Institute for International Affairs." The attending delegates believed that their own delegation's cooperation in Paris had been successful in supporting the League of Nations, a system for peacefully solving conflicts and preventing wars. This system, they were certain, could only function and lead to positive results if in the future national governments abstained from shortsighted, nationalist interests and engaged in cooperation on an international basis.

Their delegation's successful cooperation, they agreed, had been aided by positive international influence on "public opinion." With a view toward future peace conferences, the experts present postulated that they only had to continue the work of expert groups on a private basis — at least in the two English-speaking nations — to ensure the continuation of internationalist world policies. They also admitted, however, their disappointment with some aspects of the conference.[2]

In their eyes the deliberations had also clearly shown not only that the individual delegations judged certain aspects differently, but also that disagreements within the delegations had existed. This, they argued, was based partially on the lack of expertise of some delegates, and, in addition, it was the result of occasional negative pressure exerted by public opinion. The public had been disappointed about the lengthy deliberations in Paris and had pressed for speedy decisions which, in the end, often turned out to be too hasty. The envisioned "Institute for International Affairs," they postulated, would ensure com-

1. From the Council's charter in 1921; cited in CFR, *The Council on Foreign Relations: A Record of Fifteen Years, 1921–1936* (New York, 1937), 8.

2. Whitney H. Shepardson, *Early History of the Council on Foreign Relations* (Stamford, CT, 1960), 1–8.

munication among international experts in the future. It could function as a forum for discussions between experts and interested members of government and might even serve to give an internationalist slant to public opinion.[3]

It was during the numerous meetings at the Peace Conference in 1919 that Lionel Curtis, a member of the British Colonial Office, had established the first informal contacts.[4] Louis Beer in particular, a member of the American delegation and an acquaintance of Curtis from previous occasions, had shown strong interest.[5] Beer succeeded in engaging additional Americans for this endeavor, and soon a score of them participated in the founding of a postwar institution for foreign policy. Before the organizing meeting could finally be agreed upon for 30 May, additional meetings between General Tasker Bliss, Colonel Edward M. House, Archibald Coolidge, Whitney H. Shepardson, James D. Shotwell on the American side, and Lord Robert Cecil, Sir Chirol, Lord Eustace Percy and Harold Temperley, on the British side, had to take place.[6]

After Lord Cecil, head of the British delegation to Paris, had welcomed the guests on May 30, and General Bliss had been asked to take the chair, Curtis was the first to speak to the small audience. He emphasized that public opinion had prejudiced many results of the Paris Peace Conference after the internationalist mood had given way to isolationist

3. CFR, *The Council on Foreign Relations: A Record of Twenty-Five Years, 1921–1946* (New York, 1947), 5.

4. Lionel Curtis, secretary to Lord Milner in 1900 in South Africa, was one of the founding members of the periodical *Round Table*. In 1919, he was a member of the Colonial Office at the British section of the League of Nations. Curtis' biographical data, as well as those of all other individuals mentioned, were culled from so many sources that it would be too lengthy to list them all.

5. Beer was an American businessman, author of several historical studies on the English colonial system of the seventeenth and eighteenth centuries who had taught political science at Columbia University. In 1919, he was a member of the Inquiry and of the American delegation at Paris. Beer had had close contact with Curtis before 1919 and had been the American correspondent for Curtis' *Round Table*. For the Inquiry, see Lawrence E. Gelfand, *The Inquiry* (New Haven, CT, 1963).

6. Tasker Bliss, chief of staff during Word War I, headed the American delegation at Paris; Coolidge taught Eastern European history at Harvard University and was a member of the Inquiry; Shepardson, a Rhodes Scholar, was assistant to Colonel House at Paris; Shotwell taught history at Columbia University and was a member of the Inquiry; Lord Cecil headed the British delegation at Paris; Lord Percy was an emissary of the British Foreign Office at Paris; Harold Temperley, a member of the British Military Section at Paris, was a diplomatic historian at the University of Cambridge. Colonel House, special advisor to President Wilson, was not only accused of being a Marxist by an author affiliated with the John Birch Society, but was also falsely charged with being the authentic founder of the Council; McManus, *The Insiders*, 6–7.

traditions and pressure to conclude the Conference swiftly. Curtis envisioned that in the future

> molding of those settlements would depend upon how far public opinion in those countries would be right or wrong. . . . National policy ought to be shaped by a conception of the interest of society at large; for it was in the advancement of that universal interest that the particular interest of the several nations would alone be found. It [is] of all importance, therefore, to cultivate a public opinion in the various countries of the world which [keeps] the general interest in view.[7]

To reach this aim, he called upon the experts of the Conference to work in close cooperation with each other and to gain the interest of additional specialists for the "Institute for International Affairs." The task of these experts should be

> to create institutes like the Royal Geographic Society, with libraries where the members would study international affairs. The results of their studies could be put in the form of papers for discussion by the members. This would keep officials and publicists in touch with each other. Officials might often have to abstain from discussion of the papers, but there was no reason why they could not listen to them. More important still, the institutes would form centers where they could converse on these subjects.[8]

Most of the speakers of the evening supported Curtis' suggestions. Only Eyre Crowe, assistant under secretary of the Foreign Office, pointed out possible dangers that might result from a too close cooperation among government officials, institute members, and private individuals.[9] Opinions of government officials, he feared, would unduly influence the opinion of the other members and might thus dominate public opinion. Through such a mechanism, Crowe maintained, a free and independent voicing of opinion in the society at large would decay. The members of the organizing meeting concurred that such dangers existed, but they nevertheless maintained that abandoning the founding of an Institute of International Affairs would entail the much more serious danger of un- or misguided foreign policy.[10]

After some discussion Curtis, at the end of the evening, suggested the creation of a planning committee, consisting of three Americans and

7. "Minutes of Meeting at Hotel Majestic, May 30, 1919," cited in M.L. Dockrill, "Historical Note: The Foreign Office and the 'Proposed Institute of International Affairs 1919,'" *International Affairs* 56 (Fall 1980): 665–72.

8. *Ibid.*

9. Crowe was only present as a guest and did not participate in the founding of the Institute.

10. Dockrill, "Historical Note," 667.

three British experts, to work out suggestions for the founding of institutes in the United States and in Great Britain and to present their findings at a subsequent meeting. Informal talks between the men present and another meeting (held on 9 June) had to take place before 17 June, when the "Institute for International Affairs, Founded at Paris, 1919" could finally be established.[11] Until the Institutes were actually organized, however, the American and British outfits existed only formally. Making apparent what membership the Institutes should require, it was agreed that future members would have to meet high criteria to ensure that fresh and innovative ideas on foreign policy could be gained.[12]

The founding of the Institutes corresponded with the founding of the League of Nations. The Allies in Paris had made clear, through the proposed establishment of the supranational organization, that future nationalist politics would have to meet the premises of the "welfare of society at large," and the founding of the Institute of International Affairs gave support to this aim. "The proceedings at Paris have shown," a communiqué by Shepardson reads, "how necessary it is to create some organization for studying the relations of this principle to practical questions as they arise." While the task of the League of Nations was to mediate foreign policy measures of the member-states and to prevent conflict between all nations, the institutes were to coordinate public opinion in the individual countries and to provide national bases for a frictionless functioning of the League.[13]

Returning home, however, the founding members had to realize that very different conditions existed in their respective countries. In Great Britain the active work of the Institute met with support of the British Foreign Office. A residence was found swiftly and already by July of the next year the "British Institute of International Affairs" could start its activities. In August 1920, with the blessings of Lord Cecil and Foreign Minister Arthur James Balfour, its headquarters was opened.[14]

On the American side the efforts of Shotwell, Coolidge, and Shepardson soon came to a standstill. Unlike the membership in Great Britain, where most lived in the central London area, most American

---

11. James T. Shotwell, *At the Paris Peace Conference* (New York, 1937), 347, 367.

12. "Minutes of Meeting of American Institute of International Affairs, October 20, 1920," Tasker Bliss Papers, box 366, Library of Congress, Washington, D.C.

13. Shepardson, *Early History*, 3.

14. Shepardson, "American Institute of International Affairs, Memorandum, November 9, 1920," Bliss Papers, box 366.

members were scattered in Washington, New York, Boston and other cities on the East Coast. Additionally, Shotwell soon went to Europe and was not available for future organizational work for the Americans.[15]

In the United States the League of Nations had not found as much public and congressional support as it had in Europe. The Senate did not pass the Paris Treaty, and the good American-British relations experienced a setback. In this situation Shepardson had to realize that it was impossible to even obtain suggestions on the future organizational design and tasks of the American Institute from the few founding members. A common Anglo-American endeavor to educate the public on behalf of the League of Nations seemed impossible in this time of heated debates in the United States.

In a letter to Thomas Lamont, Shepardson wrote that he did not think it advisable at this time to press for more concrete steps. In this vein he apologized in March 1920 to Lionel Curtis for the inactivity of the American members with a reference to their "physical and spiritual breakdown." The venture seemed to have come to a dead end when suddenly, in the fall of 1920, the possibility of a merger with the members of another internationalist group, the Council on Foreign Relations, arose.[16]

This Council had started as a somewhat loose gathering of bankers and other members of the business community in the New York area. Invited by Elihu Root, secretary of state under President Theodore Roosevelt, some members of the elite Metropolitan Club had met on 10 June 1918, and had founded the Council as a sort of dinner club. The task of this organization was

> to afford a continuous conference on foreign affairs, bringing together at each meeting international thinkers so that in the course of a year several hundred minds in finance, industry, education, statecraft and science will have been brought to bear on international problems.[17]

---

15. Shepardson, *Early History*, 8. Shotwell collected material in Europe and contacted possible contributors to his encyclopedic *Economic and Social History of the War*, which he planned to publish for the Carnegie Endowment for International Peace. See Stephen King-Hall, *Chatham House: A Brief Account of the Origins, Purposes, and Methods of the Royal Institute of International Affairs* (London, 1937), 14.

16. Shepardson to Thomas W. Lamont, 10 February 1920, cited in Terry L. Deibel, "The Council on Foreign Relations and the League of Nations Controversy," 30 May 1970 (on page 1: *Confidential*: Not for Publication), 13–14, Hamilton Fish Armstrong Papers, box 22, Seeley G. Mudd Manuscript Library, Princeton University, Princeton, NJ; Shepardson to Curtis, 11 March 1920, *ibid.*

17. Schulzinger, *The Wise Men*, 5. The quotation is from CFR, *Handbook* (New York, 1919). The tasks proposed in March 1918 were quite comprehensive:

During occasional dinner meetings, the members discussed aspects of foreign policy and international trade. The first meetings had taken place in June 1918, and some of the following meetings were attended by foreign business partners and politicians. While the members were mainly interested in international trade, they were also eager to receive information on the political and legal framework of international commerce. They considered the security of trade and treaties important prerequisites for an undisturbed exchange of goods between nations, and favored the League of Nations as an organization that would ensure unhampered transnational business connections and a peaceful community of nations. They also placed a high value on the idealistic content of the supranational organization. When, on the evening of 25 July 1919, some speakers emphasized short-term economic advantages made possible by the League, the majority pointed out that a peaceful world was more important than short-term profits.[18]

Although this original Council had held a number of meetings on a variety of foreign policy topics, during the summer of 1920 the almost one hundred and fifty members had to admit that interest in future meetings was subsiding. The organization had a sound financial basis but seemed to be without an apparent task and international standing. In late summer of 1920, therefore, the members of this original Council offered the American Institute of International Affairs a merger under the name of the Institute.[19]

Thus, the American Institute invited its members to a meeting on 18 October 1920. It was still a "paper organization with high purposes but no locale or definite program and no finances except the $10 annual

---

1. To stimulate and organize international thought; 2. To create good will for the United States in foreign lands; 3. To discourage unjust attacks in the United States on foreign countries; 4. To cooperate and advise with existing international organizations and to encourage the formation of international forums throughout the United States.

See "Proposed Plan 'International Council or Council of Foreign Affairs or Council of International Intercourse,'" attached to Douglas L. Dunbar to Albert Shaw, 6 March 1918, Albert Shaw Papers, box 139, New York Public Library, New York, NY.

18. Deibel, "The Council," 7–8. See also folder on the Council in the Otto H. Kahn Papers, box 132, Firestone Library, Princeton University, Princeton, NJ.

19. Shepardson, *Early History*, 10. During the period between the first meeting and April of 1919, the Council met on 14 occasions. See Robert F. Byrnes, "Encouraging American Interest in World Affairs in the 1920's: The Council on Foreign Relations and *Foreign Affairs*," in: *Ostmitteleuropa: Berichte und Forschungen* (Stuttgart, 1981), 392, Ulrich Haustein, Georg W. Strobel and Gerhard Wagner, eds. Otto H. Kahn to Lindsay Russell, 4 October 1920, Kahn Papers, box 132.

dues of its 21 members." In addition to the founding members, eleven more members were welcomed. The most important topic of this meeting, however, was the merger with the Council on Foreign Relations. American presidential elections were less than a month away and the candidate of the Republican Party, Warren J. Harding, who was considered the most likely winner of this election, raised fears about a new isolationist course of American foreign policy.[20]

For internationalists and supporters of the League of Nations, this was a depressing prospect; however, Shepardson told the members of the American Institute about the Council on Foreign Relations' offer. After a lengthy discussion, the members present agreed upon a membership committee to work out the conditions of the merger. After talks with Council members, Shepardson, on 9 November, informed the members of the Institute about the latest development.[21] He told them that the Council had unanimously agreed on a merger of the two organizations; unfortunately, the Council wanted to keep the membership dues at its high level of one hundred dollars per year, which was much more than the members of American Institute were willing to pay.

Two other aspects of the merger, however, raised more concern than the question of membership dues. The founding members of the Institute had agreed in Paris that the organization should encompass the whole spectrum of political and economic thought. Shepardson considered it questionable that this would still be possible with the Council's membership as it was, composed mostly of businessmen. In addition, doubts had been raised as to whether these busy members would find it possible or would have the necessary time to take part in study or discussion groups. To create a basis for his future dealings with the Council, Shepardson asked the Institute members for their opinions on these points.[22]

In the few answers that Shepardson received, the members shared his reservations. Ray Stannard Baker (who had taken part in the meetings in Paris but did not become a member of the Institute until 1920) wrote that he did not agree with isolationist press magnate William Randolph

20. Hamilton Fish Armstrong, *Peace and Counterpeace: From Wilson to Hitler* (New York, 1971), 182. All eleven men (including Hamilton Fish Armstrong, the future editor of the Council's publication *Foreign Affairs*) invited to become members of the "Institute" accepted membership. See Shepardson, *Early History*, 10; Armstrong, *Peace and Counterpeace,* 183.

21. "Minutes of Meeting, October 18, 1920," Bliss Papers, box 366.

22. Shepardson, "*American Institute of International Affairs*: Memorandum, November 9, 1920," Bliss Papers, box 366.

Hearst that the League of Nations would mainly be supported by "international bankers," but it was, nevertheless, a fact that "the charge, however unfair, has had some effect and it will make the work of any council constituted as this . . . highly difficult."[23]

Additional responses that Shepardson solicited addressed the same concern. Professor Coolidge, one of the founding members of the American Institute, believed that a "least inglorious retreat" might be to turn the Institute over to an academic organization. A merger with an "association of bankers," he agreed with Baker, seemed very problematic. Even Hamilton F. Armstrong, who later very successfully was to guide the Council's publication, *Foreign Affairs*, for almost 50 years, feared that the members of the "old" Council were on a "far too 'sound financial basis' to care much about facts in conflict with their usual outlook," and voted "emphatically against the proposal" to merge.[24]

On 2 December 1920, Shepardson sent a second memorandum to the members. After summarizing what had taken place, he informed the members that a merger with the Council under the name of the American Institute was no longer possible. The Council, however, had meanwhile made changes in the structure and tasks of its organization, so that it now more closely resembled the organization that the founding members had had in mind.

Thus, journalists, lawyers, publishers, and members of academia were to be invited to become members, and the Council was planning to publish occasional scholarly articles and monographs "which deserved to be read on their merit as scholarly, non-propaganda statements." Additionally, the Council had agreed on a dues structure that would make memberships possible for this new group. Meanwhile, Williams College had initiated the "Institute for Politics," which had aims similar to those of the American Institute. The American Institute, therefore, seemed to be obsolete. Confronted with the alternatives of either giving up their plans completely or joining the now more attractive Council on Foreign Relations, the members agreed with Shepardson's advice to a merger on the Council's terms.[25]

---

23. Baker to Shepardson, 15 November 1920, cited in Deibel, "The Council," 18.

24. Coolidge to Shepardson, 24 November 1920, cited in Deibel, "The Council," 18; Shepardson to Baker, 17 November 1920, *ibid.* Armstrong to Shepardson, 6 December 1920, Armstrong Papers, box 57. I am grateful to Ben Primer for pointing out this letter to me.

25. Russell to Kahn, 15 November 1920, Kahn Papers, box 132. Shepardson, "Memorandum, December 2, 1920," Bliss Papers, box 366. Actually, Shepardson abandoned

While in November it had seemed that the organization envisioned in Paris was bound to fail, the work that Shepardson, Coolidge, and Shotwell had taken upon themselves now turned out to be successful after all through the possible merger with the old Council on Foreign Relations. Already by that December, both organizations agreed upon a "Committee on Policy" headed by the former Attorney General George W. Wickersham.[26] This committee, consisting of seven members,[27] was to plan the organizational set-up and the tasks of the new Council on Foreign Relations. After it met for the first time, on 3 January 1921, the committee assembled regularly in rented rooms on 43rd Street in Manhattan and invited a number of carefully chosen men to become members of the new Council. Meanwhile, Wickersham and Polk drafted a charter of the new organization and discussed possible appointees for the posts of directors.[28] When the new Council on Foreign Relations was finally incorporated on 29 July 1921, the directorate of the Council consisted of Honorary President Elihu Root, President John W. Davis, Vice President Paul D. Cravath and Secretary Edwin F. Gay.[29]

The founding of the Council on Foreign Relations in 1921, to a large degree, was based on the personal and special experience of the members of the American delegation to the Paris Peace Conference and reflected to a certain degree the work of the group of experts assembled in the Inquiry. But it was also part of a larger internationalist movement within the United States.

---

ship early in December and joined the Council to immediately become executive secretary. See Russell to Herbert S. Houston [Doubleday, Page & Co.], 9 December 1920, Kahn Papers, box 132.

26. Shepardson, *Early History*, 14–15; Wickersham to Tasker Bliss, 14 July 1921, Bliss Papers, box 367. The Republican Wickersham had served from 1909 to 1913 as attorney general.

27. Wickersham, Shepardson, William C. Grace (a manager of the old Council), lawyer Frank L. Polk (former under secretary of state), banker Paul Warburg, Edwin F. Gay (editor of the *New York Evening News*) and Columbia University professor William R. Shepard.

28. Shepardson, *Early History*, 15–17. Almost half of the old Council's membership had used the opportunity to terminate their memberships.

29. Root, a lawyer and one of the most popular Republicans of his time, had been secretary of state under President Theodore Roosevelt. He had become the first president of the Carnegie Endowment for International Peace. Davis, also a lawyer and formerly American ambassador to Great Britain, had been a Representative to Congress from West Virginia and was to become, in 1924, an unsuccessful opponent of Calvin Coolidge's for the presidency. Cravath was a senior partner of the Cravath, Swaine and Moore law firm in New York. On Davis, see also William H. Harbaugh, *Lawyer's Lawyer: The Life of John W. Davis* (New York, 1973). The Council's charter is enclosed in Grace to Davis, 7 November 1921, John W. Davis Papers, box 6, Sterling Library, Yale University, New Haven, CT.

As early as 1910, the industrialist and philanthropist Andrew Carnegie had founded the Carnegie Endowment for International Peace (CEIP), a small group composed mostly of intellectual internationalists.[30] The League of Free Nations (LFN), founded in 1918 as the Committee on Nothing at All, had tried to educate the public and supported American participation in the League of Nations in 1919.[31] In the same year that the old Council and the American Institute merged, the Woodrow Wilson Foundation was organized. This group, consisting of a number of influential politicians, members of the business community, and members of academia, defined their task as the fostering of the internationalist ideals President Wilson had originated.[32] Two years later, in 1923, the League of Nations Non-Partisan Association (LNNPA) was formed, with the help of Republican George Wickersham and the democrat and former supreme court Judge John H. Clarke, to influence public opinion in order to persuade the United States to join the League of Nations.[33]

Despite some differences all of these international groups had a somewhat homogeneous membership: they consisted almost exclusively of men from the American east coast and with few exceptions, they were Anglo-Saxon and Protestants. They had close business, cultural, and social relationships with one another, and they were mostly anglophiles. Wealthy, part of the upper class, and educated at elite schools and colleges, they had hardly any contact with the "man on the street," middle management, and small businesses. The internationalism they preached

---

30. The records of the Carnegie Endowment for International Peace can be found in the Butler Library, Columbia University, New York, NY. For the history of the Endowment's founding, see Larry L. Fabian, *Andrew Carnegie's Peace Endowment: The Tycoon, the President, and Their Bargain of 1910* (Washington, D.C., 1985).

31. After the American decision against the League, the League of Free Nations was renamed the Foreign Policy Association (FPA). See Paul U. Kellogg, *Ten Years of the Foreign Policy Association* (New York, 1929), 7–15; Wolfgang Helbich, "American Liberals in the League of Nations Controversy," *Public Opinion Quarterly* 31.4 (1967): 568–96.

32. Frank Freidel, *Franklin D. Roosevelt: The Ordeal* (Boston, 1954), 124; Edith E. Ware, ed., *The Study of International Relations in the United States* (New York, 1945), 34.

33. Clarke was associate justice of the Supreme Court from 1916 to 1922 and served as president of the LNNPA until 1928. The League of Nations Non-Partisan Association, later renamed League of Nations Association (LNA), was, until the establishment of the United Nations organization, headed by Clark M. Eichelberger. The LNA was one of the central organizations of U.S. internationalism. On these groups, see also Ruhl J. Bartlett, *The League to Enforce Peace* (Chapel Hill, NC, 1944); Raymond B. Fosdick, *Chronicle of a Generation: An Autobiography* (New York, 1958); Clark M. Eichelberger, *Organizing for Peace: A Personal History of the Founding of the United Nations* (New York, 1977), 9–10, 14–15.

addressed, at least rhetorically, all citizens of the United States. However, its primary audience was mainly only other internationalists or the members of what has been termed the "foreign policy establishment."[34]

The internationalism they advocated was an internationalism of grand ideas. A close examination of its content or aspects of its legal and practicable realization was hardly ever performed. The most important demand these internationalists made was that nations should avoid, through discussion, mediation, and compromise, any clashes or wars. As soon as concrete plans and proposals were opted for, however, the members' ability to reach a consensus was often overtaxed. Their conservative internationalism — not unusual for that time — did not envision the participation of countries outside of the United States and Europe as main actors. Such peripheral countries played no important role in their plan for a League of Nations and in the overall international arena, except possibly as markets and suppliers of cheap raw materials.

"Public opinion," for the members of these groups, had a limited definition and was synonymous with a small group of people having the means to inform and influence large parts of the public. Their idea of "public opinion" was shaped by paternalism and the firm consciousness of belonging to an elite. From their own experience they knew that senators and representatives as well as government officials would listen to them and pay attention to their opinions.

These men believed they represented the "real" public opinion, working for the good of the nation and, further, for the good of all nations, bringing enlightenment to the "uneducated." In this respect the internationalism of the 1920s and the 1930s was far removed from the bases of politics and from its constituencies.

It was common among all of these organizations to try to sway public opinion toward an internationalist foreign policy and Wilsonian ideals. Whereas the Foreign Policy Association — and also the League of Nations Association and the Woodrow Wilson Foundation — promoted American participation in the League of Nations, the Council on Foreign Relations abstained from such support. This was not only

34. The term "foreign policy establishment" describes members of organizations, such as the groups mentioned here, who were actively interested in foreign affairs. The term is related to Adler/Bobrow's "influencials" and Almond's "foreign policy elite." See Kenneth P. Adler and Davis Bobrow, "Interest and Influence in Foreign Affairs," *Public Opinion Quarterly* 20.1 (1956): 89–101; and Gabriel A. Almond, *The American People and Foreign Policy* (New York, 1950).

because of their non-partisan credo, but also because they had realized that after 1920, the term "League of Nations" had very disadvantageous connotations. The detour they took, by cultivating an interest in internationalist foreign policy and thereby fostering participation in a supranational organization, seemed to need time to mature. By biding their time, Council members hoped that an internationalist consciousness could take root and have a much stronger impact.

Therefore, the Council on Foreign Relations refrained from taking explicit positions in foreign policy debates and instead planned a studies and discussion program and the publication of a quarterly journal on aspects of foreign policy. This was not a retreat from the aims that had been envisioned in 1919 in Paris, and it did not run counter to the personal judgment of the League of Nations proponents among the Council members. In comparison with other international groups the Council was only more elite, had higher expectations of its organization and its members, and had ambitions that went beyond the League of Nations.

The public that had to be educated was therefore limited to those members of society who had influence on the media and politics and to experts in a number of important fields. The founders of the Council had envisioned the building of a foundation for a new kind of American foreign policy, which was no short-term goal. The mood of a particular administration's election campaign, in which even "uneducated" public opinion was important, should not determine the future of the foreign policy of the nation; it should be determined by a pragmatic opinion of experts, based on rational judgment and analysis.

The discussion groups of Council members and the participation of State Department officials, on the one side, and the publication of the proposed quarterly — *Foreign Affairs* — for an interested public, on the other, were used as means to achieve these aims. This combination, the members thought, should help to build a consensus, not of the broad public, but of the elites of finance and business, of academicians at prestigious universities, and of "responsible" officials in the State Department. This was to serve as the basis and legitimization of foreign policy decisions. When results of the discussion at the Council were considered important and relevant, they could be published in *Foreign Affairs*. These articles would spread important information and analyses, and they could serve indirectly as background information for the executive agencies.

The declaration of its main tasks — actually very similar to Lionel Curtis' visions in Paris, 1919, and to the original Council's credo — makes the intentions of the Council on Foreign Relations quite clear:

> To afford a continuous conference on international questions affecting the United States, by bringing together experts on statecraft, finance, industry, education and science;
>
> To create and stimulate international thought among the people of the United States, and to this end to cooperate with the government of the United States and with international agencies.[35]

35. Cited in CFR, *A Record of Twenty-Five Years*, 7.

2
The Council on Foreign Relations to 1945:
From Men's Club to Brain Trust

Through its merger with the original Council on Foreign Relations the membership and the intellectual and political spectrum of the American Institute of International Affairs was enlarged considerably. The Institute consisted of a small number of interested experts, while the old Council had been not much more than a club of well-to-do men gathering for occasional dinner meetings. Only through the influx of members from the American Institute could the new Council actually organize a discussion and study group program for its new membership, for those experts from outside and including the inner circle of New York's financial and academic community.

Study and discussion groups in the following years would not only bring together a large number of experts from industry, finance, and the academic community, but would also include foreign politicians willing, sometimes eager, to address Council audiences. Additionally, close cooperation with the State Department, to a large degree based on the work of these groups of experts, could be established. During World War II and especially through the War and Peace Studies, the Council advanced into the position of a brain trust for the Department of State.

The Council's task of "educating the public" and fostering a better understanding of foreign affairs was enhanced not only by the numerous meetings of Council members with foreign dignitaries and American politicians; frequently, published studies on aspects of international relations, especially the publication of the quarterly *Foreign Affairs*, also helped considerably. While a program for the envisioned study and discussion groups could not be launched immediately, preparations for the Council's quarterly proceeded rapidly; already by 1922, little more than a year after the Council was established, the first volume left the printing press.

Foreign Affairs

The initial suggestions to publish *Foreign Affairs* came from the Council's secretary Edwin F. Gay. Dean of Harvard Business School and, during World War I, active on the War Industries Board, Gay knew the publishing business quite well. In 1919, he had been appointed as editor of Thomas Lamont's paper the *New York Evening Post.*[1] If the Council wanted to educate the public, Gay suggested, publication of a magazine would be the most fitting thing to do. The quarterly could also serve a second purpose and function as a symbol for an *esprit de corps* for those Council members unable to participate in study and discussion groups. It was decided that the magazine should be published at least four times a year and that it was to contain original and intellectually attractive articles on foreign policy. On the question of editorship, Gay had already conferred with Isaiah Bowman. Both had agreed that Harvard professor Archibald C. Coolidge would be the most appropriate person for the task.[2]

Russia-expert Coolidge, contacted while he was traveling in the Soviet Union, did not react very enthusiastically to Gay's suggestion. Teaching classes at Harvard and directing the Widener Library occupied a large part of his time. He did not want to give up teaching, nor did he want to perform his duties for the Council's publication only half-heartedly. The employment of a managing editor, Coolidge indicated, would be a solution in this predicament. Without naming names — but having a suitable person clearly in mind — Coolidge suggested that the person should be about thirty years old and for discussion purposes should be called "A." This "fictive" person consenting to take up the assignment was soon revealed to be Council member Hamilton Fish Armstrong, who was, at the time, the correspondent for the *New York Evening Post* in Europe and acquainted with Coolidge from earlier occasions.[3]

Upon his return in early June from Europe, where he had received the Council's offer, Armstrong found that everything for his new function had been prepared. A small office on Manhattan's 34th Street had

1. Shepardson, *Early History*, 17–18; Armstrong, *Peace and Counterpeace*, 110; Thomas W. Lamont, *Across World Frontiers* (New York, 1951), 101. Gay was proposed for Council membership by Lamont. In 1922 he returned to Harvard University to teach economics. For an overview of the publication's history, see William G. Hyland, "Foreign Affairs at 70," *Foreign Affairs* (hereafter cited as FA) 71 (Fall 1992): 171–93.

2. Shepardson, *Early History*, 18; Armstrong, *Peace and Counterpeace*, 143–44; "Memo of Interview with Dr. Gay Regarding Council on Foreign Relations," 30 September 1941, Rockefeller Foundation Records (hereafter cited as RFR), 1/100/97/875, Rockefeller Archives Center, North Tarrytown, NY. Bowman was a director of the Council.

3. Copy, Coolidge to Gay, 17 March 1922, enclosure to Gay to Davis, 17 March 1922, John W. Davis Papers, box 16, partially reprinted in Armstrong, *Peace and Counterpeace*, 144–45.

been rented and the first suggestions for layout and organization of the projected periodical were already on his desk. Armstrong knew well that Coolidge would only sporadically travel from Cambridge to New York and that the major part of the work would rest on his shoulders.[4]

Before possible contributors for the important and standard-setting first issue could be approached, however, the financing of the new periodical had to be solved. The members of a newly established editorial board agreed to raise the necessary funds among Council members. The amount of $25,000, regarded as necessary to cover expenses for the first year, could be procured easily, and an offer from banker Otto H. Kahn (who obviously had been skeptical about the Council members' generosity) to cover any amount not solicited among Council members, did not have to be used.[5] After Frank D. Caruthers, Jr. of the *New York Evening Post* was persuaded to take the position of "business manager," and with Cass Canfield from the same paper "on loan" to help Council President John W. Davis win subscribers for the new magazine, the staff looked almost like a branch of the *Evening Post*.[6]

During the next weeks the managing editor was busy enticing authors for the first issue. In particular, the author for the first issue's lead article was considered with exceptional care. Armstrong tried to win Elihu Root, internationalist Republican and well-known elder statesman of the 1920s, for this important contribution. However, it turned out to be difficult to enlist him. Only after Armstrong employed the persuasive powers of his father-in-law, lawyer James Byrne, did Root concede to contribute an article entitled "A Requisite for the Success of Popular Diplomacy."[7]

Root accomplished almost more than Armstrong might have expected, since the first sentence of the essay outlined the Council's major

4. The title-page emblem for *Foreign Affairs* to this day features a horseback rider, the motto "Ubique," and the calligraphic title, designed by Armstrong's sisters Margaret and Helen. See Armstrong, *Peace and Counterpeace*, 181, 185–88.

5. Coolidge received $4,000 per annum for his work, about half of what he earned at Harvard, and Armstrong's salary amounted to $2,000.

6. Among the members of the Editorial Board were Isaiah Bowman, George Blakeslee (member of the "Inquiry", editor of *Journal of International Relations*, and since 1914 teaching history at Clark University), John W. Davis, Stephen Duggan, Edwin Gay, and George Wickersham. See CFR, *A Record of Twenty-Five Years*, 35. Within a short time, Armstrong succeeded William Grace as "general manager" of the Council. For this he received another $2,000 yearly — a stately income for a young man at the time. See Armstrong, *Peace and Counterpeace*, 185.

7. Armstrong, *Peace and Counterpeace*, 188–89.

task in American foreign relations: "The control of foreign relations by democracies creates a new and pressing demand for popular education in international affairs." This was exactly what the Council on Foreign Relations had set out to achieve. The United States would stand at the threshold to a new era, Root wrote in 1922, an era of internationalism. In the past the United States had been primarily concerned with its own affairs and, being so distant from Europe, had followed an isolationist policy. After the events of World War I and the United States' participation, however, the situation had changed dramatically. The citizens of the United States had to comprehend the special position and responsibility of their nation in the world and they had to learn what was in their interest as a nation.[8]

In addition to obtaining Root's impressive contribution, Armstrong had solicited a number of other eminent authors for essays and articles. Edvard Benes, foreign minister of the newly established Czechoslovakia (and later to become Thomas G. Masaryk's successor as president), wrote about the "Little Entente." Historian Josef Redlich, last minister of finance of the Hapsburg monarchy of Austria and Hungary, supplied an article on the "Reconstruction of the Danube Countries," and John Foster Dulles, financial advisor to the American delegation in Paris in 1919, contributed an essay on future economic problems of the European nations.[9]

That one of the articles in the first issue was published under a pseudonym must have surprised many readers. Addressing an important aspect of the new international political situation after the war, "K" outlined possibilities and problems in Soviet Russia. Hardly a secret among better-informed circles, the author "K" was no other than the editor Coolidge himself. With his contribution Coolidge directly touched upon a very important aspect of American foreign policy — the nonrecognition of the Soviet Union by the United States. This topic was being fervently discussed in interested circles and provoked heated debates in Council meetings. Coolidge, the leading expert on Russia of his time, discussed in his article the prerequisites of diplomatic relations between these two most powerful nations. The USSR, he wrote, had disavowed all imperialistic inclination but had also made clear that it

8. Elihu Root, "A Requisite for the Success of Popular Diplomacy," *FA* 1.1 (1922): 1.

9. Edvard Benes, "The Little Entente," *FA* 1.1 (1922): 66–72; Joseph Redlich, "Reconstruction of the Danube Countries," *FA* 1.1 (1922): 73–85; John F. Dulles, "The Allied Debts," *FA* 1.1 (1922): 133–55. The Little Entente had been created as a defensive pact between Czechoslovakia, Yugoslavia, and Romania to deter possible Hungarian aggressions.

had legitimate national interests. Stressing the issue of foreign trade, Coolidge asked his readers if the United States should refrain from selling harvesting machines to Russian farmers only because Americans resented the political system in Moscow. "To recognize the government of a country," he wrote, "does not imply that we admire it, it is merely to take note of an existing fact." A copy of this first issue actually found its way into the Soviet Union and was read by Lenin and Karl Radek (a member of the central committee of the ruling Communist Party of the Soviet Union). Both might have hoped that a change in American policy toward the USSR was likely. But Coolidge's arguments were without influence in 1922. Not until 1933, under the Democratic President Franklin D. Roosevelt, were official diplomatic relations with the Soviet Union established, and such ties were made for precisely these commercial reasons advanced by Coolidge, albeit in a time of economic depression and a frantic search for foreign markets.[10]

When Coolidge and Armstrong had discussed the content of the first issue, they had readily agreed that an immense interest in Soviet-American relations existed. Coolidge had indicated that he would like to contribute an essay on this topic. He believed, however, that such a contribution by the editor would raise doubts as to the non-partisanship of the magazine. Supporting Coolidge's reservations, Armstrong agreed that his article should appear under a pseudonym.[11] In this, also, the first issue set a standard: articles under such imaginative pseudonyms as "V," "E," "B," "alpha," "Kapi," "H," and "C" were published in the following years.

The quarterly was, like the Council on Foreign Relations itself, intended to provide a forum for a broad spectrum of opinion. In the preface to the first edition the editors claimed that articles "do not represent any consensus of belief . . . but we hold that . . . *Foreign Affairs* can do more to guide American opinion by a broad hospitality to divergent ideas than it can by identifying itself with one school." The editors kept their promise: over the next years, articles and essays written by very diverse authors were printed in *Foreign Affairs.*[12]

10. For a thorough account of the events leading to Coolidge's contribution, see Armstrong, *Peace and Counterpeace*, 188–95. The copy with Lenin's and Radek's comments was given to Armstrong by a former student of Coolidge's, historian Frank A. Golder. See Elisabeth Jakab, "The Council on Foreign Relations," Book Forum 3.4 (1978): 424; Armstrong, *Peace and Counterpeace*, 194. It is now in the Council Archives and was proudly presented to Mikhail Gorbachev when he visited the Council in 1992.

11. "K" [Archibald C. Coolidge], "Russia after Genoa and the Hague," FA 1.1 (1922): 133–55; Armstrong, *Peace and Counterpeace*, 192.

12. "Editorial Statement," *FA* 1.1 (1922).

Aside from financial resources and contributors, every publication needs readers. Before the first issue was ready to go to the printer in September 1922, this was another concern with which the small staff at 34th Street had to cope. The editors had hoped that at least 500 subscribers could be found. Their expectations were more than satisfied. When the first copies were mailed on 13 September 1922, the quarterly already had more than 1,000 subscribers; and, for the next issue in December, their number had grown to more than 2,700. *Foreign Affairs* apparently satisfied a demand in academic and business circles for information, solidly based opinion, and analysis on matters of foreign policy.[13]

More importantly, the first edition of *Foreign Affairs* set the standard for all following issues in its advocating a bipartisan support of foreign policy. That the Republican Root was asked to write the leading article was by no means pure coincidence. It also reflected the objective of the editors to demonstrate that the quarterly was to be, and indisputably so, non-partisan. *Foreign Affairs,* like the Council itself, was to signal that differences between the Democratic and the Republican parties in foreign policy could be mastered. As with the bipartisan foreign policy after World War II, the possibility and opportunity for an internationalist foreign policy of the United States, transcending all party lines, was to be demonstrated. This the founders of Council and *Foreign Affairs* believed to be especially important in a time when there was still heated discussion about why America did not participate in the League of Nations.

Hardly any reader, however, would have been mislead to believe that the quarterly was really indifferent to all varieties of opinions about American foreign policy. It was apparent, from the very first issue, that the Council's major aim was to promote internationalism and an active American foreign policy. The motivation for the creation of *Foreign Affairs,* Armstrong wrote in his memoirs, was explicitly, if unintentionally, laid out in Root's essay. Root had remarked that in a democracy, as opposed to a monarchy, a means existed to prevent the people from having an "erroneous" opinion. "That way is to furnish the whole people," he wrote,

> as a part of their ordinary education, with correct information upon their own rights, about the duties to respect the rights of others, about what has happened and is happening in international affairs, and about the effects upon national life of the things that are done or refused as between nations; so that the people themselves will have the means to test misinformation and appeals to prejudice and passion based upon error.[14]

13. Armstrong, *Peace and Counterpeace,* 195.

14. Root, "A Requisite," 5.

To be sure, what Root or Armstrong considered as right or erroneous opinion was never clearly defined, neither in *Foreign Affairs* nor by the Council. Only on a few very fundamental premises was there a consensus among Council members and those responsible for *Foreign Policy*: the United States, as the most powerful nation in the world, had to follow a more determined and active foreign policy; trade should be conducted with all nations, wherever possible; and access to raw materials and markets of the whole world should be secured for the United States. Root had written:

> Our people have been taught by events to realize that with the increased intercommunications and interdependence of civilized states all of our production is a part of the world's production, and all our trade is a part of the world's trade, and a large part of the influences which make for prosperity or disaster within our own country consist of forces and movements which may arise anywhere in the world beyond our direct and immediate control.[15]

Those most directly responsible for conducting and planning the international affairs of the United States, officials of the Department of State, regardless of their personal prejudices, were to guide American foreign policy pragmatically and rationally. Repeatedly, articles in *Foreign Affairs* communicated this idea of a nation led by an elite of experts — as qualified as the members of the Council believed themselves to be in their fields and judgment.

Among an interested public the first edition of *Foreign Affairs* was well received and it reached government officials, members of the business community, and members of academia with international interests. By spring of 1923, *Foreign Affairs* had more than 5,000 subscribers, a number that reached 7,000 in 1924. And in 1927 the quarterly already had 11,000 regular readers. This was to a large degree the result of Coolidge's and Armstrong's successful effort to uphold the standard they had set in the first issue.[16]

The possibility to delineate and analyze events and developments from their point of view, to foster discussion on certain aspects, or to address an interested and possibly influential public, was utilized by some Council members and many American and foreign politicians in

15. *Ibid.* Root's article was reprinted on the occasion of his death on 7 February 1937. See Elihu Root, "A Requisite of Popular Diplomacy," *FA* 15.3 (1937).

16. After Coolidge died in 1928, Armstrong succeeded him in governing the quarterly until 1971.

the following issues of *Foreign Affairs.*[17] The most important authors of that period until 1939 include Gustav Stresemann (for a short time in 1923 the German chancellor and from November 1923 until 1929 German foreign minister), Raymond Poincaré (president of France from 1913 to 1920 and 1922 to 1924), Nicolai Bukharin (editor of *Izvestia*), Leon Trotsky (at the time already in exile in Mexico), Hjalmar Schacht (German minister of finance and later president of the Reichsbank), Thomas G. Masaryk (at the time president of Czechoslovakia), Franklin D. Roosevelt, Wilhelm Marx (German chancellor from 1922 to 1925 and 1926 to 1928), German liberal author Heinrich Mann, C.C. Wu (foreign minster of the Republic of China), Viscount Kikujiro Ishii (Japanese ambassador to the United States), Wilhelm Groener (general of the Reichswehr), Cordell Hull (American secretary of state from 1933 to 1944), and Henry L. Stimson (American secretary of state from 1929 to 1933 and secretary of war from 1940 until 1945).[18]

Foreign Affairs did not — and was not intended to — reach the broader public, the man in the street. It did, however, if only on paper, support the Council's main task, which was to bring together politicians, financiers, industrialists, and members of academia for discussions and exchange of ideas. A more direct relationship with visions and experiences of the members of the American delegation and the Inquiry in Paris 1919, however, was only established by instituting a program of

17. It is hardly possible to discern if the authors really wrote these articles themselves. Quite likely, some employed ghostwriters, as Schulzinger thinks it important to point out. See *Wise Men,* 11. But this is only of secondary interest: obviously, the authors found it significant to express what was published under their name; literary merit can hardly be pivotal here. One of the authors, Raymond Poincaré, however, submitted his manuscript in his own handwriting. See Armstrong, *Peace and Counterpeace,* 209.

18. Raymond Poincaré, "The Responsibility for the War," *FA* 4.1 (1925): 1–19; *idem,* "Since Versailles," *FA* 7.3 (1929): 519–31; Nicolai Bukharin, "Imperialism and Communism," *FA* 14.4 (1926): 563–77; Leo Trotsky, "Nationalism and Economic Life," *FA* 12.3 (1924): 395–402; Hjalmar Schacht, "German Trade and German Debts," *FA* 13.1 (1924): 1–5; *idem,* "Germany's Colonial Demands," *FA* 15.2 (1926): 223–34; Thomas G. Masaryk, "Reflections on the Questions of War Guilt," *FA* 3.4 (1925): 529–40; Franklin D. Roosevelt, "Our Foreign Policy: A Democratic View," *FA* 6.4 (1928): 573–78; Wilhelm Marx, "The Rhineland Occupation," *FA* 7.2 (1928): 198–203; C.C. Wu, "Foreign Relations of the Chinese Nationalist Government," *FA* 6.4 (1928): 668–70; Karl Radek, "The War in the Far East," *FA* 10.4 (1932): 541–57; Kikujiro Ishii, "The Permanent Bases of Japanese Foreign Policy," *FA* 11.2 (1932): 220–29; Wilhelm Groener, "Germany's Military Power Since Versailles," *FA* 11.3 (1933): 434–46; Cordell Hull, "The Results and Significance of the Buenos Aires Conference," *FA,* 15.3 (Special Supplement, "Address before the Council on Foreign Relations by the Secretary of State on February 25, 1937"); Henry L. Stimson, "The United States and the Other American Republics," *FA,* 9.3 (Special Supplement, "Address of the Secretary of State before the Council on Foreign Relations on February 6, 1931").

discussion and study groups with off-the-record meetings. These groups, the Council directors hoped, would promote and help to build a foundation for a more effective and internationalist American foreign policy.

Study and Discussion Groups

Shortly after its inception in 1921, the Council aspired to accomplish its assignment "to afford a continuous conference on international questions." To this end, membership meetings, a meetings program, and discussion and study groups were initiated. For the membership meetings and the meetings program, usually a foreign dignitary or American politician was asked to present a paper followed by a question-and-answer period. The study and discussion groups were rather intimate circles of interested Council members. While discussion groups were to inform and educate members and to provide for the intellectual exchange of ideas, study groups often had the additional purpose of helping, through discussion and evaluation of background papers and memoranda prepared by outside experts or Council staff, in the preparation on a book-length study. Before any of these groups could be set up, though, the first speaker solicited by the Council provided considerable public attention for the infant organization.

Georges Clemenceau, prime minister of France during World War I, had been invited by Colonel Edward M. House and some members of the Council to visit the United States. With the lack of appropriate quarters, Council member Otto Kahn rented the Metropolitan Opera House in New York to accommodate an audience of more than one thousand. Edward House and his friends at the Council had decided that the appointments and speeches of the prime minister should be scheduled and organized through the Council as a kind of clearing board. This would ensure, they hoped, that Clemenceau would not be utilized by special interest groups or political factions for their specific concerns. The Council's directors chose Frank L. Polk, Otto Kahn, Wickersham, and Armstrong to direct this operation. They provided tickets for Clemenceau's speech in the Opera House on 21 November 1922, and arranged for audiences with the French statesman. The speech was an immense success and assured that similar invitations were frequently extended in the future — not, however, on that scale again: Clemenceau's visit had consumed almost all of the Council's and Armstrong's time, and work for *Foreign Affairs* had practically come to a standstill.[19]

19. For a very thorough account of the activities surrounding Clemenceau's visit, see Armstrong, *Peace and Counterpeace*, 198–208.

Thus, during the following years, a number of politicians addressed Council meetings: British Prime Minister Ramsey MacDonald, German Chancellor Heinrich Brüning, Japanese Foreign Minister Yosuke Matsuoka, Italian statesman Count Carlo Sforza (who had been forced to flee from fascist Italy), Mussolini's Foreign Minister Dino Grandi, former South African Premier Jan Smuts, British Foreign Minister Anthony Eden, Czechoslovakian President Beneš, Australian Prime Minister Menzies, Belgian statesman Paul van Zeeland, King George II of Greece, Soviet Foreign Minister Maxim Lidvinov, and Chinese statesman Quo Tai-Chi.[20] In addition to these prominent and internationally well-known foreign dignitaries, American secretaries of state frequented Council meetings: Charles Evans Hughes presented an appraisal of the foreign policy of the Harding administration; Frank B. Kellogg (secretary of state under President Coolidge) introduced his plan to ban war, later to be known as the Briand-Kellogg Pact; and Henry L. Stimson advanced the American non-recognition policy toward the Japanese puppet regime of Manchuria.[21]

These meetings and addresses considerably advanced the Council's reputation with the public. The harder and more important work of the Council, however, took place behind closed doors. By December of 1922, Armstrong could, in his function as general manager, inform the members that a number of small study groups had been created to research the problems of international relationships after the war.[22]

The first three groups thus organized, and discussed the national prerequisites for American foreign policy, the revolution in Russia, and international finance. Made up of eight to fifteen members, the groups met once a month in the rooms of New York's Harvard Club to discuss, over dinner, aspects of their main topics. Digests of these discussions, Armstrong had promised, would be made available for all Council members.[23]

---

20. CFR, *A Record of Twenty-Five Years,* 9–11.

21. *Ibid.*, 9.

22. Armstrong to Council members, 21 December 1922, Records of Groups I, Council on Foreign Relations Archive, Harold Pratt House, New York (hereafter abbreviated as RGCFR with the appropriate volume numbers and with the abbreviation of study or discussion group names as prefix; see also "Abbreviations" in the Appendix).

23. Schulzinger, *Wise Men,* 13. These digests of discussions constitute the major part of documents available to researchers at the Council Archives. Written by the group's rapporteurs or secretaries, they are in most cases not verbatim transcripts of what was said, but often very elaborate reports of the discussions, sometimes consisting of as much as twenty single-spaced pages. Statements are generally attributed to specific members of the group, and in most instances every member received a copy of a draft for corrections.

What internationalist ideals Council members held, became particularly evident during the discussions of the group addressing national prerequisites for American foreign policy. Contributions by Armstrong, Walter Lippmann, Gay, and Shepardson during the discussions show clearly how they envisioned a more active foreign policy. Although American participation in the League of Nations had been defeated, for these men Wilsonian ideals were not up for debate. On the contrary, Harding's election as president served only to strengthen their motivation to propagate an active foreign policy. The ideas of Wilson had not been wrong, they argued, but rather the methods he had chosen for implementation were erroneous. An already isolationist public opinion had been unduly influenced by negative propaganda as well.[24]

To support the notion that no particular foreign policy and not even an explicit internationalist policy was endorsed by the Council, the organization even gave outspoken isolationists chances to publish in *Foreign Affairs* and to address Council meetings. In the spring of 1923, Armstrong invited Senator Smith W. Brookhart (Republican of Iowa) to speak to the members. Brookhart was a prominent and vocal member of a group of senators opposing an "entanglement" of American foreign policy in Europe. Bankers Russell C. Leffingwell and Paul Warburg in particular were strongly opposed to the invitation of Brookhart to the Harvard Club, where the meeting was to take place. The senator from Iowa, they believed, was too uncouth, a dangerous demagogue, and not at all in compliance with their idealized picture of a composed and intellectually active politician. To give him the honor to speak to Council members was beyond their tolerance, and they pressed Armstrong to cancel the invitation. Armstrong found support, however, from some of the more broad-minded founding members of the American Institute, such as Shepardson, Polk, and Duggan. Isaiah Bowman reacted furiously when he heard that Warburg and Leffingwell had tried to influence Armstrong. In a letter to Armstrong he called Warburg and his friends "asses" and asked, "what has Wall Street to gain by refusing to hear even a demagogue? Certainly if he is a dangerous demagogue we ought all the more to hear him to discover why he is dangerous and just how danger-

24. Wilson's biggest mistake, they believed, was that he did not listen to the advice of a group of Republicans, among them Elihu Root, to include at least two eminent Republicans among his delegation to the Peace Conference. The Democrats within the Council took pains not to make a similar mistake, and eminent Republicans, such as Lamont and Stimson, were among its members. The Republican Wickersham was made chairman of the Council's Board of Directors and Democrat Root was chosen as honorary president.

ous he is." Finally, and after much excitement, Brookhart came to the Council, demonstrating by his appearance alone the non-partisanship of the organization.[25]

These internal quibbles were unavoidable, and probably even necessary to shape the future of the still young, though already highly regarded organization. And it did not frustrate the work of the study and discussion groups. They concentrated on post-war European problems and paid particular attention to France's conduct, which they regarded as jeopardizing the process of European political stabilization. In face of the still grim economic situation in Europe, a British-American economic alliance was proposed to help in the reconstruction. Knowing quite well that such an engagement would be costly, they suggested that Great Britain and the United States should cooperate in the ruling of the seas. This would save expenditures, which, in turn, could be used in the stabilization of Europe. When French and Belgian troops marched into the German Ruhr area on 11 January 1923, this was welcomed among study group members. Highly critical of France, they did not consider the invasion wise or even just, but they believed that Great Britain would now cease its support of France.[26] The French currency (the franc) would consequently falter, and France, dependent on outside support, would be much more open to political ideas advanced by Great Britain and the United States. Any activity in this respect, however, they warned, should consist only of economic measures; political entanglements were to be avoided. Council members would by no means have objected to political involvement, but they feared that American isolationists might utilize this to create an uproar against American involvement in European affairs, which would very much be to the detriment of a more active American foreign policy.[27] During the discussion, group

25. Bowman to Armstrong, 31 January 1923, cited in Schulzinger, *Wise Men,* 19. The more tolerant faction prevailed and *Foreign Affairs* published, if only very infrequently, articles that ran counter to any belief one would commonly attribute to the Council. See, as examples, Arthur Capper (Republican senator of Illinois), "The American Farmer and Foreign Policy," *FA* 1.4 (1923): 127–35; and Hjalmar Schacht, "Germany's Colonial Demands," *FA* 15.2 (1936): 223–34.

26. The occupation — supposed to secure the faltering German payment of reparations either by pressure on the German government or by taking over the operations of Ruhr industry — contributed to American sympathy for Germany and the fear of French militarism as a threat to peace in Europe. France's attitude was widely condemned in the United States. See the short overview by Warren I. Cohen, *Empire Without Tears: America's Foreign Relations,* 1921–1933 (New York, 1987), particularly pages 92–94.

27. "Report of Study Group C, January 1923;" and "Report of Study Group 3," 23 March 1923; both RGCFR, cited in Schulzinger, *Wise Men,* 13–15.

member Walter Lippmann criticized what he regarded as a cynical approach toward the European problems. Political and economic aspects, he emphasized, were interlinked, and both, not just the economic interdependency of American and European nations, had to be taken into account.[28]

Members of the original Council had reached similar conclusions. In January 1921, a meeting on German reconstruction had been held, with Otto Kahn describing the unraveled fabric of interdependent sectors of the European economy as a result of the war. The cooperation of nations in the interlinked world market, he maintained, had been frustrated by an ill-conceived peace treaty in Europe. John Foster Dulles, at that time a young lawyer in New York, at the same meeting called for a revision of the Versailles Treaty to the advantage of Germany. Wickersham also pointed out that a reintegration of Germany among the European economies would be in the best interests of the American economy.[29]

While in the United States the Republican administration paid tribute to public opinion and conducted a more reserved foreign policy (at least in the official diplomatic sector of foreign affairs) the Council members thought along very different lines. For them the interconnectedness of international economies and international politics was not only an honorable aim, something that had to be achieved in the future; it was already a reality. They argued that this had been neglected in the Paris peace treaties and in the Harding administration. Politicians and foreign service officials had not acted against their better knowledge, they maintained, but even worse, they had not realized their own ignorance. It was not experts who conducted policy, the Council members stated, but rather politicians with one eye always squinting at voters and party functionaries.[30]

Despite all this criticism, Council members very seldom tried to influence State Department officials directly. An exception was the case

28. Schulzinger, *Wise Men*, 13–15. Until 1937, Lippmann performed an important role in Council meetings and study groups and published a number of articles in *Foreign Affairs*. Following a love affair with Armstrong's wife Helen Byrne Armstrong, the subsequent divorce, and his marriage with her, these close ties ceased forever. See Ronald Steel, *Walter Lippmann and the American Century* (Boston, 1980), 345–66.

29. "Meeting on German Economic Reconstruction," 11 January 1921, Records of Meetings, I, Council on Foreign Relations Archive, Harold Pratt House, New York (hereafter abbreviated as RMCFR with the appropriate volume numbers).

30. Attempts to reorganize the foreign service are amply described in Robert D. Schulzinger, *The Making of the Diplomatic Mind: The Training, Outlook, and Style of United States Foreign Service Officers, 1908–1931* (Middletown, CT, 1975). Coolidge had been very active in this effort.

of State Department policy toward China and Japan. John V. A. MacMurray, assistant secretary of state for eastern affairs, was invited by a study group on Far Eastern Affairs, with the expressed intention of persuading MacMurray to favor a more lenient policy toward Japan. In the past, Japan had frequently pointed out that it had interests in China and had argued that access to raw materials was very important for the island-nation. In the United States, the myth of the China market, fostered and sustained over decades by publicists, was still widespread, and the Department of State conducted its policy in favor of China. In the last years of the Wilson administration, a banking consortium to finance the modernization of China, created under the auspices of Thomas Lamont, never really got off the ground; Lamont and his partners from J.P. Morgan rather favored highly profitable and low-risk loans to Japan. If, as in the case of the South Manchuria Railways, loans were obstructed by the Department of State, the bankers did not shy away from laundering the money through other Japanese entities. Led by banker Charles C. Batchelder, the Far Eastern Affairs group of the Council had, not surprisingly, called for a withdrawal of American interests in China and now tried to convince MacMurray — albeit without apparent results — to change American policy in favor of Japan.[31]

With Calvin Coolidge succeeding Harding as President of the United States in 1923, some Council members may have hoped that Council ideas would now actually and directly bear influence on the foreign policy of the United States. Two important Council members had gained influential positions in the State Department: Henry L. Stimson became secretary of state, and Herbert Feis was appointed Stimson's economic advisor. The members of the Far Eastern Affairs group, however, were to be disappointed if they had hoped that greater freedom of action for Japan on the Asian continent would now become possible. When Japanese troops invaded China, the American non-recognition policy made it quite clear that the United States would not condone aggressive Japanese expansion and rejected the Japanese puppet regime of Manchuria.

Another event occupying the Council between the two world wars was the social and economic disaster of the Great Depression beginning in 1929. This economic crisis had caught the American public and

31. Batchelder to Armstrong, 31 December 1924, "Far Eastern Group," RGCFR, cited in Schulzinger, *Wise Men*, 25. For the attitudes toward Japan and China, see Cohen, *Empire Without Tears*, 24, 31–32; and on the banking consortium, Warren I. Cohen, *The Chinese Connection: Roger S. Greene, Thomas W. Lamont, George E. Sokolsky and American-East Asian Relations* (New York, 1978).

many Council members by surprise. There was sharp criticism of the purely economic reactions of the Hoover administration, prompt though they were. Protective tariffs, such as the duties imposed by the Hawley-Smoot Tariff Act of 1930, were thought to be the wrong remedies for the emergency; this was, after all, a disaster which the Council members understood as an economic dilemma of international, not national trade. Discussion groups were formed by the Council and possible strategies were discussed.

As a result of these discussions, *Foreign Affairs* published articles by Edwin F. Gay, Percy W. Bidwell, and Walter Lippmann. Gay argued that the Depression was a direct result of World War I. For Bidwell the "tariff orgy of the past two years" was the reason for the dramatic plunge of the economy. Lippmann, although partially in accord with Bidwell, perceived the main reason to be economic nationalism, particularly Great Britain's nationalist economic policy. Nations had just not cooperated closely enough. During the discussions of the study group, the members could not agree on necessary and specific measures to counter the crisis and no consensus could be reached as to the reasons for the Depression. A panacea was found nevertheless: unrestricted international trade.[32]

In 1933 the Nazis, under their leader Adolf Hitler, came to power in Germany, and the Council members reacted with shock. In addition to the Japanese actions, this was another geopolitically and strategically important movement to establish a "new order." The political ideals of the national socialists were anathema to all principles the Democrats and Wilsonians held dear. The latter regarded the possibility or even likelihood of an autarchic Germany with great concern. Armstrong wrote an article for *Foreign Affairs*, describing the situation in Germany after 31 January 1933, an article which began with the dramatic and moving words, "a people has disappeared." Council criticism of the Nazis radiating to the outside world, however, remained rather sparse.[33]

32. Edwin F. Gay, "The Great Depression," *FA* 10.4 (1932): 531; Percy W. Bidwell, "Trade, Tariffs, and Depression," *FA* 10.2 (1931): 391 (Bidwell had been an economist with the U.S. Tariff Commission and later became, from 1937 until 1959, the Council's Director of Studies); Walter Lippmann, "10 Years, Retrospect and Prospect," *FA* 11.1 (1932): 53.

33. Armstrong, "Hitler's Reich: The First Phase," *FA* 11.4 (1933): 589–608. Armstrong had traveled to Germany in the spring of 1933 and had been granted, through the assistance of Hjalmar Schacht (president of the Reichsbank and contributor to *Foreign Affairs*) an interview with Hitler. See Armstrong, *Peace and Counterpeace*, 523–40.

The Munich Agreement of 1938, conceding to Germany's demands to incorporate Sudeten-Germany (a part of Czechoslovakia) into the Reich, left Council members stunned. It was a negation of all the ideals Council members had regarded as inviolable international law and self-determination of the nations. The Council members' concern about the political development in Europe was, once again, amply expressed in Armstrong's article "Armistice at Munich." The Munich Agreement, Armstrong wrote in his analysis, eerily predicting future developments, would lead to "results for the United States — economic, political, and strategic — and both of the bordering oceans and in Latin America, [that] are incalculable."[34]

War and Peace Studies

With the beginning of World War II, the Council on Foreign Relations had securely established itself as an important study organization. Leading statesmen had participated in meetings and discussion groups or had written articles for *Foreign Affairs.* When on 12 September 1939, hardly a few weeks after Germany had invaded Poland, Hamilton Armstrong and Walter H. Mallory contacted the State Department and offered the Council on Foreign Relations' support in this new political situation, they were received with great interest.[35]

Only two days before, on 10 September, Armstrong had called Assistant Secretary of State George S. Messersmith and told him about the Council's notion to set up study groups to develop medium- and long-range concepts of American foreign policy and to supply the administration, particularly the State Department, with background information. Messersmith had been American consul general in Germany when Armstrong traveled in Europe in 1933 to get first-hand impressions of the situation. "He could hardly restrain himself when he talked

34. "Armistice at Munich," *FA* 17.2 (1938): 198–290, is, at almost one hundred pages, the longest article ever published in *Foreign Affairs*; the citation is from page 199.

35. Harley Notter, ed. *Postwar Foreign Policy Preparations,* 1939–1945 (Washington, D.C., 1949), 19. See also Shoup and Minter, *Imperial Brain Trust,* 117–87; Schulzinger, *Wise Men,* 59–112; Domhoff, *The Power Elite,* 113–44; and the Council's own short account, *The War and Peace Studies of the Council on Foreign Relations* (New York, 1946). Armstrong described some of the sections written by Notter as "pretty ridiculous. Needless to say, he [Notter] has been told to write the record with Leo's name [Leo Pasvolsky] on every page, and that name only; and he has succeeded." See Armstrong to Bowman, 16 November 1948, Isaiah Bowman Papers, Milton S. Eisenhower Library, Johns Hopkins University, Baltimore, MD. Mallory had succeeded Armstrong as Council Executive Director in 1927, when Armstrong became editor of *Foreign Affairs.*

about the Nazis," Armstrong says of his encounter with Messersmith, "biting his cigar in two pieces and tossing them away in disgust as he catalogued his difficulties in trying to protect American citizens from molestation." After the blitzkrieg against Poland, the unabashed aggressiveness of the German Reich had become obvious to everyone and Messersmith found his fears confirmed that Germany's hunger for power was not yet satisfied.[36]

When the assistant secretary of state agreed to a meeting on 12 September, Armstrong and Mallory traveled to Washington, D.C. The United States, they told Messersmith, should be prepared for all eventualities and American interests in war and in peace, even at this early date, should be discussed and studied. Messersmith concurred with Armstrong and Mallory that State Department officials hardly had time to think ahead of their daily chores in order to develop long-term solutions and a future foreign policy strategy for the United States. The Council's emissaries maintained that it would be important for Council study groups to work closely with, or, even better yet, actually within the State Department. Hinting at the experience of the Inquiry in 1917 and 1918, they assured Messersmith that the Council had no desire to formulate American foreign policy, nor did it aspire to impinge on the prerogatives of the Department.[37]

Messersmith appreciated the Council's proposal and on the same day informed Secretary of State Cordell Hull and Hull's undersecretary Sumner Welles about his talks with the Council members. Aware of the fact that the State Department would not be able to create a brain trust within a short time, both supported the Council's plan. "The matter is strictly confidential, because the whole plan would be 'ditched' if it became generally known that the State Department is working in collaboration with any outside group," Isaiah Bowman wrote in November.[38]

To protect the State Department from criticism by isolationists and to demonstrate the autonomy of the Council on Foreign Relations, it

---

36. Armstrong, *Peace and Counterpeace*, 530. See also Jesse H. Stiller, *George S. Messersmith: Diplomat of Democracy* (Chapel Hill, NC, 1987), 26–55.

37. "Memorandum of Conversation: Proposed activities of the Council on Foreign Relations in the field of research and collaboration with the Department of State," 12 September 1939, Department of State, Decimal File 811.43 CFR/220, RG 59, National Archives, Washington, D.C. A copy is in the RFR, 1/100/99/898.

38. Cordell Hull, *The Memoirs of Cordell Hull* (New York, 1948) 2: 1625; "Memorandum of a conversation with Walter Mallory at 11:30 a.m., November 27, 1939," n.d., Bowman Papers; "Memorandum of Talks with Mr. Messersmith and Mr. Wilson by Mr. Mallory and Mr. Jones at Washington on January 11, 1940," handwritten note: "*Private and Confidential*," n.d., *ibid.*

was agreed to ask the Rockefeller Foundation to finance the endeavor. At first, the Foundation was not very interested in the project. Mallory and Armstrong had estimated that $100,000 was necessary to conduct the study program, a sum that soon had to be cut by half. Funding in the original amount was refused because a plan by geographer Bowman to create accurate maps as background information for discussions and decisions was perceived as unnecessary by Foundation director Joseph Willits.[39] Bowman and Mallory, who were coordinating the whole effort, tried to find other sponsors. When these could not be located and the Board of Trustees of the Rockefeller Foundation finally, on 4 December, agreed to fund the work of the study groups for the first two years with $50,000, the offer was accepted gratefully.[40] Over the next years, financed with more than $300,000 from the Rockefeller Foundation, almost one hundred men participated in the War and Peace Studies and formulated, until August 1945, more than 680 background reports and suggestions for the use of the State Department.[41]

In the meantime, Armstrong, Mallory, and a few other Council members were considering possible members to staff the study groups. In addition to Armstrong and Mallory themselves, Bowman — who had

39. Mallory and Council Director Allen W. Dulles (brother of John Foster Dulles) had discussed the Council's proposition with Willits. Mallory sent him a letter specifying the envisioned setup of study groups. See Mallory to Willits, 21 September 1939; RFR, 1/100/99/893. See also Mallory's enclosed memorandum for the Research Committee of the Council, "Project for a Study of the Effects of the War on the United States: Memorandum on Purpose, Scope, and Procedure," n.d., *ibid.* Bowman had estimated an amount of $10,000 to $50,000 for a "map program" alone. See Bowman to Mallory, 5 October 1939, Bowman Papers.

40. "Memorandum of a conversation with Walter Mallory at 11:30 a.m., November 27, 1939," n.d., Bowman Papers; "Memorandum of Talks with Mr. Messersmith and Mr. Wilson by Mr. Mallory and Mr. Jones at Washington on January 11, 1940," handwritten note: "*Private and Confidential*," n.d., *ibid.*

41. "Memorandum re. first chapter (or section) of Notter book," 15 November 1948, enclosure, Armstrong to Bowman, 16 November 1948, Bowman Papers. The "Notter book" is Notter, *Postwar Policy Preparations.* Notter had sent Armstrong the manuscript for suggestions. The Rockefeller Foundation maintained that:

> This request [to finance the program] would not have been recommended except for the warm endorsement of the State Department. This was represented by Assistant Secretary Messersmith who conveyed also the specific approval of Secretary Hull and Undersecretary Welles. . . . [T]he State Department cannot take the initiative in bringing together a group for study of the pertinent issues because political capital would be made of the action and the charge made that the government was planning to lead the country into the war or was at least considering participation in some new international supergovernment. . . . Consequently, the Department privately but not officially endorses the plan.

See Resolution RF 39110/39427, 5–6 December 1939, RFR, 1/100/99/893.

been involved from the very beginning — Whitney Shepardson, Allen W. Dulles, and Shotwell were suggested. Clark M. Eichelberger, director of the League of Nations Association, who had been proposed by Mallory, was not invited despite the fact that he was an almost ideal candidate. His activities in the Commission to Study the Organization of Peace and other internationalist organizations were regarded as being too valuable.[42]

Additional meetings between Armstrong and Messersmith took place and suggestions by Secretary of State Cordell Hull, with whom Messersmith conferred frequently, were taken into account. On 15 December 1939, Messersmith invited Council members Allen Dulles, Bowman, Alvin H. Hansen, Shepardson, Jacob Viner, Mallory, and Armstrong to his house to get the plan into final shape over dinner.[43] They agreed to form four groups of experts jointly staffed by Council and State Department members: Security and Armaments, Economic and Financial, Political, and Territorial. To deal with the daily chores and organization, each group would be outfitted with a rapporteur and a research secretary. A steering committee was established to coordinate the work of the study groups. In addition to the men present, Norman H. Davis was invited to participate and chair the steering committee. That Davis was asked to join this committee was far from being a coincidence, since he was president of the Council, advisor to and friend of President Roosevelt, and a close friend of Secretary Hull.[44]

During the next five-and-a-half years, in which the study groups worked on conceptions for American foreign policy, few changes were introduced into the organizational setup. Only one additional group, the Peace Aims Group, was established in May 1943. Headed by Armstrong, the group was financed through a special fund from the Rockefeller Foundation. As a reaction to the spreading war in Europe, the Peace Aims Group organized meetings attended by representatives of occupied Euro-

42. "Memorandum of conversation with Walter Mallory at 11:30 a.m., November 27, 1939," n.d., Bowman Papers; Clark M. Eichelberger, *Organizing for Peace*, 195–208. In early 1942, Eichelberger participated in the Advisory Committee on Postwar Foreign Policy; see below.

43. Alvin Hansen taught political economy at Harvard University and Viner was an economist at the University of Chicago.

44. The Council's own account gives 8 December as the date for the meeting. All other documents are dated 15 December. See CFR, *War and Peace Studies*, 3. Hansen and Viner served as rapporteurs for the Economic and Financial Group, Shepardson for the Political Group, Allen Dulles for the Security and Armaments Group, and Bowman for the Territorial Group.

pean countries and by the Allies. At these meetings, they could express their peace and reparations proposals, thus providing the State Department with important information for the coordination of its foreign policy aims.[45]

When the State Department created its own planning staff, the Division of Special Research headed by Leo Pasvolsky in February 1941, the War and Peace Studies were by no means obsolete; rather an additional division of labor was introduced. The planning staff was organized along the same structural lines as the Council groups, and the latter's research secretaries were integrated into the work of the Division of Special Research. With the research secretaries continuing to participate in the War and Peace Studies meetings, an intensive exchange between the two formally independent planning organizations was assured. In a design proposed earlier, the rapporteurs — having served as quasi-chairmen — were supposed to direct the appropriate committees of the State Department. Nothing came of this, however, because Dulles and Shepardson were excluded. Armstrong, in a letter to Bowman, assumed that Assistant Secretary of State Adolf A. Berle intervened in the case of Dulles because he did not like Dulles personally. And Shepardson, scheduled to work for the American war-time intelligence agency Office of Strategic Services (OSS), could not participate either.[46]

Despite this setback, the cooperation between the Council and the State Department was further enhanced when, in 1942, the Advisory Committee on Postwar Foreign Policy was established. Secretary of State Hull directed the Committee and some Council members were invited to participate. This group and its subcommittees concentrated on the United Nations organization, the successor to the League of Nations, a subject that had always received keen attention at Council meetings.[47]

In the spring of 1943, when British Foreign Minister Anthony Eden suggested that a "Committee for Europe" should be established, the

45. By 1941, plans for a "Peace Aims of European Peoples' Group" existed. At that time, however, the Rockefeller Foundation had declined funding. See "Application Council on Foreign Relations for continued support for Program of Study Groups (Interview TBK with Hamilton Armstrong, Walter Mallory and Percy Bidwell, September 15th)," 22 September 1941, RFR, 1/100/97/875.

46. Armstrong to Bowman, 16 November 1948, Bowman Papers. In his salutation Armstrong wrote: "All this between us." See also Armstrong to Bowman, 23 November 1948, *ibid.*

47. Council members participating were: Armstrong, Bowman, lawyer Benjamin V. Cohen (member of the Economic and Financial Group of the War and Peace Studies and advisor to president Roosevelt), and Norman H. Davis. See CFR, *The War and Peace Studies*, 6–7.

Advisory Committee discussed his proposal. President Roosevelt speculated that Eden's suggestion was a scheme to safeguard Britain's leading role in Europe. But Armstrong and Norman H. Davis suggested possible alternatives and the *Foreign Affairs* editor recommended proposing to Eden a plan for a new supranational organization already being discussed in the United States. Hull was approached and he asked Davis (who often served as an intermediary when others feared Roosevelt's possible scorn) to bring this proposal to the attention of the President. Roosevelt liked the idea and within a short time blueprints for a charter of the successor to the League of Nations were drafted and discussed.[48]

In his discussions with Davis, President Roosevelt proposed changes, and Davis introduced these into the discussions and revisions of drafts. Roosevelt, in August 1943, took the final draft with him to the Quebec Conference, where it was accepted by Britain's Prime Minister Winston Churchill and Foreign Minister Eden. With only minor changes, the text was taken to Moscow and signed by delegates of the United States, Great Britain, China, and the Soviet Union as the Moscow Declaration on 1 November 1943. In this document, the nations not only pledged to coordinate and cooperate in their war aims but also declared "that they recognized the necessity of establishing at the earliest predictable date a general international organization, based on the sovereign equality of all peace-loving states, and open to membership by all such states, large and small, for the maintenance of international peace and security."[49]

Always eager to prove to the Rockefeller Foundation that their money was not spent in vain, Armstrong called the Foundation's President

48. "Interviews: JHW; Hamilton Fish Armstrong," 9 November 1943, RFR, 1/100/99/897.

49. CFR, *The War and Peace Studies*, 7. Armstrong to Bowman, 28 December 1948, Bowman Papers. In this letter Armstrong also chastens Notter for his overrating of Hull's influence in drafting the document:

> I realize that in the present rush for 'credit' in this whole affair, Notter and Pasvolsky have to deal very tenderly with Secretary Hull, which means hiding the fact that he took practically no step in a matter of this sort without first consulting Norman [Davis], and that he often left Norman to 'try out' suggestions which he [Hull] felt might not be agreeable to F.D.R.

Philip E. Mosely, Research Secretary of the Territorial Group and Assistant Director of the Division of Special Research, accompanied Hull to Moscow. The text of the declaration is in U.S. Department of State, *In Quest of Peace and Security: Selected Documents in American Foreign Policy, 1941–1951* (Washington, D.C., 1951); the quotation is from page 9. The draft Roosevelt took to Quebec and Hull later took to Moscow is reprinted as "Tentative Draft of a Joint-Four-Power Declaration," 11 August 1943, in "Appendix 27," Notter, *Postwar Foreign Policy*, 553. See also: Hull, *Memoirs*, chapter 116.

Joseph Willits little more than a week later to inform him of the groundwork the Council had done for the Moscow Declaration. He told Willits about the events and emphasized the influence of Council members Bowman, Norman Davis, and Grayson Kirk, and he pointed out his own work in the process. "Armstrong is quite emphatic," Willits wrote in a memorandum of the meeting, "that without the outside members [the Council members], this diplomatic achievement would not have come off." To make sure that Armstrong had not simply exaggerated the Council members' influence, Willits contacted the Council members Armstrong had mentioned for confirmation. Still not satisfied, he called on Leo Pasvolsky and Under Secretary of State Edward R. Stettinius, Jr., to verify what the Council members had told him.[50]

Kirk backed Armstrong's evaluations. "The arrangement between the State Department and the CFR," he told Willits, "made it possible for [an] intellectual breeze from outside to blow through the State Department in a way, that the State Department, acting officially, itself would have been entirely too cautious to permit." And Bowman, so often at pains to be perceived in the right light, even compared the Council's importance to that of such celebrated institutions as the American Geographical Society (president: Bowman) and the graduate school of Johns Hopkins University (president: Bowman). He also assured Willits that, in preparing the Moscow Declaration, the documents of the Council's War and Peace Studies were "not merely significant but critical." Pasvolsky and Stettinius at the State Department were a little less emphatic but confirmed that the Council's contribution had been "extremely important" and "very essential."[51]

Willits was not very much impressed by the precise number of changes that had to be made from the first drafts to the final document nor by accounts of who introduced what minor modification, as Armstrong had deemed necessary to point out to him. Willits, like many Council members, believed that it was much more important that experts had been involved in the decision-making process in the State Department than to be able to pinpoint the influence of individuals. He appreciated the Council as an organization that could superbly serve as

50. "Interviews: JHW; Hamilton Fish Armstrong," 9 November 1943, RFR, 1/100/99/897.

51. "Interviews: JHW; Grayson Kirk," 22 November 1943; RFR, 1/100/99/897; Bowman to Willits, 23 November 1943, *ibid.*; "Interviews: JHW; Leo Pasvolsky," 29 and 30 [November] 1943 in Washington, *ibid.*; "Interviews: JHW; Under Secretary of State Edward R. Stettinius," 29 and 30 [November] 1943, *ibid.*

a recruiting ground for future advisors and officials of the executive departments. "The important thing in this," he wrote after his meeting with Armstrong, "is the series of steps from the initial growth of young men through research to the committee discussing research and political problems (in CFR) on through the policy committees of the State Dept. to active officials of government."[52]

As a rule, the meetings of the War and Peace Studies groups took place at the headquarters the Council had acquired in late 1929 on East 65th Street on Manhattan.[53] Meetings usually lasted from late afternoon until after dinner, followed by discussions often lasting well into the night. From 1940 to 1945 the group members met on 253 occasions, the Steering Committee met ten times (either at the State Department or at the Cosmos Club in Washington, D.C.), two plenum sessions were called, and ninety-six meetings of the staff took place. The outcome of all this work were 682 memoranda and drafts. These were forwarded to the State Department and found their way to other government agencies where they helped in the decision-making process.[54]

Memoranda provided by the War and Peace Studies groups fell into five categories. Particularly in the early war years, analysis of the political and strategic situation in Europe and evaluations of possible developments in a number of other areas of the world were dominant. Additionally, background information was supplied in the form of memoranda or short reports. Policy papers, the third category, consisted of detailed summaries based on the often lengthy discussions within the groups. These papers provided suggestions and possible strategies for American reactions to developments the Council members anticipated. Supplementing these special papers were memoranda of a more general nature. In these latter the framework of a war-time U.S. foreign policy and an expected peace conference was outlined.[55]

---

52. "Interviews: JHW; Hamilton Fish Armstrong," 9 November 1943, RFR, 1/100/99/897.

53. The house had been bought for $310,000, an amount raised among Council members. Donors were: James Byrne (Armstrong's father-in-law), Lamont, Leffingwell, John D. Rockefeller, Jr., Paul Warburg, John W. Davis, Norman H. Davis, and Otto Kahn, among others. See "Purchase of 45 East 65th Street," Armstrong to Council members, 18 November 1929, Philip C. Jessup Papers, box 114, Library of Congress, Washington, D.C.

54. Notter, *Postwar Policy Preparations*, 56. After World War II, sets of the memoranda were (with a few exceptions because of security reasons) distributed to a number of university libraries.

55. A list of the memoranda is in CFR, *War and Peace Studies*, 25–48.

The Economic and Financial Group was the first to have a memorandum ready for the State Department. The war was exactly six months old and the United States was still a "non-belligerent," when the memorandum, "The Impact of War Upon the Foreign Trade of the United States," made clear in what field major problems were expected. The issue of war-time trade was addressed more specifically in a number of discussions and in memoranda over the following months. "Trade Dislocations" were researched, the "Postwar Trade Role of the United States" was outlined, and "Economic Aspects of the United States' Interests in the War and the Peace" were examined.[56]

The rapporteurs of the Economic and Financial Group, Alvin Hansen and Jacob Viner, already had a blueprint at the ready in the event that Germany conquered the British Isles. Under German occupation, they assumed, the Churchill administration would flee to Canada. Americans and the British would then cooperate more closely than ever before. As equal partners they would not only conduct trade in the former British Empire but also in what remained of the French colonies. It sounded almost like the dreams of a devoted Anglophile come true when Hansen and Viner maintained that this Anglo-American "codominion" would be the substitute for the trade the European nations had enjoyed with their respective colonies.[57]

In spite of their plans, Hansen and Viner were convinced that the Allies would win the war in Europe. For the remainder of the war, the two economists proposed that British and French colonies should be accessible to American trade. Only this would insure that an economic counterweight to Germany and its satellites could be established. And the prerequisite for the success of this policy, they claimed, was unrestricted access to colonial markets. In the following years the Economic and Financial Group continued to concentrate its attention on questions of world trade. Again, the basic presumptions of many Council members was evident: the world was an interdependent system of trading nations; restrictions in international trade would generally be to the disadvantage of the nation imposing constraints and would lead to

56. Memoranda E-B 1, 1 March 1940, Council on Foreign Relations War and Peace Studies, Council on Foreign Relations Archive, Harold Pratt House, New York (hereafter abbreviated as CFRW+P); E-B 4, 1 March 1940, *ibid.*; E-B 10, 15 April 1940, *ibid.*; and E-B 14, 20 June 1940, *ibid.*

57. "Alternative Outcomes of the War: American Interests and Re-Orientation," E-B 16, 20 June 1940, CFRW+P; "Economic Trading Blocs and Their Importance for the United States," E-B 27, 10 February 1941; *ibid.* See also Patrick J. Hearden, *Roosevelt Confronts Hitler: America's Entry into World War II* (DeKalb, IL, 1987), 166–67.

unnecessary frictions; and discord could easily escalate into national conflicts and even into strife between nations. Therefore, the most-favored-nation clauses and protective tariffs had to be abolished to allow free and unrestricted liberal and international trade. Hansen and Viner had no apprehensions about the future role of the United States as a cardinal power in this system, since the United States would acquire "military and economic supremacy" within the non-German world.[58]

In April of 1940, the Economic and Financial Group advocated a more lenient policy toward Japan, and possibilities to peacefully contain Japan's expansionism were still being discussed nine months later. Not until July of 1941, when President Roosevelt prohibited all trade with Japan, did the Group change its preferences again. From there on, Hansen and Viner proposed guidelines for an effective embargo policy and argued that Japan's aggressive policy had to be contained through "peaceable means" if possible, or through force if necessary.[59]

The Armaments Group was then looking back on a number of important suggestions. A United States Navy's "goodwill mission" in the Pacific Ocean and the stationing of American troops at some bases in the Caribbean, proposed by the group led by Allen Dulles, had been transformed into actual policy. The group's formulation of a long-term structure of American foreign policy, the principal task of the War and Peace Studies groups, however, was not given much appreciation until 1941. A memorandum on the possible responsibilities of occupying forces and their functioning as a police force in occupied German territory after the fighting ceased, remained almost unnoticed at this early date.[60]

58. "The War and United States Foreign Policy: Needs of Future United States Foreign Policy," E-B 19, 9 October 1940, CFRW+P; "A Comparison of the Trade Position of a German-Dominated Europe and a Western Hemisphere-British Empire-Far East Trade Bloc," a "Supplement I" of E-B 19, 16 September 1940, *ibid.* During the preparatory discussions about the structure and program of the War and Peace Studies groups in the fall of 1939, Bowman had written: "The United States Government is interested in any solution anywhere in the world that affects American trade. In a wide sense, commerce is the mother of all wars. Commercial rivalries on the part of others inevitably lead to difficulties on the part of American traders." See Bowman to Walter H. Mallory, 5 October 1939, Bowman Papers.

59. "How Is Japan Likely to React to Economic Sanctions by the United States?," P-B 15, 8 December 1940, CFRW+P; E-B 19; "Scope of New Trade Agreements," E-B 37, 3 September 1941, *ibid.* The group also provided an elaborate and penetrating study of possible German reparations, prepared by the group's research secretary, William Diebold, Jr. Otto Nübel provides a detailed account in *Die amerikanische Reparationspolitik gegenüber Deutschland, 1941–1945* (Frankfurt, 1980), 48–73. He argues that the Council had developed the most satisfactory proposal on this question, but that Washington did not follow the Council's advice, *ibid.*, 52, 58.

60. Schulzinger, *Wise Men*, 74–75.

Other memoranda of the Armaments Group discussed mistakes that had been made during the arms reductions talks after World War I. Dulles' group concluded that treating all nations equally would ultimately lead to new conflicts in Europe. A plan for arms reductions would have to take the military and economic potential of individual nations into account. The Group maintained that the Axis powers, Germany and Italy, were to be disarmed first, followed by the smaller nations in Europe, in the Western hemisphere, and then in the Far East. Only after this had been accomplished, their memorandum ("Disarmament and Foreign Policy: An Examination of Some Basic Characteristics") of May 1940 cautioned, should the great powers reduce their arms.[61]

The Territorial Group, headed by Bowman, received major attention during this period through a contribution by Owen Lattimore. While members of the Economic and Financial Group had become disenchanted with Japan, the Johns Hopkins University China expert favored a more explicit American support for China. Rivalries between the Soviet Union and Japan, he argued, would prevail and could well be used to the advantage of the United States: if China was supported by the United States, it could defend itself against Japanese aggression on the continent. Consequently, Japanese expansionism might be deflected against the USSR to the north. Such a confrontation would be to the advantage of China, and the Chinese would doubtless be grateful to their benefactor, the United States. Chinese resentment at being used by the United States as a peon in its policy against the Soviet Union could be precluded by unconditional and generous aid to Chiang Kai-shek, Lattimore suggested. An amicable relationship between the United States and China, after a victory over Japan, would open the large Chinese market to American industries, and the raw material of this immense territory could be utilized by the United States; obviously, the myth of the China market had not yet passed away completely.[62]

Bowman's group also provided the clearest example of the influence of the War and Peace Studies groups. On 17 March 1940, the Group had forwarded a memorandum to the State Department entitled "The Strategic Importance of Greenland." Bowman's group had indicated

61. A-B 3, 1 May 1940, CFRW+P.

62. "The Soviet-Japanese Treaty of Neutrality and World Revolution in the Far East," T-B 26, 19 April 1941, CFRW+P; "Possible Effects of Agreement Between Russia and Japan," T-B 27, 3 April 1941, *ibid.*; "The Chinese Communists, the Comintern, and the Russian-Japanese Neutrality Agreement," T-B 29, 6 May 1941, *ibid.*; Schulzinger, *Wise Men*, 65–67.

that Greenland was of eminent strategic importance for transatlantic flight routes and for the gathering of meteorological information. These aspects might become extremely vital if there were active American involvement in the war, and for the safeguarding of naval transports to aid the Allies. The likelihood of Germany's invading and annexing Denmark was discussed. Greenland, a part of Denmark, would become a part of Germany, and German troops could be stationed there. Such a close geographical proximity of German forces would certainly pose a direct threat to the national security of the United States. A remedy for this hazard was found easily. Without much ado, the authors declared that Greenland was part of the Western Hemisphere and was thus protected by the Monroe Doctrine.[63]

Only a few days later Bowman was invited to the White House to discuss this aspect with the President. One day after German troops had invaded Denmark, Roosevelt announced that the United States would establish bases on Greenland and proclaimed that he considered Greenland to be a part of the American continent. Denmark's ambassador to the United States immediately met with the President and expressed his total concurrence with Roosevelt. An American consulate was established in Godthaab, the capital of the island, and American Coast Guard vessels demonstrated the presence of the United States. Hardly a year later and eight months before Germany declared war on the United States, on 9 April 1941, an agreement was signed between the United States and occupied Denmark granting the United States the right to establish military bases on the island.[64]

In this early phase of the war, the memoranda of the Political Group, just as those of the other three groups, had a less than decisive influence on policies of the Roosevelt administration. Some of the proposals, though, were put into effect, such as the opening of the Burma Road for the support of China and American protection of Dutch Guiana — the same area that had been given to the Dutch in exchange for New

63. "The Strategic Importance of Greenland," T-B 3, 17 March 1940, CFRW+P.

64. CFR, *War and Peace Studies*, 15–17; "The President Announces That the United States Will Establish Bases in Greenland, April 10, 1941," and "Note," *The Public Papers and Addresses of Franklin D. Roosevelt* (New York, 1950) 1941: 96–99. See also: Samuel Eliot Morison, *The Battle of the Atlantic* (Boston, 1950) 1: 58–64. The Council regarded this as its most decisive impact on policy-making during World War II; see CFR, *War and Peace Studies*; and CFR, *A Record of Twenty-Five Years*, 13–15. Hanson W. Baldwin, a member of the steering committee, made the matter public in his "U.S. Stand on Greenland Guided by Council on Foreign Relations," *New York Times*, 6 October 1946.

Amsterdam at the Hudson River 275 years before. Despite these few instances, high expectations the Council members may have had in influencing American foreign policies were not realized.[65]

Only in the founding of the United Nations did their discussions about organization and responsibilities have a direct and immediate impact. The group, headed by Whitney Shepardson, had suggested working for a "decisive defeat of the Axis aggressors as rapidly as possible" and for encouraging an "effective system of international security." Wilsonian ideals of a liberal internationalism were explicitly evident when the members phrased their expectations of the supranational organization in mid-1941: "The development of world order designed to promote economic progress, social justice and cultural freedom for all national groups, races and classes willing to accept their proper responsibilities as members of the world community."[66]

After the Japanese surprise-attack on Pearl Harbor, the State Department finally began to establish an independent planning organization. The Advisory Committee on Postwar Foreign Policy conducted a major part of the State Department's planning after December 1941, and the Council's input lost some of its importance. The Council was still represented in the Special Committees of the Advisory Committee through its rapporteurs, but the majority of active Council members were soon excluded from very important meetings and discussions. The strict security surrounding the War and Peace Studies was eased and Council members received mimeographed digests of discussions and could consult some of the memoranda. All members of the Council were now confidentially informed about the close cooperation between their organization and the State Department, but this relaxation of security was precisely an indicator of the diminished importance of the Council on Foreign Relations in the making of American foreign policy. What influence the Council still had was now concentrated in Armstrong, Bowman, and Norman Davis.[67]

After 1942, all study groups of the War and Peace Studies focused on the structure and responsibilities of the future United Nations organiza-

65. "Burma Road," P-B 9, 27 September 1940, CFRW+P; "White House Statement Announces Army Forces in Dutch Guiana, November 24, 1941," and "Note," *Public Papers and Addresses of Franklin D. Roosevelt*, 1941: 495–97.

66. "Basic American Interests: Preliminary Draft," P-B 23, 10 July 1941, CFRW+P.

67. CFR, *War and Peace Studies*, 18–19; Julius W. Pratt, *Cordell Hull* (New York, 1964), 718–20; Notter, *Postwar Policy Preparations*, 80, 82–83, 152.

tion. The Council members, like so many other internationalists, were convinced that the United States should not let this "second chance" to participate in a supranational organization evaporate. Preparatory meetings between Churchill and Roosevelt during the Atlantic Conference on the coast of Newfoundland in August 1941 had already outlined a United Nations organization, but this was still just an outline without substance.[68]

When the Subcommittee on International Organization of the Advisory Committee drafted the procedure for nations joining the supranational organization, the differences in beliefs held by idealists (such as Eichelberger, who had been invited to this group) and realists (such as Bowman) among the Council members participating came to the fore. Eichelberger argued that "all duly recognized independent states and dominions shall be recognized as members of the international organization." Bowman, not satisfied with this automatic membership, proposed ("off the top of his head," as Eichelberger recalled) that membership should be granted only to "qualified states and dominions," and a Security Council was to decide if a nation did, in fact, qualify. To the chagrin of Eichelberger, Bowman's suggestion was accepted after heated and controversial debate and became part of the Charter of the United Nations. In his memoirs, Eichelberger argued with hindsight that this formula was responsible for the cause of the United Nations being degraded to an instrument of Soviet and American political strategies.[69]

All members of the Subcommittee concurred that the United States, enjoying an unparalleled position in the world, would have to have more clout than other nations. They insisted that the military and economic power of the individual nations would have to be evaluated. Far from subscribing to the vision of "one world,"[70] in their deliberations

68. The term "second chance" is from the title of Robert A. Divine's *Second Chance: The Triumph of Internationalism in America* (New York, 1971). See also Clark Eichelberger's *Organizing for Peace.* For the United States' influence on the setup of the United Nations, see Ruth B. Russell, *A History of the United Nations Charter: The Role of the United States, 1940–1945* (Washington, D.C., 1958).

69. Eichelberger, *Organizing,* 199–208; the quotation is from page 202. Both nations had used their right to veto a Security Council decision and thus prevented membership of countries belonging to the opposite political camp. In an interview with Willits, Grayson Kirk praised Bowman's input and attributed little value to Eichelberger's contribution. See "Interviews: JHW; Grayson Kirk," 22 November 1943; RFR, 1/100/99/897.

70. "One World" was the title of a book published by the well-known Republican Wendell Willkie at the end of 1942 after he visited the Soviet Union and China. Inspired by a faith in a better and peaceful future and believing in the goodwill of all of mankind, Willkie imagined a unifying force that would make freedom and justice possible for all human beings. Within a short time, his book had sold more than a million copies.

they sketched out an international order surprisingly close to the system of spheres of influence and power politics of which Great Britain had so often been accused.

Quite a few members of the War and Peace Studies groups, after leaving the program, participated in the preparatory conference at Dumbarton Oaks or served in advisory positions at the organizing conference of the United Nations in San Francisco in June 1945.[71] Some of them actually attained positions of considerable influence. Philip E. Mosely (research secretary of the Territorial Group) accompanied Secretary Hull to Moscow in 1943 and was later advisor to the American Delegation to the European Advisory Commission in London. Walter R. Sharp (research secretary of the Political Group) advanced to the position of secretary-general of the United Nation's Food Conference in Quebec in 1945, and Grayson Kirk (research secretary of the Armaments and Security Group), as well as Dwight D. Lee (research secretary of the Peace Aims Group), became advisors to the American delegation during the conferences at Dumbarton Oaks and in San Francisco.[72]

Isaiah Bowman served as special advisor to the secretary of state and as a member of the Policy Committee in the State Department before he became an advisor to the American Delegation at the San Francisco conference. His confidant and friend Hamilton Armstrong, similarly assisting the American delegation as an advisor in San Francisco, had used his contacts to the State Department and was appointed special assistant to Ambassador John G. Winant in Great Britain, with the rank of minister.

Another twelve members of the War and Peace Studies groups (among them future Secretary of State John Foster Dulles) acquired influential appointments directly connected with the establishment of the United Nations or assisted the State Department. Other Council members worked for the Office of Strategic Services (for example, Allen Dulles and Whitney Shepardson), or served as officers in the Army, Navy, or Air Force.[73]

71. Other Council members were quite critical about American participation in the United Nations. Council member Russell C. Leffingwell (a colleague of Thomas Lamont at J.P. Morgan and from 1944 to 1946 president of the Council) wrote in 1944: "I do not see much good in Dumbarton Oaks [preparatory conference for the United Nations]. There can be nothing to be got out of reviving the League with another name." See Leffingwell to Lamont, 10 October 1944, Thomas W. Lamont Papers, box 104, Baker Library, Harvard University, Cambridge, MA.

72. CFR, *War and Peace Studies*, 7–9.

73. *Ibid.*; R. Harris Smith, *OSS: The Secret History of America's First Central Intelligence Agency* (Berkeley and Los Angeles, 1972), 207–208. According to the Council, more

The Council members, particularly Hamilton Armstrong, were convinced that their work had been of pivotal importance for the formation of American foreign policy during World War II. Nevertheless, Armstrong and Mallory had to strain to provide the Rockefeller Foundation with evidence, and their efforts took rather obscure forms in some instances. Bowman was only willing to report directly to Rockefeller Foundation official George W. Gray, and even this had to be off-the-record. Not even Foundation director Willits, he requested, should have access to a digest of the interview. Security was necessary, Bowman wrote, because his disclosures were confidential and he feared (once again displaying his penchant for drastic language) that someone uninitiated could take him for "an ass braying from a hillside."[74]

The Council members regarded the close cooperation with the State Department to be the culmination of their persistent efforts to secure the influence of experts in the decision-making process in American foreign policy, which they had insisted upon so ardently over the last twenty years. "The real touchstone is the usefulness of the studies for the government," the authors of the summary of the War and Peace Studies groups proclaimed in 1946. Officials at the State Department, however, perceived the Council's support as only one element in the larger area of necessary planning tasks. The Council had supplied an important portion, but it was, nonetheless, just one ingredient.[75]

Only a few propositions introduced in the study groups were based on new concepts; most of them were grounded in well-known ideas and dispositions. It was significant, however, that Council members and State Department officials could exchange and discuss ideas and reach an accord on some presumptions. They agreed that the United States

---

than two hundred of its members served in the State Department, OSS, Office of War Information, United Nations Relief and Rehabilitation Administration, War Production Board, Office of Emergency Management, and similar organizations during the war. See CFR, "Princeton Conference on Future Program of Studies, September 8–9, 1945," 5, Jacob Viner Papers, box 28, Mudd Manuscript Library.

74. Bowman to Mallory and Armstrong, 26 December 1945, enclosure, GWG [Gray] to RBF [Fosdick] and JHW [Willits], 28 December [1941], RFR, 1/100/99/898. See also Daryl L. Revoldt, "Raymond B. Fosdick: Reform, Internationalism, and the Rockefeller Foundation" (Ph.D. diss., University of Akron, 1982).

75. "List of Memoranda Issued December 1939–December 1941, with an Analysis of Recommendations," SC-B 1, 31 December 1941, CFRW+P; "List of Memoranda Issued in 1942 with Recommendations or Conclusions (dated December 31, 1941, but not listed among documents issued in 1942)," SC-B 2, 31 December 1942, *ibid.*; "List of Memoranda Issued in 1943 with Recommendations or Conclusions,"SC-B 4, 31 December 1943, *ibid.*; see also Schulzinger, *Wise Men*, 79.

should exercise influence in world politics in accordance with its position as the preeminent economic and military might. They were certain that the United States' interests spanned the whole globe and that no aspects of world politics and no region should be excluded from the design of future American foreign policy. State Department officials and Council members realized that decisions of individual nations had an impact on world politics, and thus on all nations, in a politically and economically interdependent global system.[76]

The War and Peace Studies had not only revealed that the Council was useful as a brain trust and research organization but had also demonstrated that the Council could well serve as a base for recruitment for high-level posts in the State Department and in other governmental agencies.[77]

The Council on Foreign Relations in 1945

Between 1939 and 1945 the Council, through meetings, discussion and study groups, and the publication of *Foreign Affairs*, had developed from a men's club to a brain trust. The "midwives," Armstrong, Mallory, Bowman, and Norman Davis, had worked hard to achieve this goal. A number of Council members had been associated closely with politicians and officials of the Roosevelt administration and had gained experience and contacts that worked to the advantage of the Council on Foreign Relations after World War II.

During these years, the Council also had increased its distinction on the national level. At the suggestion of the Carnegie Corporation and with its financial support, local branches of the Council on Foreign Relations, the Committees on Foreign Relations, had been founded in 1938. Francis P. Miller, a Rhodes Scholar who was formerly with the Foreign Policy Association, established in only four years twelve Committees on Foreign Relations before he joined the OSS.[78]

---

76. For post-war planning efforts, see Notter, *Postwar Policy Preparations*, and also David W. Eakins, "The Development of Corporate Liberal Policy Research in the United States 1885–1965" (Ph.D. diss., University of Wisconsin/Madison, 1966), summarized as "Business Planners and America's Postwar Expansion," in *Corporations and the Cold War* (New York, 1969), 143–71, David Horowitz, ed.

77. Aside from the State Department, the War and the Navy Departments, the War Production Board, and the Office of the Vice President had profited from *War and Peace Studies* memoranda. See CFR, "Princeton Conference," 3.

78. CFR, *Report of the Executive Director, 1938–1939*, 11; Francis P. Miller, *Man From the Valley* (Chapel Hill, NC, 1971), 40–42, 79, 84–88, 105. From 1940 to 1943 the Democrat Miller was a member of the Political Group of the War and Peace Studies. See "Preface," *ibid.* See also Harbaugh, *Laywer's Lawyer*, 356.

Influential members of the business community and academia in regions other than New York or the East Coast now had the opportunity to participate in Council activities. By way of the Committees they could join the network of elites concerned with foreign policy. The activities of the Committees, however, were guided by the Council on Foreign Relations. Sometimes topics under discussion were considered important by members of the local groups, but in most instances the Council on Foreign Relations recommended possible subjects for discussion. Miller and (as soon as the Committees could function without outside help) committee officers, made sure that the Council branches observed strict membership criteria. "Men who occupy positions of leadership in their communities" were selected and invited to become members.[79] The Committees met regularly in their own quarters in their own particular cities, and their members were invited to the annual membership meetings of the Council on Foreign Relations in New York. Committee members did not have a direct influence on the work of the Council, but they helped considerably to spread ideas and suggestions emanating from the Council on Foreign Relations. The Council was thus able to dampen prejudices Midwest elites might have had against the "East Coast establishment" and could influence public opinion throughout the United States. By the end of World War II, the Council could muster twenty committees that served as "listening posts to sense the mood of the country," as Miller put it.[80]

Opinion polls the Council received from these listening posts were published and distributed to Council members and politicians as well as to State Department officials. When Miller edited the first report, *Some Regional Views on our Foreign Policy*, in 1939, Committees already existed in Cleveland, OH; Denver, CO; Des Moines, IA; Detroit, MI; Houston, TX; Louisville, KY; Portland, OR; and St. Louis, MO. The members had discussed "The Tradition of America Political Isolationism vis-à-vis Europe," "The Closing Door and the Far East," "The Impact

79. For the Council itself, it was expected that prospective members held "a business, professional, or official position making it possible to influence opinion on matters of foreign policy." See "Criteria for Membership," in CFR, *Report on Membership Policy and New Procedures for Admission* ([1954], n.p.). Four years later the requirement was abbreviated to: ". . . position having to do with international problems." See CFR, "Procedures for Admission and Membership," enclosure, Arthur H. Dean to John D. Rockefeller, 16 June 1958, Office of the Messrs. Rockefeller Records, JDR, World Affairs 5, 187.1 #3, Rockefeller Archives Center.

80. John W. Davis to Arthur Sweetser, 21 November 1946, Arthur Sweetser Papers, box 45, Library of Congress. This long report was sent to all Council members on the occasion of the Council's 25th anniversary. Miller, *Man From the Valley*, 87.

of Other Forms of Government Upon Democratic Institutions," and "The Current Expansionist Policies of Japan, Germany, and Italy."[81]

The opinions Committee members expressed in their meetings in 1939 were, like the topics for discussion themselves, quite vague. The Des Moines Committee maintained that "the two most vital national interests are the maintenance of peace and the preservation of liberalism," and the Houston Committee argued that "our opposition to a foreign policy pointing toward war seems to be as definite as our disapproval of any interest in imperialism or in aggressive expansion whether political or economic." Similarly, the Houston Committee summarized that it was of vital importance that American foreign policy should safeguard "the chief good of America, our democratic way of life, the realization of the democratic ideals and principals which make our American society worth preserving."[82]

Since the initiation of the War and Peace Studies in 1939, the Council had thus considerably extended its activities and the number of members had increased. When the widow of Council member Harold I. Pratt, at the end of 1944, donated her house at the corner of 68th Street and Park Avenue to the Council, this gift was most gratefully accepted. A number of offices, meeting rooms, and a library in the three-story building improved the operations of Council staff and Council members considerably after the house had been repaired and newly furnished. Funds for the renovation and maintenance of the Harold Pratt House were provided by Council member John D. Rockefeller, Jr., so that the Council could move into its new rooms by the spring of 1945.[83]

---

81. In a letter to Clark Eichelberger, Council member W. Harold Dalgliesh summarized what expectations the Council had for the committees:

> The Committees serve a two-fold purpose: They stimulate the interest of their members in our foreign relations, and they help to keep the Council informed of the state of public opinion concerning international problems in the community. . . . A digest of the viewpoints expressed in the discussions is furnished by the Secretary to the Council; this report at the discretion of the Council's staff may be sent as a confidential document to the Department of State.

See Dalgliesh to Eichelberger, 9 January 1946, Clark M. Eichelberger Papers, box 18, New York Public Library.

82. Francis P. Miller, ed. *Some Regional Views on Our Foreign Policy* (New York, 1939), 55, 92, 122.

83. Letters to John D. Rockefeller, no sender, 6 June 1944, Offices of the Messrs. Rockefeller Records, JDR, World Affairs, 4; Jakab, "The Council," 435. Pratt had been director of Rockefeller's Standard Oil Company. A marble plaque, placed in the entrance hall of the Council headquarters, still reads: "The Harold Pratt House, given

Almost as if to belatedly compete with the conception twenty-five years previously of the Council's sister organization in Great Britain, the Royal Institute of International Affairs, the Harold Pratt House enjoyed a grand opening on 6 April 1945. Secretary of State Edward Stettinius, Jr., felt called upon "to bear witness, as every Secretary of State during the past quarter of a century, to the great services and influence of this organization in spreading knowledge and understanding of the issues of United States foreign policy." Hamilton Armstrong could only very indirectly corroborate this allusion because the unconditional surrender of the United States' most ruthless enemies, Germany and Japan, was still a few months hence, and the memoranda of the War and Peace Studies were still kept confidential. Thus, only the celebration of the opening of the house on 68th Street could reward the Council members for the work they had done for their country.[84]

In this new abode, the offices for *Foreign Affairs* could also take up a little more room. The periodical had won new readers constantly and in 1945 had more than 17,000 subscribers. Some of the articles in the magazine may only have been of interest to specialists and experts, but all readers knew that the information and analysis *Foreign Affairs* contained were usually grounded soundly on expertise, evidence, and intellect. This was most certainly one of the reasons why *Foreign Affairs* was highly regarded by politicians and members of academia and the business community.[85] To provide the interested public with even more information, the Council published reference books such as a *Foreign Affairs Bibliography* and, after 1927, a *Political Handbook and Atlas of the World*, as well as a *Survey of American Foreign Relations* (the title of the latter was changed to *The United States in World Affairs* in 1931).[86]

---

to the Council on Foreign Relations, by Harriet Barnes Pratt in memory of her husband Harold Irving Pratt, 1877–1939, a member of the Council 1923–1939."

84. CFR, Proceedings at the *Opening of the Harold Pratt House* (New York, 1945), 9, 5. Among the two hundred persons donating money for the maintenance of the Harold Pratt House Fund were Bowman, Hornbeck, Lamont, Warburg, Secretary of War Henry L. Stimson, Assistant Secretary of Commerce William A. M. Burden, Assistant Secretary of State William L. Clayton, Director-General of UNRRA Herbert H. Lehman, David, John D., Jr., John D. III, and Nelson A. Rockefeller (the latter assistant secretary of state), and the companies of IBM, the Chase National Bank, the National City Bank, and Standard Oil Company (New Jersey). See *ibid*, 14–16.

85. CFR, *Report of the Executive Director, 1944–1945* (New York, n. d.), 15. (Until 1947 these reports to the members were reproduced only in mimeographed form and restricted as *"Confidential for members."*)

86. Over the years, these publications had different editors: Hamilton F. Armstrong, William F. Langer, Walter Lippmann, Whitney Shepardson and Janis A. Kreslins. Publication of *United States in World Affairs* ceased after 1941; only after the end of World War II was this series continued.

By publishing these handbooks, reference volumes and the quarterly *Foreign Affairs*, the Council members followed their mandate to foster an internationalist public opinion. They regarded the War and Peace Studies as an important and constructive influence on American foreign policy. The founding members of the Council had worked to implement an internationalist liberal policy of the United States after World War I and had established the Council as a means to that end.

In the summer of 1945 conditions were quite different from the period after World War I. The United States had emerged from the Second World War as the most powerful economic and military nation in the world. Concentrating during the war on post-war planning, the Council members now saw their task as the struggle for a "just and lasting peace." This was a responsibility, they believed, which had to be taken as seriously as the war had been. They would certainly have agreed with their executive director Walter H. Mallory that the Council would have to continue its support for the State Department after the fighting had ceased. "The mere enumeration of the crucial questions which must be answered by the United States in the next few years," wrote Mallory in his annual report to the members in December of 1945, "makes it evident that those with special knowledge and experience should continue to help in any way they can to get private expert judgment built into political policy. The Council in peace and in war, must provide facilities for stimulating such work and for making it available to those who formulate our national program of foreign relations."[87]

When the Council on Foreign Relations, strengthened by its experiences during World War II, set out to help win the peace, however, it was confronted with the Cold War. Thus, the Council restructured and reorganized its study and discussion groups. The close cooperation with the State Department had been an exciting experience for many Council members. It evidently had led to the recognition of the Council as an important, if not pivotal, outside group in the process of the formulation of American foreign policy. But this collaboration with the administration had also had its disadvantages. The number of Council members actively involved in the War and Peace Studies had been relatively small while the majority of members had gained little from the Council during these years. Staff members had spent a major part of their time on the War and Peace Studies program. Because of its confidential nature, however, the program's reports and memoranda could

87. CFR, *Report of the Executive Director, 1944–1945*, 9.

not be used openly for the education of the members. Additionally, it had become evident that the Rockefeller Foundation would not continue its financial support for the project after the war had ended.

Preparing the Council for the Cold War

Thus, before the new study year began in the fall of 1945, twenty distinguished Council members[88] met in Princeton, New Jersey to reorganize the Council's activities for the post-war world. Walter Mallory had asked Bowman, the chairman of the Council's Committee on Studies, to organize the weekend meeting to design the future of the Council.[89] To Mallory's distress, representatives of both important foundations regularly financing Council activities (Joseph H. Willits of the Rockefeller Foundation, and Devereaux Josephs of the Carnegie Corporation) had to decline. Bowman was busy for the weekend and the president of Brown University (in Providence, RI), Henry B. Wriston, could not even be persuaded by the tempting postscript in Mallory's invitation, that "we will keep Saturday afternoon free for golf, so bring your clubs," to attend the meeting.[90]

---

88. Participants were: Frank Altschul (New York investment banker and secretary of the CFR, 1944–1972), Armstrong, Hanson W. Baldwin (military and naval editor of the *New York Times*), Percy W. Bidwell (director of studies of the Council, 1937–1953), Arthur H. Dean (with the law firm of Sullivan and Cromwell — the same firm the Dulles brothers belonged to — since 1923), William Edwin Diez (administrative secretary of the Steering Committee of the War and Peace Studies), Thomas K. Finletter (partner of Coudert Brothers and secretary of the Air Force, 1950–1953), Columbia University professor Carter Goodrich, Alvin Hansen, Clarence E. Hunter (vice-president of New York's Liberty National Bank from 1928–1949 and treasurer of the CFR from 1942–1951), Grayson Kirk, Mallory, Arthur W. Page (vice-president of American Telephone and Telegraph and son of Walter Hines Page, the well-known American ambassador to Great Britain during World War I), Winfield Riefler (special assistant to the American ambassador in London, from 1942–1944, responsible for Economic Warfare), Beardsley Ruml (trustee of the philanthropic Laura Spelman Rockefeller Fund and in a leading position in a number of other internationalist organizations), William H. Schubart (with Lazard Frères and Co. Bank, and, during World War II, assistant to the Office of Economic Warfare), Harold Sprout (political scientist, advisor to Office of War Information, State and Navy Departments), Frank Tannenbaum (professor for Latin American history at Columbia University), Jacob Viner, Edward P. Warner (vice-chairman of the Civil Aeronautics Board, 1941, 1943–1945, and recently elected president of the Provisional International Civil Aviation Organization). All members of the War and Peace Studies' Steering Committee were thus present or, as Bowman and Wriston, had been invited but did not attend.
89. Referring to the termination of the War and Peace Studies in December 1945 and the continuation of the Council's work, Walter H. Mallory wrote: "The question of how to win the peace was still unanswered. Hence the job of the Council was to reorganize its groups rather than demobilize them." See CFR, *Report of the Executive Director, 1945–1946* (New York, n.d.), 8, "Confidential for Members."
90. Copy, Mallory to Wriston, 16 July 1945, Bowman Papers; Mallory to Bowman, 21 August 1945, *ibid.*; Mallory to Willits, 26 September 1945, RFR, 1/100/97/877.

The first topic on the agenda on the morning on 8 September was an evaluation of past Council activities. Armstrong, taking the chair, told the men present that the Council had reached a point where new activities had to be conceived and planned. In a few days, on 20 September, the Council's Committee on Studies would have to decide if the remainder of the funds the Rockefeller Foundation had appropriated for the Council for the year should be used for continuation of the War and Peace Studies or, if it turned out to be more advisable, to discontinue the project and expend the Council's energy, and the Foundation's money, on the study of post-war problems.[91]

First, however, the editor of *Foreign Affairs* attempted to evaluate the productivity of the War and Peace Studies program. Armstrong told his audience that 361 meetings had taken place, on average attended by fifteen members. They had worked more than 21,000 hours in the service of the nation. The Council, Armstrong maintained, "was entitled to feel that it had performed a notable public service, during the war." Now it was high time, he continued, "to try to put the lessons which could be derived from that work to good account for the future."[92]

One development had become apparent during the course of the war: the national interest of the United States was no longer restricted to some regions and countries or to some specific problems. It now encompassed political and economic developments on the whole planet. The Council, Walter Mallory continued, had to take this new situation into account. From the wide array of all possible issues, it should choose subjects for its study and discussion program that offered the most practical implications. Additionally, he suggested, the study groups should be coordinated to avoid overlapping and duplication of work with other research institutions and universities.[93]

During the afternoon and the discussion of possible cooperation with other organizations, specific subjects for study groups were to be adopted. As a basis for discussion, William Schubart had prepared a memorandum suggesting eleven areas of concentration. Very soon, however, the Council members turned their attention to study and discus-

91. CFR, "Princeton Conference," 1. Copies of this digest prepared by Grayson Kirk were quite likely sent to all men present and to the Council's officers. A copy is attached to Mallory to Willits, 26 September 1945, RFR, 1/100/97/877.

92. CFR, "Princeton Conference," 2.

93. *Ibid.*, 6–7.

sion groups that would entail more than just one geographical area.[94] Although it was not realized at the time, the discussion reflected a decision between short-term and long-term studies. Whereas groups considering clear-cut issues and aspects would be able to take immediate concerns and requests raised outside the Council into account, groups studying whole regions would have to concentrate on long-term plans and problems. Additionally, Walter Mallory argued, it would be "far more difficult to elicit satisfactory reports and memoranda from the geographical committees." The Council staff was interested in such reports and memoranda, because they could be forwarded to the State Department or might be published as articles in *Foreign Affairs* or even as monographs.[95]

A passionate discussion on this problem ensued between Edward Warner and Mallory. Warner, supported by Carter Goodrich, argued that specific subjects would lend themselves much better to discussions and would produce results more easily. Alvin Hansen and Beardsley Ruml emphasized pragmatic aspects, and Hansen Baldwin maintained "that it would be important to agree upon a series of subjects for functional organization which would mesh together with the regional groups in such a way as to minimize or avoid duplication and conflict." To bring the discussion to a close, Armstrong finally suggested a compromise: five or six regional groups could be established. These would have a larger membership than usual and would convene only when imminent problems arose or when an "unusually competent person" was to address the group. Armstrong's proposal met the accord of the Council members, and the discussion could advance to specific projects for individual groups.[96]

Spurred by the deployment of atomic bombs over Hiroshima and Nagasaki little more than a month before, the Council gave priority to the problem of the influence of nuclear weapons developments on the United Nations' potential to prevent wars. Military expert Baldwin suggested that this discussion should encompass probabilities for weakening or strengthening the United Nations. At variance with the opinions of American military officials, his suggestion developed from the conviction "that there would be only a brief period before the use of these newest technical discoveries would become the common property of all

94. William H. Schubart, "Thoughts on the Further Usefulness of the Council on Foreign Relations," August 1945, enclosure, Mallory to Bowman, 21 August 1945, Bowman Papers; a copy is in the Jessup Papers, box A116.

95. CFR, "Princeton Conference," 17–19.

96. *Ibid.*, 19–20.

the great powers."[97] The development of nuclear weapons would certainly influence the organization of American armed forces and had to be taken into account when conceiving a future American foreign policy.

Thomas Finletter (personal assistant to Secretary of War Henry L. Stimson during World War II) maintained that this subject was closely related to the topics "National Power and Foreign Policy" and "American Foreign Policy after San Francisco," which had been suggested for other study groups. Again a discussion ensued. Ruml, Warner, and Bidwell called for a group researching "objectives of American foreign policy" in general. The findings of this group could provide a basis from which the other groups could then operate. The other members, however, did not agree and the proposal was not discussed further.[98]

As the discussion continued, it became obvious that the men present had problems with precisely defining individual areas for study and discussion groups and then making distinctions among them. Bidwell's solution to this particular problem was the suggestion to establish "country groups." He received support from those who believed that the Council membership would more readily participate in broadly defined groups. After further discussion, five functional groups and six regional groups were picked from the wide range of all possibilities proposed.[99]

An increase in Council activities superseding the War and Peace Studies also required an enlargement of the Council staff. Mallory, who during the war had to take care of only four groups, would have been overtaxed by the expected increase in the number of Council groups.[100]

97. Shortly before, Baldwin had published an article entitled "Atomic Bomb Responsibilities" in the *New York Times.* He accused the Truman administration of wasting time and argued that international control of atomic energy should be instituted speedily. Atomic energy would have been an extraordinary scientific achievement, he maintained, but the victims at Hiroshima and Nagasaki starkly portrayed the end of moral leadership for the United States. See *New York Times,* 12 September 1945.

98. CFR, "Princeton Conference," 21–24.

99. *Functional Groups*: 1. Objectives of American Foreign Policy; 2. National Power and Foreign Policy; 3. Organization of Peace; 4. Organization and Formulation of U.S. Foreign Policy; 5. Economic Questions: Industrialization, Trade, Financial Policy, International Air Transport. *Regional Groups*: 1. Japan and China; 2. Germany and Central Europe; 3. Russia; 4. Latin America; 5. British Commonwealth; 6. France. See CFR, "Princeton Conference," 24–31; CFR, "Topics for Future Studies," enclosure, Mallory to Bowman, 21 August 1945, Bowman Papers; "Inter-Office Correspondence; From: RFE to JHW [Willits], *Subject*: CFR Princeton Conference," 24 September 1945, RFR, 1/100/97/877.

100. The Council had had problems during the war keeping the regular groups functioning. Only 86 members participated in the study groups for the year 1944–1945

He therefore suggested that the Council hire additional staff members. A Steering Committee, similar to the body operative during the War and Peace Studies project, was proposed to coordinate the groups' work. The Council's Committee on Studies, chaired by Bowman,[101] was informed of the results of the conference, and on 20 September it decided to reorganize the study groups of the Council as had been suggested.

Thus, nine study and discussion groups could be created or revitalized for the post-war period. The groups "National Power and Foreign Policy" and "American-Russian Relations," were to attract many Council members. "The Organization of Peace" group paid special attention to the influence of atomic weapons technology on the development of the United Nations, and the "Economic Aspects of American Foreign Policy" group concentrated on problems of financial credit and investment in the post-war period. As the discussions at the Princeton Inn had suggested, a study group on the "Formulation and Administration of American Foreign Policy" was founded. Additionally, regional groups — "British Commonwealth and Empire Affairs," "Far Eastern Affairs," "Latin American Affairs" — were established. In particular, a regional group on "Western European Affairs" (continued as a study group on "The Problem of Germany") received much attention during the next few years.[102]

These study and discussion groups can be divided into different regional and thematic areas. Thus, the meetings of important study and discussion groups will serve as guidelines for the following discussion of Council activities, but deliberations in other groups will be taken into account as well. With the beginning of the Cold War setting the stage, the new definition of the relationship between the United States and the Soviet Union was the paramount issue. Next to this strand running through almost all Council meetings, some other facets are accentuated and can be

("Legal Problems of Reconstruction," "International Business Arrangements," "United States Relations with Argentina, Brazil, and Mexico," and "United States Relations with Russia"). See CFR, *Report, 1944–1945*, 9–12.

101. The other members of the Committee on Studies were Armstrong, Allen Dulles, Finletter, Page, Ruml, Riefler (by that time economist at the Institute for Advanced Study at Princeton University), John H. Williams (economist at Harvard University), and Wriston. Only three of these men had not been present at the conference: Dulles, Williams and Wriston.

102. CFR, *Report, 1945–1946*, 8–14. Bidwell had already maintained at the Princeton conference that "a better result could be achieved by a study group devoted, for example, to the problem of Germany, but which was instructed to examine this problem as broadly as possible in the general western European setting." See CFR, "Princeton Conference," 30.

distinguished. These are primarily the reflections on Europe (Germany and European Recovery), Asia (Japan and China), and, as almost a second broad issue, the United States' future role in world politics.

In these first years after World War II, Germany became the major battlefield of the confrontation between the two disparate social, economic, and political systems represented by the United States and the Soviet Union. Formerly the common enemy, Germany was rapidly transformed to an agent in the slowly escalating, or — more precisely — resurfacing conflict between the U.S. and the USSR, rendering the wartime cooperation useless. Hence, analysis and delineation of the development of the Soviet-American relationship breaks off with the evolution of the Truman Doctrine and events preceding the inauguration of the Marshall Plan. The issue will be picked up again after discussions within the Council on European rehabilitation and Germany have been depicted.

In a dialectical system of interdependent decisions and events, this demarcation is necessarily artificial. It yields, nonetheless, a greater clarity of description and analysis by allowing concentration on individual topics and problems. Wherever necessary for understanding the argumentation, deliberations in Council groups concentrating on other geographical or political fields will be related. Inevitably in this period, groups on the Soviet Union and on Europe overlapped in topics of discussion, participants, and invited speakers.

3
The Soviet Union and the United States:
Allies or Potential Enemies?

In the early Cold War years, opinions on the possible interests of the Soviet Union and on an adequate American foreign policy vis-à-vis the USSR, within the Truman administration as well as within the Council, were scattered over a wide spectrum ranging from naive sympathy to irrational distrust. As Thomas G. Paterson has outlined, a number of miscellaneous factors, in addition to more obvious reasons, influenced the decision-making process in American foreign policy during these years: distorted images of reality, fears, irrationality, personality in style, supposed lessons from the past, traditional political ideals, bureaucratic lethargy, domestic restraints, public opinion, and economic and military interests.[1]

Deliberations within Council groups reflected these diverse elements. Discussions and papers were sometimes grounded in insecurity and lack of factual knowledge. This frequently led participants to revert to often poorly defined ideals: open door policy, free and democratic institutions, and capitalism. These ideals were frequently regarded as a panacea for all of the perceived ills of world politics.

Shortly after the fighting had ceased in Europe and Japan, it became obvious that the Soviet Union was likely to disregard what American politicians and Council members alike believed to be axiomatic prerequisites. Additionally, distrust of any kind of different social order, only slightly obscured by the experience as allies in the war against Nazi Germany, surfaced again.[2] Those few Council members who had been impressed through the New Deal era and the Roosevelt administration with its liberal attitude toward the USSR — one based on a belief in the

1. Thomas G. Paterson, *Soviet-American Confrontation: Postwar Reconstruction and the Origins of the Cold War* (Baltimore, 1973), ix.

2. For the Russian Revolution as one of the pivotal events shaping this distrust, see N. Gordon Levin, Jr., *Woodrow Wilson and World Politics: America's Response to War and Revolution* (New York, 1968).

possibility of peaceful coexistence — soon lost their influence in the Council, as did their like-minded peers in the Truman administration.[3]

The American government faced a difficult situation after 1945: the traditional objectives of U.S. foreign policy, namely multinational free world trade[4] in Europe, Asia, and Latin America, were hopefully to be sustained. At the same time, a means had to be found to absorb the USSR, with its very different social and economic order, into the system of international politics. To achieve this, some Council members soon maintained, it would become necessary to break the economic, intellectual, and social blockade the Soviet Union had erected against the West, without at the same time antagonizing this ally. A free contest of systems, many officials in the State Department and most of the Council members hoped, would show without doubt that the capitalist system was superior to socialism, simply because it provided more goods for consumption and a better "way of life."

The Council on Foreign Relations in its self-adopted role as a brain trust of American foreign policy could have given invaluable advice and guidance in this respect. Eminent experts among its members (political scientists and historians, economists and members of the business community well-acquainted with the situation in Europe, the Soviet Union, and the prerequisites and possibilities of international trade) met for many rounds of meetings. Unfortunately, some of the discussions soon became little more than airings of prejudices and group members' attempts to defend their preconceptions. Results supposed to serve as guidelines for American foreign policy were rather scant. Within the "Study Group on American-Russian Relations," internal strife between those members more inclined to cooperation with the USSR and those favoring a confrontational course, prevented the publication of a final report of the group's findings compiled by George S. Franklin, Jr., which

3. How Franklin D. Roosevelt would have conducted his foreign policy after the war can only be guessed. Interpretations of historians in this respect differ and are, of necessity, based on "counter-factual" interpretations. It seems certain, however, that Roosevelt was willing to make concessions to ensure the goodwill of Soviet leaders.

4. This trade had always been only "relatively free" because of protective tariffs in the United States and elsewhere. As the idealized and ideological basis of American foreign policy, however, it never vanished. For the correlation between foreign policy and foreign economic policy, see William H. Becker and Samuel F. Wells, eds., *Economics and World Power: An Assessment of American Diplomacy Since 1789* (New York, 1984), and a contemporary evaluation in Thomas C.T. McCormick, ed., *Problems of the Postwar World* (New York, 1945).

the group's chairman, William Schubart, had hoped would contribute to a sensible American foreign policy.[5]

The Council might thus have wasted an opportunity to positively influence post-war politics. State Department officials attending group meetings could sometimes gain little more than a confused understanding of the possible intentions and potential of the USSR. The business community, an integral part of the open door ideology and the idea of a peaceful contest of systems, was in many cases no less insecure, divided, and uneducated about the USSR than the man in the street and many State Department officials. In this regard, discussions within the Council reflected the development within the American administration. Both factions had a clearly defined goal — peace — but were ambivalent about the ways and means to reach and protect this aim.[6]

Some Council members maintained that the leaders of the USSR had exhibited a considerable measure of goodwill. They counted on peacefully integrating this powerful nation into supranational institutions such as the United Nations and the system of free international trade. Bankers and lawyers among the Council members criticized the "naive hopes" of their peers, who were mostly from the world of academia. They advocated what they called a more "realistic" approach toward Soviet interests and actions. With the exception of Council members such as William Schubart and George Franklin, they did not believe that the common goal — lasting peace — would be sufficient to overcome the differences between the dissimilar social and economic systems, and some even doubted the Soviet Union's will to secure peace.

Even before official policy in Washington disposed of what was still left of its strategy for a peaceful coexistence, these Council members called for a very guarded approach toward the Soviet Union and even urged that the United States should prepare itself for armed conflict with the USSR. The dispute within the Council evolved, from the end of 1945 through 1946, from a restrained attitude of confrontation among the more conservative Council members that coexisted with a somewhat naive hope for a better world among the more liberal Council members, to an inclination of most members toward military preparedness for a major confrontation.

---

5. Franklin functioned as rapporteur of the group. William H. Schubart to Frank Altschul, 15 June 1946, USR/RGCFR-XVIIA.

6. E.O. Czempiel, *Das amerikanische Sicherheitssystem 1945–1949* (Berlin, 1966), 60–62.

When in March of 1945 the United States and the Soviet Union were still allies in their fight against the Axis Powers and the war in Europe was two months from resolution, the Study group "United States Relations with Russia" met for the first time.[7] The chairman of the group, Lazard Frères banker William H. Schubart, addressed the members with words disclosing his great hopes that the USSR would open itself to international liberal trade. He even saw signs of development toward democracy:

> It seems reasonable to suppose that if economic and political cooperation between Russia and the United States could be developed in peace as military cooperation between the two nations has been developed in war, the world might look forward to an era of relative stability and considerable prosperity.

Although he realized that the political system of the Soviet Union was a dictatorship and that trade and industry were controlled by the administration, he believed "that Russia is moving toward democracy and may intend to take her place among the great trading nations of the world."[8]

Schubart, as a banker more used to the world of trade and finance, had planned at first to concentrate only on those aspects of American-Soviet relations familiar to him. He had given a draft of his address to Bidwell. "It seems to me increasingly important," the director of studies wrote, urging Schubart to also reflect on other topics, "that we should be able to break down the intellectual blockade with which the Russians have surrounded themselves." Schubart added this suggestion to his speech, pointing out that justifiable doubts existed as to whether the Soviet Union was honestly interested in an exchange of ideas.[9]

Some time before the meeting took place, all study group members had received "Three Views as to Russia's Future," an essay written by Raymond L. Buell, the former president of the Foreign Policy Association (FPA). On the evening of 21 March, the author was invited to expand on his treatise. In what he had termed "Thermidor Theory," Buell compared the situation in the USSR with conditions that had existed in France shortly before Robespierre was toppled on 27 July

7. Council members used the terms Russia and Soviet Union interchangeably. Invitations for participation in the study group were mailed in the first weeks of March. See Schubart to John H. Hazard, 7 March 1945, USR/RGCFR-XVID.

8. "Schubart's opening remarks" (handwritten notes), Draft, 12 March 1945, USR/RGCFR-XVID; Digest of Discussion (herafter cited as DD), "First Meeting," 21 March 1945, 1, *ibid.*

9. Bidwell to Schubart, 13 March 1945, USR/RGCFR-XVID; DD, 21 March 1945, 1, *ibid.*

1794, the ninth of Thermidor. The Soviet Union, likewise, was on its way to becoming a bourgeois liberal state, and it would cooperate with Great Britain and the U.S., as soon as the Western nations proposed such cooperation, Buell predicted. This at least was the expectation, Buell claimed, of the majority of officials within governmental agencies. The restraint the USSR had displayed in Poland, Finland, and in the Balkan states, was seen as an indicator for such an attitude.[10]

Another theory Buell introduced, the "Universal State Theory," followed an analytical approach "meta-historian" Arnold J. Toynbee had introduced in his multi-volume work, *A Study of History*, examining twenty-one "civilizations" over a period of six thousand years. A "civilization" would change, Buell maintained, when a "crazy minority" broke up the crust of the old order. As soon as a time of unrest developed, this group would change into a repressive class establishing a "universal state." This, in turn, would again allow a "crazy minority" to establish a new order. Although World War II had drawn to a close and a time of unrest had developed, Buell admitted that he could see no drastic changes in the power structure within the USSR. Unlike Schubart, he and the other members could not detect a development toward democracy: "The Russians seem definitely to believe that they are already more democratic and free than we are. They call those who oppose them, as for example in Russia and Poland, fascists." "Dr. Buell," Franklin wrote in his digest of the discussion, somewhat irritated, "said he could not explain the reasons for their so believing."[11]

Although many members agreed with Buell's evaluation, many were critical. Joseph Barnes of the New York *Herald Tribune* was doubtful as to whether Soviet foreign policy followed strict rules or paid attention to domestic developments. The formation of American policy toward the Soviet Union and toward the change in Europe after the war, he maintained, would at least have some impact on Soviet politics. Buell's argument that influential groups within the USSR, namely the Red Army (which had won privileges and powerful positions after the war with Finland), would oppose an opening to the west, was challenged by Edward C. Carter, the general secretary of the Institute of Pacific Relations. Together with Barnes he emphasized the prospects a friendly policy toward the USSR might entail. "There is tremendous interest and

10. Buell was research director from 1927 to 1933 and president of the FPA from 1933 to 1938. "Material for Discussion, First Meeting—3/12/45," USR/RGCFR-XVID.

11. Arnold J. Toynbee, *A Study of History* (New York, 1935–1961) 12 volumes. DD, 21 March 1945, 2, 5, USR/RGCFR-XVID.

enthusiasm for this country in Russia," he argued, "and there is a great desire to catch and surpass us. This interest is a capital asset in the inter-cultural area."[12]

The study group itself suffered from the lack of Soviet interest in exchanging information informally. In organizing the group and in his early planning to invite Soviet emissaries to attend group meetings, Schubart had encountered only unwillingness to participate and to accept the Council as an important forum. During the war, the Council had conducted a number of meetings with officials of the Canadian and British embassies and consulates in the U.S. Now, it was taken for granted that the USSR would also have an interest in a similar opportunity for exchanges with American experts. When Percy Bidwell, on 14 January 1944, invited the secretary of the Soviet Embassy, Vladimir Basikin, to such a meeting, his invitation was rejected. Three weeks later, Bidwell and Schubart, in a meeting with Ambassador Andrei Gromyko, again tried to persuade the Soviets to participate in Council groups — to no avail.[13]

Thus, Schubart's study group had to work without Soviet participation. Its work had to be based on second-hand data and on the personal experiences of American journalists, bankers, lawyers, and a few industrialists, experiences which in most cases had occurred years before. These rather scant data led to discussions often dominated by prejudices and preconceptions, widely lacking in expertise and an analytical understanding of the ideological and traditional bases and perspectives of Soviet policy toward the U.S. Suggestions for a future American policy toward the Soviet Union were hardly advanced by these deliberations; rather, the meetings turned out to be merely a process of synchronizing the "correct" view of the USSR among Council members.

In this situation, the members' reaction to this first meeting remained rather subdued. Too little agreement was achieved about the aims and tasks of the group. This changed very little at the second meeting, when one of the most important aspects of the relationship between the two nations was discussed, a topic that should have interested members from finance and banking especially: the six billion dollar credit the

---

12. During the time of McCarthyite witch-hunt, Carter was accused because of his "Sovietophile" attitude. In the 1930s he had been in the USSR a number of times and had not regarded the Soviet Union as a totalitarian state. He had defended Stalinist purges and the German-Soviet Nonaggression Pact of 1939. He remained a Russophile until his death in 1954. DD, 21 March 1945, 6–7, USR/RGCFR-XVID.

13. Schulzinger, *Wise Men,* 115.

USSR had requested for the rehabilitation of its war-torn industries and economy. John Scott, of *Time/Life*, lamented that "we 'do not know what we want.' Each member of the gentlemen present knew what his firm wanted, namely dollars and export business with the Russians and others. But collectively the dollar means something only in terms of some imported commodity or gold. As a group," he stated regretfully, "that crowd should have been able to define our national commercial desires better than almost any group I know." Scott thought it possible that the credit could be a means to induce changes in Soviet political behavior: "If we could buy permanent peace for six billion it would be a bargain if we could be sure." A more thorough and fruitful evaluation of this aspect could only be expected, he believed, if the group discussed the subject of credit in a meeting centered exclusively on this topic.[14]

The question of an American contribution to Soviet economic rehabilitation was not a new topic in 1945.[15] At least some of the members present (through their close connection with the Department of State during the war) might have known about consultations Council member W. Averell Harriman had had on this subject in 1943 when he was American ambassador to Moscow.[16] A number of times, in 1943 and in 1945, the United States had offered the USSR help in reconstructing its economy after the war. The Soviet Union had suffered enormously and Anastas I. Mikoyan (commissar for external and internal trade) and Foreign Minister Molotov had supported the proposal. Officials in the U.S. regarded economic aid as a means to strengthen the economic and political ties with their eastern ally. Additionally, they hoped that the resulting increase in trade would facilitate a smooth change from war economy to peace economy for the United States itself.[17]

14. Scott to Bidwell, 27 April 1945, USR/RGCFR-XVID.

15. The Economic and Financial Group of the War and Peace Studies, for example, had prepared a report entitled "Postwar Economic Problems: International Relief, Labor Problems and Social Legislation, International Trade, International Commodity Problems, Monetary Reconstruction, International Long-Term Investment," 1 April 1942, E-B 49, CFRW+P. Of the members of the "United States' Relations with Russia" study group, Bidwell, Schubart, and William Diebold had participated in the Economic and Financial Group.

16. Harriman had been named ambassador by Roosevelt in October 1943 and remained at this post until February 1946. For a delineation of events, see Paterson, "Diplomatic Weapon: The Abortive Loan to Russia," chapter 2, in *Soviet-American Confrontation,* 33–56. The credit is mentioned in almost all studies of Soviet-American relations of this period, but interpretations and evaluations differ widely.

17. Harriman had told Mikoyan that the trade between the two nations being fostered by the credit would be "in the self-interest of the United States" and would help "to be able to afford full employment during the period of transition from war-time to peace-

To the surprise of Harriman, Molotov presented, on 3 January 1945, a formal request for a credit of six billion dollars for the purchase of pipes, rails, wagons, locomotives, and other goods of industry. The conditions the USSR proposed were considerably more favorable than the U.S. was prepared to accept: the credit was to be paid back in small sums after a moratorium of nine years, and with only two and a quarter percent interest. Although Harriman and his colleagues were surprised that the Soviets suddenly pressed these proposals, they did not want to dismiss them out of hand. If the Soviet desire was declined, they feared, a chance to procure political concessions from the USSR might be lost. In agreement with Harriman's thinking, William L. Clayton, undersecretary of state for economic affairs, and a number of other State Department officials, had hoped that the Soviet Union would be prepared to make such concessions in Eastern Europe, the Balkan states, in its policy at the United Nations, or in the problematic situation in Iran in accordance with American desires.[18]

Unexpectedly, however, the credit was not taken up by the White House before July 1945, when Harry S. Truman, the successor to President Roosevelt, asked Congress to increase appropriations for the Import-Export Bank by seven hundred million to 3.5 billion dollars. Of this, one billion dollars was earmarked for the Soviet Union.[19] The Council members were informed of this development when Council member James Reston (who had superb contacts with the State Department) mentioned the credit in an article in the *New York Times.*

The discussion of the credit issue on 24 April had not satisfied discussion leader Scott, and chairman Schubart put the issue on the agenda for the next meeting on 22 May. Economist Alexander Gerschenkron, member of the board of governors of the Federal Reserve System and an expert on economic relations with the Soviet Union, was invited as speaker and discussion leader for this third meeting of the study group.[20] Realizing that the USSR was possibly on its way to

---

time economy." See W. Averell Harriman, "Certain Factors Underlying Our Relationship with the Soviet Union," 14 November 1945, quoted in Paterson, *Soviet-American Confrontation,* 35. See also Harriman to Secretary of State, U.S. Department of State, *Foreign Relations of the United States, 1944* (in the following abbreviated *FRUS* followed by year and volume number), 4: 1034–1035.

18. *FRUS, 1945,* 5: 939–40, 942–45, 966.

19. Paterson, *Soviet-American Confrontation,* 42.

20. Gerschenkron was invited with the usual promise that "no reporters will be present, and no publicity will be given to the proceedings." See Bidwell to Gerschenkron,

becoming the most influential power in Europe and Asia, Gerschenkron told the group: "Unless we can achieve understanding, the world can hardly fail to shift from crisis to crisis, finally culminating in the catastrophe of another world war." Tying the Soviet Union to the system of international trade, he argued, would likely prevent this from happening and it might, additionally, secure American employment in the long run.

After the ensuing discussion had turned to the question of whether the Soviet economic system would permit exports at all, and a debate of possible consequences of trade between free market societies and planned economies, Frank Altschul turned the attention again to the issue of the credit for the USSR. Like Gerschenkron, he maintained that a credit should depend on the political and military situation. Such a credit, he cautioned, could considerably enhance the war potential of the USSR. Bidwell, regarding this disapproving analysis as too far-fetched, reproached Altschul's hard-line attitude with the argument that a close affiliation of the USSR with the international trade system as a result of the credit was more likely to enhance the peace potential of the USSR. To move forward in the discussion, Bidwell proposed to draft a working paper for the next meeting called for 6 June.[21]

Full domestic employment, it was agreed at that meeting, was assured for the next three or four years and did not depend on an expansion of economic ties with the Soviet Union. An integration of the USSR into the international trading system would not only have positive aspects, members argued, but also contained the risk of disrupting world trade. Rehabilitation of the war-torn country would be possible without help from the outside because the people were used to a low standard of living and priority would be given to investments in heavy industry anyway. Large exports of goods from the USSR were not very likely, it was anticipated, and only the expenditures of American tourists might constitute a considerable export of American capital to the Soviet Union. The members agreed that trade with the USSR should be reduced to a minimum and that possibly harmful agreements and treaties were to be avoided. A clear consensus, however, on guidelines that might be supplied to officials in Washington could not be reached.[22]

---

5 May 1945, USR/RGCFR-XVID. In 1945, Gerschenkron published his *Economic Relations with the U.S.S.R.* (New York, 1945).

21. DD, 2 May 1945, 2, 6, 8, 11, USR/RGCFR-XVID. Bidwell to Altschul, 24 May 1945, *ibid.*; Bidwell, "The Problems of Trade Policy in American-Russian Relations: A Working Paper for Discussion, 4th Meeting, 6/6/45," 24 May 1945, *ibid.*

22. DD, 6 June 1945, 2-6, 11, USR/RGCFR-XVID. Susan J. Linz argues, in her study on the possible impact on the Soviet economy of a one billion dollar credit in 1946,

Until the end of September, no further meetings of the group took place and rapporteur Franklin used the time to work on a final report summarizing the results of the group meetings during this customary summer break. When on 25 September, East Asia expert Owen Lattimore[23] was invited to discuss the future role of the USSR in that region, Schubart summarized what he believed to be the consensus among the group members:

1. Russia and the United States will be the two great powers of the post-war world;
2. Russian policy is flexible and likely to be determined by national rather than ideological considerations;
3. World communism is likely to be revived as a primary Russian interest policy only in the failure of international cooperation;
4. We would like to believe Russia is interested in international cooperation, though she will not make any unnecessary concession to bring it about;
5. She is determined to have friendly governments on her Western [*sic*] border to insure her security in case of failure of international security arrangements;
6. Enduring cooperation with Russia must be based on understanding and we must, therefore, break down her intellectual blockade;
7. Russia must not meddle in our internal affairs or use her foreign trade monopoly to dislocate free economies;
8. Russia must carry out her agreements with us in spirit as well as in form, and we must be just as careful to carry out scrupulously our agreements with her;
9. We must make a real effort to understand Russia's viewpoint and particularly her need for security after three centuries of bitter experience.

In addition to this evaluation, Schubart stated his support for a recognition of acquisitions of areas that had become part of the USSR

---

that it would have contributed little to the gross national product of the USSR (4.7 to 6.5 billion rubles). See Linz, "Foreign Aid and Soviet Postwar Recovery," *Journal of Economic History* 45 (December 1985): 947-54.

23. Lattimore headed the Walter Hines Page School of International Affairs of Johns Hopkins University. In 1943 Lattimore had been accredited as President Roosevelt's personal emissary to Chiang Kai-shek. McCarthy-era accusations against Lattimore — also documented in his autobiographical *Ordeal by Slander* (Boston, 1950) — are delineated in Stanley I. Kutler, *The American Inquisition: Justice and Injustice in the Cold War* (New York, 1982), 183–214. In the spring of 1945 Lattimore had published his study *Solution in Asia* (Boston, 1945).

over the last six years — including the Baltic states, parts of Finland, Romania, and Prussia.[24]

The group chairman may have been inspired to conduct this moderate appraisal of Soviet intentions by a paper Vera M. Dean of the Foreign Policy Association had given almost three weeks before, on 6 September, at a meeting of the Council's Steering Committee.[25] Arguing that Soviet Foreign Minister Molotov could have been invited to be one of the chairpersons of the founding conference of the United Nations at San Francisco, Vera Dean during that meeting expanded on her argument regarding the primary importance of closely tying the USSR to international organizations.[26] To the chagrin of some Council members, she could see no great differences between the actions of the United States and the Soviet Union in the political arena:

> We complain bitterly about her [the USSR] failure to arrange prompt free elections in Eastern Europe, but we have done no better in Italy.
>
> We demand bases for our security in the Pacific. Russia feels that she must have certain of the Baltic countries for her security and for the same reason that she must make sure of friendly governments in Eastern Europe.

Again, it was Fran Altschul who expressed great distrust of the USSR during the heated discussion which followed. When the question was raised as to how strong the American ties to Great Britain should be, he repeated the slogan of Britain as the "first line of defense" of the American continent; a slogan repeatedly proclaimed before and during World War II by the Committee to Defend America.[27] To Bidwell's objection

24. DD, 25 September 1945, 1–2, USR/RGCFR-XVID.

25. The Steering Committee, assigned to monitor the draft of the final report, had met on 4 May 1945, 28 July 1945, 6 September 1945, and later on 1 October 1945, 18 October 1945, 15 November 1945, 26 November 1945, and 15 February 1946. Vera M. Dean, because of her moderate attitude toward the USSR, was later accused of being a "fellow traveler" of communism. See Julius Epstein, *The Case Against Vera Micheles Dean and the Foreign Policy Association* (n.p., 1947). See also Minutes of Meeting, Executive Committee of the FPA, 22 January 1947, Frank R. McCoy Papers, box 73, Library of Congress, and the additional correspondence and pamphlets in this collection.

26. She argued similarly in *The United States and Russia* (Cambridge, MA, 1948).

27. In the summer, Altschul had circulated a proposed outline for a contribution to *Foreign Affairs.* He argued strongly in favor of a American policy "based on frank avowal of Anglo-American solidarity." Council staffers Mallory, Bidwell, Armstrong, and Byron Dexter (Armstrong's assistant) were startled that Altschul was prepared to give up the United Nations even before that instrument had had a chance to start operating. Altschul believed that American security was imminently threatened by the USSR. At that time, the staffers still regarded this evaluation as overly pessimistic, and

that it would be very difficult to reach an agreement among three partners when two had already agreed to close cooperation, the financier from Wall Street responded adamantly: "We and Britain are inevitably tied together and you can't change the facts of the situation."[28]

Lattimore had little that was new to tell the group members on this 25 September. Only when Major George Fielding Eliot raised the subject of the military situation within the USSR did discussion erupt.[29] The atomic bomb had changed the power relations in favor of the United States and Great Britain, and Eliot argued that the leaders of the USSR would most certainly press for a speedy development of their own atomic weapons. This would be true especially if they had the feeling that "we are likely to push them around if they do not have such weapons." Incidentally, only a few days earlier Secretary of State James F. Byrnes had created exactly such a suspicion at the Council of Foreign Ministers' conference at London. In a conversation, Molotov had asked Byrnes if he had an atomic bomb in his pocket. Byrnes had responded "jokingly" that Southerners like himself would always carry "our artillery in our hip pocket. If you don't cut out all the stalling and let us get down to work, I am going to pull an atomic bomb out of my pocket and let you have it."[30]

Contrary to what passed for common knowledge, Eliot knew that there was no single "atomic secret" and that Soviet scientists undoubtedly would find the means to develop such a weapon without very great difficulty. Along with Secretary of War Stimson, he believed that an international agreement on control of atomic energy would be essential for the security of the United States. Until this was achieved, the superior military might of the Western nations might have a positive impact on Soviet foreign policy.[31]

---

the possibility of publication of such an article was rejected. See "Memorandum for Mr. Armstrong," 20 July 1945, Armstrong Papers, box 2. For the Committee to Defend America, see chapter 7.

28. "Steering Committee, Study Group on U.S. Relations with Russia," 6 September 1945, 4, 6–7, USR/RGCFR-XVIIA.

29. From 1922 to 1933 Eliot was with U.S. Army Intelligence. He published studies on military subjects and became military and naval correspondent of the New York *Herald Tribune* (1939 to 1946).

30. DD, 10 October 1945, 2, USR/RGCFR-XVID. See also the quotations from Byrnes, Molotov, Harriman, and General Dwight D. Eisenhower on this topic in Thomas G. Paterson, *On Every Front: The Making of the Cold War* (New York, 1979), 89.

31. DD, 10 October 1945, 1–2, USR/RGCFR-XVID. He thus came to conclusions similar to Hanson Baldwin's. See also the chapter "Pax Atomica: The Myth of the Atom-

When Schubart once again introduced the credit the USSR had requested into the discussion, Altschul again raised considerable doubts as to the trustworthiness of the Soviet Union. "How can we logically aid her industrial reconstruction if we don't want her to have the atomic bomb?" he asked. As before, the study group members could not agree on an answer to this important question. The dilemma was obvious: if the credit was useful in inducing more cooperation with the USSR, it was advisable to aid reconstruction. If the Soviet Union was secretly preparing for aggression, American aid would nourish a dangerous enemy. Thus, it might be more advisable to wait and see if the Soviet Union showed a readiness for cooperation. This in turn bore the risk of inadequate support of positive developments — but it also was an approach that would make American aid less of a juggling act with priceless eggs. Torn between the desire to tie the USSR closer to the United Nations organization on the one hand, and the fear of a possible enemy on the other, the Council members regressed in their arguments and ideas to the well-worn ideal of "peace and prosperity." That the USSR believed a *cordon sanitaire* to be indispensable for her security remained an enigma to some members. Eliot maintained that the importance the Soviets attached to a few hundred square miles of territory, in a time of long-range bombers, guided missiles, and atomic bombs, might indicate that the Soviet leaders had not learned the lessons of the past. He also found it difficult to envision "how Russian security need could justify domination of countries which wanted to be free in any event."[32]

Vera Dean, Owen Lattimore, and George Eliot had provided support for the more liberal members of the group, so that men such as Frank Altschul (at least in the digests of discussion) appeared almost cantankerous. Now, at the last meeting, on 23 October, the discussion leader was more to the taste of those who mistrusted the USSR. Michael Karpovich, a former member of the diplomatic mission to the United States of the Aleksandr F. Kerensky government of the short-

ic Secret," in Gregg Herken, *The Winning Weapon: The Atomic Bomb in the Cold War* (New York, 1980), 97–113. Nobody knew just how long the Soviet Union would take to develop its own atom bombs; estimates ranged from six months to six years. See Stephen Duggan (director of the Institute of International Education) to Schubart, 15 October 1945, USR/RGCFR-XVID.

32. DD, 10 October 1945, 5–8, USR/RGCFR-XVID. In 1945, the explosions on Hiroshima and Nagasaki had an immense impact on most contemporaries and on the group members. A vastly superior weapons system seemed to have been created, making all conventional weapons obsolete. For the impact on American society, see Paul Boyer, *By the Bomb's Early Light: American Thought and Culture at the Dawn of the Atomic Age* (New York, 1986).

lived Russian Republic[33] and later historian at Harvard University, seemed to discard the last sparks of hope that the USSR could be dealt with as a potentially well-meaning partner. Soviet policy was a mixture of revolutionary, traditional, and nationalist elements, he maintained, painting a picture of the nation cunningly following its legitimate course of action (control of the Chinese Eastern Railway, accessions in the north and partially in the west) and illegitimate aims (occupation of Port Arthur, accessions of northern East Prussia, eastern Galicia, and northern Bukovina). Karpovich agreed that the USSR had security interests, but he saw no reason for the Soviet Union to be as unyielding in its policy toward Eastern Europe as it had been in the past. The relationship between the USSR and Great Britain had never been so good, he argued, and the relationship with the U.S. could be established on a solid and positive basis — advantages he could not believe the leaders in Moscow would give away wantonly. The Harvard professor could only explain this attitude, forecasting an analytical approach George F. Kennan was to use in his famous "long telegram" in 1946,[34] with the help of terminology borrowed from psychology.[35]

As a guideline for American policy toward the Soviet Union, Karpovich suggested being resolute on existing agreements and treaties: "It is time for us to be firm in Eastern Europe and to cease making concessions. The Russians agreed to establish democracy in that area, and they knew well what we meant by democracy. We must insist that they stand by their agreements." To gain influence in the Balkans and to establish the Dardanelles as an international trade route,[36] however, concessions by the U.S. would be necessary. The Soviet leaders had doubts about the motivation of the United States, and rightly so, Karpovich maintained, when Pacific islands were being declared trust territories of the United States or when the U.S. prevented Soviet participation in the control of

33. Kerensky had established his government on 14 September 1917. Shortly thereafter, he had to flee from Russia when the Bolsheviks gained power. See Karpovich's statement about his background in DD, 23 October 1945, 1, USR/RGCFR-XVID.

34. In his "long telegram" (reprinted in *FRUS, 1946*, 4: 696–709) and later in his article "Sources of Soviet Conduct," *Foreign Affairs* 25 (July 1947): 566–82, Kennan had maintained that neurotic and psychological elements were partly responsible for the political behavior of the USSR.

35. DD, 23 October 1945, 1–4, USR/RGCFR-XVID.

36. Karpovich did not know that almost to the day, one year before, Churchill and Stalin had agreed upon their respective spheres' of influence (using exact percentages) in the individual Balkan countries. See Albert Resis, "The Churchill-Stalin 'Percentages Agreement on the Balkans,' Moscow, October 1944," *American Historical Review* 83 (April 1978): 372.

occupied Japan.[37] He was even prepared to cast aside the sacrosanct Monroe Doctrine to gain greater influence in Eastern Europe and to give the Soviets the impression that the U.S. was a partner with equal rights in negotiations.[38]

For some of the study group members this analysis was too far-fetched. Buell, for example, could see no possibility of reaching an agreement with the USSR. "Russia," he said, "is a totalitarian state existing under a reign of terror, concentration camps, and forced labor. There can be no effective cooperation with her unless we can somehow obtain a free flow of ideas resulting in a change of regime." He did not expect, however, such a change in the near future. Within the next ten years he expected the USSR to be involved in another war, especially if the Soviet Union could win over Germany or Japan as allies. Anticipating arguments State Department officials would raise two years later in support of the necessity of the Marshall Plan, he argued that this might be likely, "if we make . . . serious blunders such as letting the Japanese starve this winter." Even for Karpovich, such ferocious charges against the Soviet Union were too much. However, Buell was supported, at least in part, by Altschul and some other hard-liners among the members.[39]

During past discussions the disagreement between those who favored international cooperation and believed that goodwill was important, and those who distrusted the Soviet Union and advocated that the U.S. should prepare itself for a conflict, remained on the level of friendly discussion of conflicting opinions. Friction erupted sharply, however, when the liberal George Franklin submitted his manuscript of the final report of the study group meetings. Distinctions between the two factions within the group then became clearly visible, especially through attacks by Frank Altschul against Franklin.

Before the discussions on Franklin's report in May of 1946 began, the group members had another opportunity to compare their opinions on the USSR and their ideas about an adequate U.S. foreign policy against recent developments. James Reston, well-informed *New York Times* journalist,[40] had accompanied the American delegation to the first Gen-

37. Even Secretary Byrnes realized that the United States' uncompromising position in Japan had invited embarrassing comparison with Soviet rule in Eastern Europe. See James F. Byrnes, *Speaking Frankly* (New York, 1947), 102.

38. DD, 23 October 1945, 4–6, USR/RGCFR-XVID.

39. DD, 23 October 1945, 7, USR/RGCFR-XVID.

40. Invitation, Franklin to Reston, 27 February 1946, USR/RGCFR-XVID. For Reston's role in the Truman Doctrine and the Marshall Plan, see Joseph M. Jones, *The Fifteen*

eral Meeting of the United Nations at London in January 1946 and agreed to share his impressions with a combined meeting of the study groups on "United States Relations with Russia" and "United States Foreign Policy" in March of 1946.[41]

There was not much news Reston could share with the Council members present, but he gave strong support to their expressed fears about a lack of expert guidance in American foreign policy. The American delegation, he reported, "was most inadequately constituted and prepared." Only one meeting of all delegation members had taken place during the journey to Great Britain, and only two more during their five weeks in London. Almost as if to legitimize the existence of Council study groups, he pointed to the lack of a clear-cut advance definition of the American position for the negotiations.[42]

The use of veto power by the USSR during the conference, and its threat to invoke the veto at a second meeting, had led to speculations about possible consequences and caused concern among the Council members. Reston had to remind them that it was the United States that had favored the veto so that it could block decisions and resolutions. He reiterated that little was known about the motives and reasons of Soviet behavior, but it was clear that its actions were based on fear, not on aggression. The Soviet negotiators possessed few bargaining skills, and their persistence regarding military bases and political influence in Eastern Europe indicated that they did not understand the new developments in weapons technology, especially the atomic bomb and its influence on military strategy.[43]

Reston's well-balanced deliberations contributed little toward reaching a consensus among the study group members. In this situation, George Franklin's assignment to summarize evaluations and opinions within this very diverse group became impossible to accomplish. But in early 1946, he still believed he was on the right track. Preliminary drafts of the report had already been sent to the members in January, and ini-

---

Weeks (February 21 - June 5, 1947) (New York, 1955). Reston's own evaluation of the influence of the press on American foreign policy can be found in his *The Artillery of the Press: Its Influence on American Foreign Policy* (New York, 1967), published by the Council on Foreign Relations.

41. DD, 19 March 1946, USR/RGCFR-XVID.

42. Reston was very critical in his analysis of the potential of State Department officials: "Given our present policy-making personnel, there is little chance of our exercising any effective leadership." See DD, 19 March 1946, 3, 5, USR/RGCFR-XVID.

43. DD, 19. March 1946, 2, 6, 4–8, USR/RGCFR-XVID.

tial reactions by group members John H. Hazard and Stephen Duggan had been positive. Even Karpovich, with some reservations, was "favorably impressed."[44] If Franklin now expected that opposition to his report could be overcome, he was to be bitterly disappointed during the last meeting of the study group on 21 May 1946: Altschul lined up the resistance to the document.[45]

In his report "United States Relations with the U.S.S.R.," Franklin had formulated a rather benevolent evaluation of Soviet policy based on an attitude of friendly cooperation and coexistence with the USSR — and he had not spared the United States from criticism. The German-Soviet Nonaggression Pact of 1939,[46] he wrote in his historical background of the political situation, had been sharply criticized by all democratic nations. But, he asked, had the USSR been the only one guilty of fostering developments leading to that treaty? Ever since Hitler came to power in Germany, Soviet leaders had suggested "effective measures to combat aggression. . . . The democratic powers, though hostile to aggression, did nothing." He defended the Soviet annexation of Lithuania, Latvia, Estonia, and Bessarabia with the argument that these regions had previously belonged to the Russian empire and had shielded the country from attacks by enemies from the west and the north. As long as the Soviet Union had not developed atomic weapons, he suggested doing everything within reason to create a climate of trust between the Soviet Union, the United States, and Great Britain. Based on an acceptance of the *modus vivendi*, the United States should not disregard the differences between the two nations but should, nevertheless, develop an understanding of the Soviet position and should attempt to work closely with it.[47]

---

44. Hazard to Bidwell, 28 January 1946, USR/RGCFR-XVIIA; Karpovich to Franklin, 19 February 1946, *ibid.*; Duggan to Schubart, 22 April 1946, *ibid.* The final draft was sent to the members in the second week of May 1946. See Franklin to G. Raymond Walsh, 3 May 1946, USR/RGCFR-XVID. At that time, Franklin obviously anticipated further antagonism. He wrote to Walsh: "The Report [*sic*] takes a rather more pro-Soviet slant than many of our members feel justified, and I know we shall need able support from the less conservative members of the group." See *ibid.*

45. Franklin had already received some warning that Altschul would do everything possible to prevent publication of the report. See Franklin to Duggan, 19 February 1946, USR/RGCFR-XVIIA.

46. USR/RGCFR-XVIIA, 17–19, 21, 8 April 1946. A secret addition to the German-Soviet Nonaggression Pact of 23 August 1939 provided for the division of Poland and the Baltic nations between Germany and the Soviet Union.

47. Franklin, "United States Relations," 19, 76–77. The exact number of atomic warheads in American arsenals at that time is still undisclosed. Based on circumstantial evidence,

From the point of view of present-day liberal analysis, Franklin's evaluations were by no means "soft on communism" and seriously took into account the issue of security for the United States:

> Cooperation between the United States and the Soviet Union is as essential as almost anything in the world today, and unless and until it becomes entirely evident that the U.S.S.R. is not interested in achieving cooperation, we must redouble, not abandon, our efforts, when the task proves difficult. Cooperation, however, does not mean that we should knuckle under, or allow ourselves to become weak. We must bend every effort to make this country strong, prosperous, and happy, to relieve cyclical unemployment, and to show the world a way of life that people everywhere will wish to emulate. . . . The United States must be powerful not only politically and economically, but also militarily. We cannot afford to dissipate our military strength unless Russia is willing concurrently to decrease hers. On this we lay great emphasis. . . . We must know what are the really essential objectives of our foreign policy, and for these we must stand firmly. . . . We must take every opportunity to work with the Soviets now, when their power is still far inferior to ours, and hope that we can establish our cooperation on a firmer basis for the not so distant future when they will have completed their reconstruction and greatly increased their strength. . . . The policy we advocate is one of firmness coupled with moderation and patience.[48]

The evening of 21 May began unusually, even for meetings of study groups of the Council. After a few introductory words and noting that Theodore Switz and Altschul were Franklin's main critics, the chairman read a letter Altschul had sent him the day before.[49] In this letter, Altschul praised Franklin but also pointed out that Franklin and he viewed the Soviet Union and its intentions from quite different perspectives. Franklin's analysis, Altschul maintained, was much too favorable toward the USSR and much too generous in its evaluation of the motivation of Soviet foreign policy. For Altschul, the time of negotiations and compromises was over, and he believed the USSR was already in conflict with the "Anglo-American world." To rely only on the faith

---

however, scholars have concluded that fifteen months later, in July of 1947, not more than twenty-nine atomic warheads were available. See David Rosenberg, "American Atomic Strategy and the Hydrogen Bomb Decision," *Journal of American History* 66 (June 1979): 67–68. Herken relates estimates of six to twenty-four warheads. See *The Winning Weapon*, 372–73, footnote 8.

48. Franklin, "United States Relations," 78–80.

49. Copy, Altschul to Schubart, 20 May 1946, USR/RGCFR-XVIIA. The letter is reprinted in DD, 21 May 1946, 2–3, USR/RGCFR-XVIIA. Theodore M. Switz, of Encyclopaedia Britannica Films, Inc., like Altschul, was very critical of the USSR.

that the Soviet Union would not use the chaos in Europe to later utilize Germany as a spearhead for new aggressions, that the USSR would not expand its influence in the Near East toward the Persian Gulf, and would not use its strategically advantageous position in Manchuria to disturb the political situation in China, as he maintained Franklin had done, would surely be dangerous. He, at least, could not agree to publication of this document by the Council.[50]

The debate did not reveal new insights and neither Altschul nor Switz could convince other members, even though Switz compared the USSR with Nazi Germany and called the policy proposed by Franklin "appeasement," suggesting the nation should prepare for another great war. Seventeen of those present were still willing to publish the report under their names. Only four had reservations and stipulated that their partially differing opinions should be added to the published report. Even in the face of this defeat, Altschul threatened to "violently oppose releasing it as a Council document."[51]

"The vote is an interesting comment on the increasingly common assumption that nearly all business and banking leaders are openly hostile to Russia," Joseph Barnes of the New York *Herald Tribune* wrote to Edward Carter. Even a proposed revision of the concluding chapter by Franklin could not soothe Altschul. In June, the Committee on Studies, headed by Isaiah Bowman, cast a final vote on publication. Staffed with old friends of the banker and Council secretary Altschul, the Committee had little sympathy for Franklin's report.[52]

Bowman, Hamilton Armstrong, Arthur W. Page, and Winfield Riefler voted against publication. Comforting words from Allen W. Dulles, who remained undecided, faded against Bowman's crushing commentary: Bowman wrote Franklin that he believed the report to be outdated and, even worse, to be mostly "ordinary off-the-cuff opinion that does not represent fresh analysis or thought. . . . A report on so an important a theme for so many meetings of a substantial group of men,

---

50. *Ibid.*

51. DD, 21 May 1946, 8, USR/RGCFR-XVID. Publication of the report was supported by, among others, Schubart, Barnes, Curtis, Duggan, and Kirk.

52. Barnes to Carter, 30 May 1946, USR/RGCFR-XVIIA. Switz, fearing that his letter would get into the wrong hands and would thus endanger his travels to the USSR where he was to conduct business, nevertheless believed his country to already be involved in a dangerous conflict: "THE 3rd WORLD WAR — the war between the U.S.S.R. and Western Christendom — IS ALREADY VIGOROUSLY BEING WAGED AGAINST US [*sic*]." See Switz to Schubart, 13 June 1946, *ibid.*

will be taken as the measure of the work of the Council on Foreign Relations," he feared. "Neither scholars nor policy-makers in Washington will consider this report as either excellent or useful."[53]

It is quite possible that the Council thus missed an opportunity to give guidance to American policy-makers through constructive advice. The next few months did show a move of American foreign policy away from a cooperative attitude toward a policy of confrontation. Precursors to this change had already been visible as early as the end of 1945. Many officials at the State Department, among them Dean Acheson and James Byrnes, had advocated a firmer line toward the USSR in the summer of 1945, after symptoms of the incompatibility of policies on the future of Germany and Eastern Europe had become clearly visible. At the Foreign Ministers' Conference in Moscow in December, Secretary Byrnes had indicated that a compromise over Eastern Europe was possible, but he was soon reproached by the President. "I am tired of babying the Soviets," Truman had jotted down when he prepared for a meeting with his secretary of state.[54]

If the leaders of the USSR had followed a course of cooperation with the Western world, a change in this policy seemed to be clearly announced in early 1946, when, in a speech on 9 February 1946, aired by Radio Moscow, Stalin spoke in a confrontational spirit. To legitimize the necessity of a new five-year plan, he depicted an encirclement of the USSR by capitalist powers, heavily armed foes of the socialist system.[55] Many in Washington and many Council members interpreted Stalin's speech as a barely disguised political declaration of war against the United States and Great Britain.[56]

As a staff member of the American embassy in Moscow, George F. Kennan was asked to supply the State Department with an analysis of

53. Dulles to Franklin, 24 June 1946, USR/RGCFR-XVIIA; Bowman to Franklin, 24 June 1946, *ibid.*; Memorandum, Armstrong to Percy Bidwell, 27 June 1946, *ibid.*; Franklin to Percy W. Bidwell, 27 June 1946, *ibid.* In his *Annual Report of the Executive Director, 1946–1947* (New York, 1947), Walter Mallory wrote that "preparation of a joint group report on a matter as controversial as U.S. policy toward the Soviet Union was an almost impossible task." See *ibid.* 30.

54. Harry S. Truman, *Memoirs: Years of Decision* (Garden City, NY, 1955), 552.

55. The speech was reprinted on 10 February 1946 in the *New York Times.* In view of the release of the "Novikov Telegram," in the fall of 1991, George F. Kennan argued that Stalin may not have been prepared as late as September 1946 to commit himself to a hostile policy vis-à-vis the USA, as Molotov was advocating. See his "Commentary," in "The Soviet Side of the Cold War: A Symposium," *Diplomatic History* 15 (Fall 1991): 541.

56. See, among others, Bruce R. Kuniholm, *The Origins of the Cold War in the Near East: Great Power Conflict and Diplomacy in Iran, Turkey, and Greece* (Princeton, NJ, 1980), 310; Walter Millis, ed., *The Forrestal Diaries* (New York, 1951), 134–40.

Soviet politics. On 22 February 1946 he sent his "long telegram" to Washington in which he stated that the USSR would not be able to compromise and cooperate internationally and delineated the danger the Soviet Union posed to the United States.[57] Whereas in September 1945 Schubart had perceived the national interest of the USSR as the main stimulus of its foreign policy (contrary to a foreign policy that was based on ideological grounds), Kennan believed it to be irrationality and conformity to the party line of a Marxist-Leninist *Weltanschauung.* "In summary," he wrote,

> we have here a political force committed fanatically to the belief that with US there can no permanent modus vivendi, that it is desirable and necessary that the internal harmony of our society be disrupted, our traditional way of life be destroyed, the international authority of our state be broken, if Soviet power is to be secure.[58]

Kennan later wrote in his memoirs that much of his telegram sounded like one of the brochures commonly published by the fervently anti-communist Daughters of the American Revolution and that he later studied it with "horrified amusement."[59] But unlike such pamphlets, his deliberations were received enthusiastically in Washington and served as an impetus for a development in foreign policy that had already been in the making for some time. The "long telegram" served as an intellectual legitimation to cast aside a line of politics inherited from the Roosevelt administration that now seemed to be obsolete. The well-known "Iron Curtain" speech former British premier Winston Churchill gave at Fulton, MO came only a few days later, its content and tenor welcomed by President Truman and Secretary of State Byrnes.[60]

At the same time a crisis in Iran reached its climax. On 19 January, the Iranian administration had accused the USSR at the United Nations

57. Kennan, *Memoirs, 1925—1950* (Boston, 1967), 292–93. A mere routine answer to the request was not what Kennan had in mind. He used the opportunity to deliver his considered evaluation of the situation in the Soviet Union: "It would not do to give them just a fragment of the truth. Here was a case where nothing but the whole truth would do. They had asked for it. Now, by God, they would have it." See *ibid.*

58. "Annex C," *ibid.*, 557. The complete text is reprinted in *FRUS, 1946,* 4: 696–709.

59. Kennan, *Memoirs*, 294. For the wide distribution of the telegram, see Kuniholm, *The Origins of the Cold War,* 312, particularly footnote 23. It seems quite likely that through their contacts with State Department officials some Council members had access to copies of the telegram.

60. Churchill gave his speech on 5 March 1946. For Truman's and Byrnes' knowledge about the content of the speech and their later denials that they knew what Churchill was to say, see Fraser J. Harbutt, *The Iron Curtain: Churchill, America, and the Origins of the Cold War* (New York, 1986), 161–63.

Security Council of interference in internal Iranian affairs. During the ensuing confrontation among the United States, Great Britain, and the Soviet Union over oil drilling concessions, the USSR had supported the communist Tudeh Party in its struggle for the national autonomy of the northern Iranian province Azerbaijan. In August 1945 military clashes occurred between government troops and the rebels.

When on 2 March 1946 the deadline (agreed upon in 1942) for withdrawal of Soviet, British, and American troops from Iran had passed, there were still soldiers of the Red Army on Iranian soil. Again, the Security Council was called upon and a meeting was scheduled for 26 March. The Soviet Union tried to delay the meeting, but they did not succeed. To prevent disturbing the delicate negotiations over drilling concessions (in which the presence of the Red Army certainly was to press Soviet interests), the Soviet delegation left the meeting of the Security Council — for the first time in the history of the United Nations — to prevent a resolution. A few days later, an agreement was reached between the USSR and Iran, granting oil drilling concessions to the USSR provided that all foreign troops left the country and the Iranian parliament ratified the treaty. The Soviet Union — anxious to establish political influence on its southern border and eager to gain access to the Iranian oil — had in the eyes of many Americans appeared to be an aggressive, expansionist power, wantonly breaking treaties to gain influence and new satellites.[61]

Thus, when the meetings of the group continued in November 1946, the deliberations had a quite different basis. Council member DeWitt C. Poole may have expressed what a large number of group members believed when he wrote that ". . . in 1945 there had accrued to Soviet Russia an almost unmeasured good-will in the western world. . . . Within short time these advantages had been cast away by a deceitful and grasping diplomacy and unilateral action of cynical and brutal type." Poole was not surprised: "It is not an accident that it has turned

---

61. The agreement was never ratified. In November, the United States had already supplied Iran with miliary aid in excess of 10 million dollars. A comprehensive description is in Paterson, *Soviet-American Confrontation*, 177–83. See also David S. Painter, *Oil and the American Century: The Political Economy of U.S. Foreign Oil Policy, 1941–1954* (Baltimore, 1986), 111–16. Kennan, invited to participate in the deliberations of the study group on 7 January 1947, supported the thesis that the USSR was eager to gain oil concessions diplomatically and would evade military engagement and additional conflicts. The occupation of Iran's northern province Azerbaijan by the Red Army had had a civilizing impact, Kennan maintained, and American support for the country would hardly turn out to be constructive. See DD, 7 January 1947, 9–10, SFP/RGCFR-XXIIC.

out so. The Russian course issues naturally from a background of fanaticism and dictatorship."[62]

Even the chairman, Schubart, stated openly that he no longer believed that "a lasting peace can be established or that Communism can live with the Capitalist System, or vice versa."[63] During the first few meetings it also became clear that the attitude of the group as a whole, similar to that of the broader public and the officials at the State Department, had changed. Contributions such as "Leadership and Control in the Soviet Union" and "The Soviet Economic Position and Its Future Potentialities," indicated this new direction.[64] When on 7 January 1947 George Kennan, who only shortly before had gained final endorsement as the most eminent expert on the Soviet Union within the State Department, offered his analysis of Soviet foreign policy — "The Soviet Way of Thought and Its Effects on Foreign Policy" — more than three-fourths of the group's members participated at the meeting.[65]

Kennan's reports and analyses from Moscow had gained Secretary of Navy James V. Forrestal's attention.[66] Three months after sending his famous report from Moscow, Kennan had been transferred to the newly founded National War College in Washington, D.C., to serve as deputy for foreign affairs. In December, Forrestal asked him for his evaluation of a background memorandum on the correlation between Marxism and Soviet policy. When Kennan spoke to the members of the study group at the Council, he was in the midst of this work — not on

62. Poole to André Visson (*Reader's Digest* consultant for international affairs), 22 August 1946, DeWitt C. Poole Papers, box 1, State Historical Society of Wisconsin, Madison, WI. Poole was a member of the Foreign Nationalities Branch of the OSS and became one of the founding members of the anti-Soviet propaganda radio program, Voice of America.

63. Schubart to Franklin, 14 October 1946, SFP/RGCFR-XXIIC.

64. *Ibid.*, 31. Speakers and discussion leaders were Geroid T. Robinson on 22 November 1946 and Abram Bergson, professor at the Russian Institute of Columbia University, on 20 December 1946. See DD, 22 November 1946, 5, SFP/RGCFR-XXIIC. Abram Bergson addressed possibilities and prerequisites for reconstruction in the USSR. See DD, 20 December 1946, *ibid.*

65. Of the forty-five members, thirty-two were present. See DD, 7 January 1947, 1, SFP/RGCFR-XXIIC, and list of members, *ibid.*

66. See Kennan, *Memoirs,* 298, and Ronald Steel's "Introduction to the Torchbook Edition," xi, in *The Cold War* (New York, 1972) by Walter Lippmann. For Kennan's career in general, see Anders Stephanson, *Kennan and the Art of Foreign Policy* (Cambridge, MA, 1989).

the evaluation that he had been asked for, however, but on a memorandum of his own on this subject.[67]

At the Council meeting Kennan stressed, reminiscent of his "long telegram," three determinants of Soviet foreign policy: "(1) 'ideology,' (2) Russian traditions and national habits of thought, and (3) internal circumstances of Soviet power." The ideology of the leadership of the USSR was undoubtedly Marxism-Leninism, Kennan argued, but this served only as a guideline for politics, sometimes no more than a linguistic vehicle; neither Marx nor Lenin could have foreseen the political developments in the USSR. Russian traditions and traditional ways of thought, he told the members present, were the primary bases for important decisions and unfortunately were often misjudged as not important by the United States. These two determinants of foreign policy would constitute today's ideology in the Soviet Union. The third determinant, the domestic political situation in which all political opposition had to be denounced as hostile to socialism and supported by foreign powers, so that it could not threaten the credibility of the regime, had led to the public assumption in the Soviet Union that the nation was surrounded by enemies. It would be wrong, Kennan argued, to take the Soviets for cynics or habitual and blatant liars: the leaders of the Soviet Union actually believed in the ideology of Marxism-Leninism and the task of world revolution. As he already had indicated in his "long telegram," Kennan told his captive audience, American policymakers were dealing with fanatics.[68]

His analysis, he said, should not lead to discouragement about American foreign policy, and, he comforted his listeners, "other Russian traits of character [make] . . . it perfectly possible for the U.S. and other countries to contain Russian power, if it [is] . . . done courteously and in a non-provocative way, long enough so that there might come about internal changes in Russia." Kennan regarded a get-tough policy as being unsuitable. The U.S. should take an honorable and self-assured stance in world politics. As long as the United States made clear that it set virtuous targets and was willing to pursue these, the USSR would not

67. John L. Gaddis, *Strategies of Containment: A Critical Appraisal of Postwar American National Security Policy* (New York, 1982), 25; Kennan, *Memoirs*, 354–55. In July of 1946 he had written a "Draft of Information Policy on Relations with Russia" depicting the unfavorable relations existing between the U.S. and the USSR, but also suggesting: "In general, keep cool, avoid hysteria. Relations will remain difficult but need not become hopeless if we keep a steady hand." See Dean G. Acheson Papers, box 27, Harry S. Truman Library, Independence, MO.

68. DD, 7 January 1947, 1–4, SFP/RGCFR-XXIIC.

challenge the U.S. Kennan, by and large, was optimistic about the future relationship between the two nations, especially if the United States was firm in future negotiations. Even regarding the question of control of atomic power, he believed that the USSR would, in the long run, agree to American proposals. When Altschul asked if atomic bombs in the hands of the Soviets would change their foreign policy, Kennan predicted that no such change would occur; and, hinting at the deployment of atomic bombs against Hiroshima and Nagasaki, he maintained: "They know that that [using atomic weapons against cities] would defeat their aims and that no one wins in an atomic war. They are wiser than we are in that sense."[69]

None of the men present could have realized that this lecture would lead directly to one of the most important and controversial publications in the history of the upcoming Cold War: the article "Sources of Soviet Conduct," in the July 1947 issue of *Foreign Affairs*, written by a certain "X."[70] Similar in theme and tenor to the "long telegram," this article served a broader interested public and provided an intellectual and avowedly systematic and pragmatic basis for future American policy vis-à-vis the Soviet Union, and it served as a basis of the actual American strategy of a limited and "cold" war.[71]

Three days after Kennan was a guest of the study group, Hamilton Armstrong, in his function as editor of *Foreign Affairs*, asked Kennan for a contribution to the periodical. Armstrong had not participated in the meeting of 7 January but other members of the study group had related Kennan's reflections to him. Also, Kennan had spoken about the USSR not only in New York but on a number of other occasions. For a lecture at Yale University, his contribution had been mimeographed, and Armstrong had received a copy of the "exceptionally interesting" paper.[72]

---

69. *Ibid.*, 4–9.

70. Kennan's article is discussed in Thomas G. Paterson, "The Search for Meaning," in *Makers of American Diplomacy* (New York, 1974), 553–88, Frank Merli and Theodore A. Wilson, eds.; and, in an evaluation thirty years later, in John L. Gaddis, "Containment: A Reassessment," *Foreign Affairs* 55 (July 1977): 873–87.

71. "Introduction" of the editor in *American Civil-Military Decisions: A Book of Case Studies* (Birmingham, AL, 1963), 19, Harold Stein, ed.

72. Armstrong to Kennan, 10 January 1947, George F. Kennan Papers, box 28, Mudd Manuscript Library; handwritten note by Armstrong to his assistant Byron Dexter, Kennan to Armstrong, 4 February 1947, Armstrong Papers, box 33. Kennan recalled a conversation with Armstrong at a Council dinner (with Kennan as the guest of honor) which he believes led to Armstrong's written request for a contribution for *Foreign Affairs*. See Kennan to Michael Wala, 24 October 1986. The documentary evidence and the short interval between his presentation and the letter makes this implausible.

Kennan took his time in responding to Armstrong's request. On 4 February he finally answered Armstrong's letter and told him that he would be prepared to contribute an article, but only under a pseudonym. As a government official he was in no position to contribute "anything of value" under his own name, he claimed. In the meantime Kennan had finished his memorandum for Secretary of the Navy Forrestal, who considered Kennan's manuscript "extremely well-done."[73] After Kennan had contacted Forrestal's office and submitted the proposal to the State Department's Committee of Unofficial Publications (which had to clear all written work of State Department officials prior to publication), his essay for Forrestal was allowed to appear under a different title in *Foreign Affairs.*[74]

Immediately, the essay created considerable excitement. Many readers saw their doubts about their former ally, the Soviet Union, confirmed. For some time, in newspapers and magazine articles, voices had been raised saying quite openly that the USSR was the new — and possibly old — enemy. President Truman had asked both houses of Congress for economic and military aid to Greece and Turkey and had contended that foreign powers were responsible for the civil war in Greece. Truman's offer to aid "free peoples who are resisting attempted subjugation by armed minorities or outside pressure" was a clear warning to Moscow.[75] The interested public seemed only to wait for Truman or the State Department to formulate a clear-cut line of policy toward the USSR, but nothing of that sort came forth. The speech of Secretary of State Marshall on 5 June 1947, in which he offered aid for the reconstruction and rehabilitation of all European countries, only confused the situation further: officially the Soviet Union was not excluded from the United States' offer, but hardly anybody could envision Congress granting appropriations for aid to the Soviet Union.

73. Kennan to Armstrong, 4 February 1947, Armstrong Papers, box 33. A carbon copy is in the Kennan Papers, box 28. Kennan, *Memoirs*, 355. His memorandum, dated 31 January 1947, was entitled "Psychological Background of Soviet Foreign Policy."

74. Kennan to John T. Connor (special assistant to Secretary Forrestal), 10 March 1947, Kennan Papers, box 28; Marx Leva (Connor's successor) to Kennan, 12 March 1947, *ibid.*; Kennan to E. Eilder Spaulding (chairman, Committee of Unofficial Publications, State Department), 13 March 1947, *ibid.*; Spaulding to Kennan, 8 April 1947, *ibid.* Armstrong sent the galley proofs to Kennan on 15 May 1947. See Armstrong to Kennan, 15 May 1947, *ibid.*

75. "Special Message to the Congress on Greece and Turkey: The Truman Doctrine," 12 March 1947, *The Public Papers of the Presidents of the United State: Harry S. Truman, 1947* (Washington, D.C., 1963), 176–80.

The pseudonym "X" did not protect Kennan's identity for long and soon it was an open secret that he was the author of this article. That he had not voiced the official opinion of the administration was disregarded and the failed attempt to conceal Kennan's identity only fostered the belief that a thinly disguised official statement had been made through an unofficial channel. A high official in the State Department, it seemed, who had been named the director of the Policy Planning Staff, had in seemingly clear language outlined the basis of American policy. The wording Kennan had used to acknowledge the difficulty of this topic and his analysis of the dichotomy of determinants and variables, however, left plenty of room for different and even divergent interpretations.[76]

Walter Lippmann, one of the most highly regarded and renowned journalists of his time, reacted immediately. In a series of commentaries in his column "Today and Tomorrow" in the New York *Herald Tribune*, he attacked Kennan.[77] Lippmann regarded Kennan's article as a continuation of the dangerous view, first surfacing in the Truman Doctrine, that military clashes with the USSR were unavoidable. He interpreted the article in *Foreign Affairs* as a call to contain Soviet interests around the globe. This was misleading, he maintained, and only distracted policy-makers and the interested public from the more important site of the clash between the United States and the Soviet Union: the major problem between the two great powers was not in a distant corner of the world but in Germany, in the center of Europe.[78]

Not surprisingly, Kennan believed that he had been misunderstood. He respected Lippmann and was baffled by his harsh judgment. Lippmann believed Kennan to be one of the authors of Truman's speech of 12 March 1947 and regarded Kennan's "long telegram" as a corner-

76. Arthur Krock reported a few days after *Foreign Affairs* was published that the article came from an official source. See *New York Times*, 8 July 1947. The wide distribution of the memorandum Kennan had written for Forrestal and also Kennan's own latitude in this incident had provided for a quick disclosure of the author's identity. When Louis P. Lochner (editor of the *Goebbels Diaries*) asked Kennan in May for a copy of his "Psychological Background of Soviet Policy" (after a friend had shown him the study), Kennan wrote that he had no spare copy left and "you will soon see it appearing anonymously in *Foreign Affairs* under another title." See Lochner to Kennan, 11 May 1947, Louis P. Lochner Papers, reel 13, frame 242, State Historical Society of Wisconsin, Madison, WI; Kennan to Lochner, 20 May 1946, reel 13, frame 244, *ibid.*

77. The series was published from 2 September to 2 October 1947 in the Tuesday, Thursday, and Saturday editions. Later that year, all twelve articles were published by Harper and Brothers under the title *The Cold War: A Study in U.S. Foreign Policy* (New York, 1947).

78. Lippmann, *Cold War*, 5–52.

stone of the confrontational attitude of U.S. foreign policy. In his column, Lippmann now formulated, with very few modifications, counterpositions that Kennan actually would have regarded as accurate. Although he was quite unhappy, Kennan did not publish a rebuttal, and a long letter he wrote to Lippmann to illuminate the misunderstandings was never mailed. Sacrificing the precision that had prevailed in the discussions at the Council meeting, Kennan had used elegant formulations to convey his analysis. In his memoirs he accused himself of "egregious . . . errors" that had led to the "greatest and most unfortunate . . . misunderstandings." But neither Kennan nor any other State Department official in 1947 regarded a correction as necessary; the article and its common interpretation agreed much too well with the developing foreign policy of the United States.[79]

In addition to these implications for the formulation of American foreign policy, the publication of the article turned out to be fortunate for the Council: "Sources of Soviet Conduct" was widely discussed and long excerpts were reprinted in *Life* and *Reader's Digest*.[80] The prestige of *Foreign Affairs* and the Council on Foreign Relations increased considerably.[81]

While Armstrong and Kennan were still discussing Kennan's contribution and trying to convince the State Department to approve publication, the study group was continuing its work. At the next meeting in January, for example, Philip E. Mosely, professor at the Russian Institute at Columbia University, summarized the experience of the American delegations with their Soviet counterparts, and reported about the different strategies at the negotiations and explained a number of details of the negotiations.[82]

---

79. Kennan, *Memoirs*, 359–61; Steel, "Introduction," xiv.

80. Kennan, *Memoirs*, 356. Harry H. Harper, Jr., a staff member of *Reader's Digest*, had participated in the group meeting of 7 January. It is quite likely that he arranged for the reprint in this popular, conservative, and widely read magazine.

81. Russell C. Leffingwell, member of the Board of Directors, wrote to Council member Thomas W. Lamont: "Thirteen [*sic*] essays in criticism of one magazine article by a not very anonymous career man in the State Department seems a little out of proportion. Well, Walter [Lippmann] gave Ham's [Hamilton F. Armstrong] magazine some very valuable free advertising." See Leffingwell to Lamont, 1 December 1947, Lamont Papers, box 104. As a result of increasing interest in foreign policy, *Foreign Affairs'* circulation had improved considerably after 1945 (by 2,100, from 17,179 to 19,301 copies). Then, until mid-1947, circulation dropped by 100 copies. The Marshall Plan, the "X" article, and NATO provided for another increase of 1,100 copies by June of 1948. See CFR, *Annual Report of the Executive Director, 1947–1948* (New York, 1948), 12.

82. DD, 29 January 1947, SFP/RGCFR-XXIIC.

Three weeks later, on 19 February, Abraham A. Feller reported on Soviet participation in the United Nations. He explained that at first, the Soviets had taken the supra-national organization as a "formalized and strengthened big-power alliance." To their great surprise, they realized during the first meeting in London that the organization had turned out to be an anti-USSR league. After a short period, which Feller termed as a period of "diplomacy by insult," they had changed their tactics and used the United Nations and especially the General Assembly to "market" the more attractive parts of their ideology. People in the United States too easily forgot "that our political liberties, especially freedom of the press (under which anyone who has a million dollars can print a newspaper) and freedom of speech" had little meaning for some other peoples. "We overlook the fact that for many peoples Russia has a more important kind of freedom, which is freedom of colored and colonial races. This is a point which the Russians have exploited very effectively." As Reston had done in an earlier meeting, Feller pointed out that the right to veto a decision of the Security Council by any of its five permanent members,[83] which had been blamed by the American press as the major reason for the ineffectiveness of the United Nations, was considered to be just as important by the United States as it had been by the USSR. The Soviets knew "that if the veto is ever really in danger the U.S. will come forward to support it."[84]

The evening of the next group meeting was overshadowed by an important and special event. President Truman had addressed both houses of Congress and, with barely disguised anti-Soviet rhetoric, had called for a military and economic aid program for Turkey and Greece. Hardly three weeks before, on 21 February, "Great Britain had . . . handed the job of world leadership, with all its burdens and all its glory," as one of the officials involved later wrote, "to the United States." At that time, the British embassy in Washington had transmitted two letters in which it informed the State Department that, because of economic problems, Great Britain would not be able to continue its military aid to the two Mediterranean countries.[85]

83. China, France, Great Britain, the Soviet Union, and the United States.

84. DD, 19 February 1947, 1–3, SFP/RGCFR-XXIIC. Historian Michael T. Florinsky, professor in the political science department of Columbia University, inquired at the meeting if anyone knew which nation had requested the veto power. Mosely had the correct answer: "The veto was in the draft for the UN organization that the United States circulated two months in advance of the Dumbarton Oaks conference [in the fall of 1944]." See *ibid.*, 4.

85. Jones, *The Fifteen Weeks*, 7. Jones was at that time special assistant to the assistant secretary of state for public affairs.

Truman's carefully prepared speech, soon to be called the Truman Doctrine, had been cleared with a number of politicians in the Senate and the House of Representatives. "A militant minority," the president had said, "exploiting human want and misery, was able to create political chaos." The existence of the Greek nation was endangered by terrorist activities supported by communists. No other country was able or willing to support Greece and measures of aid through the United Nations were not possible, Truman asserted. Although the Soviet Union was not named directly, it was obvious that the installation of administrations friendly to the Soviet Union in Poland, Romania, and Bulgaria was depicted by Truman as a threat to the security of the United States. Truman promised that the United States would support nations in their resistance against foreign and domestic foes.[86]

When Percy E. Corbett of the Institute of International Relations at Yale University met with the Council members on 12 March, certainly none of the men present had missed the news and had already reflected upon the Truman speech.[87] More so than in preceding meetings, the inclination of the group members was aimed toward confrontation with the Soviet Union. Reflecting this inclination, Chairman Schubart asked if Truman's speech was not an admission that American policy was bent on confrontation, "a potent argument in Russia in substitution of much we tried to deny in respect to the 'capitalist encirclement' of the Soviet Union." Corbett agreed with Schubart but also maintained that American aid to Greece, Turkey, and other countries in a similar situation could also be regarded as "a reasonable part of the protection of our way of life."[88]

During the same discussion, Colonel Herman Beukema of West Point Military Academy questioned an aspect of the speech that Truman had only hinted at, i.e., the comparison between fascism and communism. The argument that Soviet foreign policy was only intended to provide security for its own territory seemed to him to be merely a cover for "actual grabs of territory, coinciding with an internal fifth column attack." Corbett disputed these analogies between fascism and communism as being absurd. However, there was no stopping the members

86. "Truman Doctrine," 12 March 1947, *Public Papers*, 176–80; Jones, *Fifteen Weeks*, 148–70.

87. Additionally, the impact of Truman's speech had been filtered through press briefings, and the president and Senator Vandenberg had simultaneously, on 10 March 1947, announced that Truman would address a joint session of the houses of Congress.

88. DD, 12 March 1947, 6, SFP/RGCFR-XXIIC.

from attaching even more farfetched and old labels to the villain: Henry V. Poor, a former member of the American diplomatic corps, compared Hitler's *Mein Kampf* with Marxism-Leninism. Corbett's scholarly and academic explanations of the possible validity of differing definitions of terms such as "free elections" or "democracy" in disparate social systems, and his assertion that the communist doctrine was "quite different from the doctrine of *Mein Kampf*," very soon put him in a helpless position similar to that of a liberal intellectual accused of being a "fellow traveler" during the McCarthy era. When historian and Russia-expert Florinsky asked if he could not see "an important difference between Russian attempts to spread their system and our own," the professor hastened to assure everyone that he was "a convinced Western democrat."[89]

At the last meeting of the 1946/47 year,[90] James W. Riddleberger, chief of the Division of Central European Affairs of the State Department, described the actual problems of Soviet occupation in Germany. At the State Department, George Kennan and his Policy Planning Staff, of which Riddleberger was a member, had meanwhile started working on a framework for rehabilitation and reconstruction of the war-torn European economy.

Before the war Germany had been an eminently important factor in the interconnected, interdependent network of national economies in Europe, Riddleberger summarized. In recognition of this fact, in September 1946, Secretary of State Byrnes had in his important speech at Stuttgart already officially introduced the changed concept of American policy by declaring that the United States would increase the level of industry in Germany.[91] General Lucius D. Clay, military governor of the American occupation zone, had even before that date departed from the guidelines of the directive of the Joint Chiefs of Staff, the well-known document JCS 1067, which had been partially based on premises of the Morgenthau Plan.[92]

89. *Ibid.*, 9–10.

90. The meeting took place on 22 May 1947. It was preceded by a meeting with Walter L. Wright, Jr., a former president of Robert College at Istanbul and professor at Princeton University in 1947. The uneventful meeting closed with a call by Wright and Florinsky to support the "Truman policy with its modifications." See DD, 2 April 1947, SFP/RGCFR-XXIIC.

91. Excerpts of Byrnes' speech are reprinted in U.S. Congress, Senate, Committee on Foreign Relations, *A Decade of American Foreign Policy* (Washington, D.C., 1949), 522–27.

92. For the meeting between Roosevelt and Churchill at the second Quebec conference in September 1944, Morgenthau had prepared a memorandum on the future treatment of Germany which included a policy that would make Germany a pastoral and agrar-

The four "D's" of JCS 1067 — demilitarization, denazification, decartelization and democratization — could not be translated very easily into the day-to-day chores of occupation. The residue of the Morgenthau Plan obstructed the preservation of German industry — not to speak of strengthening or rebuilding German production capabilities — and was in sharp contrast to the necessities of occupation and the political aims of the United States. The stunningly high costs of occupation had to be financed by the American taxpayers. The directive — "assembled by economic idiots," as the financial adviser to Clay, Lewis W. Douglas, maintained — did nothing to alleviate this burden.[93]

Against the background of these developments, Riddleberger reported that the USSR had a maximum aim — "lasting political and economic control over the whole of Germany" — and a minimum aim — "neutralization of Germany as a source of aggression." Now the Soviet leaders found themselves in a possibly threatening situation: the consensus of Allied policy vis-à-vis Germany, that — in their understanding — had been agreed upon at the meeting in Potsdam in July 1945, seemed doomed. In this situation, Secretary of State Marshall had returned, in April 1947, disillusioned from the Council of Foreign Ministers' Conference in Moscow. An agreement on the future treatment of Germany and on economic unity of the zones of occupation, favored by the Americans, had not been reached. "The patient is sinking while the doctors deliberate," Marshall described the situation shortly after his return to the United States in a national radio broadcast on 28 April. He announced that the United States would provide, if necessary, for rehabilitation and reconstruction of Europe without help from the other Allies.[94]

---

ian nation. These ideas had hardly reached the public when opposition to the plan was raised in the press. Only two weeks after Roosevelt and Churchill had initialled Morgenthau's memorandum, Roosevelt withdrew his support and put the blame on Morgenthau: "Henry pulled a boner . . . ." See Frank A. Ninkovich, *Germany and the United States: The Transformation of the German Question Since 1945* (Boston, 1988), 21–22. See also Harry G. Gelber, "Der Morgenthau-Plan," *Vierteljahrshefte für Zeitgeschichte* 13 (1965): 372-402.

93. See Lucius D. Clay, *Decision in Germany* (Garden City, NY, 1950), 19. For the development of JCS 1067, see Paul Y. Hammond, "Directives for the Occupation of Germany: The Washington Controversy," in *American Civil-Military Decisions*, 314–460. The text of JCS 1067 is reprinted in U.S. Department of State, *Documents on Germany, 1944–1985* (Washington, D.C., 1985), 15–32. The quotation is from Robert D. Murphy, *Diplomat Among Warriors* (Garden City, NY, 1965), 281. Council member Lewis Douglas was appointed ambassador to the Court of St. James in February 1947.

94. U.S. Department of State, *Bulletin*, 11 May 1947, 919. On his way to Washington, he had stopped at Berlin and met Clay. See Forrest C. Pogue, *George C. Marshall: Statesman 1945–1959* (New York, 1987), 197–200.

Riddleberger could not provide the members with additional information on this probability and the discussion turned to the somewhat chaotic Soviet strategy to levy and ship reparations to the USSR. The study group members wondered about the ineffective, reckless, and destructive handling of the transportation of dismantled machinery and whole factories to the Soviet Union.[95] Altschul, always eager to point out the repressive Soviet system in Poland and other East European nations, turned the discussion to the question of borders between Poland and Germany. He had to realize, however, that his colleagues believed that this question was a closed issue. The Potsdam agreement had included the relocation of Germans from parts east of the Oder-Neisse line to what was to remain of Germany, an agreement that could hardly be regarded as temporary. The other members of the group agreed that there was nothing to gain if the United States pressed this point. A separate German state west of the Oder, Riddleberger argued, would hardly be viable economically; its only chance was a "European confederation."[96]

With this subject, the study group turned to a problem that had already been discussed for some time in a different study group. The crushed and defeated Germany had in the first months after "V-E" day only been of secondary interest to foreign policy. Nazism had been defeated and it was widely assumed that the disillusioned Germans, hungry and hopeless, would not put up any resistance to the victorious powers. It was presumed that denazification and "re-education," undertaken with the effectiveness of the war machinery of the Allies, would soon re-create a democratic nation that would rejoin the community of nations — albeit, as a partner with limited rights.

All nations that had fought the Axis powers had agreed that Germany should never again be a threat to peace and that its potential to unleash another war should be destroyed eternally. But very soon, Germany had become of prime importance for the future strategies of the Soviet Union, Great Britain, and the United States. Here, in the former focus of inter-European trade and political developments, the different social and political systems and ideologies of the United States and the Soviet Union clashed and led to disagreements that policy-makers in Washington and Moscow may have thought to be conflicts of the past. The division of Germany in the following years turned out to be a symbol and expression of the division of Europe and the world into two hostile blocs of power.

95. DD, 22 May 1947, 1–5, URS/RGCFR-XXIIC.

96. *Ibid.*, 4–5. He thus mentioned what only a few days later would be recommended by Kennan's PPS and Under Secretary of State for Economic Affairs William L. Clayton in discussions within the State Department.

4

Europe and Germany:

"Political Economy in the Literal Sense of that Term"[1]

Allied troops were still fighting in Europe when the Council on Foreign Relations began to discuss and study possibilities for the economic and political rehabilitation of the liberated countries after the fighting ceased.[2] The European infrastructure of roads, railroads, and waterways had been nearly totally destroyed by the war. Staple foods could hardly be transported to areas of need, and as early as April 1945, some Council members doubted if the military would be the best choice to organize and structure the economic recovery of Europe. German prisoners of war in American and British internment camps were fed sufficiently, but the military hesitated to deal with civilians. The United Nations Relief and Rehabilitation Agency (UNRRA) was prevented from providing aid to former enemy countries, and reports in the press about stockpiles of luxury goods in Germany had led to the assumption of the broader public that the supply of food there posed no problem.[3]

When the Council reorganized its study groups for the post-war period, among the regional groups was one group on "Western European Affairs." Chaired by Allen W. Dulles, the former chief of the OSS in Germany, this group continued the work that had been launched with the study group on "Economic and Political Reconstruction."[4] Larger than the usual discussion groups of the Council, with 20–40 instead of 15–20 members, the regional groups functioned mainly as forums for Council members, State Department officials, and foreign politicians. They supplied reports and information and thus contributed to the members' knowledge on conditions in the various regions of the

1. George Kennan's definition of the essence of American aid to Europe. See Kennan to Acheson, 23 May 1947, *FRUS, 1947* 3: 231, under the subheading "Clarifying Implications of 'Truman Doctrine.'"

2. During the war a Council group consisting of American and British members had discussed the future of Europe. In March 1945 a similar group was set up with officials from the U.S. Department of State and the British embassy. See Percy W. Bidwell to Carl W. Ackerman (dean at Columbia University), 22 March 1945, EPR/RGCFR-XVIB.

3. DD, 5 April 1945, EPR/RGCFR-XVIB.

4. Council, *Report, 1945–1946*, 12–14.

world. Allen Dulles, however, also utilized his group to establish an influential podium for his views on the future American policy toward Germany. His point of view was based on his experiences during and after the war, first in Switzerland, and then in Germany.

In November 1942, Dulles had been sent to conduct intelligence operations on Germany from his station as chief of the OSS mission in Bern, Switzerland. His greatest success during that time was "Operation Sunrise," the surrender of the German forces in Italy on 28 April 1945. Negotiations between emissaries of SS-General Karl Wolff and Dulles had begun two months earlier but had been hampered in early April by Russian demands to be involved in the talks and by accusations that Great Britain and the United States were scheming for a separate peace with Germany. After President Roosevelt died on 12 April 1945, Dulles had to discontinue his contact with the Germans. The SS-General — cynically expressing his "sincere and deeply felt condolences" with the "highest respect for the majesty of death" — had anticipated difficulties and wrote to Dulles that he feared the negotiations might be thwarted. With the Germans set on the course of capitulation, however, President Truman finally decided to accept the surrender.[5]

Immediately after Germany's unconditional capitulation on 8 May 1945, Dulles established the OSS mission in Germany and served as its chief until August 1945. At that time Dulles probably still believed in the possibility of a continuation of war-time cooperation with the Soviet Union, even after his frustrating experience with Soviet misgivings about his negotiations with Wolff in Switzerland. But in Germany, he was repeatedly hindered in his work by Soviet colleagues and became quite disillusioned. Americans could scarcely move about freely in the Soviet zone of occupation, and to their dismay discovered that many moderate German socialists returning to their homes in Eastern Germany disappeared — quite possibly killed or sent to Siberia.[6]

Frustrated with this experience and enlightened by his first-hand encounter with Soviet occupation policy, Dulles' reaction to the developing distrust between the United States and the Soviet Union was not

---

5. Wolff had coyly crossed out his letterhead introducing him as SS-Obergruppenführer and General of the Waffen-SS, Highest SS- and Police-Leader and Authorized General of the German Forces in Italy. See Wolff to Dulles, Allen Dulles Papers, box 22, Mudd Manuscript Library. Dulles' own account of "Operation Sunrise" is his *Secret Surrender* (New York, 1966).

6. Leonard Mosley, *Dulles: A Biography of Eleanor, Allen, and John Foster Dulles and Their Family Network* (New York, 1978), 179–88.

to try to clear up misunderstandings and to treat the ally as a rational partner in international affairs by fostering Soviet engagement in international organizations. He stuck to his immediate field of experience, Germany, which had taught him to be more pessimistic about U.S.-Soviet relations. One of the reasons he agreed to chair the Council discussion group was certainly his desire to induce the public and the administration to change U.S. policy toward Germany. Earlier than many of his peers in the United States, Dulles had concluded that Germany was at the focal point of the future political, strategic, and economic situation of Europe and consequently of the post-war world. Germany was vitally important for European economic restoration and it was the site where the future predominance of the Soviet or of the American economic and political systems in Europe would be determined. Dulles was certain that clashes between the USSR and the U.S. were almost inevitable and only "insulating the two systems" promised a chance for lasting peace; without this, dangerous conflicts were imminent.[7]

An exceptionally large membership (close to one hundred) drawn from all quarters of the Council's elite composition, demonstrated the tremendous interest in this topic. It also revealed the strategy Dulles and his associates at the Council used as a common practice: all group members received digests of the proceedings, and even if only a fraction of the members attended the meetings, it was assured that the important information — the message Dulles and his friends wanted to get across — would reach all one hundred members and could then be disseminated further.[8] Under Dulles' chair, the study group was used to spread the conviction that the economic reconstruction of Germany was imperative and only the degree of rehabilitation was up for debate. Undoubtedly, Germany had to be prevented from ever again being able to attack her neighbors, but Germany was also needed in the rehabilitation of the European economy as a whole.

Dulles told the group members at their first meeting that the Joint Chiefs of Staff directive 1067 (JCS 1067), issued to General Eisenhower in early 1945 to provide for firm demilitarization and denazification, hampered adequate improvement of the German economy. Dulles, by no means a "friend of Germany," detested Nazism fervently and was, like most of his peers at the Council, an anglophile. He simply wanted

7. "Memorandum for J.F.D. [John Foster Dulles]," 14 May 1946, John F. Dulles Papers, box 28, Mudd Manuscript Library.

8. Only for the meeting on 28 May 1946, when twenty-five members attended, were the names of members present recorded.

to put Germany back to work. "Europe as a whole," he argued, "cannot get back to anything like normal conditions, not to speak of any prosperity, with a completely disorganized Germany."[9]

Economic consolidation in Germany thus had first priority for Dulles. "Germany ought to be put to work for the benefit of Europe and particularly for the benefit of those countries plundered by the Nazis," he maintained. The greatest handicap in the attempts to reinvigorate regional industry, transportation, and administration was the rigid denazification policy of the American occupying forces. In their venture to reinstate communal administrations, the Americans had to realize that hardly any useful individuals, when treated according to the guidelines of this policy, could be hired. "We have already found," Dulles complained to the Council members, "that you can't run railroads without taking in some [former Nazi] party members."[10]

Dulles' assessment that stern deindustrialization as a security measure against Germany was a flawed concept was shared by many of his associates at the Council. DeWitt C. Poole, among the American embassy personnel in Moscow during the Russian Revolution and until recently involved in the interrogation of German politicians, argued that it was time to free Germany from "indiscriminate de-Nazification + unrelenting de-industrialization."[11] In addition, Chicago lawyer Laird Bell, who had been deputy director of the Economic Division of the Office of Military Government in Germany, maintained that JCS 1067, as a guideline for occupational policy in Germany, was ill-proposed and based on political presumptions long surpassed by events. Bell fought, according to his own judgment, a "one man crusade against [JCS] 1067."[12]

Invited by Dulles to address a group meeting on 6 February 1946, Bell maintained that "our essential objective in Germany is to prevent

9. DD, 3 December 1945, 5, WEA/RGCFR-XVIIIE; Manuscript "Talk at Council, 12/3/45", Allen Dulles Papers, box 21; Dulles spoke on "The Present Situation in Germany."

10. DD, 3 December 1945, 5, 1, WEA/RGCFR-XVIIE.

11. Poole addressed "The Position of Germany in Europe", DD, 21 January 1946, WEA/RGCFR-XVIIIE; Poole to Dulles, 8 February 1946, Allen Dulles Papers, box 21. This hand-written five-page letter was copied and, without indication of the author, was used as a discussion paper for the group. See Dulles to Poole, 11 February 1946, *ibid.* Poole had already spoken on "The Future of Germany" at a Foreign Policy Association meeting on 19 January 1946. See DeWitt C. Poole Papers, box 11, State Historical Society of Wisconsin.

12. Bell to Dulles, 28 January 1946, Allen Dulles Papers, box 23. For the JCS directive see Paul Y. Hammond, "Directives." The text of JCS 1067 is reprinted in Department of State, *Documents on Germany, 1944–1985*, 15–32.

the Germans from plunging the world into another war. We could have done this by killing off the sixty-five or seventy million Germans still left, a course we fortunately have no intention of adopting." Another possibility, Bell had learned from recent talks in Washington, was to "police the Germans more or less indefinitely." Neither prospect was feasible, and crushing Germany would only induce bitterness, resentment, and revenge — feelings that might lead to another war, thus achieving the very opposite of what was intended.[13]

Among Americans (in the general public as well as among the interested and attentive public) the attitude toward Germany, Bell believed, was still guided mainly by "war hysteria with vengeance as its principle ingredient." Something had to be done to change this perspective to allow for some modification of U.S. policy. Thus, after the study-group meeting on 6 February 1946, Bell, Dulles, and a few other members got together to "see whether there was anything we could do to help get the right slant to public opinion on Germany."[14]

Additionally, and through the good services of Dean G. Acheson, then under secretary of state, Bell was able to meet with State Department officials James Riddleberger, Charles P. Kindleberger, and John Kenneth Galbraith.[15] JCS 1067 was not very helpful, all agreed, and the State Department wanted to implement changes. Officials feared, however, that doing so openly would arouse the "residual power of the Morgenthau group" within the administration. Not much on this issue had appeared in the press, and Bell urged that newspaper articles "on the general thesis that the Morgenthau plan is being junked" should be written.[16]

The State Department was not certain about its future policy toward the Soviet Union and Germany, but it wanted to avoid unnecessary tension. Riddleberger indicated that the Department's political advisors agreed with him on the necessity of change in the deindustrialization policy; the "youngsters on the economic side" would do what they were

13. DD, "The United States Policy in Germany," 6 February 1946, 1–5, WEA/RGCFR-XVIIE.

14. DD, "The United States Policy in Germany," 6 February 1946, 1–5, WEA/RGCFR-XVIIE. Dulles to Bell, January 3, 1946, Allen Dulles Papers, box 23.

15. Kindleberger's role will be discussed below. During the war, Galbraith had been director of the U.S. Strategic Bombing Survey, and in 1946 he was the State Department's director of Economic Security Policy. Trained at Princeton and Harvard, the economist later took up a job with *Fortune*. See also his autobiography, *A Life in Our Time* (Boston, 1981).

16. Bell to Dulles, 9 February 1946, Allen Dulles Papers, box 23.

ordered to do, leaving only the president and Secretary of State Byrnes to be won over.[17]

In the following months a number of speakers in addition to Laird Bell addressed the study group on topics related to the rehabilitation of individual European countries. Charles M. Spofford and Charles Poletti, both former members of the Allied Military Government in Italy, made reports on the situation in that country, and Pierre Mendès-France, minister of finance of the preliminary French government (1944 to 1945), talked about the situation in France.[18] Arthur H. Dean, partner at the law firm Sullivan and Cromwell (with which Allen Dulles was affiliated), lectured on "The Program of Reconstruction in Holland." Posing as a Dutch politician, he expressed what Dulles and his associates believed and feared: "You [the Americans] don't want German industry to get going because you fear another war in 25 years, but as a result of your policy, you are promoting civil war and communism today."[19]

Two weeks later, the discussion at a group meeting on 28 May 1946, with *Newsweek* editor Malcolm Muir as the speaker, turned out to be almost a nucleus of future American policy in Europe.[20] European reconstruction, it was maintained, was important to the fabric of international economic ties and to the well-being of the United States. A speedy and effective restoration of the European economies depended upon German economic rehabilitation, which in turn was only achievable if Germany were treated as an economic unit. Russia, however, was preventing this. The division of Germany was a fact, members stated, and a Western European federation, including the three western zones of Germany, should be established. Asked if this would not violate the Potsdam agreements, the Council members were informed by Dulles that, if unification of Germany was offered "to Russia and she turned it down, then Russia and not the United States would be in the position of rejecting the Potsdam formula." He suggested "offer[ing] the Soviets a feasible plan,"

17. Riddleberger to Poole, 5 February 1946, marked *PERSONAL AND CONFIDENTIAL*, Armstrong Papers, box 40; Poole to Dulles, 8 February 1946, Allen Dulles Papers, box 21.

18. Spofford and Poletti addressed "Basic Economic and Political Problems in Italy," DD, 6 March 1946, WEA/RGCFR-XVIIIE. Mendès-France spoke on "The Financial and Economic Problems of France," DD, 23 April 1946, WEA/RGCFR-XVIIIE.

19. DD, 15 May 1946, 5, WEA/RGCFR-XVIIIE.

20. Muir had been invited, together with thirteen other newspaper and magazine editors and correspondents, by Secretary of War Robert P. Patterson to a tour of Europe. See DD, "The Political and Economic Situation in Central Europe," 28 May 1946, 1–5, WEA/RGCFR-XVIIIE.

but in the event that the Soviets did not accept it, the United States should "work out a constructive policy for western Germany."[21]

Some time before the United States offered economic unification with other zones of occupation in July 1946, the Council members thus advocated a unification of the three western zones of Germany; and, long before Secretary of State Byrnes' well-known speech in September 1946, in Stuttgart,[22] they called for the revitalization of German industry. The future treatment of Germany, they knew quite well, was the major issue at the beginning of the Cold War, and it forced decisions upon the American government that would necessarily lead to discord with the Soviet Union.

In the fall of 1946, the Council's attentiveness toward Germany rose considerably. Two study groups for the years 1946/1947 were established. Under the leadership of Charles Spofford, a group discussed "Reconstruction of Western Europe" and, with David Rockefeller as the group's secretary, Dulles continued his work on the "The Problem of Germany." The economic situation in Europe since May 1945 had not recovered as much as had been hoped. Coal mining had broken down, and attempts to supply the population with food and other necessities were still insufficient. Many Council members agreed, in the fall of 1946, that American help in the reconstruction of Europe was necessary. Only the type of help and the allocation of resources was still discussed controversially. Rehabilitation was hampered by very severe weather conditions during the winter of 1947, coal mining broke down almost completely, and the supply of food, especially in Germany, was catastrophically low. People froze and starved to death. Many Council members agreed that reconstruction without American help would be impossible. Questions such as "What are the causes of the slow progress . . . toward political stability and better business conditions? What American policies can help most?" and "How can these policies be framed so as to safeguard and advance the interest of the United States?" show this concern clearly. These questions also reveal, however, the Council's inclination to give special attention to advantages and concerns of the United States.[23]

21. DD, 28 March 1946, 3–4, WEA/RGCFR-XVIIIE.

22. For Byrnes' speech, see John Gimbel, "Byrnes' Rede und die amerikanische Nachkriegspolitik in Deutschland," *Vierteljahrshefte für Zeitgeschichte* 20 (1972): 39–62.

23. CFR, *Annual Report, 1946–1947*, 15.

At the same time, the Council, aided by the Department of State, conducted an opinion poll among members of its local chapters, the Committees on Foreign Relations.[24] The Council found that most respondents believed that a unified and prosperous Germany would not be a threat to future peace, provided "demilitarization takes place and . . . the German people establish and support democratic institutions." Germany should be encouraged to participate in international trade and American policy should assist the development of Germany's industry to that end. However, the revival of the German economy should not take precedence over denazification. Of the respondents, forty-four percent considered making "sure of thorough denazification, perhaps at the expense of delaying the revival of the German economy" a primary concern, whereas forty-five percent deemed more critical the pursuit of "a more lenient policy in the belief that the defeat of Germany has so discredited Nazism that its reconstitution is no longer an appreciable danger." One respondent cautioned that "anyone who entertains the idea, 21 months after the surrender, that the German people have become sufficiently denazified, is sadly deluded." Arguments against thorough denazification at the expense of the revival of German industry were just as emphatic. One member, at least, was ahead of his time when he argued that "we are no longer fighting Nazism; we are fighting communism and [a more lenient denazification policy] is the only way to combat that." Council staff members summarized the poll and concluded that "denazification and the revival of the German economy are [regarded as] equally essential."[25]

The Council considered these findings important enough to warrant publication and general distribution. In early spring of 1947, just in time for the beginning of the Moscow Conference in March 1947, advance copies of the report (entitled *American Policy toward Germany*) were directed to the State Department and to officials of the U.S. Military Government in Germany. "Copies were available at the Moscow Conference and were found to be helpful, according to individuals who were present," the Council's *Annual Report* for 1946–1947 proudly claimed.[26]

24. Joseph Barber, ed., *American Policy Towards Germany* (New York, 1947), 14–15. In November 1946 Barber had called upon Francis Russell at the State Department to help with the questionnaires. Russell put Barber in touch with Shepard S. Jones, acting chief of the Division of Public Studies, who was to help the Council. See Barber to Russell, 27 November 1946, Decimal File 811.43 Council on Foreign Relations/11–2746, National Archives RG 59; Russell to Barber, 12 December 1946, *ibid.*

25. Barber, *American Policy Toward Germany*, 4–5, 15.

26. CFR, *Annual Report of the Executive Director, 1946–1947* (New York, 1947), 52.

At this same time, Dulles' group had accepted a special task. During the summer of 1946 the newly founded Nederlandse Genootschap voor Internationale Zaken had invited the Council to participate in a conference to be held at Baarn in early October 1947. It was to be followed by a similar symposium in April 1948 which would attract preeminent foreign affairs delegates from Europe to discuss the topic of post-war Germany. Percy Bidwell, director of studies of the Council, was to represent his organization, and the Council's Committee on Studies wanted to give him thoroughly researched background information first.[27] Fearing that the participation of only Western European organizations might create the impression that such a meeting was aimed against the Soviet Union, the Committee on Studies persuaded the Dutch to also invite organizations from the USSR, Poland, and Czechoslovakia.[28]

In gathering data on the economic situation of Germany, the group swiftly turned to the question of the supply of food. John Kenneth Galbraith told his captive audience that the European infrastructure was not as problematic as it had been and that the main cause of the slow progress of rehabilitation was now, in addition to the shortage of money, the lack of food supplied by the United States. "We have eaten too much," was how Galbraith explained the insufficient exports.[29] To make things worse, the British, whose zone of occupation contained the very heart of the German economic potential, were unable to reorganize the economic and political life there.[30] Galbraith had argued in autumn 1946 that credits to Europe could be a main foreign policy instrument. At the core of this policy, he had asserted, was the reconstruction of German industry, particularly coal production at the Ruhr, in the interest of Europe as a whole.[31]

---

27. Financing of the operational costs and travel expenses was made possible by a Rockefeller Foundation grant. Mallory had asked at the beginning of January 1947 for $8,000 and received $6,000. See RFE to Willits and ME, 4 March 1947, RFR, 1/100/98/889; "Inter-Office Correspondence," 5 March 1947, *ibid.*, 1/100/97/889; RA SS 4725, 25 April 1947, *ibid.*, 1/100/98/889.

28. Dulles to Shepard Morgan (Chase National Bank), 24 October 1946, PofG/RGCFR-XXIB; DD, 12 November 1946, 1–2, PofG/RGCFR-XXIC. The conferences took place in Baarn, from 6 to 11 October 1947, and in Scheveningen, from 11 to 17 April 1948. The contributions of these groups were printed in Percy W. Bidwell, ed., *Germany's Contribution to European Economic Life* (Paris, 1949).

29. Barely a year later President Truman called for a nationwide drive to cut the consumption of food. See Theodore A. Wilson and Richard D. McKinzie "The Food Crusade of 1947," *Prologue* 3 (Winter 1971): 136–52.

30. DD, 12 November 1946, 2, 5, PofG/RGCFR-XXIC.

31. John K. Galbraith, "Recovery in Europe," *Planning Pamphlets* 53 (Washington, D.C., November 1946): 28, 30–35.

"It will require imports of food, and several years of credit, to prime the pump with raw materials and some machinery" to revitalize German industry, economist Karl Brandt of Stanford University's Food Research Institute wrote to Shepard Morgan after the groups' meeting on 12 November 1946. "Recovery in Denmark, Holland, France and Switzerland particularly is impeded and delayed so long as the cadaver of Germany sends its stench of decay into all these countries." In addition, addressing an issue of even more importance to the group, Brandt stated that, "if in two decades Western Europe gradually slides into the Russian political and economic orbit, the decision on it matures nowhere else but in Germany."[32]

In the wake of Secretary Byrnes' Stuttgart speech, arguments for a thorough reindustrialization were advanced, but it was also debated whether it would prove necessary to reunite the eastern parts of Germany (which were under Soviet and Polish administration) with the rest of the nation for Germany to be self-sufficient. During the discussion on the evening of 12 November, John J. McCloy (assistant to Henry Stimson during the war and a member of the group since the fall of 1946) claimed that to render Germany incapable of aggression in the eyes of the other European nations, it would be necessary to "restore Germany but prevent her from becoming dominant economically in Europe." Theologian Reinhold Niebuhr added that "a viable economy in Germany would do more to eliminate Communism than anything else." When talk again turned to the reunification of Germany, DeWitt Poole maintained that there was no prospect of cooperation with the Soviet Union in this respect. "Germany had been unified only since 1870," he argued, and the "United States' policy should favor the partition of Germany . . . the public should be weaned away from the idea of the necessity of unification."[33]

The group's work soon parted from the exclusive task of providing background material for the conference at Baarn. Rapporteurs Carl E. Schorske and Hoyt Price had been assigned to write an informative account of the basic facts and principles of American policy toward Germany for general circulation in the United States. Additionally, a policy statement for the State Department was to be prepared. Not surprisingly, the same problems that had arisen with Franklin's report for the study group on the Soviet Union quickly resurfaced.[34] Percy Bidwell

32. Brandt to Shepard Morgan, 22 November 1946, PofG/RGCFR-XXIC.

33. DD, 11 December 1946, PofG/RGCFR-XXIC.

34. Economist Price, who had been assistant to General Clay's political advisor Robert Murphy, was put in charge of writing the economic parts. Schorske had been chief of

considered neither Schorske nor Price competent enough to compose such a sensitive document. Nevertheless, several drafts were discussed but soon rejected until the group members agreed to use Allen Dulles' introduction to the meeting of 10 January as the basis for the group's statement for the State Department.[35]

Dulles had outlined the danger of domination of Western Europe by the Soviet Union if Germany were to become a satellite of the USSR. It was far too early, he maintained, to be certain that Germany was on its way to becoming a democracy. This process could last years, possibly decades. In light of this, American policy should not be guided by feelings of revenge, he wrote: "Germany belongs predominantly to the culture of the West and not to the area of Slav civilization." Fear of disturbing the uneasy balance in the relations between the Soviet Union and the Western Allies had delayed resolution of the main issues until the rapid deterioration of the situation in Europe threatened. It was essential, Dulles emphasized, that at the forthcoming conference of foreign ministers at Moscow "a beginning be made toward measures of reconstruction and toward tracing out a program for the future." A disarmed and neutralized Germany should be established, which "although a part of western Europe, would not be a legitimate cause of apprehension to Russia."[36]

At the 10 January meeting, some of Dulles' statements raised discord among the group members, in particular with regard to assuring that a neutral and strong Germany would not again commit military aggression. Heated discussion ensued. Schorske and Price were delegated to edit their draft for the next meeting on 29 January so as to address this concern, but since very few of the group members who had been present at the previous meeting were in attendance on 29 January, the deliberations made little progress. Overall, Shephard Morgan argued, the draft by Schorske and Price was still too negative, only repeated well-known facts, and contained far too many platitudes.[37]

The discussion on 10 January did nothing to clarify the controversial parts of Dulles' suggestions, and the members instead tried to reach a

---

the Central European Section of the OSS during the war and was to be responsible for the political and social parts.

35. Bidwell to Dulles, 12 December 1946, PofG/RGCFR-XXIC; DD, 10 January 1947, 1, *ibid.*

36. Dulles, "United States Policy with Respect to Germany: I. Introductory Statement," dated 10 January 1946 [*sic*, 1947], PofG/RGCFR-XXIC; DD, 10 January 1947 [*sic*, 1947], *ibid.*

37. DD, 10 January 1946 [*sic*, 1947], PofG/RGCFR-XXIC; DD, 29 January 1947, *ibid.*

consensus on a definition of what Germany actually was.[38] At the end of the meeting the members seemed hardly to have agreed on any issue at all. Nevertheless, Price revised his draft and Poole contributed a manuscript which, he claimed, could serve as an example for a careful declaration by the Council. "Such a statement," he believed, "would have a good chance of being read top-side in the State Department as an exposition by a representative and highly informed group." Time was running out; the Truman Doctrine was in the making and the meeting of foreign ministers at Moscow would convene shortly. The group members were asked to submit their comments on Price's manuscript by 28 February to assure that "the final draft [is] in the hands of the Secretary of State shortly after the first of March, at the latest."[39]

With a less tangible aim, the discussion group "Reconstruction in Western Europe" had started its work. Led by Spofford, it did not so much discuss particular aspects, as the group on "The Problem of Germany" did, but rather considered the situation in Europe as a whole. The two groups cooperated closely, were addressed by the same speakers, and some Council members participated in both groups. Thus, as with Dulles' group, the discussion group members realized quickly that economic revival was the foremost issue and imperative for the consolidation of the political situation.

For the first meeting, the topic was the various political currents and parties in Europe and their popular support. Political scientist Arnold Wolfers of Columbia University demonstrated to the members just how diversified the political landscape in Europe was in comparison with the that in the United States. Addressing the situation in Germany, Wolfers maintained that the Communist Party had only a very few supporters and that the conservative groups on the far right were also of little importance to the political life in the occupied nation. Only the Social

38. One member defined Germany as "that area where Germans lived and historically have lived;" Poole maintained that there existed no "Germany" as such; Dulles argued that the term should refer to the four united zones; and another member proposed that the hypothesis of a unified Germany should serve as the basis for discussion. See DD, 29 January 1947, PofG/RGCFR-XXIC.

39. Poole to Bidwell, 4 February 1947, PofG/RGCFR-XXIB; Price to Members, 24 February 1947, *ibid.* Dulles' "Introductory Statement" eventually served as the core of his article, "Alternatives for Germany," *Foreign Affairs* 25 (April 1947): 421–32. See also his footnote, *ibid.*, 421. Schorske's and Price's monograph was published under the title *The Problem of Germany* (New York, 1947). The anticipated memorandum for the State Department had been an important factor in convincing the Rockefeller Foundation to extend its financial support. See "Inter-Office Correspondence," 5 March 1947, RFR, 1/100/97/889.

Democrats — "the only party which can be said to have survived Fascism and the war with unchanged standing, program, and membership" — and the Christian Parties had been able to obtain a considerable number of votes during the last elections.[40]

In France, the situation was different. There the communists had more influence not only in the administration but also in the labor unions. At the same time, however, the French were much more nationalistic than the Germans. In Italy, as well, the communists had considerable political influence. However, in both Italy and France, chairperson Spofford saw a revival of right-wing or even fascist movements as a much more likely and dangerous threat. The only way to wean potential supporters away from these radical parties, Arnold Wolfers maintained, was economic revival. During the ensuing meetings, discussions and papers on the prerequisites and potential of economic recovery and related issues should, consequently, dominate the gatherings of the group.[41]

At the meeting on 25 January 1947, a State Department official addressed the dearth of food supplies in Europe. The harsh winter of 1946/47 had worsened the situation. In view of the hunger and starvation in Europe, he concluded that the Germans had eaten more during the war than any other Europeans. In the fall of 1945, when supplying food had become more difficult and only an average of 1,550 calories per person per day could be distributed, Germans had lost some weight, "but they had it to lose." Far removed from the actual situation, the official complained about the generosity of German workers who shared their rations with their wives and children. This, he maintained, was a difficult problem, and only the distribution of one meal to miners on the job had successfully impeded this "unfortunate generosity." But plans existed, worked out by nutritionists, for a redistribution of the scant supplies. This would entail that older people would possibly die prematurely and the common consumer would have to make do with an absolute minimum, but the workers could then receive what they needed. The question of how many Germans one wanted to feed was not only a moral problem. In other parts of Europe, he asserted, the sit-

40. DD, 18 December 1946, 1–3, RWE/RGCFR-XXB. In addition, George Franklin had supplied the members with a compilation of "Important Western European Elections Since V-E Day." See enclosure, Franklin to Members, 16 December 1946, Carnegie Endowment for International Peace, Records, Baker Library, Columbia University, New York, NY (herafter CEIPR) #64563 and #64564.

41. DD, 18 December 1946, 3, 5–6, RWE/RGCFR-XXB.

uation was much worse. The interdependence of the supply of food and productivity would have to be a major concern for American policy in occupied Germany.[42]

After these depressing reflections, the group turned to more practical matters. The economy in Europe should be revived, all agreed, and developments after Secretary of State Byrnes' speech at Stuttgart in September 1946 had been quite promising. The major problem was the inadequate supply of coal. Without coal, machines did not run, heating was not available, and the railroads had no fuel. Transporting American coal to Germany was too expensive, British mines did not produce enough surplus coal for export, and the German mines in Silesia, now under the Polish administration, could not be utilized. The Ruhr area, the assembled experts and members of the group acknowledged, was thus the key to the future of Europe.[43]

American military governor Lucius D. Clay was aware of Germany's importance and had very early on used the contradictory implications of directive JCS 1067 to execute a more lenient deindustrialization policy in Germany than many would have favored. During the Potsdam Conference, in July and August 1945, it became apparent that the U.S. wanted to leave Germany with at least a minimum of industrial power to ensure its economic existence. This notion was reinforced when in December the State Department revealed its ideas about reparations and a peace treaty with Germany.[44]

At Potsdam it had been agreed that the Allies would issue, within the following six months, a plan to address these problems.[45] After lengthy negotiations on a score of individual questions and extremely controversial discussions regarding the level of German coal production, it was decided that Germany should be allowed approximately seventy percent of its 1936 industrial capacity. Clay, however, was not very eager to put

42. Kindleberger to Franklin, 25 January 1947, RWE/RGCFR-XXB; DD, 28 January 1947, *ibid.* The situation was not as rosy — at least not for the German population — as the State Department official seemed to indicate. In March 1946 the Germans in the American zone received, on the average, 1,250 calories per person, in the British zone 1,015, and in the French zone only 940 calories per day. See Michael Balfour, *Viermächtekontrolle in Deutschland, 1945–1946* (Düsseldorf, 1959), 202–10.

43.DD, 28 January 1947, 3, 7, 9–10, RWE/RGCFR-XXB.

44. See Nübel, *Amerikanische Reparationspolitik*, passim; and also John Gimbel, *The American Occupation of Germany: Politics and the Military, 1945–1949* (Stanford, CA, 1968).

45. Documents on the negotiations at Potsdam are reprinted in the *FRUS, Potsdam* volumes. See also the chapter "Die Konferenz in Potsdam," in Nübel, *Amerikanische Reparationspolitik*, 174–201.

these guidelines into effect. His attitude was similar to that of many Council members who believed that the German economy was of prime importance for the economic rehabilitation of the whole of Europe. In addition, experts within the State Department had realized that a low level of industry in Germany would entail spending millions of dollars of American taxpayers' money to maintain a minimal standard of living in the occupied area.[46]

During the winter of 1946/47, the notion of revitalizing Germany's economy gained a good deal of support in the United States. Herbert Hoover headed a commission, initiated by President Truman, to research the economic situation in Germany and the rest of Europe. Hoover reached a conclusion similar to those of the military government in Germany and the Council members in New York: "The whole economy of Europe is interlinked with German economy through the exchange of raw materials and manufactured goods. The productivity of Europe cannot be restored without the restoration of Germany as a contributor to that productivity," Hoover wrote in his final report in March 1947.[47]

By that time, America's relationship with the Soviet Union had changed drastically. President Truman's speech of 12 March had created considerable excitement, although it was still not yet clear how Truman's statements would be transformed into actual policy. During the last group meeting before the customary summer recess, on 19 May, this new situation was the focus of attention. This time, three speakers discussed American economic aid in a larger context. Again it was apparent that most of the men assembled regarded American aid as a means to gain political influence, whereas only a minority understood foreign aid as purely economic policy. Reaffirming his conviction that American aid would help to stabilize the political situation in Europe, Arnold Wolfers maintained that a low standard of living in Europe might well lead to an increase of power of leftist parties, and that American policy should certainly favor conservative movements. The Truman Doctrine had been perceived in Europe as an announcement of anti-communist policy on the part of the American administration, but it had not yet led

46. Bruce Kuklick, *American Policy and the Division of Germany: The Clash with Russia over Reparations* (Ithaca, NY, 1972), 172–74; Paterson, *Soviet-American Confrontation*, 240–44.

47. Herbert Hoover, *The President's Economic Mission to Germany and Austria*, Report No. 3, 2, dated 18 March 1947, quoted in Feis, *From Trust to Terror*, 267, footnote 1. See also Michael J. Hogan, *The Marshall Plan: America, Britain, and the Reconstruction of Western Europe, 1947–1952* (New York, 1987), 33–35.

to stability. Wolfers summarized the prevalent opinion among the group members by stating that political consolidation depended primarily on support given to the economy.[48]

A State Department official attending the meeting did not agree with Wolfers' evaluation. The political situation, he argued, was of the greatest importance, and U.S. policy should be guided primarily by supporting parties and politicians who were at the center of the political spectrum before American economic assistance should be considered. Also, he maintained, Germany should be induced to export: "[T]he taxpayers have a right to receive some return in the form of exports from the occupied zones or from countries to which we give or lend our economic assets." A policy he regarded as "proper and practical" should demand that the population in the Ruhr area prove that it was able and willing to export goods; only then should economic help be provided. John Kenneth Galbraith disagreed with this notion. Like Karl Brand, he believed that a substantial economic aid program conducted by the United States was necessary and would be most timely.[49]

A consensus was reached with little trouble regarding the issue of whether the United States should aid only countries friendly to the U.S. "Humanitarianism is not a proper basis for the allocation of economic aid. Direct benefits must accrue to the United States," it was argued, and one member maintained that only the strongest and most active of the United States' supporters in Western Europe should be assisted; thus, Poland, Yugoslavia, and Romania should all be excluded from American aid. The United Nations, Arnold Wolfers insisted, should not be involved in the aid program, and "[i]f the program of the United States is to prevent countries from going Communist, it should be done openly." Frank Altschul even regarded the United States as being in a "prewar world, making preparations of a political, economic, and military nature to protect vital national interests." This evaluation, however, and his critical assessment of the USSR did not preclude his hope for a peaceful solution. Economic and political stability, he asserted, had to be the aspiration of American policy. More gloomily, Russell Leffingwell, of J. P. Morgan and Company — seldom a participant at the group meetings — postulated that "the key problem now is to arrest this process of disintegration, no longer for the sake of humanitarianism, but to save ourselves."[50]

48. DD, 19 May 1947, 1–3, RWE/RGCFR-XXB.

49. *Ibid.*, 4, 6.

50. *Ibid.*, 5–10.

Proposals and evaluations of economic aid by the groups' members corresponded closely with designs developed by other organizations and State Department officials during that period. The foreign policy of the United States in the two years following World War II was a mixture of measures inspired by ideas of free trade, "peace and prosperity," and repeated (although half-hearted) attempts to dissociate itself from the USSR. Politicians in Washington were convinced not only that their views on foreign economic policy — or at least their notion of free multilateral trade — would benefit all nations, but also that the "American way of life" would best suit all the peoples of the world. The Soviet Union, a respected ally for a long time, did not conform with any of these ideas. In particular, the Soviet definition of democracy did not correspond with what Americans commonly understood as a democratic system of government; and, in addition, many Americans were unable to accept that the Soviet leaders themselves might honestly regard their political system to be preferable to the American style of democracy. There was still a feeling that the Soviet leadership might be comprised of cynical dictators. The Soviets, in turn, schooled in the theories of Marx and Lenin, probably regarded the interrelation of economy and society as much more important than their American counterparts believed.

American policy toward the Soviet Union was by no means unswerving. In some instances, the U.S. gave in to Soviet requests, while at other times sanctions were inflicted. Deliveries under the Lend-Lease bill had been suddenly canceled in 1945, and ships had even been recalled from the high seas.[51] The previously discussed post-war credit came to naught, although the Soviets had reason to believe that the U.S. would favor this for its own interests. After extensive negotiations Great Britain had received a credit amounting to $3.5 billion, provided the country reduced trade barriers, but a proposal for a credit to Poland was recalled only one month after it had been made. Financing of the rehabilitation of European economies was thus hampered by the burgeoning disagreements between the U.S. and the USSR. In February 1946, the credit to the USSR had again been discussed, and the Americans put the unresolved issue of political dominance in Eastern Europe and Soviet membership in the World Bank on the agenda to demonstrate that a credit would depend on concessions in these areas. Concurrently, the Iranian

51. Most historians interpret the termination of Lend-Lease as legally correct but politically unfortunate. See Feis, *From Trust to Terror*, 228; George C. Herring, Jr., "Lend-Lease to Russia and the Origins of the Cold War, 1944–1945," *Journal of American History* 56 (June 1969): 97–105; and idem, *Aid to Russia, 1941–1946: Strategy, Diplomacy, the Origins of the Cold War* (New York, 1973), 180–236.

crisis was developing, Kennan's "long telegram" received wide attention within the administration, and Winston Churchill used the phrase "Iron Curtain" in the presence of President Truman. The still unsettled question of control of atomic energy and the continuing conflicts in occupied Germany had poisoned the relationship for a long time. Truman's speech of March 1947, in its tenor more anti-Soviet than many in the administration had anticipated, and the return of the disillusioned Secretary of State Marshall from the Moscow Foreign Ministers' Conference in April added to the discord between the former allies.[52]

Very soon after Truman's speech, journalists and concerned individuals had claimed that a broader aid program than the one proposed by the president for Greece and Turkey, would be necessary in Europe because of the desperate situation.[53] A policy would have to be devised that would stabilize the European economies without an excessive drain on the domestic budget and, at the same time, prevent the USSR from gaining dominance in Europe — without further alienating the Soviets.

Some groups within the administration had discussed a broadly based program of rehabilitation for the European economies prior to 12 March. By spring of 1947, $9 billion had already been spent through various agencies on the war-torn regions. However, these measures had not solved the problems. Dean Acheson, one of the advocates of the aid program to Greece and Turkey, asked Secretary of War Robert P. Patterson on 5 March 1947 to request a subcommittee of the State-War-Navy Coordinating Committee (SWNCC) to study the questions of the feasibility and prerequisites of a more encompassing aid program.[54]

52. Special Assistant to the Secretary of State Charles E. Bohlen — certainly not a man to be accused of being soft on communism — was "somewhat startled to see the extent to which the anti-Communist element was stressed" in Truman's address. See Bohlen, *The Transformation of American Foreign Policy* (New York, 1969), 87; Jones, *The Fifteen Weeks;* Ronald Steel, *Pax Americana* (New York, 1967), 21–23. Truman's address is reprinted in *Public Papers of the Presidents, Truman, 1947*, 176–80.

53. Officials regarded responses by prominent journalists such as Walter Lippmann and Drew Pearson as being very important. See Eben A. Ayers Diary, entries for 12 and 13 March 1947, Ayers Papers, box 26, Truman Library. See also "Excerpts from Telephone Conversation between Honorable James Forrestal, Secretary of the Navy, and Mr. James Reston of the New York Times. 13. March 1947," Joseph M. Jones Papers, box 1, Truman Library.

54. Acheson to Patterson, 5 March 1947, *FRUS, 1947* 3: 197. Already in mid-January Greece asked the Import-Export Bank for a $25 million credit. See Memorandum of Conversation, "Greek Request for Urgent Financial Assistance," dated 14 January 1947, U.S. Department of State: Office Files of the Assistant Secretary for Economic Affairs and the Under Secretary for Economic Affairs (Clayton-Thorp) 1944–1948, box 4, Truman Library.

The hastily drafted report, issued on 21 April and still oriented toward Truman's vaguely formulated policy, advocated taking "positive, forehand, and preventive action in the matter of promotion of United States interest through assistance" and advised giving priority to such countries or regions "which are vital to our national security and our national interest . . . which contain or protect sources of metal, oil and other natural resources, which contain strategic objectives, or areas strategically located, which contain a substantial industrial potential, which possess man power and organized military forces in important quantities."[55]

The Joint Strategy Survey Committee of the Joint Chiefs of Staff quickly expressed this military-strategic component more drastically: "If assistance is given," it maintained, "it should, in each instance, be sufficient to positively assist the nation to achieve or retain a sound economy . . . to maintain the armed forces necessary for its continual independence and to be of real assistance to the United States in case of ideological warfare." Accordingly, neither the USSR nor countries under its influence could profit from American aid. Germany, however, was regarded to be of prime importance because of its strategic and politically pivotal position in Europe and because the country was "the natural enem[y] of the USSR and communism." As to the possibility of the U.S. keeping the strategic aims of its aid program secret, they stated that "[t]he Soviets will *correctly* interpret a program of United States assistance as aimed at containing them."[56]

The members of the SWNCC had also taken military and strategic components into account, but they had refrained from "naming names." The communists in the European countries and in the USSR, they argued, would only take advantage of a worsening economic situation. Additionally, the SWNCC took into account repercussions of the situation in Europe on the domestic American economy. The usual amount of American exports could be ensured only for the next twelve to eighteen months, they claimed, and "a substantial decline in the

55. "Report of the Special 'ad hoc' Committee of the SWNCC," dated 21 April 1947, *FRUS, 1947* 3: 204–19.

56. "Memorandum by the Joint Chiefs of Staff to the SWNCC, Appendix," dated 12 May 1947, *FRUS, 1947* 1: 737, 740–41, 748. This appendix is a memorandum by the Joint Strategic Survey Committee, dated 29 April 1947; italics are mine. Marx Leva, special assistant to Secretary Forrestal, had likewise feared "a serious, immediate and extraordinarily grave threat to the continued existence of this country." See memorandum, dated 6 March 1947, enclosed to Leva to Clark M. Clifford (special assistant to President Truman), 6 March 1946, Raymond Oaks Papers, reel 2, State Historical Society of Wisconsin.

United States' export surplus would have a depressing effect on business activity and employment in the United States."[57]

The Foreign Ministers' Conference in Moscow, lasting from March through April, did not produce the results for which Secretary Marshall hoped. Obviously disappointed, he returned with the firm conviction that the Soviets were not interested in economic cooperation to solve the German situation. On the contrary, they seemed to be planning to include Germany and other European countries in their sphere of influence as soon as the desperate situation turned chaotic. Immediately after his return from Moscow on 28 April, Marshall created within the State Department the foundation for a policy that would not need confirmation by all of the Allies. The State Department scrambled to get a grip on the deplorable situation in Europe, to prepare the public for the change in policy, and to get representatives and senators into the fold and prepare them for the large expenditures that a widened foreign aid program would entail.[58]

Shortly thereafter, Under Secretary of State Dean Acheson used the opportunity of a speech to the Delta Council (a meeting of agrarians and business people in the Mississippi Valley) to indicate that a new policy of the U.S. was in the making. It had become increasingly apparent that Truman's offer to Greece and Turkey was only an additional part of a piecemeal foreign aid policy, and his vaguely formulated offer to help all subjugated peoples was regarded as quite unrealistic. Acheson in his address pointed to the interdependency of the economies of Japan and Germany, which he called "two of the greatest workshops of Europe and Asia," and spoke of the economic revival of Europe and Asia. He called for an increased effort (if necessary without the cooperation of all Allies) to revitalize the economies in these countries. His reflections, meant to help further the change in American foreign policy, did not receive much attention. There was still no clearly defined policy evident, "[u]nless", as Russel Leffingwell wrote, "Acheson's swan song in Mississippi [could] be regarded as such. If that was an announcement of a major policy it was an odd thing to choose the speech of a retiring Undersecretary [*sic*] at a remote point as the opportunity for announcing it."[59]

57. "Report 'ad hoc' Committee of the SWNCC," *FRUS, 1947* 3: 210–11.

58. Calls for such measures had already appeared in the "published" opinion pages. Walter Lippmann in particular had repeatedly called for economic aid. See Jones, *Fifteen Weeks*, 181–83, 226–29; see also Steel, *Lippmann*, 440–41.

59. Department of State, *Bulletin*, 18 May 1947, 991–94. The speech was given on 8 May. Acheson's summary of developments leading to his speaking engagement and the

Acheson's primarily economic-political analysis not only corresponded with the evaluations of Council members but was also supported by many other State Department officials. Council member William L. Clayton (at that time under secretary for economic affairs), having returned in May 1947 from a trip to Europe, was evidently impressed by the destruction he had seen. The only source for sufficient aid, he believed, was the United States. "Without further prompt and substantial aid from the United States," he wrote in a memorandum to Secretary Marshall dated 27 May, "economic, social and political disintegration will overwhelm Europe. Aside from the awful implications which this would have for the future peace and security of the world, the immediate effects on our domestic economy would be disastrous: markets for our surplus production gone, unemployment, depression, a heavily unbalanced budget on a background of a mountain of war debt." He did not regard the participation of UN agencies in administering an aid program to be advisable. In the last sentences of the memorandum he warned that "we must avoid getting into another UNRRA. *The United States must run this show.*"[60]

In the meantime, George Kennan's Policy Planning Staff had produced its first results. Ordered to devise a framework for the economic aid program and not very much interested in specific issues or in in-depth analysis, Kennan and his staff collected information and contemplated possible procedures.[61] Kennan's "hobby," analyzing the role of psychological factors in politics, was employed again when the PPS submitted its preliminary report on 23 May. The very announcement of the United States' offer to help would be an essential stimulus to the hopes of the Europeans, he claimed. Kennan saw the United States' role as that of a paternalistic friend and donor, offering help but leaving the task of allocation and administra-

---

lack of press coverage are delineated in Acheson to Jonathan Daniels, 9 September 1949, Acheson Papers, box 29. See also "Office Memorandum," Francis H. Russell to Humelsine, dated 9 September 1949, *ibid.* Leffingwell to Lamont, 23 May 1947, Lamont Papers, box 104. Leffingwell did agree with Acheson. He also regarded "German coal and iron, German labor and skills" as "vital to the European economy." See Leffingwell to Lamont, 21 May 1947, *ibid.*

60. "Memorandum by the Under Secretary of State for Economic Affairs (Clayton)," dated 27 May 1947, *FRUS, 1947* 3: 230–32. See Clayton, "GATT, the Marshall Plan, and OECD," *Political Science Quarterly* 78 (December 1963): 493–507, where part of the document is reprinted.

61. For the PPS, see Wilson D. Miscamble, "George F. Kennan, the Policy Planning Staff, and American Foreign Policy, 1947–1950" (Ph.D. diss., University of Notre Dame, 1980). The PPS' reports for this period are reprinted in Anna K. Nelson, ed., *The State Department Policy Planning Staff Papers, 1947–1949* (New York, 1983).

tion to the needy countries themselves. "The formal initiative must come from Europe. . . . The role of this country should consist of friendly aid in the drafting of a European program and of later support of such a program by financial and other means, at European request."[62]

The necessity of reconstruction of the economies after the war was hardly a new subject in 1947, and the Council on Foreign Relations was not alone in discussing this problem. In the various War and Peace Studies groups this topic had frequently been a point of concern,[63] and in deliberations within the State Department it had often been at the center of consideration. Other non-governmental organizations had also addressed the issue during the war and did so even more intensively after the fighting had ceased. However, during the immediate post-war years, it was not envisioned as an opportunity to conduct "political economy in the literal sense of that term." At the focus of attention then was the imminent problem of conversion from a war-time to a peace-time domestic American economy and the threat of large-scale unemployment.

In this context William Clayton had argued before the Economic Club of Detroit, in May of 1945, that American foreign economic policy rested on the hope for an expanding world economy and that employment during the post-war period would depend on the export of America's excess production.[64] Banker Winthrop W. Aldrich, chairman of President Truman's Committee for Financing Foreign Trade, advanced a similar argument a year later: financing of reconstruction and foreign trade "would not only help in rebuilding the economy of the world, but would increase and stabilize employment in this country."[65]

Members and organizations of the business community were the most active advocates of an open and export-oriented post-war economic policy. The Twentieth Century Fund, one of many such groups, had asked its Committee on Foreign Economic Relations to prepare a

62. Kennan to Acheson, 23 May 1947, *FRUS, 1947* 3: 224–31. Kennan wrote the report; the other staff member had hardly any influence in its formulation. The passage quoted was used literally by Bohlen for Marshall's Harvard address. Interestingly, Dean Acheson used exactly this passage to illustrate Secretary Marshall's "genius." See Dean G. Acheson, *Present at Creation: My Years in the State Department* (New York, 1969), 233–34.

63. The first report issued by the Economic and Financial Group, for example, was entitled, "The Impact of War Upon the Foreign Trade of the United States," E-B 1, CFRW+P.

64. Department of State, *Bulletin,* 21 May 1945, 979–80.

65. "White House Press Release," dated 9 July 1946, Department of State, *Bulletin,* 14 July 1946, 112.

study on this subject. Industrialists, labor union leaders, and members of academia convened and soon came to the conclusion that revitalization of an effective multilateral trade system would be the most important prerequisite for a lasting peace. The USSR, they argued, should participate in such a system. Only labor leader Robert J. Watt — one of the two union leaders among the Council's membership in 1946 — wanted to exclude countries that did not allow a maximum of freedom in their economic system.[66] The Committee for Economic Development, the National Planning Association, and a number of other groups advanced similar statements during that time.[67]

When on 28 May 1947, Marshall, Clayton, Acheson, Kennan, and a number of other State Department officials met for discussion, it was already certain that the State Department had decided on an initiative to revitalize the European economy and that this program would be very costly. Clayton summarized his memorandum of 27 May and stressed the issue of imports from the U.S. for which the Europeans would be unable to pay. He expressed concern that, within a short period of time, the social, economic, and political structures in Europe would collapse. The United States would then lose a market for its production and the country might well slowly descend into a new depression. Only massive financial aid by the United States and close economic cooperation among the European countries, preferably through a federation like the one already existing between the BENELUX countries, could help. Clayton did not regard the involvement of Eastern European nations in this program as necessary. After discussion, it was nevertheless agreed to propose a plan including these countries, provided they "would abandon near-exclusive Soviet orientation of their economies."[68]

---

66. Members of the Committee on Foreign Economic Relations were: Council members Winfield W. Riefler and Percy W. Bidwell, Paul G. Hoffman of the Studebaker Corporation (later to become the first administrator of the Economic Cooperation Administration), Robert J. Watt of the American Federation of Labor (AFL), and Kermit Eby of the Congress of Industrial Organization (CIO). The findings of the committee were published in Norman S. Buchanan and Frederick A. Lutz, *Rebuilding the World Economy: America's Role in Foreign Trade and Investment* (New York, 1947).

67. For these organizations, see David W. Eakins, "Business Planners and America's Postwar Expansion," in *Corporations and the Cold War*, 143–172, David Horowitz, ed.; and more extensively in his "The Development of Corporate Liberal Policy Research," especially chapter 8. For the history of the Committee for Economic Development, see Karl Schriftgiesser, *Business Comes of Age: The Story of the Committee for Economic Development and Its Impact Upon the Economic Policies of the United States, 1940-1960* (New York, 1960).

68. "Summary of Discussion on Problems of Relief, Rehabilitation and Reconstruction of Europe," dated 29 May 1947, *FRUS, 1947* 3: 234–36. At the meeting on 28 May,

Participation or non-participation of Eastern European countries and the USSR in the envisioned economic aid program was one of the most important political topics, and it presented a major predicament for the administration. On the one hand, exclusion of these countries would have added to the friction between the USSR and the U.S. at a time when there was still some hope left that positive cooperation with the Soviets might be possible. In addition, the administration shunned any policy that would put the United States in the position of being responsible for the division of Europe. Also, State Department officials hoped, Poland, Czechoslovakia, and other countries could still be included in a Western European economic system. On the other hand, it was hardly feasible to expect Congress to pass appropriations amounting to about $10 to $20 billion for a program benefiting the Soviet Union or other socialist countries; just a few months earlier fervent anti-Soviet rhetoric had to be used to gain support for the relatively small amount of $400 million for aid to Greece and Turkey. Nevertheless, it was decided to invite the USSR to join the program. The conditions stated, however, made it quite likely that the Soviet Union would refrain from participation, an outcome for which the U.S. officials hoped.[69]

Only a few days after the meeting at the State Department, the secretary of state had the opportunity to initiate the American proposal. He had been invited to address the commencement ceremony at Harvard University and asked his Special Assistant Charles E. Bohlen to draft a speech. In this speech, Bohlen drew on the PPS and SWNCC reports and Clayton's memorandum to such an extent that whole paragraphs reappeared in Marshall's speech. The secretary described the destruction

---

Acheson "suggested that the ensuing 4 to 6 months be employed in . . . educating the public so that Congressional action would be sought either at a special Fall session or on January 3, 1948." See *FRUS, 1947* 3: 236. The matter of "public education" on the Marshall Plan will be discussed more extensively in chapter 7.

69. "Summary of Discussion," *FRUS, 1947* 3: 235; Bohlen, *Witness to History*, 263; Kennan, *Memoirs*, 341–43, Jones, *Fifteen Weeks*, 253. Immediately after Marshall's speech, on 6 June 1947, Kennan and Bohlen once again assured the worried secretary that he should be unconcerned that the Soviet Union might accept the American aid offer. See Bohlen, *Witness to History, 1929–69* (New York, 1973), 264–65. See also Gaddis, *Strategies of Containment*, 38, 66–67. Kindleberger, although not directly concerned with these preliminary plans but involved in the economic planning, did not believe that the aid proposal precluded Soviet participation from the very start. See "The American Origins of the Marshall Plan: A View From the State Department," in *The Marshall Plan: A Retrospective* (Boulder, CO, 1984), 7–13, Charles S. Maier und Stanley Hoffman, eds.; and also Kindleberger, "The Marshall Plan and the Cold War," *International Journal* 23 (Summer 1968): 377. See also Thorp Oral History Interview, Truman Library, 39–40. The "youngsters on the economic side," as Poole had called them, most likely were not privy to the more discreet plans and hopes of their superiors.

in Europe and the interrupted network of rural and urban production. He called upon the Europeans to specify their needs and stated that the initiative must come from Europe. He did not offer a detailed plan but only a promise that the United States would support the Europeans. Neither the USSR nor Eastern European countries were mentioned directly, and all European nations were invited to participate.

It was, nevertheless, obvious that the United States placed certain conditions on its proposal. "The revival of a working economy in the world so as to permit the emergence of political and social conditions in which free institutions can exist," Marshall declared, was the goal of the American offer, clearly an element of a capitalist economy and democracy in the American sense of that term. His intentions became more apparent when he warned that "governments, political parties or groups which seek to perpetuate human misery in order to profit therefrom politically or otherwise will encounter the opposition of the United States."[70]

The place and the occasion, reminiscent of Acheson's speech before the Delta Council, were hardly appropriate for the importance of the initiative Marshall proposed. Whereas Acheson had used the opportunity to introduce the sketchy State Department plans to an interested but not especially influential audience, Marshall used the commencement ceremonies at Harvard University for a different reason. He wanted to attract the Europeans' attention, but at the same time he was hoping to prevent an outcry of the isolationist press and members of Congress advocating a decrease in federal spending when the word spread how immensely expensive aid to Europe would be. Thus, the press was not informed about the importance of Marshall's speech, and correspondents of British papers were briefed by Acheson personally.[71]

It took a few days for the British and French foreign ministers to react to Marshall's speech. Ernest Bevin and Georges Bidault met for preliminary talks in mid-June. They informed the State Department that they appreciated Washington's offer and invited the Soviet foreign minister to Paris to discuss a consolidated response and procedure. Both had hoped that the Soviet Union would decline participation; and, from

70. Jones, *Fifteen Weeks*, 254–55; "Memorandum by Charles P. Kindleberger," dated 22 July 1948, in *FRUS, 1947* 3: 241–47; Acheson, *Present*, 232–34; Charles E. Bohlen, *The Transformation of American Foreign Policy* (New York, 1969), 88–90. The text of Marshall's speech is reprinted in *FRUS, 1947* 3: 237–39.

71. See Jones, *Fifteen Weeks*, 255–56; Kindleberger, "The Marshall Plan," 377; Acheson, *Present*, 232–34.

the scant evidence available, it is likely that Moscow was not certain how to react to the American offer. Not even three months before, the Truman Doctrine had signaled that the time of friendly cooperation was finally and officially over.

William Clayton traveled to London on 24 June to attend the first preliminary talks, and three days later the foreign ministers of the USSR, France, and Great Britain met in Paris. Molotov feared that the French and British had already conducted important negotiations with the Americans but nevertheless decided to participate. As with the credit the USSR had hoped to get from the U.S., he envisioned the United States only as a financier, a donor without the means to influence the economies of the recipient countries. He argued strongly against Germany's participation in the envisioned aid program, which Bevin and Bidault, because of the coal production of the Ruhr area, regarded as very important.[72]

Each side, Soviets and Americans, feared that the other might exert a potentially dangerous influence in Europe, gain control of Germany, and thus control the whole region. While a few officials in Washington perhaps hoped the USSR would use this last chance for cooperation, as Charles Kindleberger called it, the leaders of the Soviet Union may have perceived the negotiations in Paris as a last opportunity to find out whether they would be accepted, alongside France and Great Britain, as equal partners. Marshall's statement, that the United States would only lend "friendly aid in the drafting of a European program and of later support of such a program," could have been misinterpreted. The very next sentence, however, which stated that this would be done only "so far as it may be practical for us to do so," already reflected Kennan's internal comment on the aid program as "political economy in the literal sense of that term."[73]

During the negotiations in Paris it became rapidly apparent that the aid program was much more than just friendly aid among partners with equal rights. The United States declared that information on internal economic data of participating nations and influence in the allocation of resources was a prerequisite. This the Soviets could not and would not accept. Molotov left the meeting after the fifth and last round of dis-

72. Reports of the American ambassador in Paris and additional documents in *FRUS, 1947* 3: 268–309, provide some information on the negotiations at this meeting. See also Paterson, *Soviet-American Confrontation*, 215–18.

73. Kindleberger, "The Marshall Plan," 377; *FRUS, 1947* 3: 239.

cussions on 2 July, but not before accusing the British and French of conspiring with the United States to dominate Europe politically and economically. He saw threats to the *cordon sanitaire* of Eastern European countries which protected the Soviet Union from attacks from the west. Playing on the pan-Slavist sentiment in many Eastern European nations, he claimed in his parting words that the Slav countries would again be pressed into the role as suppliers of raw materials and thus would continue to be dependent on the industrialized Western European nations and their economic policy if they agreed to America's recommendations.[74]

Bevin and Bidault, shortly after the meeting in Paris, invited all European nations — with the exclusion of Spain and the USSR — to attend a joint conference on 12 July to discuss the American aid proposal. Czechoslovakia accepted the invitation to the conference but withdrew only two days later on 10 July; it was certainly pressed by the USSR but also lured by Soviet proposals for increased trade. Poland, similarly interested, declined on July 9 for similar reasons.[75] To serve only as a financier and supplier of goods to the individual countries was not in America's interest. William Clayton, aided by the American ambassadors in Paris and London (Jefferson Caffery and Lewis W. Douglas), prodded the emissaries of the sixteen participating nations to establish a common organization and to cooperate closely with each other. Clayton let the Europeans know that they would forfeit American economic aid if they were not ready to accept American wishes in this regard. The Committee for European Economic Cooperation (CEEC), which would later develop into the Organization for European Economic Cooperation (OEEC), was founded and was immediately accused by the Soviets of being a machine of American imperialism and dangerous to the sovereignty of the peoples of Europe.[76]

74. For the text of Molotov's statement and excerpts from Bevin's and Bidault's responses, see *New York Times*, 3 July 1947, 4. Paterson, *Soviet-American Confrontation*, 217–18.

75 The Czechoslovakian Prime Minister Klement Gottwald had flown to Moscow and instructed his administration in Czechoslovakia by telephone on 10 July to announce the withdrawal. See *New York Times*, 11 July 1947, 1; and *New York Times*, 13 July 1947, 1.

76. Paterson, *Soviet-American Confrontation*, 126–36, 220; LaFeber, *America, Russia and the Cold War, 1945–1966* (New York, 1967), 50; Clayton, "GATT," 502. See also William F. Sanford, "The Marshall Plan: Origins and Implementations," U.S. Department of State, *Bulletin* 82 (June 1982): 24; and Robert D. Landa, Office of the Historian, Department of State, under the heading, "The Soviet Vetoes," correspondence and memoranda of the State Department and the ambassador in Paris, in *FRUS, 1947* 3: 335–428.

On 22 September 1947, the final report of the CEEC was published and, after contingency aid of $597 million to Italy, France, Austria, and China[77] had checked the most desperate needs, Congress appropriated $12.3 of the requested $17 billion in March of 1948 for the next four years.[78] In terms of international public relations, the Marshall Plan was an outstanding success: the division of Europe and specifically Germany, fostered by Soviet as well as by American politics, was soon attributed solely to the leaders of the USSR. "It is not a philanthropic enterprise," Allen Dulles wrote in his book on the Marshall Plan, "[i]t is based on our view of the requirements of American security . . . this is the only peaceful course now open to us which may answer the communist challenge to our way of life and our national security."[79]

Against the background of these developments, a Council discussion group "The Marshall Plan," a sub-group of the "Western European Affairs" group, was established on 6 November 1947, to observe the aid program's progress at monthly meetings. At the same time, preparations for the European Recovery Program (ERP) were well under way. Sir Oliver Franks, a member of the British Finance Office during World War II, had led the meetings of the CEEC and was now with a delegation of that committee in Washington to promote support for the Europeans' requests. Before his return to Europe, he agreed to address the members of this newly founded group.[80]

Franks confirmed that William Clayton had been responsible for most of the cuts of the $28 billion proposal by the Europeans. Franks reported on the meetings of the CEEC and told the Council members why the United Nations' Economic Commission for Europe (ECE) had not been regarded as suitable to execute the Marshall Plan. Clark Eichelberger and other Council members supporting the United Nations had

77. The Senate had voted 83 to 6 and the House 313 to 82 in favor of the interim aid program that had been introduced on 17 November in a special session of Congress. See also U.S. Congress, House, Committee on Foreign Affairs, *Hearings on Emergency Aid*, 80th Congr., 1st sess.

78. The Europeans had set the figure at $28 billion. In Paris, Clayton, Douglas, and Caffery cut this amount down to $22 billion. Truman asked Congress on 19 December 1947 for appropriations. The Senate voted 69 to 17 on S. 2202 — introduced by the Senate Committee on Foreign Relations, chaired by Arthur Vandenberg — on 13 March 1948, and the House, after limiting appropriations to the first year, approved the measure by 329 to 74 votes on 31 March.

79. Allen W. Dulles, *The Marshall Plan*, edited and with an introduction by Michael Wala (Oxford/Providence, 1993), 116. Dulles completed the manuscript in January 1948 but never published it.

80. DD, 6 November 1947, MP/RGCFR-XXIVA.

hoped that the ECE would be used to manage American economic aid. State Department officials, however, had not liked that notion. They preferred direct control of the administration and allocation of aid and goods by the United States and would have approved of Clayton's statement that "*the United States must run this show.*"[81] Franks told the audience that an additional reason had existed for bypassing the UN. Some of the sixteen participating nations were not members of the United Nations, and Italy, as a former enemy country, would have been excluded from aid distributed through the supranational organization. It had been agreed in Paris, nevertheless, to work closely with the UN and its agencies wherever possible.[82]

Some of the group members were particularly interested in the amount of aid the Europeans had requested. They did not, however, go into detail to find out how the sum of $22 billion had been arrived at in Paris. When Altschul addressed the probable conditions set by the United States, Franks expressed his hopes that such American stipulations would have a "positive" character, but he also indicated that all this clearly depended on the good-will of the American administration and Congress.[83]

The speaker at the next evening's meeting, the vice-chairman of the House Select Committee on Foreign Aid, Christian H. Herter (Republican of Massachusetts), promised to provide more informative details. Herter had proposed to establish the House committee on 15 July (H. Res. 296, 80th Congr.), and soon after its creation, the members went on a fact-finding tour to Europe. After their return, the committee produced twenty-four preliminary reports in addition to a final report.[84] Two discussion group members, Allen Dulles and Winfield Riefler, were consultants to the committee. Dulles' major input in these activities was his preliminary report delineating the legal and administrative phases of the aid program. The State Department had initially advocated a Marshall Plan agency under the control of the Department. The House Select Committee on Foreign Aid, the Bureau of the Budget, and a

81. "Memorandum," dated 27 May 1947, *FRUS, 1947* 3: 232.

82. DD, 6 November 1947, 3, 6–7, MP/RGCFR-XXIVA. For hopes of the Soviet leadership that the ECE would function as the administrator of the aid program, see Paterson, *Soviet-American Confrontation*, 227–31; Kennan, *Memoirs*, 338–41.

83. DD, 6 November 1947, 6–8, 10, MP/RGCFR-XXIVA.

84. Herter to Dulles, 4 August 1947, Allen Dulles Papers, box 30; Charles A. Eaton to Dulles, 8 August 1946, Allen Dulles Papers, box 29. See also "Statement by Allen Welsh Dulles, February 24, 1948, Committee on Foreign Relations, House of Representatives," n.d., Allen Dulles Papers, box 36.

number of politicians and experts, however, favored an independent organization. The Business Advisory Committee, established by President Truman and headed by W. Averell Harriman, reached similar conclusions. Senator Vandenberg's opinion finally tipped the scale. To ensure his support of the recovery program in Congress, the administration accepted his proposal to establish an independent administration with close ties to Congress and to the executive branch. Truman included these recommendations in the proposed legislation which accompanied his message to Congress on 19 December 1947.[85]

At the group meeting, Herter explained the difference between the findings of the Committee and the concepts the State Department had favored, and the members discussed the question of providing the amount of aid necessary to the recovery program during its first year. The members of the group agreed that the primary task of the United States was more political than economic,[86] but such "Political Aspects of the Political Recovery Program" were not discussed intensively before 2 February 1948, when Council member John Foster Dulles was a guest of the group.

The Republican, who had anticipated an imminent "worldwide struggle primarily between western (Christian) civilization and communism" as early as March, 1947, offered a harsh evaluation of American foreign policy. "Up to the present time," he stated, "Americans had had no clear notion of what they wanted in the way of foreign policy . . . the result was that the war ended without our knowing clearly what we wanted in Europe." He gave a short, albeit partially erroneous, account of the developments leading to Secretary Marshall's speech at Harvard University,[87] and he expressed his anti-communist sentiment (an attitude that, after he was appointed secretary of state in 1953, became even more pronounced). The current situation in Europe, he maintained, "is

85. DD, 12 January 1948, 1–2, MP/RGCFR-XXIVA. Seven of the nineteen members of the Business Advisory Committee (Harriman Committee) were members of the Council. Vandenberg had asked an independent research organization, the Brookings Institution, to draw up a plan for the administration of the ERP funds. See Sanford, "Marshall Plan," 25–28; Eakins, "Business Planners," 165–66; and Kim McQuaid, *Big Business and Presidential Power: From FDR to Reagan* (New York, 1982), 154–59.

86. DD, 12 January 1948, 2–15, MP/RGCFR-XXIVA.

87. DD, 2 February 1948, 1, MP/RGCFR-XXIVA; Memorandum, "*SECRET*," dated 7 March 1947, John F. Dulles Papers, box 32. John Foster Dulles had assumed that Marshall had had the idea for the aid program at the Moscow meeting of foreign ministers and that he had thought of a possible Harvard address on his trip back to the United States. The reactions, Dulles maintained, had surprised Marshall.

the third illustration in 30 years of the push of despotism which comes from the East [meaning the USSR] and knocks off the European countries one by one until we come to help them." To prevent this from happening again, he warned, it was imperative that the individual nations cooperate very closely and that such a European cooperation soon also include fascist Spain. Even though President Truman had maintained that he could see no difference between totalitarian regimes ("Nazi, Communist or Fascist, or Franco, or anything else"), officials in the State Department argued in 1947 that Spain should be integrated into a European economic community to support and accelerate rehabilitation. William R. Herod of General Electric supported John Foster Dulles' evaluation. Herod had recently returned from a trip to Spain and asserted, somewhat naively, that he had not seen anything that he could declare "morally bad." General Electric had some branches in the country, labor organizations existed, and the workers had been able to voice their opinions freely.[88]

John Foster Dulles expressed his hopes that a Western European economic community, in addition to purely economic ambitions, would also be able to break open the Iron Curtain and that some nations still within the Soviet sphere of influence, particularly Czechoslovakia, could be included in this system. Western Germany, he argued, should be integrated into the European community not as a federal republic but as a number of smaller individual states yet to be created. Support for his idea of a military alliance of the Europeans — guided by Article 51 of the Charter of the United Nations providing for defensive organizations — was received from some of the members present at the meeting. Colonel G. A. Lincoln of West Point went even further and suggested American military guarantees for Europe. This, he argued, would ultimately become necessary in the wake of the Marshall Plan aid.[89]

---

88. DD, 2 February 1948, 3, 7. MP/RGCFR-XXIVA. The Truman quote is from *Public Papers of the Presidents, Truman, 1947*, 198. On the discussion of including Spain, see especially LaFeber, *America, Russia*, 56, 105, 125–26. Hamilton Armstrong was very much opposed to including Spain. On 1 April 1948 he cabled to Senator Vandenberg: "We cannot logically oppose communist totalitarianism through ERP and collaborate with fascist totalitarianism in Spain. . . . Franco is one of Communism's best propaganda allies in Europe." See telegram, Armstrong to Vandenberg, Armstrong Papers, box 48.

89. DD, 2 February 1948, 4–5, 9, MP/RGCFR-XXIVA. On 12 May, Lieutenant General Lauris N. Norstadt, deputy chief of staff, Operations, U.S. Air Force, talked about the "Strategic Implications of Our European Aid Program." Only one copy of a digest of his remarks was produced, sent to the chairperson, and soon destroyed. See Franklin to Spofford, 22 June 1948, MP/RGCFR-XXIVA.

Meanwhile, the study group addressing "The Problem of Germany" was still discussing procedures to control the former enemy, a topic that would engage the Council until the early 1950s. One of the young Council staff members, William Diebold, provided the group members with a summary of the memoranda the individual groups of the War and Peace Studies program had produced, and a list of possible methods to control Germany. Diebold held that a consensus existed that Germany should be barred from establishing a standing army and from the production of weaponry. His major concern was whether these two mandatory limitations would be sufficient to control German militarism. If necessary, Diebold asserted, restrictions on imports, restraints on stockpiling strategically important raw materials, and limitations on the production of certain goods might be required. Control of the industrial Ruhr area was another possibility to ensure that Germany would never again turn into a threat to Europe and the rest of the world.[90]

To provide additional insight in this matter, John Foster Dulles, informed the group members at a meeting on 6 January 1948 about the relations between the Allies regarding the future of Germany. At that time the western Allies were already well on their way toward establishing a European defense community. General Matthew B. Ridgway and his British and French partners had taken the first steps toward such an organization, and during a meeting it had been stated that a defense community without German participation would not make much sense. Nevertheless, John Foster Dulles and the group members still discussed measures to contain potential German aggressiveness.[91]

New York Times journalist Shephard Stone doubted that this discussion still made much sense because Germany was a divided nation and the Soviet zone of occupation could not be included in any proposition. William Herod even asked his peers if the group was concentrating on the right topic, since the relationship with the USSR appeared to be much more important to discuss than Germany, which was only a secondary problem. John Foster Dulles' response to these arguments was direct: "As a practical matter . . . for the time being we shall have to write off eastern Germany." The French, who still feared Germany's Prussian bearing, were much more willing to go along with the other European nations on this basis, now that the Soviets were burdened with Prussia.[92]

90. William Diebold, Jr., "Preliminary Survey of Proposals for the Control of Germany," dated 2 January 1948, PofG/RGCFR-XXVA.

91. DD, 6 January 1948, PofG/RGCFR-XXVA. Feis, *From Trust to Terror*, 286.

92. *Ibid.*, 2, 3, 14.

Before the group met again one month later, a poll was taken among the Council's local chapters (the Committees on Foreign Relations) on their opinion of the Marshall Plan. It had revealed that 95 percent of all respondents agreed with the secretary of state that the United States should undertake a long-term aid program. The Committee members did not believe his statement, however, that this "policy is directed not against any country or doctrine." They were certain that "American policy is, and should be, directed against Communism."[93]

The revival of the European economy and the success of the Marshall Plan were considered of such importance to the well-being of the nation, that they were even "willing to put up with necessary consumer and production control[s]" in the United States. Marshall's cautious statement that the role of the United States should only "consist of friendly aid in the drafting of a European program and of later support . . . by financial and other means" was not accepted without reservations. The U.S. should avoid controls that recipient countries might interpret as unwarranted intervention in internal affairs. Since the United States provided the aid, however, the United States would be "entitled to adequate guarantees of its proper use." Utilization of the scientific knowledge and skills of the Germans, as well as incorporating Germany in the European Recovery Program, was regarded as of the utmost importance to European recovery.[94]

Percy Bidwell was surprised at the lack of serious disagreement regarding the inclusion of Germany in the Marshall Plan. The same lack of opposition, he maintained at the group meeting on 11 February 1948, was to be found among the European nations. The only explanation he could think of was that these nations hoped to receive a certain share of the goods Germany would produce. In this context, some group members argued, more pressing than the issue of German participation was the question of future control of the Ruhr. During the war, American and international policy had tended to favor internationalization of the Ruhr as a precaution and a measure of control over Germany's war potential.[95]

In early 1948, with German and largely European recovery depending on coal production in this area, the Ruhr became an additional issue of discord among the Allies. The Foreign Ministers' Conference in late

93. Joseph Barber, ed., *The Marshall Plan as American Policy; a Report on the Views of Community Leaders in 21 Cities* (New York, 1948), 4–5.

94. *Ibid.*, 5.

95. DD, 11 February 1948, 4, PofG/RGCFR-XXVA.

1947 had explicitly revealed that no unified Allied program for Germany could be expected. The Soviet Union was asking for participation in the control of the Ruhr area and the United States feared that a possible Soviet-inspired revolt in this region would impede German and other European reconstruction. Different measures of internationalization, decartelization, decentralization, socialization, and control were discussed among the Council members. Eminent historian George N. Shuster aptly summarized the discussion when he opted for the Ruhr to be linked closely to the three western zones, both politically and economically. If the communists tried to gain control, the area could easily be cut off from the rest of Germany to ensure that the industrial potential would not be used against democratic nations. To assure economic rehabilitation, "the Ruhr should be granted priority to the fullest extent possible." Nevertheless, Reinhold Niebuhr wondered "whether the issue [to control the Ruhr area] was a real one." It seemed to him that "the dividing line between Russia and the United States runs right down the middle of German[y]." As long as that remained true, he maintained, the United States would likely stay on in Germany and there would be "no need for a special regime to keep the Ruhr out of Russian hands."[96]

DeWitt Poole had insisted already in December of 1946 that there would be no way to prevent the division of Germany, and he again outlined a caustic vision of the future. Developments of the last few years and the policies the Marshall Plan would soon put into effect would certainly advance the division of Germany. Both of her parts were already isolated from each other more drastically than Germany and France had been before the war. The cohesion of the German people, he claimed, would nourish a political force "to bridge the Elbe. . . . Fine! Some day that force will be ripping holes in the Iron Curtain. Given a West European confederation of the kind suggested [by the American government], later adherence by trans-Elbian components will be highly desirable."[97]

Before the second conference of preeminent foreign affairs institutes in the Netherlands took place in April of 1948 (for the preparation of which the study group had originally been founded), the members had a final meeting on 9 March 1948. The Ruhr area was again at the center of discussion, and William Herod argued that the national security of the United States was endangered if economic development in that

96. DD, 11 February 1948, 4–5, PofG/RGCFR-XXVA. Shuster to Bidwell, 24 February 1948, *ibid.*; Sherman to Bidwell, 16 February 1948, *ibid.* Shuster taught at Hunter College, New York City.

97. Poole to Diebold, 2 March 1948, PofG/RGCFR-XXVA.

region (to support the United States' action to contain Soviet expansionism) failed to take place. However, his call for a change of deindustrialization, denazification, and decartelization policy had long been surpassed by the actual policy the United States maintained toward Germany.[98]

At the second Dutch conference, held this time in Scheveningen from 11 April until 17 April, Bidwell, accompanied by William Diebold, again represented the Council. The Dutch had followed the Council's advice and invited Eastern European institutes. In addition to delegates from the Milan Institute for International Studies, two emissaries from Poland participated. The delegates agreed that it was not reasonable to just let millions of Germans starve to death. It seemed inconceivable that Germany's own resources would be sufficient to solve the problem of reconstruction in the near future, and yet it was also impossible to expect the United States to feed the Germans indefinitely. Yet, the Polish and French delegates did not agree with their peers that future policies regarding Germany should be less restrictive and that a positive German contribution to intra-European trade and economic rehabilitation was of pivotal importance.

The fear of a rekindled German militarism among the delegates was of more significance than the prospect of increased trade and production. French and Polish delegates argued that Germany's economic potential should be placed under strict controls. In addition to checking German militarism, the Council suspected that the French and Polish alike feared the competition of German products in domestic and other markets. Echoing Molotov's statement of July 1947 in Paris, the Polish delegates maintained that their country — as had been the case before the war — would again be restricted to supplying raw materials. When the Polish delegates were asked why Poland had backed out of the Marshall Plan, they hinted vaguely at political reasons.[99]

The Marshall Plan, clearly the topic receiving the most attention during these years, also stimulated the founding of another group within the Council. Expertly staffed and financed with $55,000 by the Rockefeller Foundation, it was meant to research conditions of the newly established administration for the Marshall Plan, the Economic Cooperation

98. DD, 9 March 1948, 2, 8, PofG/RGCFR-XXVA.

99. Council, *Annual Report 1947–1948*, 40–44; see also Bidwell, *Germany's Contribution*; and on Polish fears of German competition, see Anderson, "Poland and the Marshall Plan 1947–1949," *Diplomatic History* 15 (Fall 1991): 478. The Rockefeller Foundation provided $3,700 for the second conference in the Netherlands. See RA SS 4803, dated 19 January 1948, RFR, 1/100/98/889.

Administration (ECA).[100] Dwight D. Eisenhower became the chairman of that study group on "Aid to Europe," and "whatever General Eisenhower knows about economics," journalist Joseph Kraft quoted a member of the group as stating, "he has learned at the study group meetings." The Rockefeller Foundation went even further and suggested that the study group "served as a sort of education in foreign affairs for the future president of the United States."[101]

Eisenhower at that time was president of Columbia University and "did not cut much of a figure," as historian Robert H. Ferrell described his tenure. Eisenhower served in this position from June 1948 until December 1950. This interlude between his service as General of the Army and his new post on 19 December 1950 as supreme commander of the Allied Forces in Europe has received very little attention, and the time at Columbia was not a very enjoyable episode in Eisenhower's life. The General had to entertain and serve as a fund-raiser, and "his calendar quickly filled with luncheons, dinners, and meetings." There are strong indications, however, that this period may have served as part of "the political education of General Eisenhower," as one of his biographers has termed it.[102] He had to deal with an environment that was not comparable to his experiences as soldier in a military setting. Because he was not a peer in intellectual discussions with the faculty, a "gulf between the president's office and the academic disciplines" might well have existed and never have been bridged during his stint as president of Columbia. Eisenhower, nevertheless, learned to function in a civilian setting and to head an administration in the non-military sector of the public sphere, and he surely broadened his perspectives.[103] When the

100. On Eisenhower's work at the Council, see also Michael Wala, "Dwight D. Eisenhower at the Council on Foreign Relations," *Reexamining the Eisenhower Presidency*, (Westport, CT, 1993), 1-15, Shirley A. Warshaw, ed..

101. For Eisenhower's career, see Stephen E. Ambrose, *Eisenhower: Soldier, General of the Army, President Elect, 1890–1952* (New York, 1983), especially chapter 24; and for his presidency, Fred I. Greenstein, *The Hidden Hand Presidency: Eisenhower as Leader* (New York, 1982), and Richard A. Melanson and David Mayers, eds., *Reevaluating Eisenhower: American Foreign Policy in the Fifties* (Urbana, IL, 1987), to name just a very few of the many volumes written on Eisenhower. Kraft, "School for Statesmen," 64–68; "Excerpts from Trustees Confidential Monthly Report," dated 1 January 1953, 39–40, RFR, 1.2/57/440.

102. Robert H. Ferrell, ed., *The Eisenhower Diaries* (New York, 1981), 148; Blanche Wiesen Cook, *The Declassified Eisenhower: A Divided Legacy* (New York, 1981), 61.

103. Dwight D. Eisenhower, *The Papers of Dwight David Eisenhower: Columbia University* 10 (Baltimore, 1984), xviii. Grayson Kirk's responsibilities as the provost of Columbia were not made easier by Eisenhower's inexperience with problems of academic administration; Kirk to Michael Wala, 1 October 1990.

opportunity arose, Eisenhower grasped the chance to learn more about economics and foreign policy and about the interdependency of military, economic, and political matters in foreign affairs. Despite his time-consuming obligations as university president from 1948 to 1950, he missed only two of the twenty meetings of the group.[104]

The study group Eisenhower was to head was founded when Franklin A. Lindsay, assistant to Paul G. Hoffman, the administrator of the ECA, asked his friends at the Council on 1 May 1948 to establish a large-scale research program on the European Recovery Program. Although the Marshall Plan was hardly a month old, Lindsay did not believe the administration would launch such a study in the immediate future. Keeping a broad outlook while forming guidelines and evaluations and working without the pressures of day-to-day work faced by the ECA, were highly desirable arrangements for a research group. Lindsay counted on Council President Allen Dulles and the Council's staff to help the ECA formulate long-range plans. Immediately, discussions and planning began on how such a study group could be organized, conducted, and what aspects should receive primary attention. However, another six months would pass before all preliminary discussion and difficulties in organizing the study group were solved.[105]

Dulles had his reservations about the program and was not certain that the State Department would react favorably to this undertaking, which could easily develop into a new War and Peace Studies project. Just to be on the safe side, the Council contacted Richard M. Bissell, Jr. (assistant administrator of the ECA), Theodore Geiger (special assistant to Bissell for policy), and Lincoln Gordon (head of the ECA's internal study department), to discuss the plan with them.[106] All three liked the idea of a Council investigation and proclaimed a "keen interest," and the ECA's administrator Paul Hoffman wrote in mid-June in support of the Council's idea. The Council on Foreign Relations' Committee on Studies approached the proposal with much more caution than some other Council members and their friends at ECA may have hoped. A

104. Eisenhower did not attend meetings during his convalescence at Key West, 28 March 1949 to 12 April 1949 (he had fallen ill on 21 March) nor during his vacation at Augusta National Golf Club, Augusta, GA, 20 January 1950 to 26 January 1950.

105. Lindsay to Dulles, 1 May 1948, Allen Dulles Papers, box 36. Dulles and Lindsay had met earlier that week in Washington.

106. Theodore Geiger to Michael Wala, 8 January 1992. Bissell was to join the study group in May 1950 after leaving the ECA. See Mallory to Eisenhower, 10 May 1950, Dwight D. Eisenhower Pre-Presidential Papers (EPP), box 28, Eisenhower Library, Abilene, KS; Bissell to Eisenhower, 15 May 1950, *ibid.*

memorandum on the plan, together with a copy of Hoffman's letter, was sent to all members of the Committee and was discussed during one of the next meetings.[107]

During these preliminary discussions, John H. Williams of the Federal Reserve Bank argued against an "inside job" for the ECA. He feared that the Council might later become a scapegoat for mistakes the administration had made. Nevertheless, he agreed to consider serving as chairman of the group. A subcommittee of the Committee on Studies was to select and invite members to participate in the group's work. Background material would be provided by the Council's staff, but the group, the Committee on Studies maintained, should primarily depend on the "wisdom and judgment" of its members.[108]

At the Committee on Studies meeting on 7 October 1948, the plan for the study group received its final approval. It was decided that the Council would work completely independently of the ECA and that a book, based on research the group would conduct, should be published.[109] When Percy W. Bidwell proposed that the group would need a "shrewd and capable person with political wisdom as well as economic knowledge to serve it," Winfield Riefler, economist at the Institute of Advanced Studies at Princeton University, suggested that Dwight D. Eisenhower was the "obvious chairman." The committee "strongly endorsed" his suggestion because it "believed that a distinguished non-partisan investigation of the most important problem before our country today might give the General just the type of connection with public affairs which would be most useful to him, as well as close contact with some of the individuals whom he must get to know as president of Columbia." After considerable discussion, the Committee requested

107. Memorandum, Dulles to Mallory, 4 May 1948, AE-RGCFR/XXXA; Geiger to Dulles, 3 June 1948, *ibid.*; copy, Dulles to Hoffman, 15 June 1948, *ibid.*; Hoffman to Dulles, 22 June 1948, *ibid.*; Bissell to Dulles, 7 July 1948, *ibid.*; Dulles to Bissell, 12 July 1948, *ibid.* Copies of all these letters are in the RFR, 1.2/57/440.

108. "Minutes of Meeting of Subcommittee of the Committee on Studies of the CFR," dated 4 August 1948, AE/RGCFR-XXXA; "Committee on Studies Meeting," dated 7 October 1948, *ibid.*; "Committee on Studies Meeting," dated 29 November 1948, RFR, 1.2/58/444. To cover the expenses for the study group, Executive Director Walter Mallory had asked Henry Ford II for a Ford Foundation grant. In May 1948, the Rockefeller Foundation supplied $50,000, so no further appeals to Ford were necessary. See Mallory to Eisenhower, 31 December 1948, AE/RGCFR-XXXA; Bidwell to Mallory, 3 May 1949, *ibid.*; Resolution 49010, RFR, 1.2/57/440.

109. On the basis of the study group's deliberations and background papers, Howard S. Ellis later wrote *The Economics of Freedom: The Progress and Future of Aid to Europe* (New York, 1950).

that Allen Dulles, Henry M. Wriston, and John W. Davis ask Eisenhower to accept the chair.[110]

Dulles, Wriston, and Davis were well-chosen representatives to sway Eisenhower to become chairman of the group; Dulles was the highest representative of the Council; Davis, a former president of the Council, had been a Democratic candidate for U.S. President; and Wriston, as president of Brown University and president of the Association of American Universities, was one of Eisenhower's colleagues. This truly bipartisan and eminent trio was able to persuade the general when they met with him on the afternoon of 3 November 1948 in his office at Columbia.[111]

Eisenhower, however, took his time to decide the scope of his involvement and had his assistant Kevin C. McCann scrutinize the Council. Arrangements could not be made before 18 November for McCann to meet with Dulles, Wriston, and Walter Mallory. "We hope," Mallory wrote to McCann, "that after a chat here you will lunch with us so that we may have ample opportunity to explain in detail what we have in mind."[112] The schedule for meetings would be arranged with McCann, and it was agreed that the group would start working in January 1949. There is no account of what was said at these meetings, but Eisenhower must have been duly impressed. A handwritten note on a letter to Under Secretary of State Robert A. Lovett reads: "Recently I undertook an assignment with the Council on Foreign Relations on representations made to me that you and your department were deeply interested in the work."[113]

The agenda the group was about to research was extensive and involved economic as well as military aspects. It was assumed that Europe would still have major economic problems at the end of American

110. "Committee on Studies Meeting," dated 7 October 1948, 7, AE/RGCFR-XXXA. It is very likely that the possibility of Eisenhower eventually running for the presidency of the United States was addressed during the lengthy discussion.

111. These names appear on Eisenhower's desk calendar for the 3 November 1948 meeting. See Eisenhower, *Papers of Dwight David Eisenhower: Columbia University* 11 (Baltimore, 1984), 1575.

112. Mallory to McCann, 8 November 1948, EPP, box 183; "Note," dated 8 November 1948, Armstrong Papers, Addition, box 121. McCann did not make a good impression on the Council members he met: he only drank water and would not have anything to eat for lunch; Diebold Interview, 23 August 1990. See also Wriston Columbia University Oral History Interview, 7.

113. Eisenhower, *Papers of Dwight David Eisenhower* 11: 1578. Mallory to Eisenhower, 26 November 1948, EPP, box 183. Eisenhower to Lovett, 20 December 1948, EPP, box 72.

aid. Determinants for the economic independence of Europe were to be discussed as well as the question of military support to ensure the safety of Europe. Under Eisenhower's chairmanship, however, the discussions turned rapidly to military aspects and to the problems a military buildup might cause for the economic reconstruction of Europe.[114]

Bissell had sent the Council a long list of possible research topics of primary interest to the ECA, such as trade and economic relationships between the European states and their economic relations with the world market. However, the twenty topics were exclusively of an economic nature and a thorough research would certainly have overtaxed the Council's normal conduct of study groups. At the first group meeting, though, it became obvious that discussion of military aspects would dominate the meetings. Economic implications were mostly discussed in the background material and memoranda the Council staff provided. At the subsequent meetings, economic matters were addressed, but Eisenhower usually dominated the discussion and routinely turned the attention to political and military matters.[115]

Eisenhower's difficulty in following deliberations and theoretical arguments of economists and bankers and the more technical aspects of investment, inflation, and devaluation was one reason for this emphasis on military aspects. The general knew his shortcomings and, on one occasion, freely admitted, "that I know so little about such things [the possible effects of pound sterling devaluation] that my opinion is properly deemed to be next to worthless."[116] Another reason, however, was the change of American aid policy toward Europe over the preceding few years. The Marshall Plan had originally been envisioned as "political economy in the literal sense of that term," to once again use George F. Kennan's words. It was a measure that was to promote American interests and American ideas about political constellations in Europe,

---

114. William Diebold to Michael Wala, 2 October 1990.

115. "Suggestions for the Council on Foreign Relations' Research Project," signed "TG/dg," n.d., enclosed to Bissell to Dulles, 7 July 1948, AE/RGCFR-XXXA. Kirk to Wala, 1 October 1990.

116. "Excerpts from Trustees" Confidential Monthly Report," dated 1 January 1953, 40, RFR, 1.2/57/440. Eisenhower had almost no time to read the memoranda and went "to each class with my lesson totally unprepared." See Eisenhower to Philip D. Reed (chair of the Board of General Electric), 3 April 1950, EPP, box 97. He was usually picked up at Columbia by Arthur S. Nevins (who had helped Eisenhower with his war-time memoirs and was hired upon his suggestion by the Council), or Council staff members and was briefed on the way to the Council's headquarters at 68th Street and Park Avenue. Eisenhower to Leffingwell, 11 July 1949, EPP, box 71.

without, at the same time, actively provoking an open clash with the USSR. Even before the European Recovery Program had passed Congress, American and European military leaders nevertheless realized that economic aid would not suffice and that a defense community would have to be established to deter Soviet aggression.

The British and French foreign ministers (during the first discussions on the Marshall Plan in 1947) had raised the issue of a defense treaty. Together with their American partners, they negotiated during the remainder of the year how such a military program could be established. In the meantime, it had become obvious that cooperation with the USSR in Europe was nearly impossible. The Communist coup in Czechoslovakia in February 1948 — which prompted a swift passage of the Economic Assistance Act by Congress — added to the difficulties. Lucius D. Clay cabled in the beginning of March from Berlin that the situation over the last few weeks had become dangerous and that a very serious, possibly military, conflict with the USSR seemed imminent.

In the United States, negotiations and discussions between Secretary Marshall and Under Secretary Robert A. Lovett, on the one side, and Senators Arthur S. Vandenberg and Tom Connally, on the other, began in the first weeks of April 1948.[117] On 19 May 1948, after deliberations by the Senate Committee on Foreign Relations, Senator Vandenberg proposed a resolution of Congress asking for a defense treaty between the United States and the Western European nations in accordance with Article 51 of the United Nations' charter. When Vandenberg asked the Senate on 11 June to vote on his resolution, the USSR had already choked off access to the Soviet sector in Berlin for the Western allies. After the currency reform in the three Western zones of Germany was announced on 19 June, the thirteen-month blockade of the city began.[118]

The main question politicians in Washington discussed in the following months regarding the North Atlantic Treaty Organization (NATO) was whether rearmament of European countries would prevent effective economic rehabilitation. President Truman, in his famous quotation, called the Marshall Plan and the Truman Doctrine "two halves of the same walnut," and the military alliance, undoubtedly, was the third

117. Feis, *From Trust to Terror,* 306–308; Lovett Diary and Daily Log Sheet, entries 21 and 28 April 1948, Brown Brothers and Harriman Papers, State Historical Society of New York, New York, NY; Memorandum of conversation between Marshall, Lovett, Vandenberg, and John F. Dulles, 27 April 1948, John F. Dulles Papers, box 37.

118. The Senate voted 64 to 4 in favor of the resolution (Senate Resolution 239).

"half." The communist coup in Czechoslovakia in February, the Vandenberg Resolution and the Berlin Blockade in June of 1948, and the beginnings of official consultations about a European Defense Community and NATO all had shifted attention away from economic issues. With General Eisenhower as chairman of the group, the discussion in this setting even more rapidly moved from an economic and political emphasis to deliberations on military aspects.

The members of the study group were well-informed about the latest developments in Europe when they discussed the very strong interdependence between the Marshall Plan and the Alliance at their first meeting on 10 January 1949. Eisenhower maintained that both the Marshall Plan and NATO were directed to ensure "democracy in the enterprise system." J.P. Morgan partner Russell C. Leffingwell, although agreeing on most ideas with Eisenhower, had doubts as to whether simultaneous economic reconstruction and rearmament would be possible. Eisenhower was much more positive: the Europeans would maintain that this was infeasible, but a supply of raw materials and the right impetus would show what was really possible. A buildup of armed forces was imminent, Eisenhower maintained, and it was certain that Soviet aggression at this time could only be stopped at the Pyrenees and the English Channel. This evaluation was not to be mentioned in public, he warned, because it would take away every hope for Western Europeans and might endanger the economic success of the Marshall Plan.[119]

The group members did not believe that war with the Soviet Union was imminent, at least not until the European Recovery Program had been completed. In asking for a vote if they believed that the USSR, even accidentally, would unleash a war, Leffingwell told the other group members that George Kennan had argued that the Soviets might create a crisis that could not be controlled in order to achieve their political goals.[120]

Europeans would receive psychological support and security through the conclusion of the defense treaty, Hamilton Armstrong maintained, that would be much more important than any weapon they might acquire. Eisenhower himself reported that the Truman administration was willing to do everything possible to support and strengthen a Western European defense community. This was the case in spite of the reluc-

119. Memorandum, "Studies on Aid to Europe," n.d., enclosure, Mallory to Eisenhower, 26 November 1948, RFR, 1.2/57/440; DD, 10 January 1949, 5, 4, 13, AE/RGCFR-XXXA. William Diebold wrote most of these digests.

120. DD, 7 March 1949, 3, AE/RGCFR-XXXA. A majority of the group members regarded this danger as "great" or "considerable."

tance of some members of the administration to restrain the United States' freedom of action by such an alliance. "If Western Europe is overrun by the Russians," Eisenhower shocked his audience, "we are on the way to extinction." He proposed a rough outline of a domino theory of Western Europe and said that the United States would be surrounded by enemies if it were not prevented: "If Western Europe goes, Africa is in danger, then South America. Much of Asia is already lost or in jeopardy." This made the economic recovery of Western Europe all the more pressing, since it would serve "[to] strengthen the war potential of these countries against an overt military attack, and simultaneously . . . keep their economies strong enough so that they may not be susceptible to communist infiltration from within."[121]

Additionally, Eisenhower reminded the group members, the region did possess a large and competent pool of skilled labor and a large industrial capacity. It would also have great influence on large regions in the world through its colonies. A political community of the Western European nations would be of the utmost importance and would have implications far beyond successful economic aid through the Marshall Plan.[122]

Within the administration it was still heatedly discussed whether Spain and Germany should be members of the military alliance, whereas the Council members easily formed a consensus regarding this issue. "Whatever we may think of its economic significance or internal politics it [Spain] is of tremendous military importance, commanding the entrance to the Mediterranean and protected on the north by the Pyrenees," General Eisenhower argued, adding that "it is a sound military principle to choose one enemy at a time and choose first the one most dangerous to you." The Soviet Union and communism, the most dangerous enemies to which Eisenhower referred, supposedly not only endangered the Western European countries from the outside but from the inside as well. Council members were convinced that the Marshall Plan and NATO would ensure domestic security in the participating countries and would prevent communist coups. In France and Italy in particular, it seemed possible that the communists could come to power through elections. A better standard of living and stable political institutions, Council members were certain, would prevent this.[123]

121. Memorandum, "Studies on Aid to Europe;" DD, 10 January 1949, 5, 4, 11, 13, AE/RGCFR-XXXA.

122. DD, 10 January 1949, 6, 7–10, AE/RGCFR-XXXA.

123. DD, 10 January 1949, 7, 11, AE/RGCFR-XXXA; DD, 7 March 1949, 10, AE/RGCFR-XXXA.

This scenario applied not only to Europe; the group members agreed that NATO should be part of an entire system of U.S. military alliances spanning the globe. At a meeting on 7 March 1949, Eisenhower proposed to draft a memorandum on the subject. It was supposed to demonstrate to government officials and politicians, shortly before the North Atlantic Treaty was to be signed, that similar treaties or agreements would be necessary in other regions. He suggested forwarding such a memorandum to Secretary of the Navy James F. Forrestal for the National Security Council or to Dean Acheson, who had recently been named secretary of state. The memorandum called upon the president to extend the Truman Doctrine "to include a flat warning that aggression in any form, in any part of the world, will always be considered as 'dangerous to our peace and safety.' This is the language of James Monroe, and we believe that it now applies to the whole world." Only three days later, on 10 March 1949, Eisenhower handed the memorandum to Under Secretary of State James Webb.[124]

Even the rearmament of Germany was considered a reasonable measure to avert this danger. McGeorge Bundy, assistant to Henry L. Stimson and coauthor of his memoirs, *Active Service in War and Peace*, had prepared a working paper on the political equilibrium in Western Europe. Rearmament of Germany, Bundy wrote, was being proposed only by "irresponsible men." Hanson Baldwin, military editor of the *New York Times*, believed that this evaluation was hardly realistic. The Federal Republic of Germany had just been established, and Baldwin thought it inconceivable that an independent nation could be prevented from having an army.[125]

Eisenhower pursued a somewhat different line of argument in this respect; the question was, who did the United States fear more, the Germans or the Russians? Treating Germany as a neutral power would drive it into the arms of the Soviet Union and thus would unnecessarily increase the number of potential enemies. After Baldwin mentioned political means to check Germany's drive for yet another war, Bundy somewhat sarcastically referred to the 1930s, when political guarantees had existed to no avail. Economist Jacob Viner of Princeton University

124. DD, 7 March 1949, 12, AE/RGCFR-XXXA; "S–2," dated 9 March 1949, *ibid.*

125. DD, 27 June 1949, 14–17, AE/RGCFR-XXXA; McGeorge Bundy, "Working Paper on the Problem of Political Equilibrium," memorandum M-13, dated 16 June 1949, AE/RGCFR-XXXIIA. Only after the loss of the American monopoly in nuclear weapons in September 1949 and the beginning of the Korean War in 1950 did United States officials push more openly for German rearmament.

summarized the whole problem: "We fear a possible German menace, but we also have thoughts about Germany as a potential ally." Eisenhower counseled patience, because the danger a strong and reunited Germany certainly posed to the security of all nations was "a reason not to hurry the unification of Germany." When the emotional background of fear of the Germans had eased, everyone would agree to embrace Germany as an ally. Although group members Allen Dulles and Hamilton Armstrong advised a slower pace in shifting political attitudes toward the former enemy, and economist Emile Després could hardly envision Germany as a loyal ally to the U.S. at all, Ford International Corporation manager Graeme K. Howard wanted Western Germany immediately accepted as a member of NATO, "part and parcel."[126]

The topic of security also had indisputable implications for the Council itself. The study group members sometimes received confidential and secret information. Arthur Nevins had, in his draft "Notes on Military Aid Under the Atlantic Pact," used undisclosed information about evaluations and attitudes within the administration. Secret information not yet been cleared by the Army's Security Board had been used as a source for his analysis and description. He then feared that he had violated the law, although Council meetings were generally "off-the-record," reporters were not admitted, and the members were asked not to disclose what had been discussed.[127]

At the third meeting, on 7 March, the topic was on the agenda when some members indicated that security measures governing the distribution of Council digests of discussion were hardly efficient. After that date, distribution of digests to the nearly twenty group members and Council staffers was terminated. They could only read them shortly before meetings at the Harold Pratt House. Circulation of background material and memoranda was canceled and three of the memoranda already in circulation among the group members had to be returned to the Council. Council member Marshall MacDuffie even saw danger lurking around the next corner: secret agents of the Soviet Consulate General, across the street from the Council headquarters, could possibly

126. DD, 27 June 1949, 14–17, AE/RGCFR-XXXA. Després taught at Williams College. In a *New York Times* article on 29 December 1949, Baldwin displayed more concern about a revival of German militarism: "The moment we put arms in the hands of any great numbers of Germans," he wrote, "that moment Germany will be calling the tune, not we. The moment Germany is rearmed, she holds the balance of power — not we."

127. DD, 18 July 1949, 6, AE/RGCFR-XXXA.

spy on Council meetings. "Personally, I think the Russians could do it and are doing it."[128]

The great moment for the study group came on 11 December 1950. After some clashes in the demilitarized zone on the 38th parallel, North Korean troops had overrun almost all of South Korea within two months. The deployment of United Nations units in August (consisting mainly of American units commanded by General Douglas MacArthur) pushed North Korean troops back toward the Chinese border. On 26 November, Chinese soldiers attacked, and a long and painful retreat to the south of Seoul began.

Eisenhower, at Truman's request, had flown to Washington, D.C., and met with the president on 28 October. He had been informed that the American Chiefs of Staff were convinced that a commander-in-chief for the North Atlantic Pact forces should be named immediately, Eisenhower himself being their first choice. He came away from this meeting with the impression that, "at this moment, I would estimate that the chances are about nine out of ten that I will be back in uniform in a short time."[129]

By 11 December, at the last meeting of the Aid to Europe group that Eisenhower chaired, he knew that official announcement of his assignment as Supreme Allied Commander in Europe would be made very soon. It had been planned that Eisenhower's authority would be more restricted than he would have wished. He was supposed to go through "channels" and would have to submit his reports via the Department of State to military headquarters in Washington. Neither this setting nor the weakness of military forces in Europe added to Eisenhower's fondness for the job.[130] Henry Wriston met Eisenhower on the steps of the Council building on 11

128. DD, 7 March 1949, 1, AE/RGCFR-XXXA. Memoranda recalled were "Military Implications of a North Atlantic Pact," by Nevins, M-4, dated 28 February 1949; "Soviet Intentions," M-6, dated 4 February 1949; and "Comments on the Outline 'Soviet Intentions,'" Philip E. Mosely, M-7, dated 28 February 1949. MacDuffie to Allen Dulles, 30 November 1949, Allen Dulles Papers, box 39. Three years later, and in the midst of McCarthyite red-baiting and anti-establishment fervor, the close proximity of the Council's headquarters to the Soviet Consulate General led Emmanuel M. Josephson to suspect secret passageways existed below 68th Street, where Council members would meet with Soviet KGB agents to receive sacks full of gold and instructions from the Kremlin. See *Rockefeller "Internationalist": The Man Who Misrules the World* (New York, 1952), 4.

129. Ferrell, *The Eisenhower Diaries*, 178–80, entry 28 October 1950.

130. Memorandum, Lincoln Gordon (assistant to President Truman) to Harriman, "Subject: Immediate Dispatch of General Eisenhower to Europe," 4 December 1950, marked "Top Secret and Urgent," W. Averell Harriman Papers, box 284, Library of Congress.

December 1950 and raised the subject.[131] Wriston proposed that it would be a good idea to draft, together with the Council group, a letter to President Truman. They could let the president know what problems the group members foresaw by having allied forces in Europe.[132]

Memoranda prepared by the group's staff or outside experts were discussed as usual. Nevins' report delineated the military weakness of the French forces and Lindsay Rogers discussed the possibility that Europe might develop into a neutral third power, independent of the United States and the Soviet Union. The strength of the USSR and the relative weakness of the NATO countries were made dramatically clear to the members. They agreed that the European allies had little for defense if the Soviet Union chose to attack. All they could depend on was the hope of a will for peace in the eastern bloc, clashes between party leaders of the individual socialist countries, the generally better fighting power of NATO troops, and the atomic bomb — not a very suitable weapon in a conventional war, and a poor choice, given the fact that the USSR had detonated its first atomic bomb in 1949.[133]

In the face of these grave prospects, Wriston's idea to write a letter to the president to convey the group's impressions about the importance of military readiness was well-received. The other group members enjoyed the customary study group dinner, while Eisenhower prepared the letter to Truman. Averell Harriman, then special assistant to the president, had participated in an earlier meeting. Now he was called upon to help with last-minute corrections and delivery of the Council memorandum.[134] Eisenhower's manuscript was revised and modified, and Allen Dulles discussed the draft with Harriman to help polish the letter to President Truman in order to compose its final form.[135]

---

131. At about the same time the Committee on the Present Danger was founded, fully supported by George C. Marshall who had, meanwhile, become secretary of defense. The committee advocated universal military training and preparedness of American and North Atlantic defenses. Wriston had been one of the founding members of this organization.

132. Henry M. Wriston, "Eisenhower Study Group Letter to President Truman December 12, 1950," dated 22 April 1968, AE/RGCFR-XXXIA.

133. DD, 11 December 1950, AE/RGCFR-XXXIA; Nevins, "Limitations on Use of Available French Military Manpower Due to Lack of Equipment or Fiscal Difficulties," M-29, dated 4 December 1950 AE/RGCFR-XXXIIIA; Lindsay Rogers, "Europe as a 'Neutral' or 'Third' Force," M-28, dated 4 December 1950, *ibid.*

134. Wriston, "Eisenhower Study Group Letter," 7, AE/RGCFR-XXXIA; Dulles to Wriston, 29 December 1950, Allen Dulles Papers, box 44.

135. Wriston, "Eisenhower Study Group Letter," 6–7, AE/RGCFR-XXXIA. Memorandum, Hamilton Armstrong, dated 1 November 1962 (on the occasion of a study group "reunion" on 30 October 1962), Armstrong Papers, box 24.

In his draft Eisenhower had been quite outspoken and alarming. His evaluation, "that our country and the free world are in critical danger of defeat and the extinction of our treasured ideals," was mellowed and rephrased in the subsequent revision, to "our country and other countries still free are in critical danger." That the United States and her friends should rapidly produce "powerful military forces," was agreed upon by the group members. Eisenhower's cautioning suggestion, that this should only be limited by "national solvency," anticipated his later administration's desire for a balanced budget and his efforts to cut back Navy and Army expenditures. The Council members changed this suggestion to read "only be limited by the productive capacity of a free economy," a very different concept indeed. The group members agreed, however, on Eisenhower's call for a "strategic air strength . . . equal to an effective bombing attack against Russia," and that "about 20 U.S. divisions" should be deployed in Europe. In his discussion with Dulles, Harriman suggested deletion of the reference to twenty divisions, and the mention of capabilities for an "effective bombing attack against Russia" was changed to "an effective bombing attack in the event of war."[136]

In his cover letter to Truman, Harriman (now with official knowledge of the letter) stressed the importance of the Council "among thoughtful people in New York . . . and in helping to mobilize public opinion." However, the special assistant deceived his president in maintaining that "General Eisenhower has been active in the group, but as I understand it, did not involve himself in this letter."[137]

In the final version Truman received, Eisenhower and the group members claimed: "If our potential enemies choose to attack us in our present posture we face disastrous consequences," and "today we run the risk of global war." The national security of the United States was at stake, the military forces had to be built up speedily and effectively with minimal costs (through the introduction of universal military training), all government spending not related to a military buildup should be minimized, and a large number of American troops should be stationed

---

136. Henry B. Wriston, "Eisenhower," AE/RGCFR-XXXIA; Armstrong et al. to President Truman, 12 December 1950, President's Secretary's Files, Truman Papers (PSF), box 114; "Draft," n.d., handwritten note: "Received from Allen Dulles," Harriman Papers, box 283.

137. It is not very probable that Dulles did not tell Harriman of Eisenhower's involvement. In addition to sending a note and a copy of Truman's reply to Armstrong, Harriman sent a note and a copy of the president's comment to Eisenhower. See Harriman to Eisenhower, 16 December 1950, marked "Confidential," Harriman Papers, box 282.

in Europe. The last paragraph of this memorandum reads: "Do all things that will produce the strength necessary to carry us through the tensions of an indefinite future, without war if possible, but prepared to wage it effectively if it is thrust upon us." Truman's comment to Harriman, after reading this dramatic analysis, was rather calm: "Thanks for your memorandum of the thirteenth, enclosing me a copy of the letter from the Council on Foreign Relations in New York. It is an interesting document and I read it with a lot of pleasure."[138]

---

138. DD, 11 December 1950, AE/RGCFR-XXXIA; Armstrong et al. to President Truman, 12 December 1950, PSF, box 114; "Memorandum for the President," Averell Harriman, dated 13 December 1950, *ibid.*; "Memorandum for: Averell Harriman, From: The President," dated 15 December 1950, signed "H.S.T.", *ibid.*; the original is in the Harriman Papers, box 290. On 31 October 1962, a reunion of the Aid to Europe group took place. Eisenhower let John J. McCloy (chairman of the board of the Council) know that he "would greatly enjoy attending a meeting at the Council on Foreign Relations, and particularly a gathering of the clan of the old study group." See Eisenhower to McCloy, 30 May 1962, Dwight D. Eisenhower, Post-Presidential Papers, 1962, Principal Files (EPPP-1962), box 21, Eisenhower Library.

5
ASIA — JAPAN AND CHINA:
"A VIABLE FAR EASTERN ECONOMY ON A MULTILATERAL BASIS"[1]

Asia received considerably less attention than Europe and the dramatic developments surrounding the problems of European rehabilitation and reconstruction. In early 1946, the study group on "Far East Affairs" did not attract many Council members to its discussions on American-occupied Japan. The group, founded in 1945 and led by Owen Lattimore, in addition to examining the situation in Japan, contemplated developments in China as well. Until Mao Tse-tung proclaimed the establishment of the People's Republic of China in 1949, however, Council members were primarily interested in Japan.[2]

Japanese forces had attacked the American naval base at Pearl Harbor on 7 December 1941 — "a date which will live in infamy," President Roosevelt had vowed in his radio address to millions of Americans — when the United States was still debating whether to enter the war in Europe.[3] Japan, allied with Italy and Germany, fought fiercely against the United States and the Allies. After December 1941, the Soviet Union was repeatedly asked by the United States to participate in the fighting in the Pacific theater. When Stalin, in the summer of 1945, was finally willing to commit Soviet troops against the Japanese forces, the distrust between the Allies had already progressed too far.[4] By that time, and with their

1. CFR, *Annual Report of the Executive Director, 1948–1949* (New York, 1949), 38. The members of the discussion group on "U.S. Policy Toward China" in 1950 regarded this as the ideal solution to the problems of the Far East. It was also stated, however, that "such development in the foreseeable future was to most members difficult to envisage." See *ibid.*

2. For the developments in this region during the early Cold War, see Akira Iriye and Yonosuke Nagai, eds., *The Origins of the Cold War in Asia* (New York, 1977); Robert M. Blum, *Drawing the Line: The Origins of American Containment Policy in Asia* (New York, 1982); and, particularly for China, Dorothy Borg and Waldo Heinrichs, eds., *Uncertain Years: Chinese-American Relations, 1947–1950* (New York, 1980).

3. The most encompassing work dealing with the attack on Pearl Harbor is Gordon W. Prange, *At Dawn We Slept: The Untold Story of Pearl Harbor* (New York, 1981). The war in the Pacific is delineated in Ronald H. Spector, *Eagle Against the Sun: The American War With Japan* (New York, 1984).

4. Responding to Roosevelt's request for Soviet participation in the war in the Pacific, Stalin argued that all troops were needed in the war against Germany. During the con-

knowledge of the positive results of the atomic weapons research, American officials viewed the involvement of Soviet troops in the war in Asia with much more hesitancy.[5] The atomic bombs dropped on Hiroshima and Nagasaki finally pressed the defeated Japanese to submit to unconditional surrender and to permit occupation by American forces.

To ensure Soviet, Chinese, and British (in addition to American) participation in the control of occupied Japan, the creation of an Allied Control Council of Japan had been agreed upon in Potsdam. Very soon, however, it became apparent that the Allied Council had very little say in the actual policy of occupation; realistically, international control existed in name only.[6] Freedom of action rested in the hands of the self-conscious commander of the military government, General Douglas MacArthur. The limitations placed on his power were even less stringent than those of his counterpart in Germany, Lucius D. Clay.[7]

Since the Soviet Union did not participate in the occupation, United States officials did not perceive any threat to Japan by aggressive Soviet intentions, and the leaders of the USSR may have regarded Japan as of less importance to its sphere of influence than the Eastern European countries.[8] Frictions such as those that had developed among the Allies in Germany and Austria could not unfold in Japan because MacArthur controlled the island exclusively. The military and strategic considera-

---

ference at Potsdam, however, the Soviets announced that — provided attempts to mediate in the conflict between Japan and the U.S. failed — the Red Army would participate in the fighting by the second half of August. See Spector, *Eagle*, 552–53.

5. See the discussion in Martin G. Sherwin, *A World Destroyed: The Atomic Bomb and the Grand Alliance* (New York, 1977), 225–27. Byrnes is quoted expressing his hope that "Japan will surrender and Russia will not get in so much on the kill." See notes of Walter Brown (Byrnes' press secretary) from the Potsdam conference, and the additional documentation in footnote 23, page 268, *ibid.* For a current and comprehensive historiographical account of scholarly work on this question, see J. Samuel Walker, "The Decision to Use the Bomb: A Historiographical Update," *Diplomatic History* 14 (Winter 1990): 97–114.

6. Edwin O. Reischauer, *The United States and Japan* (Cambridge, MA, 1950), 45. In addition to the Allied Council, a Far Eastern Commission, located in Washington, D.C., had been initiated at the Potsdam conference. Consisting of representatives of eleven nations, it was to oversee the administration of occupied Japan and payment of reparations.

7. On MacArthur's notions about his task in Japan and the resulting conflicts with the administration in Washington, D.C., see Michael Schaller, "MacArthur's Japan: The View From Washington," *Diplomatic History* 10 (Winter 1986): 1–23; and idem., *Douglas MacArthur: The Far Eastern General* (New York, 1988).

8. By April 1947 "no present evidence of Soviet activity in Southeast Asia" had been detected by the State Department. See Abbot L. Moffat (State Department) in DD, "Conflicting Interests in Southeast Asia," 9 April 1947, 3, FEA/RGCFR-XXIA.

tions that had played a role in Germany and Western Europe were negligible, and the Americans could concentrate on political and economic reconstruction. Thus, the Cold War reached Japan much later than it reached Germany and Western Europe.

Ideas such as decentralizing and relocating Japanese industry and trade to the Asian mainland (particularly to China, but also to the Philippines and Australia) to ensure participation of the whole region in the envisioned economic revival, had been developed in far-away government agencies in Washington, D.C. They proved to be flawed. During the war, it had been a widely held opinion that Japanese military aggression had been merely an accident of history. A group of officials, led by Under Secretary of State Joseph C. Grew, had maintained that small incisions in the societal structure and economy of Japan would be sufficient to insure democratization of the nation. The removal of militarists from important positions, strengthening the position of the Japanese Tenno, revision of the Japanese constitution to provide for more liberalism, and tangible involvement of Japan in the multilateral world economy would serve as adequate remedies.

Very soon after President Roosevelt's death in April 1945, a different attitude developed within the State Department. Secretary of State Byrnes and his Under Secretary Dean Acheson, supported by the China experts in the State Department, maintained that Japan's militaristic tendencies were founded on tradition, feudalistic tendencies, and the very basis of Japanese culture. Only a deep cut, such as re-education and reorganization of the societal and political bases of Japan, would have a lasting impact.[9]

As with Germany and Europe, it soon became apparent that the economic vacuum that existed in Asia after the surrender of Japan could only be filled by a revitalization of Japanese industry. In his speech before the Delta Council, on 8 May 1947, Dean Acheson thus declared both Germany and Japan to be "two of the greatest workshops of Europe and Asia."[10]

9. Robert A. Pollard, *Economic Security and the Origins of the Cold War, 1945–1950* (New York, 1985), 174–75; and more comprehensively, Michael Schaller, *The American Occupation of Japan: The Origins of the Cold War in Asia* (New York, 1985). For a critical evaluation of achievements of U.S. occupational policy, see Howard B. Schonberger, *Aftermath of War: Americans and the Remaking of Japan, 1945–1952* (Kent, OH, 1989).

10. Becker and Wells, *Economics and World Power*, 348; Acheson, "Requirements," 991.

The members of the Council study group on "Far East Affairs" were informed, in four short meetings, about the most recent political developments in that region. Newspaper magnate Henry R. Luce of *Time/Life* informed them on the evening of 6 December 1945 of "The Present Situation in China."[11] Luce, who was born in China, regarded the political stabilization of China as a feasible goal. He anticipated a positive outcome from the negotiations between the nationalists, led by Chiang Kai-shek, and the communists. This would produce a strong China which would maintain friendly relations with the United States. China would then, Luce expected, fill the void that had developed after Japan's defeat. Although papers and magazines published by *Time/Life* enthusiastically greeted the Treaty of Friendship and Alliance between Chiang and Stalin on 14 August 1945, Luce was not keen on Soviet involvement in the political developments in China.[12]

The likelihood that the communists under Mao Tse-tung would rise to power in China, which was one of the major concerns of the State Department and interested circles, was regarded by Luce as negligible: "The masses have no love for the Communists." He believed that the prospect of "prosperity" would be of prime importance to China. The Chinese communists could only count on large amounts of support, Luce maintained, if the current government failed to establish the social and economic conditions that made the daily life of the populace bearable. His evaluation that "there is a chance for a real pro-Communist movement three to four years hence if the government does not produce a solution for the current social [and] economic ills" was almost prophetic.[13]

At the next meeting the chairman of the group supplied the members with his own knowledge of American policy in Japan. "Today Tokyo is a little Washington," Lattimore said, criticizing the nearly unchecked power of MacArthur on the island and the bureaucratization of occupation policy. The East Asia expert had been a member of an American commission for reparations and had visited Japan in December 1945.

11. Thomas Lamont's interests in the Far East are described in Cohen, *The Chinese Connection.* For the romantic notions of many Americans, including Luce, about China, see Sterling Seagrave, *The Soong Dynasty* (New York, 1985), *passim.*

12. DD, 6 December 1945, 7, FEA/RGCFR-XVIIIB. During the conference at Yalta, Stalin had received many concessions for his promise to enter the war in the Pacific, including the lease of Port Arthur as a Soviet naval base, participation in the operation of the Chinese-Eastern and Manchurian railroads, and acquisition of the Kurile Islands and the southern part of the Sakhalin Island. These commitments were now codified in the treaty. See LaFeber, *America, Russia,* 24–25.

13. DD, 6 December 1945, 4–8, FEA/RGCFR-XVIIIB.

The commission's task had been to decide the level of economic rehabilitation that should be granted to Japan, what resources could be mobilized to this end, and what assets still existed on the island. Lattimore advocated (not in all specifics in accordance with the Department of State, MacArthur, and the Far Eastern Commission) that only a low industrial potential should be permitted Japan and that other countries in the region should receive substantial support. The re-education program applied by MacArthur to Japan was not criticized by Lattimore; on the contrary, he argued, the process did not go far enough.[14]

The Far Eastern Commission had opted for a harsh policy against Japan, offering comments similar to Lattimore's. This policy was backed by a number of State Department officials. During the first phase of the American occupation, MacArthur also had upheld beliefs in re-education, demilitarization, and decentralization and had favored strengthening the Japanese industrial potential primarily as a means to support the economic rehabilitation of Asia as a whole. However, it was not long before criticism of this stern policy was raised. It was maintained that the objectives Americans strove for in Japan would be made more difficult to achieve under such prerequisites, that the costs of occupation would increase, and that supplying food would be more difficult. With the background of these conflicting notions in mind, historian Edwin O. Reischauer, in his presentation on 15 March 1946, tried to unravel to the study group members the chaotic arrangement of conflicting tasks and functions granted to officials and members of the Far Eastern Commission, the Allied Council, the military government, and the State Department.[15]

On 17 April, John Carter Vincent, director of the Far Eastern Affairs Division of the State Department, interpreted President Truman's directive on the American China policy of 16 December 1945 to George C. Marshall for the group members.[16] The idea behind this policy, Vincent told the audience, was to guarantee the security of the United States in the Pacific while simultaneously providing support of a free and independent China and Asia. A sovereign China, supported militarily by the United States, would serve to contain any conceivable Soviet expansion in Asia.[17]

14. DD, "The Situation in the Far East," 8 February 1946, 1, FEA/RGCFR-XVIIIB. On this issue, see also the chapter, "Japanese Reparations and Level of Industry, 1945–1950," in Pollard, *Economic Security*, 179–82.

15. DD, "The Basic Directive to General MacArthur on Japan," n.d., FEA/RGCFR-XVIIIB.

16. The members received a copy of the directive before the meeting. See William Edwin Diez (secretary of the group) to members, 28 March 1946, FEA/RGCFR-XVIIIB.

17. DD, "The President's Directive to General Marshall on China," 16 April 1946, FEA/RGCFR-XVIIIB. On Vincent, see also Gary May, *China Scapegoat: The Diplomatic Ordeal of John Carter Vincent* (New York, 1979).

During the following months, the study group continued to concentrate on collecting the latest available information on the situation in the Far East. They were puzzled when they discovered that the democratic reorientation in Japan was not supported by large parts of the island's population, but rather that it was perceived as a measure alien to Japanese political culture and dictated by foreign interests. The danger of an undemocratic society developing in Japan had not yet passed away.

The members also had to realize that the situation in China was not as hopeful as they had expected. The ongoing civil war between communist and nationalist forces had done considerable harm to the country's economic and social fabric. American financial aid for Chiang Kai-shek was squandered by the continuing fighting, and the Soviet "liberators" were removing industrial plants the Japanese had installed during their occupation.[18] It was soon becoming apparent that China was in no position to fulfill the hopes of the Council's members and those of officials in Washington for a speedy and efficient reconstruction of Asia. Council members agreed that the United States should not involve itself too deeply in internal Chinese developments and that the Chinese would instead have to solve their political disputes among themselves.[19]

At the end of 1947, when the Cold War finally reached Japan, a discussion group entitled "Occupation Problems in Japan," had Lattimore again serving as chairman, and this group succeeded the study group on the Far East. By that time, the discrepancies between the original American designs for Japanese reparations and the actual situation on the island had become striking. MacArthur had called for a peace treaty with Japan in March 1947, and in July some restrictions on Japanese foreign trade were lifted.[20] In most aspects, the study group members approved of the changes in American policy toward Japan. Only the administration's attempt to break the aristocratic Zaibatsu trust was criticized sharply and fostered heated discussion. With an eye on the domestic situation and fearful of trust-busting policies at home, some members claimed that to call an enterprise bad only because it had attained a certain size was an ill-guided policy. However, no explicit proposals were made regarding procedures that would assure that the

18. Very much to the surprise of the group members, Soviet troops had hardly dismantled any industrial plants in northern Korea, although they did so in Manchuria. See DD, 12 December 1946, 4, FEA/RGCFR-XXIA.

19. A summary of the meetings can be found in CFR, *Annual Report, 1946–47*, 36–40.

20. Invitation letter by Joseph Barber, 1 October 1947, OPJ/RGCFR-XXIVB. Schaller, "MacArthur's Japan," 14–15.

prewar and war-time Japanese ruling elites could be prevented from regaining their positions of power without first destroying their economical and societal foundations. Additionally, no consensus could be reached among the members on the issue of the level of foreign trade that should be allowed in Japan.[21]

In the meantime, George Kennan and his Policy Planning Staff, who had turned their attention away from the reconstruction of Europe and toward American policy in Japan, reached a conclusion similar to that of the members opposing decartelization. In his memoirs, Kennan wrote that the ideological basis of American attempts to decentralize the Japanese economy were so similar to Soviet notions about the ills of capitalist monopolies that the measures would have been "eminently agreeable to anyone interested in the communization of Japan." Kennan anticipated the Japanese would become easy prey for communist maneuvers after the occupying forces left the country. He believed that a peace treaty would be premature. Echoing conservative business people and politicians in Japan, he reasoned that liberalizing the international trade system and the structures of trade in Japan would do more to democratize the country and to strengthen a potential American ally in the containment of communism.[22]

Kennan had traveled to Japan in February 1948 and had steered politics in Japan, he claimed, toward a more suitable direction for containing communism. After his return to Washington, he wrote a report on his impressions which soon became part of the directive NSC 13/2 of the National Security Council of October 1948. However, not all of Kennan's suggestions were accepted by the autocratic MacArthur.[23]

Herbert Feis, advisor on international economic affairs to the State Department (who had also been to Japan), told the group members on 20 May about the implementation of this new policy in Japan. As Kennan had done, he criticized the slow advances in economic rehabilitation. He asserted that it was in the interest of the United States "to

21. CFR, *Annual Report, 1947–48*, 21–23. Some vocal members of the business community — its most ardent advocate being Harry Kern, foreign affairs editor of *Newsweek* — were alarmed by the anti-trust policy in Japan and the supposedly socialist concept that this was based on. See Pollard, *Economic Security*, 183.

22. Kennan, *Memoirs*, 374–77; the citation is from page 388. See also Michael Schaller, "Securing the Great Crescent: Occupied Japan and the Origins of Containment in Southeast Asia," *Journal of American History* 69 (September 1982): 392–414, particularly pages 395–97; and Pollard, *Economic Security*, 183.

23. Kennan, *Memoirs*, 391–92.

enhance Japan's strategic value to us vis-à-vis Russia." Some group members were still doubtful if this measure of concentration on the aspects of economic reconstruction would leave sufficient resources to assure a reorientation of Japan toward a peaceful and democratic nation.[24]

The signing of the peace treaty with Japan, as Kennan had suggested, was delayed and American troops stayed on the island.[25] With Washington now opting for Japan to become a possible ally against the Soviet Union, MacArthur had ample time for his re-education and decentralization programs. The development of the Korean War finally brought Japan into the system of Western military alliance and of Western prosperity.

In its second year, with Arthur H. Dean as chair, the group set out to discuss the "Revival of Japan."[26] Soon, however, developments on the Asian mainland caught the members' attention. The rapid and unexpected success of the communists in China surprised them, as it did the members of the discussion group "U.S. Policy Toward China." J. Leighton Stuart, American ambassador to China since 1946, addressed the question most on the minds of this latter group's members on 22 November 1949: how could Mao Tse-tung and his comrades achieve so much in so little time?[27]

Political developments in China, for Council members and State Department officials alike, were much harder to understand than the situation in Japan. American military leaders and State Department officials had believed their task in China would be comparatively simple: Japanese troops would have to be disarmed, Soviet expansion discouraged by the presence of American forces, and Chinese involvement in

24. DD, "The Road Ahead," 20 May 1948, OPJ/RGCFR-XXIVB; CFR, *Annual Report, 1947–48*, 22–23. Historian Herbert Feis had served the State Department as an economic advisor from 1931 to 1943 and was special consultant to Secretary of War Henry L. Stimson from 1944 to 1946. Before he became a member of the department's Policy Planning Staff, he taught at the Institute for Advanced Study at Princeton University.

25. The peace treaty with Japan was finally signed on 8 October 1951, at San Francisco, by 47 nations. Although the acquisitions agreed upon in Potsdam were incorporated into the document, the Soviet Union and the People's Republic of China did not sign the treaty. For a more comprehensive account, see the respective parts in Acheson, *Present.*

26. No digests of discussion of any of these meetings could be found at the Council Archives. Speakers were: Under Secretary of the Army William H. Draper, Jr., Deputy Director for Far Eastern Affairs John M. Allison, and Charles L. Kades of the Department of Navy. A very brief summary of the proceedings is in CFR, *Annual Report, 1948–49*, 33–36.

27. DD, 22 November 1949, USPC/RGCFR-XXXIVA; CFR, *Annual Report, 1949–50*, 36.

multilateral and free world trade stimulated to ensure stable political and economic conditions in the whole region. Stuart's predecessor in China, General Patrick G. Hurley, had negotiated with Mao Tse-tung and Chiang Kai-shek on 28 August and 11 October 1945 to end the bloodshed that had gone on for three decades. However, the fighting continued during the negotiations, with major clashes between the communist and the nationalist forces erupting after the Japanese capitulation on 2 September 1945. Marshall's attempts to mediate between the two parties in January 1946 had made a short cease-fire possible; but, after Chiang Kai-shek's Kuomintang occupied large parts of the country, civil war erupted.[28] Within the State Department, officials still expected revolutionaries who were disciples of the Chinese hero Sun Yat-sen[29] to leave the Communist Party of China, and Secretary Marshall hoped, even after his mediations had failed, that liberal members of the Kuomintang and the Communist Party might yet form a new national coalition.[30] Planners and military leaders in Washington, D.C. were certain that communism was contrary to the very basis of Chinese culture and world-view. The Chinese people, they believed, were, rank and file, "friends of the United States."[31]

In August 1949, the troops of the communist People's Liberation Army were about to win the civil war and Chiang Kai-shek, together with half a million of his soldiers and two million civilians, was leaving the country for the island of Formosa. The State Department just then published a "white book" on China. The authors depicted the development of Chinese-American relations since 1944 and, in line with prevailing

28. Mao Tse-tung had called on the United States in June of 1946 to discontinue its support of the Kuomintang. For the development of American policy toward China, see William W. Stueck, Jr., *The Road to Confrontation: American Policy Toward China and Korea, 1947–1950* (Chapel Hill, NC, 1981).

29. Sun Yat-sen (1866–1924) had grown up on Hawaii. Beginning in 1895, he had organized rebellion against the ruling Manchus in southern China. Sun became the first president of the Chinese republic and founded the Kuomintang. After his death, the movement split into political left and right wings. Chiang Kai-shek, after a military coup in 1925, became one of the most important leaders of the Kuomintang.

30. State Department official Abbot Moffat argued in April 1947 that "the responsible leaders of [the socialist organizations] . . . have every intention of cooperating closely with the western democracies."; see DD, 9 April 1947, 7, FEA/RGCFR-XXIA.

31. See particularly David McLean, "American Nationalism, the China Myth, and the Truman Doctrine: The Origins of Accommodation with Peking, 1949–50," *Diplomatic History* 10 (Winter 1986): 25–42. For the myth of the close relationship between the Americans and the Chinese, see Michael H. Hunt, *The Making of a Special Relationship: The United States and China to 1914* (New York, 1983); and Seagrave, *The Soong Dynasty*.

sentiments, the introduction made clear that the State Department did not see any possibility for arrangements with the communists. The communists had negated their Chinese background, it was argued, and would serve only as agents for the USSR. If China would not return to democracy, diplomatic recognition was regarded as impossible.[32]

The communist Chinese government was already well established when the group discussed with ambassador Stuart on 22 November 1949 the possibility of diplomatic recognition of the People's Republic of China. Asked if "an announcement of a clear-cut policy of non-recognition" would be the best answer to this question, Stuart maintained that this was more likely to have negative consequences. An economic blockade — proposed by one of the group members as a measure to promote unrest and dissatisfaction with the communists, which could then lead to a counterrevolution — was regarded by Stuart as very dangerous. Such suffering would only be attributed to foreigners, not to the Chinese communists.[33]

When Professor Nathaniel Peffer summarized the Council members' attitude as "agreement that China was lost to the Communists," many members disagreed. New York lawyer Colonel Harold Riegelman and Frederick C. McKee, an industrialist from Pittsburgh, PA, were particularly disturbed by this evaluation. Peffer responded to their criticism, displaying a sense of humor and exemplary wit. He asked Stuart if he believed that the situation in China could be reversed again or if Stuart knew of somebody who had been in China during the last three years and believed that this was possible. To both questions, Stuart's answer was negative. "If we do not recognize Communist China we will simply be forced to eat crow in five years," Peffer concluded. He also reminded the members somewhat sarcastically of a comparable incident: "[A]fter World War I we have chosen not to recognize a new communist country for some fifteen years. . . . That country [has] not vanished because of our action. On the contrary . . . it seems still to be very much with us."[34]

A poll among the Committees on Foreign Relations, conducted at about the same time the meeting took place, revealed that its members had reached a conclusion similar to Peffer's. Ninety percent of the 720 committee members interviewed believed that communists under the

32. Department of State, *United States Relations with China, with Special Reference to the Period 1944–1949* (Washington, D.C., 1949), particularly "Letter of Transmittal," page xvi.

33. DD, 22 November 1949, 3, 5, USPC/RGCFR-XXXIVA.

34. DD, 22 November 1949, 11–12, USPC/RGCFR-XXXIVA.

leadership of Mao Tse-tung had established themselves securely in control of the nation and that no military opposition existed within China. Also, the majority did not think it advisable to rule out American diplomatic recognition of China. Since the communists were cooperating closely with the Soviet Union, however, Committee members proposed to conduct only limited trade with the People's Republic of China. Economic support or even credit from the United States, they suggested, would only foster the spread of communism in Asia.[35]

It did take more than fifteen years for China to be officially recognized by the United States and diplomatic relations between the two nations to be established. Almost to the day, twenty-three years were to pass after Peffer's statements at the Council group meeting until the relationship between the two nations was based on normal diplomatic ties. The assessment of the majority of the Council members did not sway the "Cold Warriors" in Washington in 1949. Not until autumn, 1971, did President Richard M. Nixon's secretary of state (Council member Henry A. Kissinger) travel to China, first in his customary style of secret missions and then officially, to pave the way for the first meeting between the two heads of state.

35. Joseph Barber, ed., *American Policy Toward China: A Report on Views of Leading Citizens in 23 Cities* (New York, 1950); the results are from pages 6–8. The volume was published in April.

6

The Role of the United States After 1945:

"Maintenance of Peace, Freedom, and Prosperity" vs. "American Security, Private Enterprise, and Our Way of Life"[1]

While many of the study and discussion groups on regional aspects served mainly to inform Council members of recent developments or supply background information, other groups, concerned less with current events, discussed the United States' foreign policy in general terms and sought to formulate long-term concepts. One of the groups proposed at the Princeton meeting in 1945 studied "United States Foreign Policy: Its Formulation and Implementation." Under the leadership of Thomas K. Finletter, it was supposed to address a wide range of topics. Its preliminary agenda contained suggestions to study issues as far-reaching as the State Department's public information policy, the decision-making process in Washington, and the advisability of supporting representative democracies in regions where the Soviet Union claimed to have vital interests.[2]

During the course of group meetings, it quickly became apparent that a precise definition of what should constitute American foreign policy, other than in very broad terms, could not be achieved. Most of the members present at the first meeting on 27 November 1945 agreed that it should be the goal of the United States to create "a world of free self-governing peoples living at peace with each other." Just how this Wilsonian ideal could be translated into concrete policy, however, remained unclear. Some members believed that such cooperation as the major powers enjoyed would serve as an ample cornerstone of future

1. These two seemingly different but, from the Council's perspective, by no means mutually exclusive goals of post-war American foreign policy were advocated by members of the study groups on "United States Foreign Policy: Its Formulation and Implementation" and "Inter-American Affairs" respectively. See DD, 27 November 1945, 8, USFP/RGCFR-XIXB; DD, 13 October 1948, 11, IAA/RGCFR-XXVIIB.

2. "Tentative Agenda," 23 November 1945, USFP/RGCFR-XIXB. Finletter had been special assistant to Secretary of State Cordell Hull from 1941 to 1944, before serving as a consultant to the American delegation to the San Francisco conference founding the United Nations in 1945. He became secretary of the U.S. Air Force in 1950, serving until 1953.

arrangements, while others maintained that the very basis of Soviet policy ran counter to the concept of self-determination. A much more realistic aim, one member maintained, would be to ensure security for the United States and its allies. Thus, it was argued, the right for self-determination might have to be sacrificed in the case of India for example, to assure continuing friendly relations with Great Britain.[3]

Idealists among the group perceived these ideas as a call for a cynical, cowardly, and half-hearted foreign policy. The "Declaration on Liberated Europe," in which the Allies had stated (at Yalta in 1945) that self-determination was one of the principles of their policy, was still valid and should under no circumstances be discarded. Heated discussion and disagreement among the members erupted, they found, because a clear-cut definition of the very basis of American foreign policy was lacking within the group.[4] Consequently, the group members, like good students, set out to define what they were actually talking about.

The differences between short-term and long-term aims were addressed and the necessity to differentiate between means and aims was discussed. When a general guideline for American foreign policy was addressed in particular, however, major differences among the members arose again. Some of the members argued that the primary goal of American foreign policy should be to ensure the security and prosperity of United States citizens. This was to take precedence over the well-being and prosperity of other peoples. Other members disagreed and maintained that the welfare of Americans could only be ensured in a world in which peace, freedom, and prosperity for all was possible. It should be the goal of the United States "to make the world safe for our ideals."[5]

With no prospect of reaching a consensus regarding these very basic concepts, the study group turned to listen to speakers providing more general information. Finletter reported on the "Big Three Cooperation and U.N.," Clark M. Eichelberger gave a paper on "The United States and Trusteeships," and Walter H.C. Laves (Bureau of the Budget) summarized "How Policy Is Made in Washington." Journalist James B. Reston provided his impressions of "Soviet Policy as Seen From

3. DD, 27 November 1945, 1–4, USFP/RGCFR-XIXB. It is not possible to establish the identity of individual contributors. At the very first meeting, the members stipulated that the names of the members should not be revealed in the digests of discussion. See *ibid.*, 1.

4. *Ibid.*, 5–8.

5. *Ibid.*, 9.

London," and the president of Dartmouth College, John S. Dickey, proposed "Procedural Changes Necessary for the Effective Conduct of a Cooperative Foreign Policy." The drafting of guidelines for American foreign policy, however, was not further pursued.[6]

Another Council group, also founded at the end of 1945, was more successful in achieving its more moderate goals. The study group "Economic Aspects of American Foreign Policy" (headed by economist Winfield W. Riefler) from the very beginning invited eminent guests to the Harold Pratt House. Among others, Wayne C. Taylor, president of the Import-Export Bank, and Assistant Secretary of State William Clayton were persuaded to address the members.

In preparation for the group's program, a meeting with Riefler, Clayton, and the Council's Director of Studies Percy W. Bidwell had been held in Washington in October 1945. On that occasion, Riefler had reminded Clayton of the importance of the Council's War and Peace Studies group. He proposed to Clayton that a similar, although somewhat smaller, group of Council experts could advise State Department officials in the field of economic foreign policy. Clayton agreed that a group of knowledgeable men could certainly help the Department with constructive critique. Also, he suggested, it would be very helpful if the Council would interpret the State Department's policies to the public.[7]

It was in this tenor that Riefler addressed the group members during the first meeting. The study group had been founded, he told his audience, "to supply a sort of informal advisory board with which the administrators could consult, and to which they could express their views in confidence."[8] Opening the round of presentations, Taylor outlined the tasks of the Import-Export Bank. During the discussion that followed, economic as well as political implications of the Bank's activities were addressed.

Economic advisor Leon Henderson maintained that "the restoration of foreign trade" should be the primary task of the Import-Export Bank.

6. These meetings took place on 20 December 1945, 23 January 1946, 25 February 1946, 19 March 1946, and 8 April 1946; USFP/RGCFR-XIXB.

7. "Memorandum of conversation with Messrs. Will Clayton and Winfield Riefler in Washington, October 22, 1945," n.d., EAAFP/RGCFR-XIXA; Bidwell to Clayton, 24 October 1945, *ibid.*; telegram, Riefler to Joseph H. Willets [*sic*; Rockefeller Foundation], 8 November 1945, RFR 1/100/97/877.

8. DD, 22 January 1946, 1, EAAFP/RGCFR-XIXA. See also Bidwell to Taylor, 19 December 1945, *ibid.*

Because the credits the bank distributed came out of the American budget, however, John H. Williams (Federal Reserve Board) argued that the U.S. should be allowed to determine what a country should actually be entitled to request. Import-Export Bank credits could then be utilized to achieve political or economic influence in Eastern European countries, Taylor admitted freely. Modest amounts of credit, he argued, should be given to Poland and Czechoslovakia. Although Soviet influence in this region was obvious there was still some degree of uncertainty about the final political alliance of individual countries and the United States should not "drop the blind completely." Henderson agreed, adding that in the past the United States had "forced countries into the Russian camp" by not giving credits in a timely enough fashion to achieve sufficient influence. Asked by Riefler if the Import-Export Bank had established connections with Argentina or fascist Spain (thus touching on the quite sensitive matter of diplomatic relations with these two former allies of Nazi Germany), Taylor answered in the negative.[9]

William Clayton, a rare guest at the Council headquarters, outlined the latest developments and provided background information on the British desire for credit on 2 March 1946.[10] The credit had become necessary, Clayton argued, because, as a result of trade barriers during the war and because of the war debt, the British economy had accumulated a trade deficit of three billion dollars. Great Britain was in imminent danger of losing its important capacity as a trading nation. The prospect of reestablishing multilateral world trade, in which that nation had played an important part before the war, was endangered. Jacob Viner's evaluation was even more blunt: a credit was the only means to preserve Great Britain as a line of defense for Western ideals and as a military power with influence and prestige in the world's political arena.[11]

Different evaluations of the prospects of multilateral trade relations were advanced during the discussion, but a consensus was reached only regarding the axiom that open world trade would ensure constructive international cooperation. Consequently, the members called for a reduction of tariffs on imports into the United States. Bilateral trade agreements were regarded as dangerous. Such agreements could far too easily be uti-

9. DD, 22 January 1946, 9, 7, 6, 10, EAAFP/RGCFR-XIXA.

10. The issue of a credit to Great Britain had encountered resistance in the U.S., particularly in the Midwest. Clayton maintained that objections had been voiced mainly by individuals concerned about British competition on the international market for wool, metals, and a number of other products. See DD, 2 March 1946, 5, EAAFP/RGCFR-XIXA.

11. DD, 2 March 1946, 1–4, EAAFP/RGCFR-XIXA.

lized for political ends and could then be turned against the United States, even leading to the exclusion of that nation from foreign markets.[12]

When the group was continued in the fall of 1946 as a discussion group, Riefler limited its scope to the issue of multilateral trade from the very beginning. The reasons for this, Riefler posited during the first meeting on 21 October 1946, were obvious: Support of multilateral trade had been America's policy for some time, a preparatory conference in London was drafting rules which were to become part of the charter of the International Trade Organization (ITO), and the problem of limited world trade was at the center of contemporary international problems. Only when frictions between nations could be avoided in this matter, could a system of international organization such as the UN be able to function properly.[13]

All members of the group trusted that the proposed multilateral trade system would operate on a global scale. Soviet participation, regardless of political or economic desirability, was not considered imperative. No concessions should be made to attract the Soviet Union to such a system. A modus vivendi might be accepted, nevertheless, in trade relations with other countries with state-controlled foreign trade.[14] Most businessmen among the members disagreed with this concession during the second group meeting on 4 November. They did not consider fruitful trading relations possible with such countries. Discussion leader Jacob Viner convinced them, however, that the United States would reduce its own trade possibilities if it disallowed such trade relations. Again the members stated the importance of a reduction of tariffs on imports, but there was little hope that such a reduction was possible in the face of ardent resistance by domestic industry.[15]

It was only fitting, then, that the Council also researched the role propaganda played in American foreign policy during this period. Initi-

12. DD, 2 March 1946, 5–6, EAAFP/RGCFR-XIXA.

13. Riefler to John Chapman [*Business Week*], 1 October 1946, PMT/RGCFR-XXIIA. Multilateralism was defined by Riefler as "a highly inter-dependent system of trade, comparable in general to that which existed in the years before World War I." See DD, 21 October 1946, 1, *ibid.*

14. Riefler and Bidwell had participated in a Twentieth Century Fund (TCF) study group on the same subject. The members of the TCF's Committee on Foreign Economic Relations had agreed, however, that Soviet participation should not be precluded. See Buchanan and Lutz, *Rebuilding the World Economy*, 293–94.

15. DD, 4 November 1946, 1, 5, PMT/RGCFR-XXIIA; and CFR, *Annual Report, 1946–1947*, 26–27. See also Bidwell to Viner, 23 October 1946, PMT/RGCFR-XXIIA.

ated by Lester Markel (Sunday editor of the *New York Times*), the group "Propaganda and Foreign Policy" had set out to research possible ideas to influence and educate the American public on foreign policy issues. Since one of the major tasks of the Council was educating the public, interest in this group was keen. At its first meeting on 27 March 1947, however, the group chose a broader approach to its subject. James P. Warburg had argued that the group would have a superb chance to study the propaganda fight between the United States and the USSR, and other members had proposed also including discussion of components of propaganda within the United States. President Truman had announced what was soon to be called the Truman Doctrine barely two weeks earlier, and the Council members present realized that it would be important to examine how resulting foreign policy measures could be communicated to the public.[16]

To pay tribute to this new outline (and admittedly also to avoid "unfortunate connotations"), the study group's name was changed to "Public Opinion and Foreign Policy."[17] The discussion leaders of the second meeting (Colonel Charles A. H. Thompson of the Brookings Institution, Francis H. Russell, director of the State Department's Office of Public Affairs, and the latter's colleague in the Office of Information and Cultural Affairs, William T. Stone), had to bear the brunt of the members' criticism of the allegedly insufficient public relations performance by the administration.[18]

James Warburg had found a "striking example of complete failure" in the Truman administration's endeavor to prepare the public for the implications of the Truman Doctrine. It should be the State Department's task, Warburg asserted, to provide American citizens with the facts and to find out if the proposed foreign policy stance met with the public's consent. The State Department was obliged to provide alternative policies, he proposed somewhat naively, in situations in which it was anticipated that a particular policy might not meet with public approval.

This idealistic perspective met with little agreement among the group members. Alger Hiss (president of the Carnegie Endowment for Inter-

16. DD, 27 March 1947, 6, POFP/RGCFR-XXIIIA. Warburg, having served as deputy director of the State Department's Office of War Information from 1943 to 1945, was an expert in the field of propaganda.

17. Markel to Edward Barrett [*Newsweek*], 17 April 1947, POFP/RGCFR-XXIIIA.

18. For a discussion of the tasks of the Office of Public Affairs, see Bernard C. Cohen, *The Public's Impact on Foreign Policy* (Boston, 1973), 44–50.

national Peace and, until recently, with the State Department), put his trust in the representative character of the American parliamentary system rather than in its constituency. A system proposed by Warburg, he maintained, was academic and impossible to execute. In situations where decisions had to be made speedily, there would often not be sufficient time to use this lengthy process. In these instances the "bipartisan foreign policy" had been very helpful in reaching a consensus before a policy actually had to be decided upon by Congress.[19]

Harold Guinzburg (president of Viking Press), concurring with Hiss, cautioned that it would be important to take into consideration the reasons an administration may have for the dissemination of particular information. It would be quite possible that the executive branch merely wanted to "sell" a program instead of asking the public for its approval. This danger of manipulation was far too important to be cast aside carelessly. Russell did not respond to these references to the ambiguities and dangers of his tasks at the Office of Public Affairs. Indicating that the administration and citizens both were responsible for American foreign policy, he remarked that the State Department would indeed pay attention to public opinion. When Percy Bidwell asked if other means were available in case the State Department was not able to undertake the necessary task of educating the public, Russell indicated that "pressure groups, committees, columnists and the like" would always be willing to support the administration.[20]

After Secretary of State Marshall offered American help for the reconstruction of the European economies in June of 1947, the study group immediately concentrated on the Marshall Plan. The State Department's public relations work, it was argued at a meeting on 25 September, had once again been a failure. Important members of Congress, including Senator Vandenberg, had been informed about the importance of Marshall's speech at Harvard University two weeks after the event. British Foreign Minister Bevin had to be pushed to respond to this speech, and the news from Germany as well as a press conference by Truman at about the same time had considerably harmed press cov-

19. DD, 30 April 1947, 1, POFP/RGCFR-XXIIIA.

20. *Ibid.*, 7. Russell's evaluation was quite likely based on the State Department's experience with ad hoc "citizens' organizations" operating before the United States entered World War II. At the end of 1947, the founding of the Committee for the Marshall Plan was to confirm his appraisal of the post-war period. It also confirmed, however, the danger of manipulation of the public referred to by Harold Guinzburg. See also chapter 7.

erage of Marshall's speech. Additionally, both offices responsible for public education (the Office of Public Affairs, led by Francis Russell, and the Office of Information and Cultural Affairs, headed by William Stone) had been prevented from conducting any active public relations work. In summary, the group members believed, the task had been insufficiently coordinated and had been handicapped by antagonistic interests within the Department. The State Department's entire public relations policy and organization would have to be reconstructed to overcome these obstacles, and the current task seemed an ideal opportunity for sufficient and effective change. In this respect, it was also considered fortunate that William Benton had recently resigned from his post as assistant secretary of state. Until a successor was found, the Council would have ample time to study the problem and make proposals to the State Department for a more efficient public affairs operation.[21]

The group's decision to formulate a memorandum to the State Department had been well prepared by Markel. He had informed Percy Bidwell that he wanted to induce the State Department to do a "first class job" in the public relations work for the Marshall Plan. Guidelines for this matter, researched and developed by the Council's study group, could be confidentially forwarded to the appropriate officers at the State Department. Markel told Bidwell that the Council's Committee on Studies had already indicated its approval of this kind of support.[22]

Markel immediately contacted Secretary Marshall's special assistant, Charles Bohlen. Promising to mention the Council's proposal to the secretary of state, Bohlen told Markel that not only officers at the State Department but also the special advisor to President Truman, Clark M. Clifford, would be highly interested in the Council's plans. Robert Lovett, contacted by group member Charles Jackson (vice president of *Time*, Inc.), also endorsed Markel's proposal, stating that there was "nothing more important on the agenda than the public relations planning in the Department." During the fifth meeting of the group, on 27 November 1947, Markel proudly informed the members that even Secretary of State Marshall and President Truman had been informed about

21. DD, 25 September 1947, 1, 11–17, POFP/RGCFR-XXIIIA. During the meeting, possible candidates to succeed Benton in his position were discussed but no recommendations were forwarded to the State Department. Russell, educated at Harvard Law School, had worked for the League of Nations Association from 1929 to 1941. See Francis H. Russell Oral History Interview, 1, Harry S. Truman Library. On the issue of Benton's successor see the more extensive delineation in chapter 7.

22. Bidwell to Armstrong, 18 September 1947, POFP/RGCFR-XXIIIA.

the study group's intention to prepare a memorandum. Both Marshall and Truman had reacted favorably, even enthusiastically, and Truman had indicated that it might be difficult to select an adequate successor to Benton, the individual actually responsible for the job.[23]

"Uncoordinated and inadequate," Markel called the State Department's handling of the press in his first report to Bohlen. The printed media informed the public about foreign policy issues, but with journalists and commentators receiving inadequate information, the whole system of educating the public could not function. Benton's successor would have to pay more attention to cooperating with the press. Additionally, Markel argued, it would be of pivotal importance to coordinate the State Department's information policy, to increase the number of information programs for foreign countries, and to change the Department's structure so as to concentrate these activities in one hand.[24]

This explicit advice bore little fruit. Public relations operations for the Marshall Plan (after some initial difficulties and with the massive support of the "pressure groups, committees, columnists and the like" that Russell had mentioned during one of the group's meetings) turned out to be so extraordinarily efficient that contemporaries called it one of the biggest propaganda successes in American history. Proposals for the reorganization of public relations operations, however, had very little impact.[25] Some of the Council group's notions can be discerned in the United States Information and Educational Exchange Act of 1948, but the division of tasks below the assistant secretary level (which the Council had criticized) remained in effect. It was not until 1951 that a Psychological Strategy Board (PSB), responsible for interdepartmental and interagency programs, was founded.[26]

Robert Lovett, the designated successor to Dean Acheson as under secretary of state, had been approached by Charles Jackson during the group's initial setup and had already established contacts with the Council in the

23. DD, 25 September 1947, 19, POFP/RGCFR-XXIIIA; DD, 2 October 1947, 1, 2, *ibid;* DD, 27 November 1947, 1, *ibid.*

24. Markel to Bohlen, 6 October 1947, and the enclosed "Memorandum from Study Group on Public Opinion and Foreign Policy, drafted by Lester Markel," dated 7 October 1947, POFP/RGCFR-XXIIIA.

25. The final report of the study group was published as Lester Markel, *Public Opinion and Foreign Policy* (New York, 1949), but the information contained in this volume was available to State Department officials much earlier.

26. Burton M. Sapin, *The Making of United States Foreign Policy* (New York, 1966), 202–206.

spring of 1947. He had asked Walter Mallory to assemble a group of Council members to brief him on possible foreign policy strategies and measures. The Council could hardly decline such an opportunity to prove its excellence as a research institution and community of experts.[27]

When the meeting took place, on 12 May 1947, each Council member who was invited had prepared a short summary of important foreign policy aspects from his area of special expertise. Lovett was told that United States' political interests had become global in scope. The main objectives of U.S. foreign policy would have to be to prevent the USSR from extending its influence to all of Europe and to safeguard American security. Military expert Hanson W. Baldwin told Lovett that it would be impossible to guarantee absolute security in peace time, since this would entail the unacceptable militarizing of the lives of all American citizens and would limit individual civil liberties. American military responsibility, however, was multifaceted, ranging from the defense of the western hemisphere and the foreign possessions of the United States, to the occupation of Germany and Japan, and also to the supply of troops for the United Nations' peace-keeping forces. These military aspects, Baldwin cautioned, could not be split off from political or economic components of American responsibilities in foreign policy. When Lovett requested the members to distinguish between and point out American obligations "for which we were willing to fight" and those for which the United States should deploy other means of coercion, Hamilton Armstrong rejected such an approach. Decisions as grave as these always had to be made with the prevailing situations taken into account. This could not be done using guidelines that had been established beforehand.[28]

Grayson Kirk summarized America's political responsibilities: Germany had to be given top priority, Western influence in Greece and Turkey should be secured, and China must be safeguarded against "Sovietization." The Near East had to remain in the British and American sphere of influence because of the presence of natural resources, such as oil, and also because of the strategic position of military bases which would ensure access to the USSR.

---

27. Joseph Kraft, "School for Statesmen," 68; DD, 12 May 1947, 1–2, RMCFR-XXII. Participants at this dinner meeting were: Armstrong, Hanson W. Baldwin, Bidwell, Grayson Kirk, James Grafton Rogers (former assistant secretary of state and currently with Foreign Bondholders' Protective Council), and Joseph H. Willits of the Rockefeller Foundation.

28. *Ibid.*, 2–4. Baldwin's evaluation was based on his work as chair of the study group, "National Power and Foreign Policy." The results of that group were published as Baldwin, *The Price of Power* (New York, 1948).

Kirk, fearing civil war in France, warned Lovett that this would have a negative impact on Europe as a whole. Political change in Spain might also be dangerous. Should administrations in Spain and France be comprised of the political left, this would "decidedly not . . . [be] to our advantage," he claimed. James Rogers, former assistant secretary of state, differed sharply from Kirk's evaluation. Rogers proposed that the United States should use whatever means necessary to provide for the toppling of the fascist Spanish dictator Franco and the installment of a strong central power. Under no circumstances, however, should European countries be pressed into a decision of alliance with the United States. Insistence in this matter might close many doors still ajar and would thus jeopardize all attempts to achieve a modus vivendi. With the meeting drawing to a close, Baldwin summarized what the Council members wanted to give Lovett on the way: the first priority of American foreign policy had to be the defense of the Western hemisphere, including Greenland, Latin America, the Arctic, and Hawaii. Secondly, security of the British Isles and Iceland had to be assured. Additionally, the United States had to prevent the expansion of Soviet influence to Western Europe.[29]

These recommendations were not especially original nor altogether different from policies already devised. Council members and State Department officials to a large degree shared a common *Weltanschauung* and structure of thought after World War II. Lovett did not have to be convinced or even persuaded to follow a new path in American foreign policy but was merely confirmed in his views of American responsibilities. "I came away from this session," Lovett later recalled, "with the firm conviction that it would be our principle task at State to awaken the nation to the dangers of Communist aggression."[30]

In December, 1947, an additional Council group was formed to study the political prerequisites for the Marshall Plan. Hamilton Armstrong invited a number of eminent Council members to discuss the "political problems which must be solved concurrently with the operation of the Marshall Plan."[31] One of the first topics the group discussed was the question of participation of non-democratic nations in the European Recovery Program. During these deliberations, different evaluations within the membership soon became apparent when the principles underlying U.S.

29. DD, 12 May 1947, 12–16, RMCFR-XXII.

30. Kraft, "School for Statesmen," 68. Lovett received a copy of the digest. See copy, Lovett to Mallory, 23 May 1947, enclosed to Mallory to Willits, 26 May 1947, RFR, 1/100/97/879.

31. Armstrong to Joseph Barnes, 22 December 1947, PG/RGCFR-XXIVD.

foreign policy and its relations to the UN were addressed. A few idealistic internationalists, such as Arthur Sweetser and Benjamin V. Cohen, insisted that the Charter of the United Nations had to be the axiomatic basis of American foreign policy. Others, including Armstrong, Philip C. Jessup, and General L. L. Lemnitzer, argued that foreign policy could not always and without exception follow strict ethical standards.[32]

For the special situation of the Marshall Plan, the members argued against limitation of East-West trade. This would only serve the USSR and would secure neither political nor economic advantages for the United States. Clarifying ambiguous language used by Secretary Marshall and State Department officials, which implied that American assistance was provided mainly because of humanitarian reasons and that the U.S. had no intention of controlling the recovery program, William Diebold stated that, to the contrary, the American administration was very much interested in the control of allocation of economic aid. The group members agreed that the United States should utilize the Marshall Plan and the United Nations to gain a foothold in countries in the Soviet sphere of influence.[33]

At the close of the meeting, Armstrong summarized the group's evaluation of aid to other nations: the United States had to support a UN-member country if it was attacked by a country which was not a member of the supranational organization. If setting the UN machinery into gear took too much time, the United States should unilaterally support a country under attack regardless of its having a democratic or a non-democratic form of government. This should also be done, Armstrong asserted, in a situation in which a country was merely threatened by attack or in instances of civil war in which both sides received outside support. General Lemnitzer maintained that the degree of American involvement should always be dependent on the degree of "national interest" of the United States. Lemnitzer's views were supported by a number of group members. Unilateral actions by the United States would allow such American principles as democracy, civil liberties, and free enterprise to be disregarded if the "interests" of the United States

32. DD, 5 January 1948, PG/RGCFR-XXIVD; "Summary of Group Opinion," dated 21 January 1948, *ibid.;* DD, 26 January 1948, *ibid.* Sweetser, an ardent supporter of the League of Nations, had been a member of the American delegation to the Paris Peace Conference in 1919. He headed the United Nations' Information Office from 1946 to 1953. General Lemnitzer taught at the National War College. Cohen had been a longtime State Department adviser.

33. DD, 16 February 1948, 3, 6, 12, PG/RGCFR-XXIVD.

were threatened or if the position of the United States could be strengthened. The Council members had thereby not achieved much more than providing belated legitimization for American support of Turkey, Greece, and Europe that was already clearly stated in the Truman Doctrine and in Marshall's speech at Harvard.[34]

Armstrong's initial idea to draft a memorandum (to be written by George S. Franklin) for the use of the State Department, was never carried out. Despite group consensus in many areas, no agreement could be reached on a number of important aspects, including the American reaction in the face of a victory of the Communist Party of Italy in the upcoming elections in Italy. Quite possibly envisioning a second Greece (with democratic government troops on the one side and allegedly Soviet-financed communist forces on the other side), the Council members could not agree if they should advise President Truman to present the Italians with a warning by revealing the United States' likely response to civil war in Italy.[35] In dealing with this problem, the group found a different approach. During the group's last meeting, the members discussed how the probable communist victory in the elections could be prevented. "To give the Italians something," a battleship, for example, a colony or something similar, as John Dickey (president of Dartmouth College) later put it, was on the minds of the members. Dickey had participated in the International Trade Organization (ITO) conference in Havana, from November 1947 to March 1948. He had talked with members of the Italian delegation and had been told that the high birth rate in Italy and the increase in population was perceived as a dangerous problem by Italians. Immigration to the United States was a very welcomed means of providing an outlet for this problem, and almost every family had relatives in the U.S. and was grateful for their financial support. An official statement, Dickey maintained at the group's meeting on 10 March 1948, might be able to very subtly influence the Italian population in its behavior at the elections.[36]

---

34. DD, 26 January 1948, 6, 8, PG/RGCFR-XXIVD. The term "interests," used in this discussion, was not defined by group members.

35. In December, 1947, the State Department had prepared a speech for President Truman announcing possible American intervention in case the Communists won the national elections. Secretary Marshall helped soften the language of the speech. See James E. Miller, "Taking Off the Gloves: The United States and the Italian Election of 1948," *Diplomatic History* 7 (Winter 1983): 43.

36. DD, 10 March 1948, 1–4, PG/RGCFR-XXIVD. On 16 March 1948 the United States presented Italy with twenty-nine merchant vessels. See Miller, "Taking Off the Gloves," 49.

Dickey wrote to Dean Acheson (the still influential former under secretary of state) and outlined these ideas. An official statement by the United States should be released, Dickey advised Acheson, acknowledging the Italians' concerns by declaring that the U.S. would like to help that nation by increasing the Italian immigration quota to the United States; provided that the outcome of the Italian elections scheduled for 18 April were to the liking of the U.S. Whatever the Department decided to do in this matter, Dickey cautioned Acheson, State Department officials should not forget that 1948 was also an election year in the United States. This called for a bipartisan approach, assuring the necessary support of both political parties in Congress.[37]

Dickey's advice to the Democrat (and possible future secretary of state) Acheson to enlist Republican support in this matter was not motivated by concern for the future of bipartisan foreign policy. Many interested and informed citizens expected that the incumbent, President Truman, would not be reelected in the upcoming election later that year. "It would be unrealistic not to look forward to the possibility of a new government being in Washington in January," the chair of the Council's study group on "Inter-American Affairs," Francis A. Truslow (president of the New York Curb Exchange), maintained at the group's first meeting on 5 October 1948.[38] The Democratic Party had displayed little confidence in Truman, nominating him as their second choice for presidential candidate after Dwight D. Eisenhower had declined to run on any ticket. Additionally, the appeal of Strom Thurmond's States' Rights Party and Henry Wallace's Progressive Party to traditional Democratic voters in the south made the victory of Republican candidate Thomas E. Dewey almost certain.[39]

For Dewey, Truslow wanted to develop guidelines for a future United States Latin America policy. By 15 December, Truslow suggested, a small working group should draft a position paper for the administra-

37. Dickey to George Franklin, 17 March 1948, and enclosed excerpts from Dickey to Dean Acheson, n.d., PG/RGCFR-XXIVD. On 16 March, the Department of Justice had announced that it considered, based on a law enacted in 1919, declining to issue visa to members of Communist parties and deporting all foreign Communists already residing in the U.S. (of which quite a few were Italians). On 15 March, and later confirming this statement on 19 March, the State Department announced that Marshall Plan aid would not be granted to Italy if the Communists won the elections. See Miller, "Taking Off the Gloves," 48–49; Gaddis, *Strategies*, 67.

38. DD, 5 October 1948, 1, IAA/RGCFR-XXVIIB.

39. See Eric F. Goldman's lively depiction of that episode in *The Crucial Decade – and After: America, 1945–1960* (New York, 1960; Vintage Books Edition), 82–90.

tion that would ensure a well-coordinated and effective foreign policy vis-à-vis Latin American countries within a month. The Truman administration, Truslow maintained, had neglected this region by focusing its efforts on the main theaters of the Cold War. Additionally, discord and clashes within the different agencies and indifference among the members of Congress had hampered the establishment of a defensive alliance for the whole continent, an alliance Truslow regarded as compulsory.[40]

As with the political group, the discussion soon turned to a debate on the subject of an ethical versus a pragmatic U.S. foreign policy. Adolf A. Berle (assistant secretary of state for Latin America under Roosevelt and ambassador in Brazil until 1946), arguing for a well-defined policy, lamented that "[o]ne week the United States loves democracy and the next it kisses Peron on both checks [*sic*]. A long term basis," Berle claimed, "is needed and a philosophical and ethical thesis as well." Spruille Braden (former American ambassador to Argentina and assistant secretary of state for Latin American affairs until June of 1947), like Berle a critic of Argentine dictator Peron, even maintained that "[w]hatever the United States does and whatever be its policies it must be ethical."[41]

Nelson A. Rockefeller, a pragmatic politician, exhibited little enthusiasm for these idealistic thoughts. He argued that Latin American politicians and peoples were unable to distinguish between politics and emotions and had to be wooed emotionally by the United States. "If these people can be won over emotionally," he argued, "then perhaps they can be sold on private enterprise . . . we needn't pull any punches as to what it is that we have to sell . . . we have to sell capitalism, and we must sell it against a current which works against us all over the world." William S. Swingle of the National Foreign Trade Council described the major task of the group's discussion for a structured Latin American policy in even more grandiose terms: "Our main objective is to give guiding thoughts to government in order to preserve American security, private enterprise, and our way of life."[42]

Subgroups of the study group on "Inter-American Affairs," established to research specific topics, produced more than 47 memoranda the following few weeks, which were discussed at study group meetings.

40. See also Chester J. Pach, Jr., "The Containment of Military Aid to Latin America, 1944–1949," *Diplomatic History* 6 (Summer 1982): 241–43.

41. DD, 5 October 1948, 2, 4–6, IAA/RGCFR-XXVIIB. See also Pollard, *Economic Security*, 209–213.

42. DD, 13 October 1948, 11, 12, IAA/RGCFR-XXVIIB.

Alas, they never reached the person they were intended for: Thomas Dewey lost the election.

Despite Truman's reelection, Truslow decided to continue the study group. During a special last meeting, on 13 June 1949, the chairman proudly announced that group member Edward G. Miller, Jr., had been named the new assistant secretary of inter-american affairs. Edward Miller could have learned from his three predecessors at that post—Rockefeller, Berle, and Braden—who where among the group's members. However, attorney Miller had participated at only one of the group's meetings. Even on that occasion, his questions and contributions had been rather unimportant. Additionally, Truslow could not even supply Miller with a memorandum summarizing the group's work; the group members had not been able to agree on a concept of future United States policy toward Latin America.[43]

Too little attention had been paid to what Percy Bidwell had said at the first meeting of that group—a statement that could have been applied to most of the study and discussion groups: ". . . experience at the Council has shown that general discussions of basic policy are very time-consuming and seldom lead anywhere."[44]

By December 1950, the Council had come a long way from discussing the best possible means of achieving a peaceful and mutually agreeable modus vivendi with America's ally, the Soviet Union, in an open world where problems could be solved cooperatively within the structure of the United Nations organization. This attitude changed rapidly as the Cold War developed. At the end of 1950, the "Aid to Europe" group, led by Eisenhower, thus submitted a memorandum to the President of the United States that read almost like a call for general mobilization. Within these five years, the internationalism the Council members had advocated had been displaced by an ideological isolationism.

Some of the old-timers at the Council may have thought back to their efforts in the wake of World War I, when their aspirations had been to achieve peace and prosperity for the whole world through discussion and mediation. At that time their ideals did not have to comply with the reality of the political, military, and economic world power the

43. DD, 17 November 1948, 1, IAA/RGCFR-XXVIIB; CFR, *Annual Report, 1948–1949*, 29; dinner meeting, 13 June 1949, RMCFR-XIV; DD, 13 October 1948, IAA/RGCFR-XXVIIB. Miller had been with Sullivan & Cromwell, the same law firm to which the Dulles brothers belonged.

44. DD, 5 October 1948, 7, IAA/RGCFR-XXVIIB.

United States would become after World War II. That war, a battle against an inhumane aggressor fought with the entire might of American industrial and human potential, opened the way for the "second chance" for international cooperation for which the founders of the Council had struggled. Only five years after they had set out, though, optimistic and full of energy to achieve lasting world peace, American troops were again fighting on foreign soil and a Cold War was developing that could, quite easily, turn into Armageddon.

7
Managing the Public:
"And Our Ideas Will Control the World"[1]

The Council on Foreign Relations, it is noted in all of its publications, "takes no stand, expressed or implied, on American foreign policy."[2] Although influencing the public to achieve a better American foreign policy was one of the tasks the Council set out to accomplish at its foundation in 1921, the CFR as such maintained a strictly non-partisan attitude.

Repeatedly, however, Council members led presumably spontaneously formed "ad-hoc citizens' committees" to support the executive branch in an ongoing foreign policy. Most of these committees were formed — in sharp contrast to what was officially proclaimed — at the initiative of, and after consultation and constant informational exchange with, State Department officials. Members of the Council, frequently in collaboration with members of other foreign affairs organizations, then claimed the necessity of a certain policy and tried to convince Congress and the broader public of the urgency and significance of that policy.

The activities of the Non-Partisan Committee for Revision of the Neutrality Act (NPC), the Committee to Defend America by Aiding the Allies (CDA), and the Committee for the Marshall Plan to Aid European Recovery (CMP), therefore, should actually be considered as case studies of "private" political involvement of individual Council members rather than as the official activities of the Council itself. However, in all three committees, the strikingly high number of prominent Council members who participated and their positions and influence within the Council does not allow one to regard such participation as merely "private" functioning.

1. Council member Arthur W. Page to Henry K. Cheesen, 27 October 1947, Arthur W. Page Papers, box 16, State Historical Society of Wisconsin. Page, son of American ambassador Walter Hines Page, wrote these words during his participation at the activities of the Committee for the Marshall plan.

2. For an example, see Ellis, *Economics of Freedom*, iv.

Advocating Belligerency

Participation by Council members in propaganda operations, intended to foster a more active American foreign policy, originated at the beginning of World War II, in 1939, when the Council organized the War and Peace Studies. At that time it was not only the international political and economic scene seemed imminently threatened by Japan's, Italy's, and Nazi Germany's aggressive foreign policies; for the longer duration, these policies also posed a threat to the national security of the United States. Organizations were founded with the intent of establishing a broad political basis for a more determined American foreign policy capable of dealing with the hostile situations developing in Europe, Northern Africa, and Asia. Council members were highly influential in the formation and operation of the Non-Partisan Committee, the Fight For Freedom group (FFF), and the Committee to Defend America.

At that time many internationalist groups not only advocated the establishment of a new supranational organization succeeding the League of Nations, but also supported American participation in the developing conflict in Europe. A whole array of different but very often closely inter-connected groups and sub-groups fought against what they termed the "isolationist bloc" and the "Nye-Coughlin crowd."[3]

Contrary to what was officially proclaimed, these organizations cooperated closely with the administration. They were, to a large degree, led by the same group of men, featuring what has been termed an overlapping membership and an interlocking of officers.[4] At the same time, however, these organizations also reflected the diversity of opinion among internationalists. Some of these setups, such as the Century Group and the Fight for Freedom Incorporation, were advocating American involvement in the war and even belligerency. Others, among them the League of Nations Association, the Non-Partisan Committee for Peace Through the Revision of Neutrality Legislation, and the Com-

3. Thomas W. Lamont to General Watson (for the President [Roosevelt]) 22 September 1939, Lamont Papers, box 127. Senator Gerald P. Nye (Republican of North Dakota) had investigated the munitions industry and international banking. The findings of that investigation, although not conclusive, had led to neutrality legislation. Father Charles E. Coughlin of Michigan had been a vocal isolationist. For the isolationist movement, see Wayne S. Cole, *Roosevelt and the Isolationists, 1932–45* (Lincoln, NB, 1983).

4. For a discussion of the interlocking of officers, see Thomas R. Dye, et al., "Concentration, Specialization, and Interlocking Among Institutional Elites," *Social Science Quarterly* 54 (March 1973): 8–29. For the term overlapping membership, see Robert A. Dahl, *Dilemmas of Pluralist Democracy: Autonomy vs. Control* (New Haven, CT, 1982); and David B. Truman, *The Governmental Process* (New York, 1951).

mittee to Defend America by Aiding the Allies, to name just the most important of these organizations, had actually evolved from a "hopelessly divided" peace-movement.[5]

Only one week after Nazi Germany had invaded Poland, Council member Clark Eichelberger, the chairperson of the League of Nations Association, met with President Roosevelt. They discussed, among other topics, American neutrality and the problem of public and Congressional opinion on this issue. More then a year before that meeting, in May of 1938 — after the German seizure of Austria and in face of the developing Sudeten-Crisis — Eichelberger had already offered Secretary of State Cordell Hull help in "developing public opinion." Now, during his conference with the President, Eichelberger affirmed that he and his friends were anxious to support the government in its campaign for a revision of neutrality legislation.[6]

When the government had established its course of action in this matter, President Roosevelt directed the State Department to call on Eichelberger for support. Thus, on 19 September 1939, Eichelberger consulted with State Department official Joseph C. Green concerning a special ad hoc committee for arousing vocal public support for the government initiative. In their discussion of possible individuals to head such a committee, Green recommended a Republican from the Midwest: William Allen White, the well-known writer and editor of the Emporia *Gazette*.[7]

Eichelberger contacted White a week later, on 26 September 1939, but White was not enthusiastic. Eichelberger sent him an outline of the proposed committee, but with White still "slipping", Eichelberger even had to travel to White's home in Kansas to persuade him. Reporting to Adolf A. Berle of the State Department on 28 September 1939, Eichelberger wrote that he had only tentative acceptance from White. Finally, after being convinced that the money backing the organization would not come from "international banking and munitions money,"

5. One of the leading internationalists, Clark M. Eichelberger, used this phrase to explain the confused situation in his meeting with President Roosevelt on 7 September 1939. See Eichelberger, *Organizing*, 104. Part of this subchapter is a revised version of Michael Wala, "Advocating Belligerency: Organized Internationalism 1939–1941," *Amerikastudien / American Studies* 38 (Spring 1993): 49–59. See also Walter Johnson, *The Battle Against Isolationism* (Chicago, 1944).

6. Eichelberger to Cordell Hull, 5 May 1938, Eichelberger Papers, box 103.

White agreed to head the Non-Partisan Committee for Peace Through the Revision of Neutrality Legislation.[8]

If the J.P. Morgan Bank is considered "international banking" — which can safely be done — then White was at least partially misled. The funds for this Non-Partisan Committee, no doubt, came from private individuals. But J.P. Morgan partner Thomas W. Lamont was a key figure behind Eichelberger. In frequent communications with the White House staff, with President Roosevelt, with Eichelberger, and with other internationalists, Council member Lamont had coordinated the effort to gain public and Congressional support for a revision of neutrality legislation.[9]

Returning to New York City from his visit to White, Eichelberger established the headquarters of the new committee at the offices of the Union for Concerted Peace Efforts. Immediately telegrams were sent out, inviting prominent citizens to join. A few days later, more than 260 men and women had accepted membership in the Non-Partisan Committee "created for the special purpose of educating and mobilizing public opinion throughout the country." Utilizing the media, the Committee printed and distributed leaflets, sponsored daily news spots, sent telegrams to newspaper and magazine editors, and organized press conferences and radio broadcasts.[10]

The Committee's work was financed by a number of private citizens and various non-governmental organizations. An industrialist from Pittsburgh, for example, gave $1,300, the American Union donated $690, and Henry R. Luce of *Time/Life* contributed $500. Donations, $100 each, were received from former Secretary of State Henry L. Stimson, internationalist Republican Wendell Willkie, and Texas cotton broker William L. Clayton. The Committee was thus successful in collecting more than $8,000 during the few weeks it was operational.[11]

When it became clear that the President's bill to repeal the arms embargo portion of the Neutrality Law would pass Congress at the end

8. Henry A. Atkinson (general secretary of the Church Peace Union) to White, 26 September 1939, Eichelberger Papers, box 103; Eichelberger to Berle, 28 September 1939, *ibid.*; Eichelberger to Lamont, 13 October 1939, Lamont Papers, box 20.

9. Numerous of Lamont's letters to Roosevelt, notes of telephone conversations with the president or his staff, and correspondence with individuals involved in the endeavor can be found in the Lamont Papers, boxes 21, 127, and 137.

10. Telegram, White to James T. Shotwell (president of Columbia University), 29 September 1939, Eichelberger Papers, box 103. See also Johnson, *Battle*, 43–46.

11. "Financial Statement of the Non-Partisan Committee for Peace Through the Revision of Neutrality Law," dated 3 January 1940, Eichelberger Papers, box 98.

of October 1939, the Non-Partisan Committee for Peace had achieved its task and was dissolved. The Committee's chairperson received letters of appreciation from Secretary Hull and many others. President Roosevelt wrote to White: "You did a grand job. It was effective and most helpful." White's contribution, however, was overrated. White himself maintained that the organization had done "a good job, but Lord I had nothing much to do with it except to stand around and look wise." Characterizing himself as "a stuffed shirt," he told Lamont that he "had a few ideas which were well executed by a competent organization which I did not assemble." In fact, a small group of men around Clark Eichelberger had coordinated the committee's work from offices in New York City, providing experienced staff and office space.[12]

The Non-Partisan Committee was only the first instance of this kind of scheme in which Lamont and Eichelberger, prompted by government officials, would launch a campaign in which a prominent individual would serve as official but largely inactive leader. The organization then was basically run by the same outfit that had the previous organization. The renowned Committee to Defend America followed the same pattern.

On 29 April 1940, a luncheon was given to honor William White and to foster the internationalist sentiment. Many prominent citizens and supporters of the Non-Partisan Committee had been invited to this occasion. Present were, among others, former Under Secretary of State Francis L. Polk, Wendell Willkie, Nicholas Murray Butler of the Carnegie Endowment for International Peace, James T. Shotwell, Henry L. Stimson, and Eichelberger. Again, it was Lamont who had conferred with government officials beforehand and who had suggested to the luncheon organizers to make White the guest of honor. The subject most on the minds of the individuals present, according to Clark Eichelberger, was the war in Europe and the prospects of aid to Great Britain. However, no immediate action resulted from this meeting.[13]

After 10 May, when the German army had invaded Luxembourg, the Netherlands, and Belgium, these internationalists were roused into action. White and Eichelberger exchanged telegrams and telephone calls, discussing the organization of a revived committee. On 14 May 1940, the Executive Committee of the League of Nations Association

12. White to Eichelberger, 18 November 1939, Eichelberger Papers, box 98; White to Mrs. Olson (Eichelberger's secretary), 11 November 1939, *ibid.* White to Lamont, 25 November 1939, Lamont Papers, box 137.

13. Eichelberger to Lamont, 7 May 1940, Lamont Papers, box 21; Lamont to General Watson, n.d., Lamont Papers, box 127. See also Eichelberger, *Organizing*, 119–21.

met and authorized "[f]ull cooperation with it [the new committee] on the part of Mr. Eichelberger and the staff." The next day, Lamont called President Roosevelt and received his approval for the outlined program of the Committee to Defend America, as this second "White Committee" was named.[14]

Telegrams, inviting prominent citizens to join, were sent out only two days later and speakers of the committee came out immediately, urging assistance to Britain. Among others, James Conant, president of Harvard University, spoke on a nationwide radio program over CBS. Pointing out the dangers of a Nazi victory, he argued that the release of airplanes and other implements of war to France and Great Britain was urgent. The president of Smith college, Mrs. Dwight Morrow — mother-in-law of well-known and isolationist aviation hero Charles Lindbergh — addressed the public over NBC. As "a first line of defense," she said, British and French soldiers were fighting for the survival of democracy. Additional publicity was created by press conferences, interviews, and newspaper reports about the Committee's establishment and initial efforts.[15]

Just as with the Non-Partisan Committee, the media was utilized, leaflets were printed and distributed, daily news spots were sponsored, telegrams were sent to newspaper and magazine editors, and additional press conferences and radio broadcasts were organized. The greatest success, however, in arousing the public was an advertisement created by former pacifist Robert Sherwood — later to become a speech writer for Roosevelt. After getting the approval to run it as an official Committee ad, the playwright, a supporter of the first "White" committee, arranged for publication in eighteen newspapers with a combined circulation of over seven million for 10 June. Twenty-four additional papers reprinted the "Stop Hitler Now" ad, painting the Nazi threat in very lively colors, free of charge. Through this advertisement, the Committee received additional contributions, new local chapters were created nationwide, and new members joined already existing chapters. When President Roosevelt met the press on 11 June, he had a copy of the ad on his desk. Remarking that he would not like to endorse every phrase, he praised the Committee's actions, stating that it was "a good thing that Bill White was able to get such messages across for the education of the

---

14. Lamont to Roosevelt, 15 May 1940, Lamont Papers, box 127. In his letter Lamont makes references to a telephone conversation he had with Roosevelt the same day.

15. See Eichelberger, *Organizing*, 124; Johnson, *Battle*, 74–81. Charles A. Lindbergh, like Senator Nye, was a prominent member of the isolationist America First committee.

American people."[16] In addition, more than 2 million copies of printed material were distributed from June to October 1940 alone. The Committee arranged for speakers on radio programs and urged prominent citizens to come out in favor of aid to the Allies.[17]

At first the Committee had called only for a general support of the Allies and had favored sending planes, guns, munitions, and food. When later in June the Committee called for the supply of old destroyers to Great Britain, this again had been suggested to Committee leaders by the government. Winston Churchill had asked President Roosevelt to loan "forty or fifty" old destroyers to England on 15 May 1940, and he repeated this request on 11 June. On 29 June William White met with Roosevelt, and the President indicated that the administration was indeed interested in trading destroyers for British naval bases. Accordingly, presentation of the matter to the public was soon being discussed within the Committee and a number of other informal groups.[18]

Eichelberger, informed by White, not only introduced the plan to the staff of the Committee to Defend America, which then put a promotion program into effect, but also discussed the issue with members of the Century Group. This group — among its members Eichelberger, Henry Luce, William Clayton, Allen W. Dulles, and Robert Sherwood — took up the destroyer deal during a couple of meetings in July. The group outlined a strategy to create support for the destroyer deal, which Eichelberger subsequently introduced to the staff of the Committee to Defend America. When doubts were raised that the President by executive order alone could make the destroyer-bases deal, the Committee urged prominent New York lawyers, among them former Under Secretary of the Treasury Dean G. Acheson, to assert this right. Only two days after Roosevelt notified Congress of the completion of the Destroyer Deal, he praised Eichelberger: "You have done a swell job and we are deeply grateful to you."[19]

---

16. Papers reprinting the ad gratis had a combined circulation of about 700,000. See "Stop Hitler Now Ad," dated 20 June 1940, Committee to Defend America by Aiding the Allies Records (hereafter cited as CDAR), box 8, Mudd Manuscript Library. The "Stop Hitler Now" ad is reproduced in Johnson, *Battle*, 86.

17. "Summary of Promotion Material Distributed," dated October 1940, CDAR, box 8.

18. Johnson, *Battle*, 91; Winston S. Churchill, *Their Finest Hour* (London, 1949), 23.

19. The Century Group was named after its meeting place, the Century Club, New York. For an account of this organization, see Mark L. Chadwin, *The Warhawks: American Interventionists Before Pearl Harbor* (New York, 1970). White worried that this setup was "likely to get us in trouble." See White to Lamont, 10 December 1940, Lamont Papers, box 21. Eichelberger, *Organizing*, 131–34, 137.

A similar strategy was used with such issues as torpedo boats, flying fortresses, and lend-lease. Government officials again suggested these specific topics for the public education campaign. But vital for the Committee to actually initiate action was Roosevelt's approval. "I never did anything the President didn't ask for, and I always conferred with him on our program," William White said.[20]

With the United States' position shifting from neutral to non-neutral non-belligerent, the Committee was pursuing a course of demanding ever-increasing aid to Britain. The Committee was actually gradually moving toward advocating active involvement in the war, although this was not the policy favored by White. Discord within the Committee to Defend America evolved, and the overlapping membership of some of its officers with other organizations led to friction with the chairperson.

Some members of the Committee affiliated with the Century group had already in June 1940 called for a declaration of war against Germany. One of them, John L. Balderston — before that best known for writing the script for the 1931 movie *Frankenstein* — later was to head the Committee's confidential news service. On 5 September 1940, he outlined the Committee's program by issuing a call for the supply of tanks, planes, and ships to Britain. William White repudiated this program as soon as it was published, but Balderston, protected by Eichelberger, could continue to serve in his position. When other Committee leaders indicated that White's moderate plan of action was not in accord with reality and argued that no one would be able to guarantee that the United States could avoid active military involvement, White accused them of "ghost-dancing for war."[21]

The confrontation between the moderate White and his Committee became unsurmountable when New York mayor Fiorello LaGuardia, in December 1940, criticized White in an open letter. He accused White of giving too little support to the Allied cause and suggested dividing the Committee to Defend America into one Committee of words, which White could then go on to lead, and one Committee of deeds. To make the insult perfect, the New York chapter made LaGuardia its honorary chairperson. When some influential members threatened to resign and urged White to step down, he left the Committee later that year.[22]

20. Quoted in Johnson, *Battle* 91.

21. Copy, White to Frederic R. Coudert, 22 October 1940, Lamont Papers, box 21; White to Lamont, 10 December 1940, *ibid.*; Eichelberger, *Organizing*, 145–50.

22. Minutes of Executive Committee Meeting, 2 January 1941, CDAR, box 9; Eichelberger, *Organizing*, 145-50. The New York chapter had even before that date been out of

During that time the more brash Century group evolved into the Fight for Freedom Incorporation, a somewhat less aggressively interventionist outfit. With more than 200 members from the whole spectrum of American notables — among them Allen Dulles, Katharine Hepburn, Jehudi Menuhin, William Shirer, Kurt Weill, and the Marx Brothers — in December 1940, it maintained that the war against Hitler was also unavoidably an American war.[23]

The Committee to Defend America, after White's resignation, underwent some minor reorganization but did not alter its policy very much. When White's successor retired in May 1941, Clark Eichelberger became chairperson. By July, the Committee's membership exceeded 100,000, it had more than 750 local chapters, and well over $420,000 had been donated to its efforts. These numbers increased further until the Japanese attack on Pearl Harbor, on 7 December 1941, made the Committee's efforts and that of all other such groups unnecessary.[24]

The emergence of outspoken internationalist groups advocating revision of the neutrality legislation and aid to the Allies was by no means haphazard. It was a carefully planned effort, conducted in close cooperation with the Roosevelt administration. The main objective was not to convince the administration to change its policy or even to modify it. In most cases, moreover, these organizations were not citizens' organizations created to vocalize public opinion and sentiment.

Their cooperation with the Department of State and other governmental agencies was very close from the very outset and the two major groups mentioned were even created upon governmental suggestion. Their main task was to convince public and Congress that Americans could not stand aside in the war, that the United States had to help defeat Nazi Germany. Through professional guidance and organization

---

step with White's restrained advocacy of American aid. In late October White wrote to Coudert: "[I]f you know of any way short of assassination to shut up that New York Committee and make them get in step with the national organization, I'll be deeply and eternally grateful to you." See copy, White to Coudert, 22 October 1940, Lamont Papers, box 21. In December, Coudert was one of the first to propose that White should step down from his position. See Coudert to Lamont, 24 December 1940, *ibid.*

23. Fight for Freedom Inc., *What is the Fight for Freedom?: The Story of the First Six Months of the Fight for Freedom Committee* (New York, n.d [1940]), 4, 10, 15. A copy of the report can be found in Fight For Freedom Records, box 21, Mudd Manuscript Library. See also Chadwin, *Warhawks*, 159–263.

24. "Comptroller's Daily Cash Report," dated 18 July 1941, CDAR, box 9. See also Johnson, *Battle*, 179–202.

by experienced staff and officers from pro-League organizations, these ad hoc organizations had considerable influence on the public and Congressional attitude. Its members represented a variety of personal convictions, and came from peace organizations, pro-League groups, and from the membership of the Council on Foreign Relations.

Almost all of the members of the groups mentioned, between 1939 and 1941, slowly turned toward a more interventionist stance — some of them even openly advocating belligerency — when no shadow of doubt remained that no means short of war and American all-out aid would stop the German war-machine and its drive to crush all of Europe. Thomas Lamont, the man behind the man-behind-the-scenes Clark Eichelberger, was a realist. He was clear in his judgment about American involvement in the war. In retrospect he argued that the United States

> went to war because war was made upon her and because she came to the belated realization that Germany intended to conquer all Europe and Japan all Asia, and between them to squeeze the Americas into their own economic pattern. It was just as simple as that. That is what we are fighting for today.[25]

This should not be misinterpreted as a "cynical Wall Street remark." His evaluation was not all that far away from what President Roosevelt said in his famous "Arsenal of Democracy" address in 1940, when he cautioned that Americans "would be living at the point of a gun — a gun loaded with explosive bullets, economic as well as military."[26] Lamont, in his letter to Clark Eichelberger, went on to say:

> If we win the fight, then indeed we want to do everything we can to create the better world that we talk about. But don't let us delude ourselves into thinking that American parents are sending their sons to be slaughtered across the Atlantic and the Pacific in order to free native people or to create better worlds.[27]

But he wrote this in January 1943, more than a year after the Japanese attack on Pearl Harbor had left no avenue of non-belligerency open for the United States.

---

25. Lamont to Eichelberger, 17 January 1943, Lamont Papers, box 19.
26. Roosevelt's broadcasted fireside chat is reprinted in Thomas G. Paterson, ed., *Major Problems in American Foreign Policy: Volume II, Since 1914* (Lexington, MA, 1978), 130–33.
27. Lamont to Eichelberger 17 January 1943, Lamont Papers, box 19.

Membership, internal structure, and financial and organizational planning of the above-mentioned setups displayed such remarkable parallels that one must refer to a unified undertaking. Although the Council did not directly support these groups, proponents such as Clark Eichelberger, Henry Stimson, Robert Patterson, and Dean Acheson could at least count on the support of most Council members and rely on a pool of notables — in the form of the Council membership — as likely activists and donors. Also, many Council members were simultaneously associated with other internationalist organizations such as the American Association for the United Nations (AAUN), the Carnegie Endowment for International Peace (CEIP), and the Committee for Concerted Peace Efforts. A network of organizations existed that, despite differences in membership and tasks, was willing to actively support political measures of the Roosevelt and later the Truman administration.

The expertise of the members of these organizations predestined them to foster a global international order for the post-war world. This system should pay tribute to the increased importance the United States would acquire after the war, and it was to reproduce societal and economic structures of the United States in the global arena. Their efforts to induce the United States to play a more active role in world affairs was especially obvious when the Committee for the Marshall Plan (CMP) tried to convince Congress and the public of the advantages and necessity of a costly economic emergency program for Europe. The structure, activities, and the influence of the CMP resembled those of the NPC, FFF, and CDA, and the primary protagonists of that particular ad hoc committee were again almost exclusively members of the Council on Foreign Relations.

The Selling of the Marshall Plan

Shortly after Secretary Marshall's speech at Harvard University on 5 June 1947, the members of the Council on Foreign Relations and many other organizations realized that the State Department would face severe difficulties in launching promotional activities to market the Marshall Plan.[28] State Department officials themselves recognized and expected complications in securing American aid to Europe. William Benton, assistant secretary of state for public affairs and responsible for public relations,

28. This part is a revised and extended version of Michael Wala, "Selling the Marshall Plan at Home: The Committee for the Marshall Plan to Aid European Recovery," *Diplomatic History* 10 (Summer 1986): 247–65.

knew of these difficulties. He wrote to Laird Bell, lawyer and member of the Chicago Council on Foreign Relations, that decisive measures from the State Department to prepare the public should not be expected. He reminded Bell that it was "illegal" for the State Department to use public funds "for the purpose of influencing Congress." This task, he indicated, had "to fall on everyone who takes an intelligent interest in foreign affairs."[29]

Members of the New York Council were informed in similar fashion during the meetings of the study group "Public Opinion and Foreign Policy." State Department officials who took part in a study group meeting admitted that "*planned* public relations" work had ceased and that the Department was in a state of "confusion regarding the Marshall Plan." Secretary Marshall had ordered his press staff to refrain from providing detailed information to the press since the plan was not yet ready for public discussion; but, above all, Marshall feared a storm of protest against the high costs of the European Recovery Program.[30]

Some members of Congress were equally concerned about the insufficient capabilities of the State Department to launch an effective promotion and influence public opinion. Responding to a letter by Clark Eichelberger, the chairman of the influential Senate Committee on Foreign Affairs, Arthur H. Vandenberg, expressed his doubts. In June 1947 Vandenberg wrote: "I certainly do not take it for granted that the American public is ready for such burdens as would be involved" in providing assistance to Europe. This would remain a problem, he reflected, "until it is far more efficiently demonstrated to the American people that this (1) is in the latitude of their own available resources and (2) serves their intelligent self-interest."[31]

State Department officials had feared before Secretary Marshall gave his speech on 5 June, that the American people would consider a relief program a too generous gift to the European countries. At a meeting of the heads of State Department officers on 28 May 1947, Dean G.

29. William Benton to Laird Bell, 12 August 1947, Records of the Assistant Secretary of State for Public Affairs, box 12, National Archives, Record Group 59, Washington, D.C. (hereafter cited as ASPA). The Chicago Council was not affiliated with the New York Council.

30. DD, 25 September 1947, POFP/RGCFR-XXIIIA. Harold Stein Interview, Harry B. Price Interview Project, Truman Library.

31. Eichelberger to Vandenberg, 24 June 1947, Eichelberger Papers, box 20; Vandenberg to Eichelberger, 25 June 1947, *ibid.* This letter is also cited in Arthur H. Vandenberg, Jr., ed., *The Private Papers of Senator Vandenberg* (Boston, 1952), 381.

Acheson, then under secretary of state, had pointed out that publicity for the aid plan was necessary and that the administration itself was eager to create machinery for "intensive public education on the Marshall Plan."[32]

William Benton, in particular, was concerned about the immense task. He was aware, as he had written to Bell, that the State Department was not permitted to use tax dollars to influence Congress directly. Disregarding this restriction, however, he had his office conceive designs for a propaganda organization which would be seemingly independent of, but responsive to, State Department advice and suggestions. After initial discussions the director of the Office of Public Affairs, Francis H. Russell, drafted guidelines for a "Citizens Committee." He suggested potential members for the committee and discussed various areas in which they could operate.[33] Dean Acheson's successor in the position of under secretary, Robert A. Lovett, approved of Russell's general ideas but refused to follow up on the specific proposals to institute a citizens' committee. Probably fearful of a leak, Lovett advised Benton to recall and destroy all but the master copy of Russell's memorandum.[34]

One month later, no decisive action had been taken by the Department, and interested parties outside the government became increasingly aware that the existing information process was insufficient. Benton wrote to Marshall and Lovett on 19 September that "sharp criticism from the public — both from political and other leaders, and from the press — saying that the government is not supplying the necessary information to obtain understanding of the European economic crisis" was being raised with increasing frequency. Unpublished opinion polls, he continued, "indicate that only an insignificant minority of the American people have the remotest understanding of the 'Marshall proposal,' let alone have heard of it."[35]

---

32. Bohlen, *Witness*, 264; "Summary of Discussion," 29 May 1947, *FRUS, 1947*, 3: 235; Howland H. Sargeant (special assistant to Benton) to Benton, 12 August 1947, ASPA, box 3.

33. Office Memorandum, Swihard (special assistant to the director, Office of Public Affairs, Russell) to Sargeant, 26 August 1947, ASPA, box 3. Thomas J. Watson of IBM, H. J. Heinz II, of Heinz Corporation, and former ambassador to Great Britain John G. Winant, were among those suggested as members of the committee. Ira Mosher, president of the National Association of Manufacturers, was considered a potential candidate for the position of chairperson. See Benton to Sargeant, 28 August 1947, *ibid.*

34. Sargeant to Benton, 12 August 1947, *Secret*, ASPA, box 3; typescript addition, Sargeant to Benton, 12 August 1947, signed "l.g.," *ibid.* Unfortunately, the master copy of the memorandum could not be located at the National Archives.

35. Office Memorandum, "Subject: Information Program Concerning European Reconstruction Problem," Benton to Lovett and Secretary Marshall, 19 September 1947,

Opinions

Common ignorance and the dire state of public relations efforts during the following months were difficult problems for the State Department. Marshall, Acheson, Kennan, Clayton, and other State Department officials, who assembled on 28 May for a meeting in the State Department, had realized that the situation in Europe called for a quick implementation of the recovery program.

As a result of the war, many World War II belligerents could not easily return their industries to peace-time production to help accelerate the reconstruction of the domestic economy. Many plants had been casualties of the war, and the previously well-developed network of interdependent domestic and international markets had broken down completely. Besides the economic disaster, a severe winter and heavy rainfall during spring 1947 destroyed any hope of a sufficient harvest. The depressing and hopeless situation in Germany and Austria had turned to fatalism among the population. George F. Kennan pointed out the desperate situation in his report of 23 May. An economic relief measure by the United States, he argued, elevating the spirit of the European population, was essential and urgent. The Central Intelligence Agency (CIA) had warned since September 1945 of an increase in communist parties' influence throughout Europe and had thus added to the general understanding that actions were necessary to prevent Western Europe from falling under Soviet control.[36]

The desire for rapid appropriations for the Marshall Plan was tempered by previous experiences with a money-tight Congress. Since the election of 1946 the Republican Party, traditionally known for its fiscal conservatism, had gained a majority in both houses of Congress. When Democratic President Truman requested money for military and economic aid to Greece and Turkey in March of that year, Congress consented only after the administration and proponents of the measure had convincingly depicted the potentially menacing alternative. Anti-Soviet rhetoric alone, however, could not be used in support of the Marshall Plan. To openly exclude the Soviet Union and the East European countries from the pro-

---

ASPA, box 3. Benton's definition of the term "public," namely "political and other leaders, and . . . the press" is emblematic of the views of State Department officials.

36. Telegram, William L. Clayton (from Paris) to State Department, July 1947, cited in Fred L. Pern, "UNRRA: Fifth Council Session at Geneva," Department of State, *Bulletin* 17 (1947), 250; Trevor Barnes, "The Secret Cold War: The CIA and American Foreign Policy in Europe, 1946–1956," pt. 1, *Historical Journal* 24.2 (1981): 399–415.

jected relief program from the very outset, would not be in the interest of the policy makers. Such an exclusion would imply that the United States was responsible for the partition of Germany and Europe. With the prerequisites the United States proposed for participation in the aid program, however, the Soviet Union was very likely to decline participation, and the burden of the division could easily be shifted onto the USSR.

This strategy had some drawbacks, however, because Congress was of an anti-Soviet disposition. Marshall, Bohlen, Kennan and other high-ranking officials correctly feared that Congress would be reluctant to appropriate money for such an expensive program if it included (even if only on paper) the Soviet Union and Eastern Europe. To win time in Congress, Marshall ordered his press staff to refrain from disseminating detailed information about his proposal, and only sparse information reached the public. Although the administration was aware of the importance of the proposition, it renounced the usual extensive press briefings and played down the importance of Marshall's famous speech. Without any additional publicity Marshall's Harvard speech was released to the press on 4 June.[37]

Acheson indicated as early as 28 May the general need for publicity work, and when by the end of June Kennan dealt with the problem again in a different context, he wrote to Marshall that the Communist movement could be further weakened by an economic relief program that received "strong internal support." The "principal communist argument [is that the] U.S. public and Congress will not pack [*sic*] up a program of aid to Europe," Kennan elaborated, in a fashion similar to that in which Vandenberg had already explicated this circumstance to Eichelberger in June.[38]

Contemporary opinion polls — regularly monitored and summarized by the Office of Public Affairs in the State Department — added to the concern that significant protest might be inevitable.[39] In May

37. Marshall gave "strict orders throughout the Department of State, particularly in the press section, that there was no publicity at all given to his speech," Bohlen wrote in his memoirs. See *Witness*, 264. Also in Bohlen, *Transformation*, 89; and Charles E. Bohlen Oral History, 6, John F. Dulles Oral History Project, Mudd Manuscript Library.

38. "Memorandum prepared by the Policy Planning Staff," (Margin note: GFK Notes for Secretary Marshall 7-21-47), 21 July 1947, *FRUS, 1947*, 3: 335–36.

39. "Public Opinion Concerning European Recovery Plan," Office Memorandum, Russell to Carter (Marshall's advisor), 26 December 1947, Decimal File 840.50, National Archives, RG 59.

1947 the Survey Research Center of the University of Michigan conducted a national poll to study the public's reaction to military and economic aid to Greece and Turkey and came to some surprising results. Although three out of four persons surveyed supported the appropriation of money for war-torn countries, 70 percent of the supporters wanted conditions attached to economic aid. Phrases like "only a small amount," "if it goes to the right countries," and "if we can afford it" were repeatedly mentioned. And although Truman had painted the Communist threat quite colorfully in his speech, only 28 percent favored the support of countries "attacked by communists."[40]

Public opinion proved even more reluctant with respect to military and economic aid, specific features of the Truman Doctrine. Only eleven percent of those questioned supported military aid to Greece. Plain economic aid was generally favored over military assistance. Arguments such as "they need help," "we are able to help them," "it is a humanitarian . . . thing to do," "it will prevent war," or "it will enable them to trade with us," were often supported. Fewer than three percent of those who favored American support of Greece and Turkey generally approved of such reasons as "it will keep Russia from being the sole influence in Europe" and "it will develop democracy."[41]

Although Marshall's speech was in accord with the mood of the population, officials in the State Department operated very carefully. The Secretary of State was concerned that his proposals could be considered a "Santa Claus offer" and that in the "isolationist Midwest" a storm of protest might break loose.[42] However, Marshall's proposals were formulated in terms so general that almost every national organization could identify with his suggestion, and, although the accord of the national groups began to deteriorate when the details of economic foreign aid were discussed, most of them favored the Marshall Plan.[43]

40. Survey Research Center – University of Michigan, *Public Attitudes Toward American Foreign Policy: A Nationwide Study* (Ann Arbor, 1947), pt. 1, fig. 1, 20. Similar results are reported in "Report on Opinion: The American Majority Man: He is a Reluctant Internationalist . . . ," *Newsweek*, 4 August 1947, 32–33.

41. Survey Research Center, *Public Attitudes*, pt. 1, fig. 2; *ibid.*, pt. 2, 14.

42. Bohlen, *Witness*, 264.

43. Information on the attitude of national organizations on the Marshall Plan is taken from "Position of American National Organizations on the European Recovery-Program," 19 February 1948, Committee for the Marshall Plan, Files and Minutes, box 2, Truman Library (hereafter cited as CMPR); and Office Memorandum, Russell to Carter, 26 December 1947.

Industrial associations such as the U.S. Junior Chamber of Commerce, the National Foreign Trade Council, and the Committee for Economic Development were among the most important such organizations unequivocally supporting Marshall's proposals. Favoring the general terms of the Marshall Plan, the influential National Association of Manufacturers suggested shipping goods and merchandise instead of money to needy countries. Additionally, the Association argued, a sound currency had to be established and price controls should be suspended before any U.S. aid was provided. The U.S. Chamber of Commerce favored an aid program in which industries supported their counterparts overseas and which would be led by "outstanding leaders" of the business community. All associations agreed, however, that a program managed by the government was not very promising.[44]

A few business magazines adhering to a more narrow and domestic view of industry and trade opposed the European Recovery Program. They considered the domestic American economy to be of primary, if not sole, importance. These magazines depicted Europe as economically "finished" and argued that investments were of better use in the United States. Generally, opponents of the ERP were those business people who were not categorically opposed to trading with European countries but had general doubts about the efficiency of government programs.[45] The majority of the business community, however, might have agreed with an article in *Business Week* that argued that "industry in this country can no longer prosper with the non-Communist world suffering post-war paralysis." The author advised the business community to convince Congress that the Marshall Plan would benefit the economic well-being of both the United States and Europe.[46]

The three national agricultural associations favored the Marshall Plan and only the Farmer's Union, which had already contested the Truman Doctrine, argued in favor of a recovery program under the control of the

44. The position of the Committee on Economic Development is clearly outlined in Paul G. Hoffman's (at the time still president of Studebaker Corp.) elaborations in Senate, *Hearings on the United States Assistance to European Economic Recovery*, 848–49. For the attitude of the National Association of Manufacturers and Chamber of Commerce, see Office Memorandum, Russell to Carter, December 26, 1947, 12–16. Minutes of Meeting (hereafter cited as MM), 11 December 1947, CMPR, box 2. See also *Newsweek*, 9 June 1947.

45. Helen H. Miller, "Congress and European Recovery," *Virginia Quarterly Review*, 25 (1949): 49; Robert J. Chasteen, "American Foreign Aid and Public Opinion, 1945–1952" (Ph.D. diss., University of North Carolina, 1958), 239–45; Arthur Page to Representative Christian Herter (D-MA), 24 November 1947, Page Papers, box 16.

46. *Business Week*, 1 November 1947, 9.

United Nations. National Grange and the American Farm Bureau unswervingly supported the administration's plans for economic aid to Europe.[47]

American labor organizations approved of the government's foreign aid policies. The Congress of Industrial Organizations (CIO), in the midst of an internal power struggle between right-wing and left-wing factions within the union, declared itself in favor of a foreign aid program without referring directly to the ERP. The more conservative American Federation of Labor (AFL) explicitly championed the Marshall Plan. While the unions generally voted in favor of relief aid, organizations from the political left — Progressive Citizens of America and the American Labor Party — followed in the line of Henry Wallace and warned of possible dangers of implementing the Marshall Plan (including a possible partition of Europe and the risk of a third world war).[48]

National organizations with an internationalist inclination, such as Americans for Democratic Action, the American Association for the United Nations, and the Society for the Prevention of World War III,[49] advocated the ERP. No women's associations, veterans' organizations, or religious groups rebuked the Marshall Plan.[50]

As elaborated in previous chapters, the Council on Foreign Relations had participated in the post-war planning of the United States and had helped in the preparations of the Marshall Plan. Allen W. Dulles in his essay in the April 1947 issue of *Foreign Affairs* had summarized the Council members' opinions and had publicly stressed some time before 5 June both the necessity of economic aid and Germany's importance to European reconstruction. Other groups with tasks and goals similar to those of the Council also conducted discussions and workshops on the subject of post-war problems. The Foreign Policy Association, to name but one

47. Regarding the position of the National Farmer's Union, see Chasteen, "American Foreign Aid," 246; and Senate, *Hearings on United States Assistance to European Economic Recovery*, 926–33. For the National Grange, see Office Memorandum, Russell to Carter, 26 December, 1947, 1. On the American Farm Bureau, see House, *Hearings on United States Foreign Policy for a Post-War Recovery Program*, 940–60.

48. Office Memorandum, Russell to Carter, 26 December 1947, 2. For critiques from the political left, see James S. Allen, *Marshall Plan – Recovery or War?* (New York, 1948), and Joseph Starobin, *Should Americans Back the Marshall Plan?* (New York, 1948).

49. For details on these groups, see Lawrence Wittner, *Rebels Against War: The American Peace Movement, 1941–1960* (New York, 1969).

50. Office Memorandum, Russell to Carter, 26 December 1947; "Position," n.d., CMPR, box 2.

example, had convened a meeting at the Waldorf Astoria Hotel in New York City to discuss the topic "Germany: Keystone to European Peace."[51]

Public opinion differed dramatically from the views of organized national groups. Polls conducted throughout the general population portrayed a "general apathy of the American people toward foreign affairs." In July 1947, one month after Marshall's speech, not even half of those questioned knew of the plan to aid Europe. A representative poll was conducted by the American Institute of Public Opinion (AIPO) in October 1947. It revealed that more than half of those who knew little or nothing about the Marshall Plan opposed the ERP. Only 25 percent of the interviewees endorsed an economic aid program at all. Of the 49 percent who had heard of Marshall's proposal to the Europeans, 49 percent of the best-informed, 40 percent of the better informed, and only 34 percent of those "with vague ideas" were convinced of the necessity of the Plan.[52]

One month later, in November, the situation had not changed much, but the population was clearly better informed. By then 61 percent had heard or read of the Marshall Plan, but the same pattern was apparent: people's willingness to support the ERP was directly related to their degree of knowledge. The better informed the interviewees were, the more likely they were to endorse the Plan. Thus, of the 26 percent of persons who were exposed to the Marshall Plan for the first time through the poll, only 39 percent supported the use of twenty billion dollars of tax money to reconstruct Europe.

Also presented in the AIPO questionnaire was the relation between the ERP and the containment of communism. In contrast to a poll that had been conducted immediately after Truman's speech in March, a greater readiness to contain communism was now visible. While just over a quarter of those questioned favored public spending to allow European countries to purchase American merchandise, 47 percent of that same group advocated the development of the Marshall Plan if it could prevent the spread of communism.[53]

---

51. Dulles, "Alternatives for Germany," 432, and footnote, page 421. Brooks Emeny (president of the Foreign Policy Association) to Louis P. Lochner, 26 January 1948, Lochner Papers, box 3.

52. See Markel, *Public Opinion*, 9–11, and the opinion poll in *New York Times*, 4 January 1948, sec. 5, 5–6. Polls conducted until the end of 1947 are summarized in *Public Opinion Quarterly* (Winter 1947/48): 675–76.

53. *Ibid.*, 676. When compared to polls conducted by the Michigan Research Center, this represents a drastic change in opinion. It does, however, reflect the general political

No regional differences in attitude toward the ERP were disclosed by a similar poll conducted by AIPO in February 1948. Although it was considered isolationist, the Midwest did not differ significantly from the national average in opposition or support, knowledge or ignorance of the Plan. Significant discrepancies occurred, however, when the results were evaluated with respect to education and income. Only three percent of those considered "wealthy" but 23 percent of those considered "poor" had never heard or read of the Marshall Plan. Similar results occurred with regard to education: only three percent of college-educated but 29 percent of high school graduates and less-educated persons were not aware of the ERP.[54] The outcome of the polls clearly reaffirmed the interdependency between opinions on political measures and knowledge and information available to the population. The situation was certainly not unique to the Marshall Plan but reflected a basic attitude regarding foreign policy. It was precisely this relationship which offered politicians and representatives of interest groups, eager to "educate" and influence public opinion, an approach for their campaign for the Marshall Plan.

The mood of the public and national organizations was not as fully examined and unraveled by fall 1947 as it was later revealed by these polls, taken in February 1948. Nevertheless, officials in the State Department and members of foreign affairs organizations understood the situation. When in September 1947 two Council members, Clark Eichelberger and Alger Hiss, approached several friends and informed them of their plans to found a national ad hoc organization — comparable to the Non-Partisan Committee and the Committee to Defend America — to support the Marshall Plan, they responded with great interest.

THE COMMITTEE FOR THE MARSHALL PLAN

One month after Secretary of State Marshall's speech at Harvard, in July 1947, Clark Eichelberger had urged the Board of Directors of the AAUN to consider a citizens' committee for public support of the Marshall Plan very similar in design to the one conceived by Benton and his staff in the State Department. Eichelberger, who left for Europe a few days later, could not pursue his plan further until after his return. When he met with several board members on 26 September for lunch, some of

disposition in public opinion and reveals that the positive attitude toward the Soviet Union had been replaced by an attitude of confrontation.

54. Office Memorandum, Russell to Carter, 26 December 1947; Markel, *Public Opinion*, 55; Ralph B. Levering, *The Public and American Foreign Policy, 1918–1978* (New York, 1978), 99.

them had read Henry Stimson's article, "The Challenge to Americans" in the fall issue of *Foreign Affairs.* The former secretary of war had addressed major issues of the post-war world using arguments much like those adopted by Eichelberger and others of the AAUN. He had argued that victory and peace were not synonymous and that "close on the heels of victory has loomed a new world crisis."[55]

The AAUN members were impressed with Stimson's arguments and shared his view that arousing an anti-Communist sentiment was the wrong approach to the international situation. Adding to the existing suspicions toward Moscow would only aggravate the already tense relations between the United States and the Soviet Union. The proposed committee, they reasoned, should therefore stress the political, economic, and humanitarian advantages of the Marshall Plan. Knowing that the former secretary of war was a widely respected public figure, they "thought that Mr. Stimson should be asked to be the chairman of the proposed committee."[56]

After the meeting, Eichelberger phoned his friend and fellow Council member Alger Hiss. Hiss had just been appointed President of the Carnegie Endowment for International Peace and had been a member of the Council study group "Public Opinion and Foreign Policy." Until recently an official in the State Department, he was thought to be interested in organizing the group to promote the foreign aid program. After contacting his former associates at the State Department and talking with staff members from the office of Under Secretary of State for Economic Affairs William L. Clayton, Hiss was sufficiently encouraged to participate in setting up the committee.[57]

On 1 October 1947 Eichelberger and Hiss approached former Secretary of War Robert P. Patterson with their proposal to form a citizens' committee for the Marshall Plan. When they told him that government officials would be grateful for the support, Patterson — like Hiss and

---

55. Minutes of the Board of Directors, AAUN, 23 July 1947, CEIPR #63597; "Titles for Consideration: Support the Marshall Proposal," presented by Hugh Moore, 8 September 1947, Hugh Moore Papers, box 1, Mudd Manuscript Library. Moore was an influential member of the AAUN and had actively participated in the work of the Committee to Defend America. Eichelberger to (former Undersecretary of State) Sumner Welles, 27 September 1947, Eichelberger Papers, box 20; Henry L. Stimson, "The Challenge to Americans," *Foreign Affairs* 25 (Fall 1947): 5–14.

56. Eichelberger to Sumner Welles, 27 September 1947, Eichelberger Papers, box 20; and the attached "Memorandum on Plans for a Committee to Support the 'Marshall Proposals,'" *confidential*, 26 September 1947, *ibid.*

57. Hiss to Eichelberger, 6 October 1947, CEIPR, #63652.

Eichelberger, a member of the Council — was pleased to be asked to serve as chairman of the Executive Committee. Needing only to be reassured of State Department approval, the next day Patterson called Lovett for his views on the proposal. Lovett confirmed that such action would be welcome. When Patterson contacted Secretary of Commerce Averell Harriman, the response was equally positive.[58]

Lovett had another reason to be excited about the prospects of a group of eminent citizens in support of the administration. At the end of September, William Benton had stepped down from his post as assistant secretary of state for public affairs, thus leaving the State Department without leadership when coordinated publicity work for the Marshall Plan was most urgently needed. The search for a successor to Benton turned out to be difficult. Lovett and others within the administration hoped to fill the post with someone who had good contacts with the foreign policy establishment. The post was offered to Arthur W. Page — who was familiar with public relations tasks through previous posts as director of the telecommunications corporation A.T.& T. — and to Council President Allen W. Dulles. To the disappointment of Lovett, both declined the offer with the excuse of too many other obligations. Two other Council members, Frank Altschul and Hamilton Armstrong, received a similar offer to succeed Benton, but these men also declined the bid.[59]

Meanwhile the plans of the citizens' committee were put into action, and the men considered as Benton's possible successors — with the exception of Armstrong — were soon directly integrated into the propaganda work for the Marshall Plan. To follow through with the proposal at the AAUN meeting of 26 September, Hiss and Eichelberger informed Patterson that he should ask Stimson to serve as national chairman of the proposed committee. They told Patterson that Stimson's designation "will inevitably bring forth . . . overwhelming public support."[60]

58. Memorandum, Eichelberger to Robert P. Patterson, 3 October 1947, Patterson Papers, box 41, Library of Congress; Patterson to Stimson, 16 October 1947, *ibid.*, Lovett Daily Log, entry of 2 October 1947.

59. Page to Lovett, 21 October 1947, handwritten note by Marguerite S. Phelps, Page's secretary, Page Papers, box 16; Lovett to Page, 23 October 1947, *ibid.*; Lovett Daily Log, entry of 25 November 1947; Dulles to Lovett, 26 November 1947, *personal and confidential*, Dulles Papers, box 30, in which Dulles is referring to a telephone call by Lovett the previous day. President Truman had suggested Altschul as Benton's potential successor. See handwritten note, signed: "HST," n.d., Charles G. Ross Papers, box 7, Truman Library.

60. Memorandum, Eichelberger to Patterson, 3 October 1947, Patterson Papers, box 41.

To find out whether an attempt to approach the ailing Stimson for the post might be promising, Patterson initially turned to Stimson's confidant Arthur Page. Stimson eventually agreed to take over the chair, but he requested that he not be actively involved in the work. Page became his informal representative at the committee's activities, and although the Committee for the Marshall Plan was later often called the "Stimson Committee," Stimson's only contribution was his name and his article in *Foreign Affairs.* Informing Council member Winthrop W. Aldrich, chairman of the Board of Chase National Bank, about the plans for organizing the committee, Page wrote that this group is a "distinguished propaganda committee" and "you will certainly be asked to join."[61]

After further preparations, Patterson on 28 October 1947 asked fourteen key supporters of the Marshall Plan to attend an organizational meeting at the distinguished Harvard Club in New York two days later. Those invited included Dean Acheson, Winthrop Aldrich, Allen Dulles, Clark Eichelberger, Alger Hiss, Arthur Page, and seven other prominent Council members: William Emerson (president of the AAUN), Herbert Feis (historian and former adviser to the State Department), Herbert H. Lehman (former governor of New York and the first president of the United Nations Relief and Rehabilitation Administration), Frederick C. McKee (industrialist and former treasurer of the Committee to Defend America), Hugh Moore (industrialist and former president of the American Union for Concerted Peace Efforts), Philip D. Reed (director of the board of General Electric Corporation and chairperson of the International Chamber of Commerce), and publicist Herbert B. Swope. All of these men joined the Executive Committee of the CMP, and all except Acheson, Aldrich, and Dulles met on 30 October to organize the "public education committee" that Eichelberger and Hiss had suggested. David Dubinsky, president of the International Ladies Garment Workers Union, and Frank Altschul — who, besides his many other commitments, was vice-president of the National Planning Association — joined the Executive Committee shortly thereafter. The only invitation of a non-Council member went to James B. Carey, secretary-treasurer of the CIO.[62]

61. Page to Patterson, 14 October 1947, Page Papers, box 69; Patterson to Stimson, 16 October 1947, Patterson Papers, box 41; Patterson to Page, 16 October 1947, Patterson Papers, box 69; Stimson to Patterson, 20 October 1947, Patterson Papers, box 41; Memorandum, Page to Winthrop W. Aldrich, 2 October 1947, Page Papers, box 69; Harold Stein Interview, Truman Library.

62. Minutes of Organizing Meeting, 30 October 1947, CMPR, box 2. The text of the telegram can be found in the Acheson Papers, box 3; and in the Herbert Feis Papers, box 30, Library of Congress. In an effort to attract more labor leaders to the Council,

At that initial gathering on 30 October 1947, the committee discussed the scope of its organization as well as fund-raising problems. Eichelberger, having gained experience in this area through his service on the Committee to Defend America and a number of similar groups, submitted an outline of the organizational structure. In addition to an Executive Committee consisting of those invited to the meeting, he proposed the establishment of a general committee of several hundred "representatives of large occupational sections of the population such as farm, labor, business, etc., etc.," selected evenly from all parts of the nation.[63]

Next, addressing the problem of fund-raising, public relations counsel Harold L. Oram suggested that, after sufficient responses arrived to the invitations by telegram to join a general committee, the formation of the CMP should be announced at a press conference. Full-page advertisements would then be placed in the national press, such as the *New York Times*, the New York *Herald Tribune*, and the *Washington Post.* Immediately thereafter, Oram proposed several thousand telegrams soliciting financial support and bearing Stimson's signature be send out to potential donors. As a final step, 100,000 letters containing a reprint of Stimson's article would be mailed out to a more general public, as an appeal for additional support.[64]

As proposed by Oram, advertisements appeared in the three major East Coast newspapers, and telegrams and letters were sent to potential contributors. The advertisements contained parts of Stimson's article in *Foreign Affairs*, the names of the members of the Executive Committee, and a list of almost two hundred members of the National Council, as the general committee of the CMP was now called. In addition, the group circulated a petition for "a million signatures" urging immediate action on Secretary Marshall's proposal. In response, generous contributions started to flow in immediately, continuing without major interruption for the next four months. Although quite often individual donations were only a few dollars, some contributions by wealthy proponents of the Marshall Plan reached amounts ranging from $100 to $2,000.[65]

Carey had been invited in 1946 to become a member. The invitation remained unanswered. See "Suggested Labor Members for the Council on Foreign Relations," dated 17 May 1946, enclosure to Mallory to John W. Davis, 25 June 1946, John W. Davis Papers, box 133.

63. Memorandum, Clark M. Eichelberger, dated 30 October 1947, CMPR, box 2.

64. "Memorandum on Fund-Raising," Harold Oram, n.d., CMPR, box 2.

65. MM, 13 November 1947, CMPR, box 2. For an example of the advertisement see *New York Times*, 17 November 1947, 11. John H. Ferguson, *Report on the Activities of*

During that time the CMP established its headquarters in New York and, to stay in close touch with events on Capitol Hill, opened an office in Washington. Experienced administrators, such as political scientist Harold Stein, former CARE member George M. Eberstein, and John H. Ferguson, former assistant to Acheson in the State Department and then assistant to Eugene Meyer, the first director of the International Bank of Reconstruction and Development (IBRD), were brought in to conduct the CMP's day-to-day business.[66]

At one of the first meetings of the Executive Committee, Alger Hiss brought up the issue of women's participation in the CMP and argued "that at least one woman" should serve on the Executive Committee. Mrs. Wendell Willkie, widow of the internationally renowned fighter for a better world, agreed to head the "Women's Division" of the CMP. Although actively involved in several women's groups and a supporter of the United Nations, she did little for the committee beyond serving as a symbol of her late husband's ideas, thus attracting female and idealistic internationalists. Her participation was of importance, however, and helped to sell the Marshall Plan to women's groups and internationalists alike.[67]

Along the East Coast, chapters of the CMP, often led by prominent citizens, were quickly formed. Well-known Boston lawyer Henry Parkman, for example, headed the New England chapter. Soon branches of the CMP also materialized in Vermont, New Hampshire, Maine, New Jersey, and Rhode Island. Similar groups were founded in Philadelphia under the direction of William L. Batt, president of SKF Industries, and in Baltimore, by former Senator George C. Radcliff (Democrat of Maryland).[68]

The distinguished propaganda committee, as Page had called the CMP, hoped to generate support through a publication program —

---

the Committee for the Marshall Plan to Aid European Recovery (New York, 1948); the draft of the final report is an enclosure to Ferguson to Patterson, 5 April 1948, Patterson Papers, box 41.

66. MM, 13 November 1947, CMPR, box 2; Acheson, *Present,* 94, 240; *New York Times,* 7 March 1947.

67. MM, 26 November 1947, CMPR, box 2; *New York Times,* 16 May 1947, 20. Wendell Willkie, well-known Republican presidential candidate in the 1940 election, had published his impressions from a trip around the world in his *One World* (New York, 1943). He enthusiastically argued for a world closely interlinked and united, governed by a supranational organization. Within little more than 2½ months, two million copies of the book were sold. See John Morton Blum, *V Was for Victory: Politics and American Culture During World War II* (New York, 1976), 96.

68. MM, 26 November 1947, CMPR, box 2. Letterheads of the local chapters can be found in the Patterson Papers, box 41. See also Ferguson, *Report,* 2.

brochures, pamphlets, and leaflets — which committee members could then bring to the attention of Congress. Before November 1947 relatively little printed material on the European economic crisis or the plans for recovery was available to the broader public. Stimson's article, therefore, served the CMP well. It was an easily accessible resource, and a reprint of 200,000 copies was distributed. The committee also drew upon other articles. In cooperation with the Foreign Policy Association, a supplement of the *Washington Post* was reprinted in large quantities. More than 100,000 copies were distributed to interested citizens and internationalist organizations.[69] Written in simple language and garnished with many cartoons and charts, this special sixteen-page insert delineated the developments leading to the Marshall Plan.

One cartoon characterized the CMP members' hopes and basic ideas especially well. Entitled "Open Door," it showed a construction fence with "Help wanted for the Reconstruction of Europe" written on it; an open door in this fence identified as "Marshall Plan" afforded a glimpse of heavy machinery. This special edition was clearly printed with support for the ERP in mind. Headings such as "Our Mutual Interest Dictated Marshall Plan" and "15 Billion is a Small Ante for Such Stakes, Year's Armament Can Triple That" bluntly announced the authors' perspective. The title page itself, with a large picture of the secretary of state and the heading "This Generation's Chance for Peace," clearly indicated to the reader the positive treatment of the subject.[70]

The third of these initial CMP publications was an article entitled "What about the Marshall Plan?" by Alger Hiss. Writing for the 16 November issue of the *New York Times*, Hiss picked up on five arguments against the Marshall Plan:

> Won't American aid to Europe be pouring money down the rat hole? . . .
> Isn't Europe's trouble simply that the Europeans don't want to work? . . .

---

69. Kimball Young, "Content Analysis of the Treatment of the Marshall Plan in Certain Representative American Newspapers," *The Journal of Social Psychology* 33 (1951): 167; MM, 20 November 1947, CMPR, box 2; MM, 26 November 1947, *ibid.* Such reprints, as well as other publications issued by the CMP, were routinely mailed to the members.

70. *Washington Post*, 23 November 1947, sec. 7, 1–16; the headlines appear on pages 1 and 16, the cartoon on page 9. Charles W. Jackson, of President Truman's Executive Office, lauded the publisher of the *Washington Post*, Philip L. Graham: "You have done a swell job. In fact, I believe the November 23, supplement is the outstanding contribution to our educational job on the European Recovery Program." See Jackson to Graham, 21 November 1947, Charles W. Jackson Files, Harry S. Truman Papers, box 9, Truman Library.

> Can we afford to give more billions to Europe without wrecking our economy? . . . Can't we get along without Europe anyway? . . . Why should we support socialist governments?[71]

In answering these rhetorical questions, Hiss emphasized that the previously accomplished economic recovery of Europe had been annihilated by a devastating winter followed by spring floods. Critics of the ERP, Hiss continued, too easily overlooked these facts and blamed Europe's poor conditions on the lethargy of the population rather than on the natural disasters that had occurred. Certainly, reconstruction of Europe above all depended upon self-initiative, but this was impossible without foreign support. Food, fuel, and other resources had to be provided, means "which only the United States can supply." Also, he maintained, restoration of the now dislocated interdependent world trade would benefit not only the United States but Latin America as well. "From the political point of view," he argued, "getting along without Europe would mean the jettisoning of our finest and potentially strongest allies . . . expos[ing] 270,000,000 people and the world's second-greatest industrial complex to absorption in the vast area dominated by communist ideology and by Soviet interests."[72]

The Committee reprinted all three of these publications in large numbers and offered them to other internationalist organizations for distribution. In this initial phase of propaganda work and after the special session of Congress regarding the ERP at the end of December, the Committee added a further publication, *4 Essentials of a European Recovery Program*, to be circulated among newspaper editors, commentators, columnists, members of Congress, and the general public. The timing of this publication was by no means haphazard. The CMP wanted to make sure that it had an impact "[d]uring the time the members [of Congress] were at home for Christmas recess."[73]

The leaflet informed the reader that "European recovery is necessary for our own security and prosperity." The CMP identified the four crucial arguments in the legislative discussion of the ERP: "Effective Aid is Prompt Aid . . . Effective Aid is Aid that Will do the Whole Job . . . Effective Aid is Based on Mutual Respect and Honor," and "Effective

---

71. *New York Times*, 16 November 1947, sec. 6, 7; a copy was sent to Lovett. See State Department, Decimal File 840.50, National Archives, RG 59. Alger Hiss, *What About the Marshall Plan?* (New York, n.d.), 3.

72. *Ibid.*, 4–7.

73. For a copy, see Page Papers, box 69. Ferguson supplied this information about intentional timing in *Report*, 4.

Aid is Aid that will Bring Recovery and Self-Support and not a Hopeless Load of Debt." Keeping the tone of Hiss' article, the leaflet was designed to dispel arguments against the Marshall Plan. The *4 Essentials* closed with a dramatic and hardly modest desire: "The reward we seek from our aid program is prosperity, peace, and security; that is enough."[74]

Before the Senate Committee on Foreign Relations and the House Committee on Foreign Affairs began hearings on the ERP in 1948, the CMP issued further publications. One of these was a question-and-answer booklet — similar to Alger Hiss's article and the *4 Essentials* — which was mostly a composite of arguments against the Marshall Plan and their respective rebuttals. In addition, the leaflet addressed issues such as American supervision of the proper administration of ERP funds, economic relations between Eastern and Western Europe, participation of China in the distribution of ERP resources, the influence of the Argentine wheat prices, and similar matters.[75]

While the three initial CMP publications were aimed at the general public and potential donors as well as committee members, the *4 Essentials* was directed at journalists and members of Congress in particular. *The Marshall Plan is Up to You*, a further committee publication, addressed the common person. In an "over-the-fence-chat," as the authors called it, the booklet discussed possibilities and strategies for the creation of local sub-committees of the CMP. Following a short delineation of the development of the ERP and a few quotations by Henry Stimson and President Truman, the authors asserted that "we cannot long maintain our high standards of living and national security with Europe reduced to an economic void." Using colloquial language, the authors claimed to "explode" such "myths" and asserted that the Marshall Plan "is not going to make suckers out of us. . . . It's not going to produce disastrous inflation in this country. . . . It is not American imperialism. . . . It is not aimed against Russia."[76]

The reader was exhorted to get involved in the issue and to inform his peers at local associations, or even to organize local groups to spread information about the beneficial aspects of the Marshall Plan. "If we all

74. CMP, *4 Essentials of a European Recovery Program* (New York, n.d.). The leaflet was actually a revised and decoratively printed version of a press announcement made by the CMP on 22 December 1947. See MM, 8 January 1948, CMPR, box 2.

75. MM, 26 November 1947, CMPR, box 2. A draft of the booklet can be found in the Acheson Papers, box 5.

76. CMP, *The Marshall Plan is Up to You* (New York, n.d.), 4–5, 7.

do it, we can make tomorrow's history," the readers were assured, "full of hope, freedom and happiness. If we don't, chances are there won't be any history for anyone." The first step they could take would be to "talk," because "like atomic energy, conversation has a chain reaction." But conversations alone, the readers were advised, would not be enough. The goal had to be to spread the information through every channel of communication available: "newspapers, radio, posters, exhibits, advertising, schools, libraries, churches, and groups of all sorts." If this was not enough, everybody interested in the success of the ERP could try to win the local VIPs for the cause. "Prominent people can open doors; they can also smother a program by procrastination and domineering," read the brochure, voicing the common citizen's heartfelt feelings when it asked each person to "[u]se glamour if you can get it; don't let it use you."[77]

In the last parts of the booklet, the authors repeated their suggestions under the captions "Make It A Snowball," "Get In The Papers," "Get On The Air," "Make Them See It!" and "Give It The Personal Touch." If anyone decided to write to his elected representatives in Washington D.C., he was cautioned to write "**thoughtful, individual** letters to Congressmen and Senators. Form letters and telegrams don't work."[78]

The final paragraphs of the book told the fictitious story of Mrs. Allen, a housewife in the Midwestern town of Wichita, Kansas. The editors had chosen this character to prove to the reader that even the most modest effort could benefit this good cause. Although the authors of *The Marshall Plan is Up to You* might have considered this story superficial and simple, they deemed it appropriate in order to demonstrate the potentials that slumbered in citizens thus far undecided and overwhelmed by the task:

> She [Mrs. Allen] lacked experience in public speaking or organizing and the only group she belongs to is a mother's group connected with the local school. What can she do?
>
> Well, she can inform **herself** on the issue. Then, she can talk it over with her husband who works, say, at one of the big local plants and is a Rotarian. She can ask him to spread the word around and help her to get people interested. Next, she can chat with her neighbor who belongs, possibly, to the League of Women Voters. Mrs. Allen can find out what the League is doing. Then, at the next P.T.A. [Parent-Teacher Association] meeting she can ask some of the mothers and school teachers if they wouldn't like

77. *Ibid.*, 9–12.

78. *Ibid.*, 12–20. Bold words are in the original.

to get something going. Within a week, Mrs. Allen can probably spark a group from her mother's club, the League, the P.T.A., the local schools. Her husband may bring some people from the Rotary, some one [*sic*] will get the cooperation of the local newspaper and a campaign will be born. It's as simple as that.[79]

As with all other CMP publications, the Committee's slogan, taken from Stimson's *Foreign Affairs* article, was reprinted on the first pages: "I am confident that if the issues are clearly presented, the American people will give the right answer."[80] Only two months after its inception, the Committee could already rely on a series of publications informing the public about the benefits of the Marshall Plan. Additionally, in December, a *Statement of Purpose* was released, summarizing Stimson's article and portraying, as in the *4 Essentials*, the desperate conditions in Europe. The *Statement* gave an outline of the CMP's objectives and listed the Executive Committee and the more than three hundred members of the National Council, including each member's position in academia, business, government, or non-governmental organization.[81]

Supplementing this material, the CMP distributed a collection of government reports that was published by the Carnegie Endowment for International Peace. The committee also issued a cartoon book by Munro Leaf entitled *Who is the Man Against the Marshall Plan?* which received particularly wide notice, a bibliography of *Basic Official Documents*, and, in addition, it sent out the State Department's publication "Building the Peace," which appeared in *Foreign Affairs Outline*, no. 15.[82]

The arguments and reasoning in all of these publications advertising the Marshall Plan rarely differed. It is indicative, however, that Alger Hiss' article and the *4 Essentials* — the one originally written for the high-brow readership of the East Coast, and the other intended for circulation among editors of newspapers, commentators, columnists, and politicians — had strong anti-Soviet connotations. In publications such

79. *Ibid.*, 20–21. Bold is in the original.

80. *Ibid.*, 22–24.

81. CMP, *A Statement of Purpose* (New York, n.d.). An initial draft is in the Patterson Papers, box 41. The CMP evidently followed its own advice and used "glamour."

82. Samples are in Page Papers, box 69, and Patterson Papers, box 41. Harry B. Price, *The Marshall Plan and its Meaning* (Ithaca, NY, 1955), 56, note 10. Munro Leaf, author of *Ferdinand the Bull*, had worked for the Department of the Army during World War II, reducing complex matters to simple terms. At the end of 1946 he offered his talents to the State Department, being "anxious to work with PA [Office of Public Affairs] (without compensation and in an unofficial capacity) in doing the same thing on international policy matters." See Russell to Benton, 4 October 1947, ASPA, box 3.

as *The Marshall Plan is Up to You*, aimed at the general public, the CMP refrained from ideologically colored language.

The CMP calculated its publication and distribution strategy to correspond with the attitude of different sections of the population. With the general public taking a negative position toward the Marshall Plan as a means of anti-Soviet policy, information directed at it followed opinion polls and emphasized the humanitarian aspects of the ERP and the benefits the Marshall Plan would have for the domestic economy. A different approach was used for members of the foreign policy establishment. According to a poll conducted by the Council, a majority was convinced that, "[w]hile the Secretary's address, from which 'the Marshall Plan' has stemmed, was a statesmanlike utterance, his observation that 'our policy is directed not against any country or doctrine,' should not be taken at face value at the present time. American policy is, and should be, directed against Communism." Accordingly, this constituency primarily received publications that emphasized the anti-Soviet potential of the ERP and envisioned the economic aid program as part of American containment policy.[83]

An additional publication was deemed necessary at the end of the year, when the book *Will Dollars Save the World?* by Henry Hazlitt appeared on the market. This ardent believer in the free market economy maintained that Europe's need for help "has been greatly exaggerated" and that the United States should attack "the entire foundation of the Russian slave system" and should "defend capitalism without apology."[84]

After some discussion, CMP members found the appropriate man to respond to the charges by Hazlitt. John L. Simpson, executive vice-president of the J. H. Schroder Banking Corporation, New York City, wrote the article "Western Europe in the Balance," which appeared in the *Commercial & Financial Chronicle* on 5 February 1948. Simpson maintained that Hazlitt's arguments were "academic and theoretical" because "Europe's *main* trouble is that it has recently been a battlefield, . . . the first thing to remember, not the first thing to forget," as he claimed Hazlitt had done. In his evaluation of the communist threat Simpson went even further than Hazlitt, linking Nazis and fascists with the Com-

83. See the synopsis of the poll conducted among members of the Committees on Foreign Relations at the end of 1947 under the headline "The Principle," Barber, *The Marshall Plan*, 4.

84. Hazlitt had advanced similar arguments in his column "The World's 'Santa Claus,'" *Newsweek*, 21 July 1947, 68. Hazlitt, *Will Dollars Save the World?* (New York, 1947), 80, 88–89.

munists: "As in the balmy days of the Nazis and Fascists," he wrote, "deliberate efforts are being made to undermine the institutions and independence of these countries. . . . [T]he vigorous and well-financed Communist movement in France is something initiated and conducted from outside the frontiers."[85]

All of these publications merely repeated the basic arguments Stimson had made in *Foreign Affairs* and hardly tackled specific points. Controversial issues, such as different suggestions for the administration of the ERP or its impact on the domestic economy, were not thoroughly discussed. Consequently, the authors of the 1,250,000 copies of printed material distributed by the committee mainly stressed the humanitarian aspects of the ERP, its anti-communist potential, and the United States' responsibility to encourage "peace and prosperity."[86]

Many of these publications carried a call to add signatures to a petition that had been printed with the initial advertisement in November 1947. The collective signatures were handed over to representatives by constituents of their own congressional districts to create the impression that the entire nation was backing the Marshall Plan. For a second petition, initiated by CMP member Charles J. Symington, president of Symington and Gould Corporation, the text and layout were drafted with the help of C. D. Jackson of Time-Life and the publicity department of the CIO. To suggest that laborers and immigrants backed the ERP, three workers — a Czech, an Italian, and a Pole — handed a copy of petition signatures to chairman Charles A. Eaton (Republican of New Jersey) of the House Committee on Foreign Affairs. Yet the results of this action had very little impact and were less than gratifying to the CMP officials.[87]

Meanwhile, the State Department courted members of Congress by briefing them about every major development concerning the proposed aid program. Secretary of State Marshall convened an off-the-record conference with the members of the Senate Committee on Foreign Rela-

85. MM, 11 December 1947, CMPR, box 2; MM, 16 January 1948, *ibid.*; MM, 29 January 1946, *ibid.*; John L. Simpson, "Western Europe in the Balance," *Commercial and Financial Chronicle*, 5 February 1948, 7, 32–33. Italics are in the original.

86. Ferguson, *Report*, 7.

87. Ferguson, *Report*, 3, 8; Symington to Patterson, 15 March 1948, Patterson Papers, box 41; Patterson to Symington, 17 March 1948, *ibid.* See also Symington to Arthur Page, 15 March 1948, Page Papers, box 17. The following day Symington wrote that "from the publicity standpoint the petition was a flop." See Symington to Page, 16 March 1948, *ibid.*

tions, while President Truman invited members of the business community and journalists to the White House. Congressional committees traveled to Europe and observed firsthand the severe conditions. During the months of September and October 1947 alone, nearly one hundred delegates and about fifty of their staff visited the former German capital of Berlin and were informed, "toured," and returned to their airplanes, headed back for the United States.

"Oh, it's an assembly line, all right," admitted J. Anthony Panuch, assistant to Military Governor Lucius D. Clay, but the delegates would learn the necessary details to explain to their constituents back home why the money was necessary and why taxes could not be lowered. Most delegates returned to the United States convinced that an economic aid program was necessary and began to propound the importance of the Marshall Plan to other members of Congress. To help sway their colleagues, the State Department and CMP supplied them with briefing materials furnished by the State Department and the committee's own Washington office.[88]

CMP members maintained close and continuous contact with government departments, senators, representatives, and especially with legislators on both the Senate Committee on Foreign Relations and the House Committee on Foreign Affairs. Communications with Vandenberg, Christian A. Herter, and others served to strengthen the alliance for the Marshall Plan.[89]

In order to follow the day-to-day development in Congress, the CMP employed the International Legislation Service, an organization

88. Susan M. Hartman, *Truman and the 80th Congress* (Columbia, MO, 1971), 108–109; *Newsweek*, 18 August 1947, 12; MM, 18 November 1947, CMPR, box 2; MM, 4 February 1948, *ibid.*; MM, 26 February 1948, *ibid.*; Harold Stein Interview, Truman Library. For a list of participants at the White House conference, see "List of Persons who attended the White House Conference on Monday, October 27, 1947," Harry S. Truman Papers, OF 426, Truman Library. The citation is from Toni Howard, "Berlin Circuit: MG's Guided Tour for Congressmen," *Newsweek*, 13 October 1947, 20. See also Panuch's own depiction, in copy, Panuch to H. Stuve Hensel, 16 October 1947, Ferdinand Eberstadt Papers, box 34, Mudd Manuscript Library. Panuch refers in this letter to the *Newsweek* article and mentions the subcommittees he "processed."

89. Several MMs; reports of Harold Stein about possible changes of the ERP legislation; confidential drafts of such changes, all in CMPR, box 2; McCormack to Patterson, 26 January 1948, reprinted in U.S. Congress, *Congressional Record*, 94, 80th Congr., 2nd sess., 419. The letter also includes a CMP analysis of S. 2202 ("Vandenberg-Connally Bill") from which the ERP legislation was drawn. See *ibid.*, A1323. Patterson to Vandenberg, 9 September 1947, Patterson Papers, box 41; John Taber (Republican of New York) to Patterson, 2 December 1947, *ibid.*; copy, Christian Herter to Mrs. H.H. Bundy, 11 March 1948, *ibid.*

that provided detailed information and important guidance for the committee's work. Rachel Bell, who headed the service, wrote confidential reports on the sentiment of senators and congressmen, allowing the CMP to concentrate its efforts on stimulating grass-roots interest in the appropriate areas. As part of the accelerated efforts of the CMP in early 1948, a six-member field staff was hired in January and February 1948 when the foreign aid proposals were before Congress. Choosing areas according to the information that Bell provided, the staff visited a number of communities, mostly in the Midwest, to stimulate support.[90]

On 5 March 1948 the Committee arranged for a conference in Washington to create additional publicity for the Marshall Plan. Secretary Marshall, who had announced in January that he was willing to address such a meeting, was one of the speakers. More than 250 persons from 26 states attended, most of whom were members of the National Council. The audience was treated to a discussion panel consisting of senators, representatives, and other prominent people such as Clayton and former Wisconsin Senator Robert M. La Follette, Jr. According to Oram, the conference was "a complete success." All in all, the CMP not only received necessary additional funds but also created considerable favorable publicity on behalf of the Marshall Plan.[91] This meeting also countered the criticism of some CMP members who thought that the general membership was less than adequately represented by the Executive Committee. Evans Clark, executive director of the influential internationalist-oriented Twentieth Century Fund, for example, had voiced concern in that respect. He may have only wanted to become a member of the Executive Committee himself, but Patterson put him off until the conference in Washington and wrote: "We have to rely to a certain degree on the assumption that the Executive Committee, taken as it is from many groups, is representative of the entire Committee."[92]

The publicity work, handled by the Phoenix News Bureau, included a large number of press releases written by members of the CMP's Executive Committee and by the CMP's staff. Working with the Western Newspaper Union, the bureau succeeded in placing articles in many

90. MM, 26 November 1947, CMPR, box 2; MM, 18 December 1947, *ibid.*

91. MM, 11 March 1948, CMPR, box 2; "List of Persons Attending the Conference to be Held in Washington at the Hotel Sherman," 5 March 1948, *ibid.*; "Press Release" (abstract of the speech by William Clayton), 5 March 1948, William L. Clayton Papers, box 78, Truman Library.

92. See Clark to Patterson, 7 January 1948, Patterson Papers, box 41; Patterson to Clark, 10 January 1948, *ibid.*

country and farm papers.[93] In addition, it arranged several radio broadcasts without cost to the CMP. Committee members Herbert Lehman and Mrs. Willkie, among others, participated in these national radio programs. Pauline Mandigo, who headed the Phoenix News Bureau, reported to Clark Eichelberger that "in return for the $4,000 we received [as payment from the CMP for services rendered] over a period of four months, we secured $61,035 of free radio time for the Committee for the Marshall Plan."[94]

A nationwide broadcast on 14 December 1947 demonstrated how the CMP used the radio networks. All speakers on that program were members of the CMP who took to the air from cities all over the country: Herbert Lehman from Atlantic City; Joseph C. Grew, former Under Secretary of State, from Washington, D.C.; Charles P. Taft, brother of the isolationist Senator Robert A. Taft and president of the Federal Council on Church of Christ in America, from Cincinnati; M.I.T. president Karl Compton from Boston; Mayor Roger Lapham from San Francisco; and CMP staff member John H. Ferguson from New York City. By broadcasting from major cities across the nation, the CMP again fostered the impression that the entire nation was supporting the Marshall Plan.[95]

The Speakers' Bureau of the CMP, headed by Ruth B. Lippert, arranged for the speakers on this radio program as well as in other forums. Aside from Executive Committee members, the most prominent proponents engaged by the bureau included Representative Clifford P. Chase (Republican of New Jersey); Council member George Fielding Eliot; William L. Green, president of the AFL; Althea Hottel, president of the American Association of University Women; Senator Wayne L. Morse (Republican of Oregon); and Senator John J. Sparkman (Democrat of Alabama). These speakers appeared before women's organizations, church councils, bankers' conventions, business and merchants' organizations, and a variety of public affairs groups.[96]

---

93. MM, 13 November 1947, CMPR, box 2; MM, 23 January 1948, *ibid.*; MM, 5 February 1948, *ibid.*; Ferguson, *Report*, 7; "Mats," n.d., Eichelberger Papers, box 20.

94. Ferguson, *Report*, 7; MM, 23 January 1948, CMPR, box 2; Pauline Mandigo to Eichelberger, 12 March 1948, Eichelberger Papers, box 20.

95. *New York Times*, 15 December 1947, 14; Roger Lapham to Patterson, 8 December 1947, Patterson Papers, box 41.

96. The *New York Times* mentioned these activities in its editions of 19 November 1947, 3; 7 October 1947, 2; 19 January 1948, 18; and 22 January 1948, 2. See also *Commercial and Financial Chronicle*, 9 October 1947, 1422–23, 1442–44.

Dean Acheson went on a well-prepared publicity tour of the West and Midwest. He visited San Francisco, Portland, Spokane, and Duluth. In Minneapolis he appeared together with the city's mayor, Hubert H. Humphrey, and addressed businessmen and the local Committee on Foreign Relations. The members of the liberal Americans for Democratic Action welcomed him warmly. Other CMP members, such as Philip Reed, wrote articles and arranged public appearances for committee and State Department officials at private clubs and at meetings of non-governmental organizations.[97]

The CMP achieved its most direct influence in promoting the Marshall Plan, however, by providing and briefing witnesses for the Senate and House hearings on foreign aid. A few CMP members, such as Patterson, Acheson, and William Batt addressed congressional meetings, appearing as the representatives of the committee. Others testified as representatives of the business community or of various interest groups. These witnesses were provided not only because the CMP members thought it was necessary but also because supporters in Congress asked the committee to do so. Senator Vandenberg had urged Robert Lovett in a letter on 10 December 1947 to enlist "four or five top-level business executives as . . . aggressive witnesses" to appear before the Senate Committee on Foreign Relations. In response, Lovett had contacted Patterson. Since Patterson was in Washington at the time, Lovett dictated Vandenberg's confidential letter over the phone to Patterson's secretary, inquiring whether Patterson could not help in finding "four or five . . . powerful advocates from business . . . so that we can get them well briefed." With the help of Acheson, the Washington bureau of the CMP promptly provided the State Department with a list of possible witnesses.[98]

---

97. Acheson, *Present*, 240–41; "Memo of Mr. Acheson's Trip, Nov., 26–Dec. 6," n.d., Acheson Papers, box 4; Youngquist (Committee on Foreign Relations, Minneapolis, MN) to Acheson, 25 November 1947, *ibid.* Philip D. Reed, "Aid to Europe – and Economic Stability at Home," *Dun's Review*, 56 (January 1948): 11–12, 42–47. Allen Dulles gave a total of seven speeches. The manuscripts can be found in the Allen Dulles Papers. The Americans for Democratic Action (ADA) published only a few supportive press statements.

98. MM, 11 December 1947, CMPR, box 2; Vandenberg to Lovett, 10 December 1947, cited in Hartman, *Truman*, 160; Lovett Daily Log, entry of 11 December 1947. Lovett informed Page several days later about the activities. See Lovett to Page, 16 December 1947, Page Papers, box 69. A list of possible experts for congressional hearings is added to the Office Memorandum, Acting Legislative Counsel Carl Marcey to the Assistant Secretary of State for Economic Affairs Dallas W. Dort, 31 December 1947, State Department, Decimal File 840.50, National Archives, RG 59. Almost all experts listed were CMP members.

In January 1948 Harold Stein, director of the CMP's Washington bureau, conferred with Vandenberg's and Eaton's staff members and found that they wanted witnesses who would represent a cross-section of non-governmental organizations. And, it was indicated, they preferred "the request to appear to come from the organizations themselves."[99] Several days later Acheson sent telegrams to the proposed witnesses, stating that the CMP would "help in every way" to prepare for the hearings. Others, such as Ralph McGill, publisher of *The Constitution* (Atlanta), announced their interest in testifying and asked for "suggestions as to my statement." Still others, such as James Patton, president of the National Farmer's Union, were furnished with testimonies. A total of twenty-six CMP members, among them Carey, Dulles, Eichelberger, Green, Lehman, Reed, and Taft, appeared as witnesses before the Senate and House committees. It was essentially this group that made sure that the pro-ERP lobby was heard by the committees.[100]

The money for all this publicity, information, and printing was supplied freely by CMP members and other sympathizers. Over $162,000 in 7,500 separate donations flowed in and was spent during the five months the CMP functioned. The most notable contributors who were not CMP members were Clayton, John D. Rockefeller III, and Paul G. Hoffman. The Committee needed the funds badly. Nearly $60,000 of the total amount went toward printing and mailing expenses of the various publications. Promotion and publicity costs amounted to $24,000, and expenditures for telephone calls and telegrams were $11,000.[101]

The primary hope of the CMP became reality with the enactment of legislation for the ERP. On 2 April 1948, at the last of the weekly meetings of the CMP's Executive Committee, its members agreed to terminate operations now that the State Department's foreign aid plan for Europe was approved.[102]

---

99. Eichelberger to McKee, 3 January 1947 [*sic* i1948], Eichelberger Papers, box 20.

100. MM, 8 January 1948, CMPR, box 2; telegram, Acheson to James D. Zellerbach, 15 January 1948, Acheson Papers, box 3; telegram, McGill to Acheson, 20 January 1948, *ibid.* Patton's testimony for the Senate Committee on Foreign Relations clearly shows the influence of the CMP; syntax and the use of arguments in parts literally repeat Committee publications.

101. "Receipt and Disbursement Statement," Haskins & Sells to Committee of the Marshall Plan, 30 August, 1948, CMPR, box 1; Form A, Lobbying Act, n.d., *ibid.*; Form A, Lobbying Act, April 1948, *ibid.*; Form A, Lobbying Act, 8 January 1948, *ibid.*; see also ledgers, *ibid.*

102. MM, 2 April 1948, CMPR, box 2; telegram, Ferguson to Page, 29 March 1948, Page Papers, box 70; Page to Ferguson, 29 March 1948, *ibid.* The CMP continued to exist

CMP members had chosen to spend money, time, and energy to promote the Marshall Plan for various reasons. Some of these, corresponding closely with a similar attitude among the general Council membership, can be easily identified in their publications and internal communication. Although the economic interests of individual CMP members may have played a part, the main objective of most members was to create an international situation in which peace and prosperity through a relatively unhindered free market system was possible. They hoped that the Marshall Plan would help preserve the pre-war democratic political institutions in France, Italy, and Great Britain, and they were certain that the economic recovery program would prevent the further spread of communism in these countries. In disregard of the obvious political situation in Eastern Europe and the interests of the Soviet leadership, the CMP hoped the Marshall Plan would serve as an "open door" for Eastern European Soviet satellites to participate in inter-European and international trade, thus providing a means for these countries to break away from the Soviet orbit. In addition, they presumed that an aid program initiated and supervised by the United States would be the starting point of an earnest American commitment to the Community of Nations, eradicating the last remains of political isolationism in the United States.

The successful activities of the Non-Partisan Committee and the Committee to Defend America, in which many CMP members had taken part and which served as models for most CMP activities, had strengthened their zeal. During and immediately after World War II, many of them had joined Council study groups, dedicating much of their time and work to political and economic problems of the post-war era. Six of them had joined the War and Peace Studies and two others had participated in the work of the Committee for Economic Development. Four CMP members had been active on the President's Committee on Foreign Aid, which was directed by Averell Harriman. Thirteen CMP members belonged to the National Planning Association, four were trustees of the Carnegie Endowment for International Peace, and three others were members of the Twentieth Century Fund. Of the

---

nominally for quite some time, and in the following two years it was often discussed whether the Committee should be reactivated and how to disburse the remaining small amount of $2,500 of CMP funds. Ferguson to Patterson, 14 September 1949, Patterson Papers, box 41; note of a phone call by Harold Oram, 17 February 1949, *ibid.*; McKee to Mrs. Wendell L. Willkie, 4 May 1949, *ibid.*; McKee to Patterson, 4 May 1949, *ibid.*; Dulles to Patterson, 5 April 1950, *ibid.*; Patterson to Dulles, 7 April 1950, *ibid.*

CMP's Executive Committee, five sat on the board of the Woodrow Wilson Foundation, and four were members of the AAUN.[103]

Union officials serving on the CMP represented the more conservative faction of organized labor. Carey and Dubinsky embodied the anti-Communist right wings of their organizations and had nothing in common with the liberal left, Socialists, Communist organizations, and labor unions opposing the ERP. Their attitude paralleled that of their fellow CMP members from the business community; Carey, for example, had stated in 1945 that he was convinced of "a direct correlation between prosperity and foreign trade." To them, the Marshall Plan meant a high demand for goods, low unemployment rates and secure workplaces and, ultimately, increased bargaining power for labor. Carey and Dubinsky might have disagreed with other CMP members on many domestic and some foreign policy issues, but they could very easily agree with them on the necessity of aid to Europe. Invited to serve on the Executive Committee, they helped to create the widespread impression that all Americans, including organized workers, regardless of political, educational, and social background, supported Secretary of State Marshall and the State Department in the foreign aid program.[104]

The AAUN members had hoped earlier that the Marshall Plan would be coordinated with the activities of the United Nations Economic Commission for Europe. When they realized that the administration was reluctant to act this way, Eichelberger maintained that "we have no choice but to support adequate appropriations to provide the aid to western Europe that the Marshall Plan proposes." At the same time, he argued, "we must insist that doors be kept open for aid to Eastern Europe." With their endorsement of the Marshall plan, members of the AAUN hoped to achieve a "dual objective: Saving the economies of western Europe and resuming negotiations with Russia through the United Nations for the solution of outstanding difficulties." The imple-

103. The War and Peace Studies are discussed in chapter 2. The demographic data are taken from CMP, *A Statement of Purpose*, 4–14.

104. Regarding Dubinsky's cooperation with the CIA to provide money for activities directed against the French Communist union CGT in 1947, see Barnes, "The Secret Cold War," 413. During the conference of the World Federation of Trade Unions in Paris in November 1947, Carey prevented a resolution against the Marshall Plan. See MM, 4 December 1947, CMPR, box 2; MM, 11 December 1947, *ibid.*; Page to Carey, 5 May 1948, Page Papers, box 70. Carey's statement before the House Committee on Ways and Means in 1945 is cited in Ronald Radosh, *American Labor and United States Foreign Policy* (New York, 1969), 358–59. George Meany and William Green of the AFL and Philip Murray of the CIO were other prominent labor leaders belonging to the CMP.

mentation of the ERP, they believed, would prove the United States to be a full member of the Community of Nations and would prevent a future retreat into political isolationism. To them, as to the Council members, the Marshall Plan was an expression of a newly awakening internationalism developed during the war years that would pay justice the United States' leading role in world affairs. AAUN members were convinced, as Stimson had put it in his *Foreign Affairs* article, that "the attitude of isolationism — political and economic — must die."[105]

In addition to the economic implications, the political prospects of the ERP seemed promising to CMP members. In light of the nascent Cold War, the Marshall Plan was viewed as a measure of "political economy in the literal sense of the term," as George F. Kennan had put it in May 1947. Many CMP members argued in committee publications and in private that failure to provide assistance to the nations of Western Europe would inevitably bring about economic collapse. This, they believed, would nourish the rise of communist parties and eventually lead to communist governments in France and Italy allied to Moscow. Applying the "domino effect" theory, they assumed that with communist neighbors, other Western European nations would have difficulty resisting communism. A Europe dominated by communists was perceived as a direct threat to the national security of the United States.

Allen Dulles had made this quite clear a few days after the Marshall Plan speech. Both he and Secretary Marshall had been invited to received honorary degrees at Brown University on 16 June, where Dulles was to deliver the commencement address. Outlining the economic situation in Great Britain, France, Italy, the Netherlands, and the other West European countries, Dulles expressed his belief that "it is by restoring the economic life of a country, and by this alone, that we can meet the threat of dictatorship from a Fascist Right or a Communist Left." If the United States would concentrate aid "on those countries with free institutions," he added, the "common cause of democracy and peace" would be promoted. "We would thus," Dulles pointed out, "confront Communism, not with arms or atomic bombs, but with a restored economic life for the men and women of Western Europe."[106]

---

105. AAUN, "Statement of European Economic Reconstruction, Adopted by the Executive Committee of the AAUN," 18 June 1947, CEIPR, #63567; Eichelberger to Sumner Welles, 16 July 1947, Eichelberger Papers, box 20; Eichelberger to Alice Hill Byrne, 25 September 1947, Eichelberger Papers, box 19; Eichelberger to (former CDA official) Livingston Hartley, 5 January 1948, *ibid.*; Stimson, "Challenge," 6.

106. Kennan to Acheson, 23 May 1947, in *FRUS, 1947*, 3: 230. Dulles, "Address to the Annual Meeting of the Associated Alumni of Brown University, 179th Annual Com-

Dulles and his associates saw the Marshall Plan as an adequate means to combat communism. The aid program would stabilize the present governments, and, as Aldrich put it in an address to the annual American Bankers' Association convention, the higher standard of living resulting from American support would demonstrate most effectively the "superiority of personal freedom and the democratic way of life over the dictated and police controlled economies." Arthur Page could have spoken for all members of this coalition of corporate, labor, and liberal elites when he wrote: "We are going to keep the Russians out of Western Europe and our ideas will control the world."[107]

Despite their attitude toward the Soviet Union, CMP members remained faithful to their conviction that openly adding to the tensions between the two superpowers was undesirable and counterproductive. For example, an advertisement ("Stop Stalin Now") based on the earlier "Stop Hitler Now" advertisement by the CDA, was recalled after heated discussion. By refusing to take sides on these and similar issues, the CMP added to its bipartisan appeal and succeeded in enlisting support from citizens and national organizations from across the political spectrum.[108]

Among its National Council members, the committee could count on an almost equal number of Democrats and Republicans, as well as many members of national organizations, company presidents, international lawyers, university teachers, and former government officials. Of its general membership, fifty-five percent were from the business community, seven percent were officers of non-governmental organizations, six percent were labor union officials, eight percent belonged to academia, nine percent were from the media, seven percent were lawyers, and five percent were former members of Congress, retired government officials, governors, and acting mayors of major cities. Most Executive Committee members had been educated at elite institutions, many were affiliated with important law firms, and all were residents of the eastern seaboard of the United States. They shared a common social back-

mencement, June 16, 1947," 7, 12. A copy of the printed version is in the Dulles Papers, box 30. Marshall had left shortly after he was awarded the honorary degree (and before Dulles's speech) to attend to urgent matters in Washington.

107. Aldrich, "American Interest," 4, 5; Page to Henry K. Cheesen, 27 October 1947, Page Papers, box 16.

108. For the "Stop Stalin Now" design, see CMPR, box 2. Not surprisingly, Eichelberger was very concerned about the potential effects of such an advertisement. On 13 February 1948 he wrote to Patterson: "To use the same play on words at this time in an ad in support of the Marshall Plan, to my way of thinking, verges on warmongery." See Eichelberger to Patterson, 13 February 1948, Eichelberger Papers, box 20.

ground and a similar cosmopolitan *Weltanschauung.* Exceptions to this were the two labor union representatives and the only woman on the Executive Committee; however, they served to heighten the CMP's appeal in the public's eyes.

Since the State Department's efforts to promote the Marshall Plan were hampered by internal uncertainties, legal barriers, and accusations of using propaganda, the CMP was created to assume a considerable part of the job to educate the public. Although this period was a more innovative phase in the history of the State Department and the work on the ERP helped structure and sharpen its organizational and decision-making process, the initial stages reflected confusion.[109] The Committee was successful because the impressive numbers of prominent members attracted constant attention from Congress and the media. The widely read *New York Times,* for instance, mentioned the CMP or individual members more than sixty times during the committee's existence. The founding of the CMP received front-page coverage on 16 November 1947, and lists of its more than three hundred National Council and Executive Committee members were printed. "All this and Heaven too, in the form of newspaper publicity," wrote Pauline Mandigo while reporting to Eichelberger about her success in securing free radio time.[110]

Although the CMP's original task was to educate the public — an effort it shared with the State Department and other organizations such as the Foreign Policy Association — its main influence was elsewhere. The Executive Committee members paid attention to public opinion polls, but their perception was rather selective. They regarded as important only the opinion of those who could exert influence and vocal support on a local or national level. Benjamin V. Cohen, longtime State Department adviser, stated succinctly the determining force behind the CMP's efforts: "Our foreign policy should represent not the polling of an uninformed public opinion, but the best thought that an informed public opinion will accept." Most CMP publications therefore were distributed to other internationalist foreign policy groups and reached those citizens already

109. A vivid description of the State Department's insecurity and at times total disarray can be found in Markel, *Public Opinion.* 119. See also Harold Stein Interview, Truman Library. Accusations that the State Department was engaged in illegal propaganda activities are cited in U.S. Congress, *Congressional Record,* 80th Cong., 2nd sess., 94: 3437–38, A 225, A 678–79, A 4501.

110. *New York Times,* 16 November 1947, 1; *New York Times,* 13 March 1948, 48; Mandigo to Eichelberger, 12 March 1948, Eichelberger Papers, box 20.

interested in foreign affairs. These groups or individuals, in turn, wrote letters to their representatives in Washington, and thus helped to create the illusion that the Marshall Plan had grass-roots support.[111]

The positive reaction of Congressional leaders such as Senator Vandenberg and Representative Eaton to the State Department initiative greatly helped to produce favorable votes in the Senate and House. (The bill passed with 69 to 17 votes in the Senate and 329 against 74 votes in the House). Nonetheless, this support alone would not have been sufficient to ensure the passage of law and adequate appropriations in a Congress dominated by Republicans. The accord between these politicians, the State Department, and the majority of the foreign policy establishment and the similarity of their ideas and analyses of public opinion, were all pivotal to the successful passage of the Marshall Plan. This coalition found its organizational base in the creation of the CMP.

Representative Charles A. Plumley (Republican of Vermont) was certainly correct when he stated in March 1948 that "there was never such propaganda in the whole history of the nation as there has been for the Marshall Plan," and that this propaganda was responsible for the "overwhelming conviction among the American people and among the members of Congress, that we must have the Marshall Plan enacted right now." His evaluation of the sentiment of the American people, however, was somewhat misleading. In March, 1947, the American Institute for Public Opinion surveyed citizens' views on the Marshall Plan and found that not more than 45 percent of the general public supported aid to Europe. The public that was actually overwhelmingly convinced of the necessity of the ERP was that most directly concerned with the future of American foreign policy. A Council poll of the members of its twenty-one Committees on Foreign Relations revealed that 95 percent agreed that the recovery program was necessary. A *Fortune* poll among businessmen in early 1948 bore similarly high results.[112]

---

111. One official in the State Department called the members of the Foreign Policy Association, the Council "and all other groups like that [a] constituency of sorts" of the Department. See Cohen, *The Public's Impact*, 23. Benjamin V. Cohen, "Am I My Brother's Keeper?, Address delivered at Hotel Commodore, New York, NY," 12 November 1947, Americans for Democratic Action Papers, Series V, no. 122, State Historical Society of Wisconsin.

112. Plumley's statement can be found in U.S. Congress, *Congressional Record*, 94, 80th Congr., 2nd sess., 3437. *Public Opinion Quarterly*, 12 (Summer 1948): 365; Barber, *The Marshall Plan*, 7. *Fortune* polled 28,000 business people. See *Fortune* 37 (January 1948): 75; *Fortune* 37 (February 1948): 10.

Although outside events, such as the Communist coup in Czechoslovakia, the Soviet threat to Finland, and the upcoming elections in Italy created a favorable atmosphere for foreign aid bills in Congress, the activities of the sixteen Council members, Carey, and Mrs. Willkie in the CMP were also crucial in passing the ERP. Senators and congressmen, not easily impressed by shifts in public opinion polls nor by petitions from women's groups, were certainly influenced by the number of notables among the CMP members and by the public sentiment this group was able to elicit. In addition, the professional qualifications of many members of the CMP's Executive Committee — former government aides and officers or prominent authorities in finance, banking, and foreign policy — helped to persuade a number of senators and congressmen that "experts" were convinced of the necessity of the Marshall Plan.

Council members also participated in other similar organizations, but the Committee for the Marshall Plan represented the most explicit attempt to shape public opinion during the beginning Cold War. Energetically, persuasively, and intelligently, using lobbying, advertisement, and business strategies — skills which they knew and employed in their careers as managers and lawyers — the Council members attempted to sell the Marshall Plan to a reluctant public and a skeptical Congress. Although their activities were less successful with regard to the general public, the members accomplished their goal and induced Congress to believe that the American people overwhelmingly supported Marshall's initiative. In all of these activities the Council itself remained in the background, functioning only as a framework and recruiting base for members.

During the following years, Council members continued to join similar ad hoc organizations, but such passionate participation as in the case of the Marshall Plan was not to be repeated. In March 1948, the Office of Public Affairs and the State Department helped to institute a Citizens' Committee for Reciprocal World Trade, and its setup followed the same pattern as that of the CMP. The group was supposed to generate positive public opinion for a three-year extension by Congress of the Reciprocal Trade Agreements Act. The Trade Act allowed the President to sign bilateral agreements on lowering tariffs. As was the case with the CMP, lists of possible candidates were drawn up and proposals for the chairperson were suggested to the Office of Public Affairs.[113] Council

113. William Clayton indicated that he would accept the chair, but the initiators feared that the entire action would then look too much like a State Department arrangement. See Melvin J. Fox (CEIP) to Hiss, 2 February 1948, CEIPR Addition, box 6, Folder "A. Hiss, Gen. Correspondence, 1948, Melvin J. Fox;" E.B. Syre to Fox, 16 March 1948, *ibid.*; "Appointment List of Fox," CEIPR, #97623.

members Altschul, Hiss, Eichelberger, and Henry Wriston joined the Committee, but members of lesser eminence in Council affairs, such as Gerard Swope, Thomas J. Watson of IBM, and W. Randolph Burgess, held leading positions. The Committee received part of its financing from the Committee on International Economic Policy, a subgroup of the CEIP headed by Aldrich.[114]

The National Committee for Free Europe once again followed the same model. Council members DeWitt Poole and Altschul, with the assistance of Allen Dulles, Arthur Page, and Charles Spofford, founded this group in 1949 to support the administration's containment policy. Henry Stimson, by that time seriously ill, was again suggested as chairperson. Surprisingly, the motion came from George F. Kennan, who had met with Poole. Kennan advised Charles Bohlen to ask the secretary of state for support in recruiting Stimson.[115] Over the following few years, however, this group developed into a major tool for anti-Soviet propaganda as the Cold War intensified and, although its origins were similar to those of the other groups, it could hardly be considered an ad hoc organization.[116] Its brainchild, Radio Free Europe, went on the air in Germany and, supported by the CIA, broadcast in the respective native languages to Eastern Europe while Lucius D. Clay launched a Crusade for Freedom in 1950.[117]

---

114. Of its 81 members, 30 belonged to the Council. Letterhead of the Citizens' Committee for Reciprocal World Trade, Charles P. Taft Papers, box 311, Library of Congress; Swope to Altschul, 25 March 1948, Frank Altschul Papers, Folder "Citizens' Committee for Reciprocal World Trade," Herbert H. Lehman Suite, School of International Affairs, Columbia University; Memorandum, "Subject: Interim Report," W.H. Baldwin to Swope, 5 April 1948, *ibid.* See Acheson to Swope, 2 February 1949, State Department Decimal File 611.0031/2-2/49, National Archives, RG 59. See also the documents in the Cordell Hull Papers, reel 51, Library of Congress.

115. Kennan to Bohlen, 18 April 1949, Records of Charles E. Bohlen, box 1, National Archives, RG 59. An irony of history is that Kennan at the time was residing in the township of East Berlin, PA.

116. The Committee was controlled from its beginning by intelligence organizations. Frank G. Wisner, chief of the Office of Public Guidance, which was integrated into the CIA in 1950, pushed for its creation. See Kennan to Bohlen, 18 April 1949, Records of Charles E. Bohlen, box 1.

117. Joseph C. Crew to Charles P. Taft, 27 May 1949, Taft Papers, box 153, and the further correspondence and memoranda in this archive, box 153; correspondence, memoranda, and MM in the Altschul Papers, Folder "National Committee for Free Europe" and Folder "Radio Free Europe." Altschul considered Radio Free Europe of extreme importance and spent a good deal of his time on it. See "Notes on RADIO FREE EUROPE," dated 30 November 1949, *ibid.* Clay to William Clayton, 20 December 1950, Clayton Papers, box 102. See also Domhoff, *Who Rules America?*, 65; Victor Marchetti and John D. Marks, *The CIA and the Culture of Intelligence* (Dell Book Edition, New York, 1980), 152–56.

Finally, the Committee on the Present Danger, founded with the initiative of the Department of Defense to sell an increase in military spending to the public, also could count on a series of Council members such as Altschul, Clayton, and Henry Wriston.[118] "This is the same gang who sold us the Marshall Plan," Representative John T. Wood (Republican of Idaho) complained.[119] A highly effective, successful, and influential group with a limited task, carrying out propaganda activities for the State Department with a large number of eminent Council members as its officers, as had been the case with the Committee for the Marshall Plan, however, was not seen again.

118. Memorandum, Tracy S. Voorhees to Altschul et al., 17 January 1951, Altschul Papers, Folder "Committee on the Present Danger," Correspondence; Altschul to Voorhees, 19 January 1951, *ibid.* See also Clayton Papers, box 92 and box 102 for digests of discussion and other information he received.

119. Cited in William M. Tuttle, Jr., "James B. Conant, Pressure Groups and the National Defense, 1933–1945" (Ph.D. diss., University of Wisconsin – Madison, 1967), 389.

8
The Council on Foreign Relations and the Decision-Making Process in U.S. Foreign Policy

Theoretical Models

The beginning of the Cold War brought dramatic changes in the international constellation of power. During that period, from 1945 to 1950, the division of the world into two hostile blocks of power was inaugurated. Repercussions from that time, even now that the Cold War has been declared over, are determining the present state of the world. The means of destruction amassed today, resulting from the armaments race that had been unleashed during that period, still threaten the life of every being on this planet — despite recent developments in the international arena.

Historians, political scientists, and sociologists are looking for explanations for these developments while examining the factors that influenced decision-makers in those years. In this process, scholars have researched global as well as domestic determinants, because, in addition to external factors, the internal structure of society and the cooperation of its parts has an impact on the decision-making process in global matters. The study of the role of an elite organization, such as the Council on Foreign Relations, must also address the status of that organization within society, its composition, and its influence. A meticulous analysis of discussions and decisions within the Council and its connections with those agencies in which decisions were actually made — within the confines of limited sources — has to be conducted *before* the historians' legitimate and necessary tool of interpretation can be employed to evaluate the role and the degree of influence such an organization may have had.[1]

1. The term "elite" will be used in this study to define a group of individuals who hold positions regarded to be eminent by the group's peers and a large part of society. All members of the Council can thus be described as part of an American elite. The Council is an oligarchic or "closed" elite because the organization itself determines criteria for the eligibility of prospective members and limits their number, and has provided that membership is by invitation only. A prospective member has to be nominated by a

Until the early 1960s, analytical concepts in history, sociology, and political science, in the United States and in other western countries, were to a large part marred by a prevailing anti-Soviet Cold War ideology. The Soviet Union was regarded by "traditionalists" as a ferocious and expansionist enemy that the United States had more or less successfully checked in its ruthless drive for world domination. Not until critical scholars began to question the impeccability and self-righteousness of American foreign and domestic policy did historians and other scholars termed "revisionists" develop innovative approaches. In this process, diplomatic history based only on official statements and memoranda was rejected as insufficient.[2]

Detailed studies uncovered that Thomas A. Bailey's hypothesis that the idealized concept of a pluralist American society would also hold true in the nation's foreign policy, i.e., that U.S. foreign policy is a literal reflection of the interest of the American people, had to be dismissed.[3] The influence of societal elites, "interest groups," ethnic groups, and particularly the prerequisites of a capitalist economy had to be taken into account. William A. Williams contributed immensely to our understanding of the forces underlying United States foreign policy through his hypothesis that the interests of domestic economic stability and of an expanding American economy characterize U.S. actions abroad. Taking the issue a step further, Gabriel Kolko asserted that the interests of the American ruling class were reflected in U.S. foreign policy.[4]

Council member, and seconded by another member. After this process, the Council's Membership Committee decides whether the proposed new member is to be invited.

2. For a extensive delineation of Cold War historiography, see Howard Jones and Randall B. Woods, "Origins of the Cold War in Europe and the Near East: Recent Historiography and the National Security Imperative," *Diplomatic History* 17 (Spring 1993): 251–76. I concentrate in the following on approaches that have direct implications for the study of organizations such as the Council on Foreign Relations.

3. Raymond G. O'Connor, "Thomas A. Bailey: His Impact," *Diplomatic History* 9 (Fall 1985): 305. See also William Widenor, "The Role of Electoral Politics in American Foreign Policy Formation: Are Historians Meeting the Conceptual Challenge?" SHAFR *Newsletter*, 16 (December 1985): 3–29, particularly pages 11–12.

4. William A. Williams, *The Tragedy of American Diplomacy* (New York, 1962); Gabriel Kolko, *The Roots of American Foreign Policy: An Analysis of Power and Purpose* (Boston, 1969); and the many studies and articles based on these analytical approaches. See also the historiographies of Walter LaFeber, "'Ah, If We Had Studied It More Carefully:' The Fortunes of American Diplomatic History," *Prologue*, 11 (Summer 1979): 121–31; Charles S. Maier, "Marking Time: The Historiography of International Relations," in: *The Past Before Us: Contemporary Historical Writing in the United States* (Ithaca, NY, 1980), Michael Kammen, ed., 355–87; "Symposium: Responses to Charles S. Maier, 'Marking Time: The Historiography of International Relations,'" *Diplomatic History* 5 (Fall 1981): 353–82; and J. Samuel Walker, "Historians and the Cold War Origins: The

These two concepts, the influence of societal elites and the economic determinants of foreign policy, served as the basis for a number of historical studies in the 1960s and 1970s. In the wake of these studies, and supported by earlier research conducted by political scientists,[5] the notion that public opinion or "the man in the street" was the driving force behind foreign policy decisions had to be rejected. It had become apparent that "manipulation of the public" was a much more appropriate term to characterize the relationship between the administration and its constituency.[6]

Both of these major concepts, "traditional" and "revisionist," were soon challenged by studies asserting that high-level officials had far less influence than commonly presumed. Graham T. Allison asserted in his 1971 study, *Essence of Decision*, that advisors and the bureaucracy, the so-called "career-officers," influenced and determined decision-making during the Cuban Missile Crisis. This claim was dismissed, however, when subsequent studies showed that recommendations by career-officers were quite frequently rejected by their superiors.[7] Additionally, this interpretation slighted the element of the 60 percent "in-and-outer's" from business, law firms, and academia among officials in high positions at governmental agencies, who served for a few years and then returned to their previous occupations.[8]

New Consensus," in: *American Foreign Relations: A Historiographical Review* (Westport, CT, 1981), Gerald K. Haines and J. Samuel Walker, eds., 207–36.

5. Particularly James N. Rosenau, *Public Opinion and Foreign Policy* (New York, 1961); see also the discussion in Domhoff, *The Higher Circles: The Governing Class in America* (New York, 1970), 148–53.

6. See also Cohen's discussion in *The Public's Impact*, 1–26; and Melvyn Leffler, "Symposium: Response," 368.

7. Graham T. Allison, *Essence of Decision* (Boston, 1971). See also Thomas J. McCormick, Jr., "Drift or Mastery?: A Corporatist Synthesis for American Diplomatic History," *Reviews in American History* 20 (December 1982): 322. "Where officials stood did not always depend on where they sat (the secretary of defense, for example, did not argue for a military solution during the Cuban Missile Crisis)," wrote Walter LaFeber in his "'Ah, If We Had Studied It More Carefully,'" 129.

8. The 60 percent figure is based on Minter, "The Council," 117. Minter examined 502 officials in high positions (from the American president to the assistant secretaries at State, War, Navy, and Defense Departments; under secretaries at Treasury and Commerce Departments; Joint Chiefs of Staff, White House assistants, ambassadors to France, Germany, Great Britain, and the USSR; and heads of such agencies as ECA and the Import-Export Bank) during the period 1945 to 1972. More than half of these "in-and-outer's" — a term used by Richard Neustadt in *Presidential Power: The Politics of Leadership* (New York, 1960) — were members of the Council. See Minter, "The Council," 135, 118. Richard J. Barnet (a Council member himself) combined Allison's concepts and C. Wright Mills' "power elite" (see below) and postulated a bureaucratic elite, the "national security managers," who determined American foreign policy in col-

Since the early 1980s, some American historians (most notable among them John Lewis Gaddis) have suggested constructing a synthesis for the study of U.S. foreign relations. This "post-revisionist" concept or "new consensus" proposed to combine the "traditional" approach with "revisionist" elements.[9] Many historians associated with the "revisionist" school have rejected Gaddis' notion, which they regard as "orthodoxy plus archives." The latest attempt to create such a synthesis, the national security imperative proposed by Howard Jones and Randall B. Wood, met a similar fate.[10]

Inspired by Thomas J. McCormick,[11] a number of scholars of American foreign relations have developed a systematic analytical framework that takes the "revisionist" concept a step further without understanding economic factors and the involvement of elites in the decision-making process in a deterministic manner. This "corporatist" approach of American foreign relations has proven to provide an excellent framework particularly in those areas of foreign relations in which the influences on the decision-making process and the process itself are closely scrutinized.[12]

laboration with "corporations." See *Roots of War: The Men and Institutions Behind U.S. Foreign Policy* (New York, 1973, Penguin Books Edition). Barnet mentioned the Council only in passing, arguing that membership would be "a rite of passage for an aspiring national security manager." See *ibid.*, 49. For a similar evaluation, see Irving L. Janis, *Victims of Groupthink: A Psychological Study of Foreign-Policy Decisions and Fiascoes* (Boston, 1972), particularly the chapter, "The Making of the Marshall Plan," *ibid.*, 167–81.

9. John Lewis Gaddis, "The Emerging Post-Revisionist Synthesis on the Origins of the Cold War," *Diplomatic History* 7 (Summer 1983): 171–90; and earlier J. Samuel Walker in: "Historians and the Cold War Origins." See also Gaddis' discussion of the corporatist approach in his "The Corporatist Synthesis: A Skeptical View," *Diplomatic History* 10 (Fall 1986): 357–62. A recent study following this approach is Pollard, *Economic Security.*

10. Warren F. Kimball, "Response to John Lewis Gaddis, 'The Emerging Post-Revisionist Synthesis on the Origins of the Cold War,'" *Diplomatic History* 7 (Summer 1983): 198. See also Michael J. Hogan's critique in "Corporatism," *Journal of American History* 77 (June 1990): 153. Jones and Wood, "Origins of the Cold War," and the commentaries on their essay in *Diplomatic History* 17 (Spring 1993): 277–310.

11. Thomas J. McCormick, "Toward a New Diplomatic History: Social History, Revisionism, and the Corporatist Synthesis," Colloquium Paper, 22 June 1981, Woodrow Wilson International Center for Scholars; and *idem.*, "Drift or Mastery?," 318–30.

12. The most notable study using this approach for the early Cold War is Michael J. Hogan's *The Marshall Plan.* Gaddis, a critic of the corporatist approach, agreed that "corporatist analyses tend to be applied successfully to . . . the late 1940s. . . ." See Gaddis, "Corporatist Synthesis: A Skeptical View," 359. See also Michael J. Hogan, "Corporatism: A Positive Appraisal," *Diplomatic History* 10 (Fall 1986): 363–72; *idem.*, "Corporatism;" and Joan Hoff-Wilson, "Symposium: Response," 377–82.

In other areas of concentration and levels of analysis, a number of scholars have recently proposed additional systematic analytical approaches to explain American foreign relations. Most of these concepts are complementary but some are in competition with one another. The study of American foreign relations obviously remains a changing and challenging field of concepts and analytical systems to explain why and how particular decisions were made, the question that is at the very heart of every historical inquiry.[13]

In the historical analysis of an organization such as the Council on Foreign Relations, the dangers of committing a fallacy are many when the study is guided by narrow concepts of influence or of power. If the evaluation involves an attempt to single out who or what has the most power or the most influence to determine a foreign policy decision, one can easily make the mistake of attaching more importance to one's subject than is warranted and disregard the position of that particular organization in the larger context of all other such groups.[14] Neglecting various potentially influential factors in the decision-making process besides those of the organization studied could lead to an evaluation that greatly exaggerates the organization's influence.

To dismiss the influence of the Council from the very outset as negligent and to thus ignore all other analytical tools besides the system of multi-archival research, however, might produce a rather simplistic account of Council activities without providing satisfying answers to questions at the core of the Council's very *raison d'être*.[15] To clarify contradictions in Council members' activities and to be able to specify the members' *Weltanschauung* beyond a reasonable doubt, it would be imperative to research the philosophy of each individual member. The sources, however, are much too scant to study in this amount of detail. It would probably be necessary to interview each individual thoroughly on his or her personal convictions on a variety of topics to gain meaningful data, a task that is impossible to accomplish more than forty years after the events being analyzed took place. However, to merely relate contradictions in Council activities and disagreements among Council

13. See the essays in "A Round Table: Explaining the History of American Foreign Relations," *Journal of American History* 77 (June 1990): 93–180; and in "Writing the History of U.S. Foreign Relations: A Symposium," *Diplomatic History* 14 (Fall 1990): 553–605.

14. McCormick, "Toward a New Diplomatic History," 2.

15. Despite Schulzinger's claim that he would provide an answer to the issue of the Council's influence, his *Wise Men* hardly addresses this crucial matter.

members and to consider this to be a sufficient analysis of Council activities, is as flawed as disregarding such differences in favor of an alleged homogeneity of opinion among the members.

An additional mistake that could easily be made is to declare the Council to be representative of a social group within American society and thus to come to an evaluation of the United States as a whole. The Council, with its high number of members from the business community, could then be perceived as an agent of business or financial interests and the "owning class." Shoup and Minter, as well as Kolko (who also studied other organizations) have proposed such an evaluation. This can only be argued, however, if the large number of academics and the labor leaders participating in Council groups are considered to be dominated by business members and when the disagreement among Council members on many issues of foreign policy discussed in the preceding chapters is discarded as negligible.

Thus, William Minter defined his United States "ruling class" by using the concept of an "owning class." This part of society, Minter argued, had private ownership of the means of production and generated income through these possessions. That this system of private ownership had not been changed in the U.S. was evidence enough for Minter to conclude that the "owning class" had the political means to protect its assets and could thus be termed the "ruling class." Because it controlled politics, the "ruling class" also controlled the nation's foreign policy.[16]

Despite his painstaking research of the personal background of two hundred randomly selected Council members and of all Council officers for the period from 1922 to 1972, revealing that not more than 11.5 percent of the members and 15.2 percent of the Council's directors privately owned some means of production, Minter argued that the Council was an instrument of the "owning class."[17] The logic of this claim could be proved only through the notion that members of the boards of directors of large corporations and top-flight managers had to be counted among the "owning class," because, Minter argued, it was very unlikely that they pursued interests other than those of the "owning class" proper.

If an organization such as the Council is studied almost exclusively in a situation of international crisis in foreign policy, an inaccurate evalua-

16. Minter, "The Council on Foreign Relations," 316–17. See also C. Wright Mills' criticism of such simple and deterministic argumentation in *The Power Elite* (New York, 1959), 277.

17. Minter, "The Council," 337. No significant deviation between Minter's meticulously accrued database and the information on Council members for the period from 1945 to 1950 could be detected and Minter's data will be used in the following evaluation.

tion of its influence is almost predetermined. Shoup's and Minter's study of the Council's activities concentrated on the period of World War II.[18] This was a time when the Council, responding to an international emergency with extraordinary effort, found unusual responsiveness in an administration well aware of its own limitations in long-term planning. In the instance of the War and Peace Studies' proposal to safeguard Greenland under the provisions of the Monroe Doctrine, evidence for direct, concrete, and most likely exclusive influence can be detected. The Charter of the United Nations organization and the creation of the International Monetary Fund was drafted with the help of Council members. Regarding reparations, another fundamental topic of the Council, however, the Council's elaborate and well-argued proposals were not (as Otto Nübel has shown) transformed into actual policy, a fate shared by many other recommendations.[19] Shoup and Minter could not provide proof based on solid and conclusive evidence, furthermore, for their suggestion that the Council was responsible for American foreign policies to "have been and . . . [to be] against the interests of the majority of the American people and the people of the world."[20]

The pluralist analytical concepts of Robert A. Dahl and David B. Truman, proposing that the equilibrium created by the struggle of a large number of groups to promote their individual and dissimilar interests (with the administration serving as little more than as an umpire) would determine American foreign policy, does not reflect reality. Under close examination, concrete evidence for the postulation of a pluralist foreign policy is missing. In addition, exclusive connections between government agencies and interest groups — in this study, between the State Department and the Council on Foreign Relations, through participation in study and discussion groups and by recruitment of Council members for government positions — were neglected.[21]

---

18. See also Domhoff's study of the War and Peace Studies in *The Power Elite*, 113–144. He goes beyond Shoup and Minter and analyzes the Council's involvement in the creation of the International Monetary Fund. See *ibid.*, 159–81.

19. Nübel, *Die amerikanische Reparationspolitik*, 48–73.

20. Shoup and Minter, *Imperial Brain Trust*, 278–80. One State Department official interviewed by Bernard C. Cohen stated that, for a more recent period, the Department did in fact utilize organizations such as the Council to provide background information and to disseminate information supporting measures anticipated and initiated. However, he could not recall any incident in which such an organization had direct and exclusive influence over — or even controlled — the decision-making process. See Cohen, *Public Impact*, 93.

21. For examples, see Dahl's study of city power structure in *Who Governs?* (New Haven, CT, 1961), and, more recently, his *Dilemmas of Pluralist Democracy: Autonomy vs. Control* (New Haven, CT, 1982); also see Truman, *The Governmental Process.*

Thus, James N. Rosenau, the most notable advocate of this thesis, described the Committee for the Marshall Plan as a citizens' organization that was created spontaneously and which affirmed public consensus in favor of the European Recovery Program. The Committee's close affinity with the Department of State and its function as a propaganda agency was overlooked by Rosenau. Similarly, Rosenau did not mention that, with very few exceptions, almost all national organizations favored the Marshall Plan before the Committee for the Marshall Plan was created, whereas the majority of the American people did not approve of the Marshall Plan as late as March 1948. The same corrections apply in the cases of the Non-Partisan Committee for Peace and the Committee to Defend America, mentioned by V.O. Key. As with the Committee for the Marshall Plan, these groups were initiated and supported by the administration to provide domestic legitimization for a foreign policy that was already endorsed by the vast majority of elites from internationalist organizations, labor unions, and the business community.[22]

Heinz Ulrich Brinkmann has shown in his study of "public interest groups" that it is difficult to ascribe influence or success even to organizations that have a clear-cut goal.[23] Unlike the "public interest groups" studied by Brinkmann, the Council had no explicit goal it pursued — even though the Council members may have believed this to be the case in their promotion of the United States' "national interest." The concept of "national interest" is much too ill-defined (and did not receive a definition by Council members) and far too vague to be comparable to the goal to ban the use of nuclear energy, for example.[24]

Priscilla Roberts proposed studying the Council on Foreign Relations as part of the "American establishment." Studies of "the establishment" were necessary, she maintained, including in this term the "power elite," the "governing class," the "foreign policy establishment," and also the "corporate elite."[25] At first glance, this appears to be a promising

22. James N. Rosenau, *National Leadership and Foreign Policy: A Case Study in the Mobilization of Public Support* (Princeton, NJ, 1963), 23; Key, *Politics, Parties, and Pressure Groups* (New York, 1964), 114–16. On the activities of the NPC, CDA, and CMP, see chapter 7.

23. Heinz Ulrich Brinkmann, *Public Interest Groups im politischen System der USA: Organisierbarkeit und Einflußtechniken* (Opladen, 1984), 29–31; see also Jeffrey M. Berry, *Lobbying for the People: The Political Behavior of Public Interest Groups* (Princeton, NJ, 1977), 272–84; Dahl, *Dilemmas*, 21.

24. For a definition of "public interest groups," see Brinkmann, *Public Interest Groups*, 6–11.

25. Priscilla M. Roberts, "The American 'Eastern Establishment' and Foreign Affairs: A Challenge to Historians," part I, SHAFR *Newsletter* 14 (December 1983): 9-28; Part

approach; it would have the advantage of incorporating all eminent organizations and individuals in one analytical framework. A number of "collective biographies" could be produced, shedding light on the world-view of individual members of "the establishment."[26]

When examined more closely, however, this concept has more disadvantages than advantages. The general methodological problem the term "elite" raises is not addressed by the establishment concept, and Roberts herself is not quite certain what and who should constitute this "establishment." Additionally, the differences and divergent interests of individual organizations and their members in the highly complex process of decision-making is obscured by this amalgam of diverse factions of society.[27] Consequently, Roberts' proposal has received little attention in the field.

G. William Domhoff has produced the most elaborate analysis of the Council on Foreign Relations and its function in the American society. He has suggested that through the Council "the power elite formulate general guidelines for American foreign policy and provide the personnel to carry out this policy," and argues that, during the post-war planning of World War II, the Council was "the elite core of the internationalist perspective that projected a very large role for the United States in the post-war world. Its function was to create and organize the policy goals of the internationalist segment of the ruling class."[28]

Drawing on C. Wright Mills, Domhoff combined an institutional analysis with a class analysis by "redefin[ing] the power elite in such a way that it included active, working members of the upper class and high-level employees in private institutions controlled by members of the upper class, and then explored the extent to which the members of

---

II, SHAFR *Newsletter* 15 (March 1984): 8-19. See also Roberts' dissertation, "The American 'Eastern Establishment' and World War I: The Emergence of a Foreign Policy Tradition," Ph.D. diss., King's College, University of Cambridge, 1981.

26. This term has been used mainly by journalists. An example of a collective biography is Walter Isaacson and Evan Thomas, *The Wise Men: Six Friends and the World They Made, Acheson, Bohlen, Harriman, Kennan, Lovett, McCloy* (New York, 1986). For the American establishment, see Leonard Silk and Mark Silk, *The American Establishment* (New York, 1980), with a long but not very informative chapter on the Council on Foreign Relations entitled, "Mission on Sixty-Eighth Street: The Council on Foreign Relations." See also John B. Judis, "Twilight of the Gods: The Rise and Fall of the American Establishment," *Wilson Quarterly* 15 (Autumn 1991): 43–55.

27. On the term "elite", also see Klaus von Beyme, *Die politischen Theorien der Gegenwart* (Munich, 1986), 242–68.

28. Domhoff, *Higher Circles*, 122; *idem.*, *Power Elite*, 114.

this power elite overlapped with those encompassed by Mill's concept." The upper social class's separation from other citizens is indicated by their marriages, attendance at certain schools, memberships in particular clubs, and source of income. "There is an interacting and intermarrying upper social stratum or social elite in America that is distinctive enough in its institutions, source and amount of income, and life-style to be called an 'upper class,'" he argued.[29] This group formulated, through a "set of interlocking policy discussion groups, foundations, think tanks, and university institutes," the economic and social policy of the United States, which, in turn, was transformed into "public opinion" by these same institutions. In addition to their influence on political parties and candidates through their financial contributions, these institutions also served as recruiting grounds for positions in the executive branch of government, thus securing the continuation of influence which made the "upper class" the "ruling class."[30]

If the Council on Foreign Relations were to be classified as a part of this network of the upper social class, the Council membership would have to show a significant homogeneity among its members. This homogeneity could be assumed to be particularly high in the Council, because membership was by invitation only. In addition, the number of members was quite limited. In 1945, the Council had only 642 members, a total that increased to 902 by 1950. The rather cumbersome membership process mentioned earlier should have been able to assure a high degree of homogeneity.

The majority of Council members (62 percent) came from the American East Coast, and about 50 percent attended an elite (Ivy League) university. A reference in the *Social Register* (according to Domhoff, evidence of belonging to the social upper stratum) could be claimed by 37 percent of the Council's members and half of the Council's directors. Also, half of the members were affiliated with eminent clubs. This ratio supports Domhoff's hypothesis and the findings of this

29. Domhoff, *Power Elite*, 1; *idem.*, *Who Rules America Now?*," 17–51; the quotation is from page 49.

30. Domhoff, *Who Rules America Now?*, 82, 116–56. Mills called that label a "badly loaded phrase." See Mills, *Power Elite*, 277. A good overview of criticism on Mills' concept is G. William Domhoff and Hoyt B. Ballard, eds., *C. Wright Mills and the Power Elite* (Boston, 1968), which also provides valuable insights into the editors' own positions. Thomas R. Dye proposed an evaluation similar to Mills' but with a higher rating for institutionalized power than Domhoff. See Dye, "Oligarchic Tendencies in National Policy-Making: The Role of Private Policy-Planning Organizations," *The Journal of Politics* 40 (May 1978): 310.

study for the early Cold War period concur with his sociological analysis.[31] No evidence could be found, however, that the Council's homogeneity in its membership was reflected by a homogeneity of policy recommendations. The Council, as Domhoff has accurately observed, "is far too large for its members to issue policy proclamations as a group."[32]

Only a small portion of Council members regularly participated in Council activities. According to Minter's findings, thirty percent of the Council's directors and even 70 percent of the general membership had never taken part in study and discussion groups. With regard to the actual attendance of individual members at group meetings, this ratio was yet lower. The number of businessmen who joined varied considerably, and quite often they attended only a few of the meetings. Council staff and experts, in particular, and the group's members from academia attended such meetings much more often. As was shown in the preceding chapters, the discussions of Council groups hardly indicate a significant homogeneity in opinion among members of the business community. Many active Council members rather perceived themselves as internationally and socially enlightened experts representing only their educated, intellectually sound, and considered judgment. The Council members' negative opinion of labor leaders participating in Council study and discussion groups (see below), accordingly resulted not so much from an anti-labor attitude, but much more so from their experience that union officials tended to act not as individual experts but rather as representatives of an organized group of society and were thus unable to cooperate on an equal footing with the other Council members.

Despite the concurrence of this study's findings with many of Domhoff's sociological data and a number of his conclusions, and in view of the Council activities discussed in the preceding chapters (particularly the lack of evidence for direct influence of the Council as an organization), the most promising analytical system to understand the Council's function in the foreign policy decision-making process seems to be the corporatist approach as it has been developed by a number of scholars in the field of American foreign relations. It is oriented along the lines of what Philippe Schmitter has defined as corporatism — the

31. Minter, "The Council," 326–55. See Domhoff's studies, *Who Rules America?*, 71–73; *The Higher Circles*, 112–23; *The Powers That Be: Processes of Ruling-Class Domination in America* (New York, 1978), passim.; *Who Rules America Now?*, 85–88.

32. Domhoff, *Who Rules America Now?*, 88.

system of societal communication of interests.[33] Analytical concepts by themselves, such as interest group pluralism, categories of social classes, ruling classes, and even "power elite" seem unable to explain the reality and complexity of American society and the decision-making process in U.S. foreign relations. A system that includes and recognizes larger entities and organizations (business organizations, labor unions, and agricultural organizations, in addition to "interest groups" and public opinion as embodied in elections) as components in the political process, offers a more promising approach.

The corporatist approach also provides a more sufficient analytical concept for studying the organizational dimension of the decision-making process than does a concentration on "national opinion leaders" or a particular elite. The functional elites of the business community, organized labor, academia, and the State Department, in their pursuit of what they saw as societal interests, collaborated in the shaping of foreign policy by using corporatist strategies. In this strategy, collaboration is coordinated by creating "a pattern of interpenetration and power sharing that often make it difficult to determine where one sector leaves off and the other begins." In this cooperation government departments and the business community played more important roles than labor and national agricultural organizations.[34]

Elites originating from these functional groups often have more in common with each other than with their organizational constituency. These are Barnet's "national security managers," Chadwick's and Divine's "internationalists," Mills' "power elite," Domhoff's "higher circles," and Priscilla Roberts' "establishment."[35]

Pluralist traditions and structures still exist in the American political system and cannot be ignored despite the concentration of decision-making processes in the hands of a few groups. Neither can Congress be disregarded as an important factor in this process. Through the direct

---

33. Philippe C. Schmitter, "Still the Century of Corporatism?" in: *The New Corporatism* (South Bend, IN, 1974), Fredrik B. Pike and Thomas Stritch, eds. See also Ellis W. Hawley, "The Discovery and Study of A 'Corporate Liberalism,'" *Business History Review* 52 (Autumn 1978): 309–20; and Winfried Steffani, *Pluralistische Demokratie: Studien zur Theorie und Praxis* (Opladen, 1980), and his criticism of Schmitter, *ibid.*, 61–65. In addition, see William A. Kelso's delineation of "corporate pluralism" in *American Democratic Theory: Pluralism and ITS Critics* (Westport, CT, 1978), 19–25.

34. The term "national opinion leaders" was created in 1963 by Rosenau, *National Leadership.* Hogan, "Corporatism," 154.

35. See the studies mentioned in the preceding notes; Divine, *Second Chance*; and Chadwick, *Warhawks.*

election of senators and representatives, their respective constituencies are able to exert a potentially critical influence. This becomes important when foreign policy is highly dependent on the appropriation of financial means and the "power of the purse" of the House of Representatives becomes vital. The activities of ad hoc committees (discussed in chapter 7), therefore, were orchestrated to convince members of Congress that the American public and eminent national organizations supported a particular policy and that the politicians would not jeopardize their own reelections if they voted in favor of these measures. Additionally, interest groups exercised influence on decision-making to promote their special interests, and published opinion also had an impact.[36]

It can be stated, nonetheless, that during the beginning of the Cold War the cooperation between government agencies and large functional groups was more significant than these pluralist properties of the American decision-making process. These latter groups did not act autonomously and in competition with one another. They pursued close relations through formal and informal contacts and were hierarchical and elitist rather than democratic in their internal structure and membership. By cooperating closely with each other, they shaped American foreign policy through consensus-building and self-regulation.

Membership and Functions of the Council on Foreign Relations

The main role of the Council on Foreign Relations in this interplay of societal functional groups was the continuous attempt to form a consensus among the participants of Council study and discussion groups. At these occasions, they contemplated proposals and evaluations and discussed their suggestions with State Department officials attending the meetings. Plans and concepts were examined by experts and scholars in the light of possible effects, practicability, and the likelihood of generating legislative approval. This was seldomly done in a highly formalized fashion. In most instances, the group members and their guests engaged in conversation and informal discussion. That the content of the meetings and individual contributions were kept confidential only heightened openness and willingness to disclose information and to voice opinions.

36. During the period from 1945 to 1950, the cooperation between eminent commentators and journalists — such as Lippmann, Reston, and Baldwin — on the one side, and State Department officials on the other side (often through the vehicle of the Council on Foreign Relations), worked superbly.

When the Council was founded in 1921, the prospect of informed and stimulated discussion was one of the major reasons for the merger of the old Council with the American Institute. The members of the old Council realized that their meetings rarely accomplished anything worthwhile, since they lacked the participation of scholars and government officials, and that their organization was about to become yet another men's club for New York's wealthy business people interested in foreign affairs. Although the Council on Foreign Relations developed its capacity as a research organization, it still featured the characteristics of a club. Some members even listed their affiliation with the Council in biographies such as *Who's Who,* under the heading, "club memberships." The Council's membership criteria, the rather elite position it adopted in relations with similar organizations, the exclusion of women from the membership until 1970, and the provision that half of the membership had to be composed of residents of the New York City area, enhanced this impression.[37]

Officers of the Council tried to draw into the Council's membership experts from outside business and academia. Journalists, editors, and clergymen were equally regarded as vital for a foreign policy sustained by all functional elites. Members of the business community, however, constituted the largest part of the Council's membership. Comprising about 30 percent of the membership, their relative dominance remained constant over the years. During World War II, one fourth of the members served with the government, a number that declined to less than 20 percent in 1950. Initially, 25 percent of the membership were professors and presidents of elite universities. Close to 10 percent of the men were journalists or held eminent positions in print media or radio. Only 5 percent headed institutions such as the Carnegie Endowment for International Peace, the American Association for the United Nations, and the Rockefeller Foundation, or were labor leaders or representatives of agricultural organizations such as the American Farm Bureau Federation.[38]

---

37. Against strong opposition, the Council admitted five women in 1970. Frank Altschul and Arthur Dean were among the most outspoken critics, with Dean arguing: "If you let one woman in, how can we keep our wives out?" See Lukas, "The Council on Foreign Relations," 130; Campbell, "The Death," 48. William Diebold stated that members also feared their wives' jealousy when they attended meetings until very late at night with women present; William Diebold, Jr., Interview, Century Club, New York City, 20 September 1988. By June 1992, the membership exceeded 2,900. Of these, 15 percent were women and 8 percent were minorities. See CFR, *Annual Report, July 1, 1991–June 30, 1992* (New York, n.d.), 102–105.

38. The data are taken from Minter, "The Council." The annual reports only categorized members as "Resident," "Non-Resident," "Resident Academic," and "Non-Resident Academic" members. Here the term "academic" refers to Council members — mostly members of academia, journalists, officials of non-governmental organizations, and

In 1945 only two labor leaders were members of the Council: David Dubinsky and Robert J. Watt of the American Federation of Labor. The relationship between Council officers and labor was quite ambivalent at that time. On the one hand, most Council members did not regard organized labor very highly and were hardly eager to include them in their ranks. On the other hand, however, they understood the increased significance of labor unions, particularly in the wake of World War II, and the importance of labor in any attempt to promote an American foreign policy supported by all functional elites. In May of 1946, the Board of Directors of the Council decided that this warranted the inclusion of more labor officials in the Council membership; however, only a few carefully chosen and trustworthy (i.e., conservative) union leaders were asked to join. Of these, only two, Solomon Barkin of the Textile Worker's Union of America and the CIO's Michael Ross, accepted the Council's invitation. Four years later only David Dubinsky, the anti-communist president of the International Ladies Garment Workers Union, was still among the members.[39]

Council officials were obviously disappointed by the lack of interest among labor leaders in participating in the Council's activities. It was important to build bridges between the Council and organized labor, the frustrated Isaiah Bowman wrote, but the efforts had turned out to be "a waste of time." Labor leaders had been invited to Council meetings before, but then they had either declined the invitation, did not show up, or had arrived too late and had not spoken at the meetings. "Our Labor leaders," as opposed to their British colleagues, Bowman reflected, "are not yet sufficiently mature to engage in an objective and cooperative study with other groups."[40]

Overlappings of affiliations and interlockings with various organizations and institutions were thus commonplace among Council members.[41]

---

government officials — who paid reduced membership fees as agreed at the merger of the old Council and the American Institute in 1921.

39. "Suggested Labor Members for the Council on Foreign Relations," dated 17 May 1946, enclosure to Mallory to John W. Davis, 25 June 1946, Davis Papers, box 133. Sidney Hillman, president of Amalgamated Clothing Workers of America, and Walter P. Reuther, president of United Automobile Workers, had been proposed as possible candidates by Whitney Shepardson. Council director John W. Davis adamantly opposed these recommendations. See Davis to Mallory, 8 July 1946, *ibid.*.

40. Bowman to Arthur W. Page, 20 March 1947, Bowman Papers. William Diebold confirmed the lack of interest in the Council among labor leaders; Diebold Interview, 17 September 1985.

41. This phenomenon is described as "overlapping membership" (Truman, *The Governmental Process*) or "interlocks." On the Council's "interlocks" with other notable organizations, see the data in Harold Salzman and G. William Domhoff, "The Corporate

Short biographical sketches of some eminent Council members may not be conclusive but do give an indication of the extent of this phenomenon:

> Dean G. Acheson: A.B. Yale; lawyer; secretary to Supreme Court Justice Louis D. Brandeis, 1919–1921; practiced law until 1933; under secretary of the treasury in 1933; again, practiced law, until 1941; assistant secretary, and after 1945, under secretary of state until 1947; secretary of state from 1949 to 1953; fellow of the Yale Corporation; Metropolitan (Washington) and Century (New York) clubs.
>
> Winthrop W. Aldrich: J.D. Harvard; financier; chairman of the board, Chase National Bank, 1934–1953; ambassador to England; chairperson of the American Heritage Foundation; chairperson of the President's (Truman) Committee to Finance Foreign Trade; chairperson of the Committee on International Economic Policy of the Carnegie Endowment for International Peace; Century Club.
>
> Frank Altschul: B.A. Yale; financier; chairperson of the Board of Directors of General American Investors, affiliated with Lazard Frères and Lehman Brothers; vice chairman of the National Planning Association; Metropolitan and Century clubs. Brother-in-law of Herbert H. Lehman.
>
> Isaiah Bowman: Ph.D. Yale; member of the "Inquiry;" president of Johns Hopkins University since 1935; member of the Board of Directors of American Telephone and Telegraph (AT&T); chairperson of the National Research Council; American delegate to the Dumbarton Oaks conference; advisor to the American delegation to the founding conference of the United Nations organization, San Francisco, 1945; Century Club.
>
> William A.M. Burden: A.B. Harvard; financier; with Brown Brothers and Harriman 1928–1932; vice president, Defense Supplies Corporation, 1941–1942; assistant secretary of commerce for air, 1943–1947; special assistant to the secretary of air force, 1950–1952; Metropolitan and Century clubs.
>
> Lewis W. Douglas: B.A. Amherst College; Democratic member of the House of Representatives, Arizona, 1923–1925; representative from Arizona to the U.S. Congress, 1926–1934; president of Mutual Life Insurance, 1940–1947, chairperson of the Board of Directors, 1947–1959; special advisor to General Lucius D. Clay, German Control Council, 1945; president of the English Speaking Union, 1946–1947; ambassador to Great Britain, 1947–1950; Metropolitan club. Brother-in-law of John J. McCloy.
>
> David Dubinsky: president of International Ladies Garment Workers Union, 1932–1966; member of the Board of Directors of the Willkie

Community and Government: Do They Interlock?" in *Power Structure Research* (Beverly Hills, 1980) G. William Domhoff, ed., 227–38.

Memorial, 1945; consultant to the United Nations' Economic and Social Council, 1946; member of the Trade Union Advisory Committee on International Labor Affairs of the Department of Labor; member of Labor's Committee for the Election of Truman, 1948; delegate to the international Confederation of Free Trade Unions, London, 1949.

Allen W. Dulles: M.A. Princeton, 1916; diplomatic service, 1916–1926; LL.B. George Washington University, 1926; lawyer, with Sullivan & Cromwell; advisor to the State Department; chief of OSS mission in Switzerland, 1942 to 1945; chief of OSS mission in Germany until November 1945; legal advisor for the Interim Committee on Headquarters of the U.N., 1946; consultant, Joint Committee on Atomic Energy, 1947–1948; senior staff consultant, House Select Committee on Foreign Aid (Herter Committee); head of Committee of Three, shaping the CIA, 1948; deputy director of plans, CIA; director of CIA; Metropolitan and Century clubs.

Arthur W. Page: A.B. Harvard, 1905; vice president and editor of *Worlds Work*, 1913–1927; vice president of AT&T, 1927–1947; director of Continental Oil Company and Westinghouse Electric Company; member of the Board of Trustees of the Carnegie Corporation, Metropolitan Museum of Modern Art, Educational and Development Fund of the Farmers Federation; chairperson of the Joint Army and Navy Committee of Welfare and Recreation, 1942–1946; advisor to Secretary of War Stimson; director of the Free Europe Committee; Metropolitan and Century clubs.

Philip D. Reed: B.S. University of Wisconsin –Madison, 1921; various positions (assistant to president, director, chairman of the Board of Directors) at General Electric, 1926–1942, 1945–1959; War Production Board, 1942; deputy chief, and later chief, of U.S. Mission for Economic Affairs, London, 1942–1945; advisor at UN founding conference at San Francisco, 1945; member of the Business Advisory Board at the Department of Commerce, 1940–1950; trustee, Committee on Economic Development since 1946.

With very few exceptions, all Council members had received a college education. Almost 50 percent had been educated at elite universities such as Harvard, Yale, Princeton, and Columbia, and more than a third had earned a graduate degree. A number of these men guided their alma maters as presidents, as members of the board of trustees, or as members of the governing board.

Membership in prominent clubs, frequently regarded as a sign of prestige, was widespread among members. About 25 percent were members of the Century Club and more than 10 percent were affiliated with the Metropolitan Club in Washington, D.C. Among the Council's directors, this number was even higher. Two-thirds of them belonged to the Century Club and one third were associated with the Metropolitan Club. The factors of education and club membership, however, although reflecting wealth and social status, were of minor significance in choosing an individual to become a Council member. More important in this respect was his position in the business community, academia, government, and at eminent foundations and other such non-governmental institutions. Thus, a number of Council members were affiliated with large internationally operating firms such as United States Steel, Mobil Oil, Standard Oil (NJ), IBM, ITT, and General Electric.

From the commercial banks, directors of Chase Manhattan Bank, J.P. Morgan & Company, First National City Bank, Brown Brothers, Harriman & Company, and the Bank of New York were frequently Council members. Of the investment banks and firms, members of Morgan Stanley, Kuhn and Loeb, Lehman Brothers, and General American Investors were among the members. Additionally, a number of partners of eminent law firms and insurance companies, as well as individuals affiliated with business organizations (such as the Business Council and the Committee for Economic Development) had been recruited by the Council.[42]

A number of Council members were trustees of the Rockefeller and the Ford foundations as well as the Carnegie Corporation. The media were represented by journalists and editors of the *New York Times*, *Washington Post*, *Wall Street Journal*, *Time*, *Newsweek*, *Fortune*, and *Business Week*, and by executives and journalists of the radio networks CBS and NBC.[43]

In addition, quite a few Council members were affiliated with the Brookings Institution, Foreign Policy Association (FPA), American Association for the United Nations (AAUN), and the National Planning Association. And half of the trustees of large internationalist organizations, such as the Carnegie Endowment for International Peace,

---

42. The number of these "interlocks" is in each case larger than four. On these "interlocks" and "overlaps", see Domhoff, *Who Rules America Now?*, 86; and Salzman and Domhoff, "The Corporate Community and Government," 237. See also Eakins, "Business Planners;" McQuaid, *Big Business*; Karl Schriftgiesser, *Business and Public Policy: The Role of the Committee for Economic Development, 1942–1967* (Englewood Cliffs, NJ, 1967); and *idem.*, *Business Comes of Age*.

43. Salzman and Domhoff, "The Corporate Community and Government," 237. On the foundations, see also Edward H. Berman, *The Influence of Carnegie, Ford, and Rockefeller Foundations on American Foreign Policy: The Ideology of Philanthropy* (Albany, NY, 1983); David Horowitz and David Kolodney, "The Foundations: (Charity Begins at Home)," *Ramparts* (April 1968), 38–48.

Twentieth Century Fund, Woodrow Wilson Foundation, and the World Peace Foundation, were members of the Council.

These organizations themselves, however, were kept at a distance from the Council. Council members and members of these groups worked together closely in substantial numbers only in ad hoc groups when promoting a particular foreign policy. Although officers of foreign policy organizations, such as Clark M. Eichelberger of the AAUN and Brooks Emeny of the FPA, were members of the Council, they participated very infrequently in Council groups. An extensive interchange of staff or experts or other close cooperation with the Council was not undertaken, whereas collaboration among such foreign policy organizations as FPA, AAUN, and CEIP was more common.[44]

Council officials regarded overtures for closer cooperation more as a threat than as an offer to complement Council activities. Proposals by the FPA to work with the Council more closely and to merge regional chapters for a combined effort, for example, were fended off vehemently. The FPA's president, Brooks Emeny, repeatedly urged the Council to coordinate its activities with the operations of other organizations. In 1944, he suggested opening the Council's Committees on Foreign Relations to a broader public and merging their efforts to educate the public with those of local FPA chapters. The directors of the Rockefeller Foundation, who financed the Council as well as the FPA and other similar organizations, considered Emeny's proposal but did not follow up on it, fearing that the FPA president might become too influential.[45]

None of these attempts "to get together," as Hamilton Armstrong called it, were received well by Council officers. During World War II, Russell Leffingwell argued against the proposed cooperation with the Foreign Policy Association. "If I'd wanted to sit down with those people," he wrote to Bowman, "I would have joined them." Percy Bidwell was even more disrespectful in his evaluation of FPA activities. Explain-

44. Thus, a large number of internal memoranda of other such organizations can be found among the Carnegie Endowment Records at Butler Library (Columbia University) and the AAUN Records (as part of the Eichelberger Papers at the New York Public Library).

45. Raymond R. Fosdick to John D. Rockefeller, Jr., 30 August 1944, Records of the Office of the Messrs. Rockefeller, box 4; copy, George S. Messersmith to Brooks Emeny, 7 August 1944, enclosure to Messersmith to Hamilton Armstrong, 7 August 1944, Armstrong Papers, box 38; Joseph H. Willits, Inter-Office Correspondence, "Letter from Brooks Emeny," dated 3 January 1946, RFR, 2/200/336/2272; Brooks Emeny to John D. Rockefeller, Jr., 28 March 1946, Messrs. Rokefeller, box 4; "Interview: Brooks Emeny," dated 29 April 1946, RFR, 2/200/336/2272.

ing the differing publication policies of the Council and the FPA to the members of the study group on Public Opinion and Foreign Policy, he declared that "[t]he Council has very rarely issued pamphlets, preferring to leave this field to the Foreign Policy Association." After opening Council membership to women and younger individuals, Walter Mallory's verdict was even harsher: "The organization [the Council] more and more assumes the character of the Foreign Policy Association. Perhaps fifty years is all a select organization can last, especially in these *permissive* years."[46]

The partial list of overlapping memberships and the general composition of the Council's membership reveals the high degree of interconnection and interpenetration among organizations. It also gives an indication of the Council's recruitment strategy. In most cases, individuals were invited to become Council members after they had acquired eminent positions in business, in the executive branch of government, in academia, and in other institutions and organizations. This was regarded as a guarantee that they would prove useful for the Council's role in the decision-making process. Recruitment of Council members for positions in non-governmental organizations, in business, or in the executive branch of government, solely because of their affiliation with the Council, most probably occurred very rarely. To be a member of the Council, nevertheless, was an indicator of the potential usefulness of a candidate.

"Whenever we needed a man," John J. McCloy (assistant secretary to Secretary of War Stimson and later American high commissioner for Germany) recalled, "we thumbed through the roll of Council members and put through a call to New York."[47] This certainly was an exaggeration, but the number of Council members recruited by the U.S. government's executive branch, nonetheless, is remarkable. Out of a list of 122 officials of the Truman administration in high positions (including the president, the secretaries and assistant secretaries of the State, War, Navy, and Defense departments; under secretaries at the Treasury and Commerce departments; Joint Chiefs of Staff, White House assistants, ambassadors to France, Germany, Great Britain, and the USSR; and heads of such agencies as the ECA and Import-Export Bank) in 1945,

46. Armstrong to Bowman, 27 October 1947, Bowman Papers. Leffingwell's letter is quoted in Schulzinger, "Whatever Happened," 282. For Bidwell's statement, see DD, 27 March 1947, 2, POFP/RGCFR-XXIIIA. Mallory assumed that George S. Franklin (his successor as the Council's director of studies after 1953) "couldn't control . . . the 'progress'" he had initiated, and that "[v]ery few seem to have any intestinal fortitude among our so-called leaders." See Mallory to Armstrong, 2 August 1972, Armstrong Papers, box 37.

47. Quoted in Kraft, "School," 67.

fourteen were members of the Council. By 1950, this number increased to thirty-four, and by 1955, to forty-six. This increase was in part a result of the expansion of government activities in foreign relations, in addition to the administration's drawing on the pool of Council members already proven to be acquainted with the field. Such notables as George F. Kennan, Dean Acheson, and Dwight D. Eisenhower were invited to become members only after they had acquired their prominent positions and esteemed reputations.[48]

In addition to being drafted for government service, Council members were often nominated to serve on advisory committees in their function as representatives and experts of functional groups (such as those in business, organized labor, and agriculture). The President's Committee on Foreign Aid was led by Council member Averell Harriman. Of the additional nineteen members of that Committee, seven were affiliated with the Council. The House Select Committee on Foreign Aid was guided by Council member Christian A. Herter, and the President's Committee on Financing Foreign Trade was chaired by Council member Winthrop W. Aldrich. This does not suggest, however, that the Council, through well-placed agents, influenced these groups, however tempting this evaluation may be.[49]

Paul G. Hoffman was most certainly not drafted to head the ECA because of his Council membership but because Senator Arthur Vandenberg insisted on his appointment. John J. McCloy (whom Richard Rovere, in a satirical article, dubbed the chairperson of the board of directors of the "establishment") had excellent connections with the War Department and had been president of the International Bank for Reconstruction and Development before being made High Commissioner; these were much better qualifications than his affiliation with the Council.[50] Allen Dulles' involvement in the shaping of the American peace-time

48. Minter, "The Council," 137–40. Surprisingly, in view of Eisenhower's exceptionally close affiliation with the Council, the percentage declined during his administration (from the 42 percent during the Truman administration, corrected by the number of Council members resting their memberships) to 40 percent. During the Kennedy administration the proportion increased to 51 percent, and attained its highest mark during the Johnson administration with 57 percent. See Minter, "The Council," 122. On the relation between the Council and the Kennedy administration, see Arthur M. Schlesinger, Jr., *A Thousand Days* (Boston, 1965), particularly pages 116–17; and David Halberstam, *The Best and the Brightest* (New York, 1972; Fawcett Crest Edition), *passim.*

49. See also Domhoff, *Who Rules America Now?* 133; and Eakins, "Business Planners," 164, 161. See also chapter 7.

50. Richard H. Rovere, "Notes on the Establishment in America," *The American Scholar* 30 (Fall 1961): 489–95; *idem.*, "Postscript: A 1978 Commentary," *The Wil-*

intelligence agency, the CIA, and his heading the agency from 1953 to 1961, were most likely due to his previous intelligence experience during World War I and at the OSS and not to his presidency of the Council.

In other instances it seemed quite possible that Council membership served as what Richard Barnet termed a rite of initiation for a position related to foreign policy.[51] Membership in the Council certainly proved one thing: the member was interested in foreign affairs and was regarded by his peers to be useful in this field. Regarding skills for the job and the potential to accomplish assignments, however, other qualification undoubtedly were considered more important.

The Council's efforts to inform the "interested public" of developments in foreign relations was accomplished through the publication of the journal *Foreign Affairs*, handbooks, and monographs.[52] Publication of studies and articles, frequently resulting from the efforts of study and discussion groups, was thus aimed at broadening the consensus on foreign policy beyond that of participants in Council groups. Additionally, the handbooks published by the Council (which were proofread by State Department officials to ensure accuracy) served as reliable and timely sources of information on current events.

No serious author has argued that, through these publications, the Council controlled American foreign policy. It would also be rather farfetched to maintain, for example, that the Council had inaugurated the containment policy by publishing George Kennan's "X" article in the July 1947 issue of *Foreign Affairs.* The Truman administration was already proceeding along the lines proposed in Kennan's article and had already received an intellectual legitimization through Kennan's "long telegram" in February 1946 and in his widely circulated paper written for Secretary of the Navy Forrestal, in January 1947, of which the "X" article was only a reprint. "Sources of Soviet Conduct," which was the article's real importance, replayed this process for the broader public.

Quarterly 2 (Summer 1978): 182–84. "Oh, no, not me," protested Wall Street lawyer McCloy, who had been born to poor parents in Philadelphia, "I was not really a part of the Establishment. I was from the wrong side of the tracks." Quoted in Isaacson and Thomas, *The Wise Men*, 27.

51. Barnet, *Roots of War*, 49.

52. The term "interested public" included individuals among the "foreign policy public," "national opinion leaders," "foreign policy establishment," and "internationalists" who were not members of the Council but showed an interest in foreign affairs. See Ernest R. May, *American Imperialism: A Speculative Essay* (New York, 1968); Adler and Bobrow, "Interest"; Divine, *Second Chance*; Rosenau, *National Leadership*; and Cohen, *The Public's Impact.*

Books published by the Council seldomly provoked protests, as did the studies *Challenge to Isolation* and *The Undeclared War*, authored by William L. Langer and S. Everett Gleason. For these studies, Langer had received $139,000 from the Rockefeller Foundation through the Council. He used his good connections in the State Department to gain access to documents not yet released to the public in writing his salutary history of American involvement in World War II.[53]

The renowned "revisionist" historian Charles A. Beard vehemently attacked what he termed a "court history." He accused the Rockefeller Foundation and the Council of blocking critical historians' examination of Langer's evaluations by failing to secure access to the documents Langer had used. The Council was not shaken by this criticism. Beard's evaluation of history was "based on a theory," Isaiah Bowman maintained, and thus could not be taken very seriously. "By temperament," Bowman argued, "he is incapable of understanding the nature of the political process that is involved in attaining a better world order."[54]

In addition to *Foreign Affairs*, handbooks, and monographs, Council members were informed about the results of study and discussion groups through the *Annual Report*, which was written by the Council's executive director. Summaries, often two to five pages in length, were printed together with information regarding internal Council affairs and accounts of cooperation with other organizations. In addition to informing the members about their organization, the annual reports thus also contributed to the Council's effort to foster a consensus on foreign policy.

Direct influence of the Council and its members on State Department officials, to the extent that this can be judged by documentary evidence, memoirs, and recollections, was rather scant. Conversations at dinner parties and over the telephone, informal discussions at receptions, and short meetings at lunches were favored and frequently used methods of exchange of information of the individuals studied. The

53. Resolution 47315, dated 1 February 1950, RFR, 1.2/58/444; CFR, Committee on Studies Meeting, 29 November 1948, *ibid.*; CFR, Committee on Studies Meeting, 16 November 1949, RFR, 1.2/57/440. On Langer, see also his autobiography, *In and Out of the Ivory Tower: The Autobiography of William L. Langer* (New York, 1977).

54. Schulzinger, *Wise Men*, 129–135; For Beard's critique, see *Saturday Evening Post*, 2 October 1947. Bowman to Mallory, 6 October 1947, Bowman Papers; Langer, *In and Out*, 210–13. In the case of William L. Shirer's *The Rise and Fall of the Third Reich* (New York, 1960), also written with Council support, this cooperation did not provoke any criticism. See Shirer to Armstrong, 12 October 1958, Armstrong Papers, box 43.

Council's traditional dinner break during the study and discussion group meetings consciously provided a relaxed, informal setting.[55]

This important type of communication left few records, making it difficult for scholars to determine whether these conversations resulted in any kind of influence. Notes of informal conversations and meetings are the rare exception and none of the individuals studied (with the exception of Robert Lovett, whose daily log contains scarcely more than a short note as to the person calling and the subject of communication) kept notes of telephone conversations.[56]

In the correspondence of Council members (for example, that of Bowman, Allen Dulles, and Armstrong), frequent references can be found to conversations and meetings with State Department officials such as Dean Acheson, Archibald MacLeish, Francis Russell, and Robert Lovett. This indicates that many more contacts between Council members and State Department officials existed, a number far exceeding the total number of meetings recorded in the sources. No substantial number of Council memoranda (one type of documentary proof for such meetings and exchange of information), however, could be found among the State Department documents accessible to researchers.[57]

Concepts discussed by the Council's study and discussion groups in the period studied were not especially original or altogether different from policies already devised, nor did these groups propose policies very different from those already anticipated or launched by the Truman administration. The change in the U.S. deindustrialization and denazification policies in Germany, advocated by Allen Dulles, had already been partially put in operation by Lucius D. Clay and his staff. Dulles maintained constant contact with government officials and could communicate his views through more direct channels than the Council. The major objective for the study group, therefore, was to change the attitude among elites toward Germany; from the view of Germany as an aggressive enemy that had to be prevented from ever again becoming a

55. "A great many important things happened at social occasions," Willard Thorp recalled without specifically referring to the Council. One could meet with interested individuals and foreign politicians and could informally discuss and reach agreement on details. See Thorp Oral History, 54–59; the quotation is from page 56.

56. See Lovett Daily Log, which contains numerous entries regarding meetings for lunch or dinner with Senator Vandenberg, Baldwin, Armstrong, and others.

57. Cohen related that individuals (such as McCloy, Acheson, Kennan, and the Rockefeller brothers) had access to State Department officials, often long after they had left office, and that they frequently served as informal advisors. See *The Public's Impact*, 84.

menace to peace, to a view of Germany as the key to the fight against economic breakdown and the spread of communism in western Europe. Even the Aid to Europe group, led by Dwight Eisenhower, probably had little more impact than serving as a valuable education for the future president of the United States on the complexity and diversity of American foreign relations.

A decisive and direct influence by the Council during the early Cold War years could not be detected. Council members and State Department officials generally shared a common world-view and structure of thought after World War II. The Council continuously offered its services to the State Department. It provided an abundant supply of (sometimes rather sketchy) long-range concepts that could be developed without the pressure of daily chores State Department officials faced. Memoranda were forwarded to Department officers, officials were invited to participate in study and discussion groups, and Council members frequently met with officials on formal and informal occasions. The State Department could presume that Council proposals and concepts were supported by a large part of the functional elites concerned with foreign policy. That these proposals were not directly reflected in U.S. policy statements, would seem initially to be evidence of a lack of influence on the part of the Council. Only a lack of *direct* influence, however, can be inferred; proposals might well have "floated around" before being incorporated in policy measures without evidence of the original source.[58]

Similar to the Council's weekly discussion and study group meetings, the less frequent dinner meetings and the few full-membership meetings at the Harold Pratt House in New York City were often used as forums. Speakers could impart their ideas to an interested public, advocate their causes, and further the development of favorable opinion among the elites. Council members received information and could in turn convey their impressions through the manifold channels of communication available to them. Probably more influential than speeches at these meetings were the informal discussions at dinners or over cocktails that followed. Through its function as a forum the Council was influential, although the extent varied with each issue, and the influence was rarely direct in nature.

---

58. Willard Thorp recalls, without specifically naming the Council, that memoranda were often not immediately included in policy decisions, but "the idea floated around." See Thorp Oral History, 32.

The constant reiteration of the claim that the Council was an important and influential organization, an impression the Council and its members made efforts to foster, may have induced politicians and government officials to spend some of their valuable time with the Council. Again, the Council's function went beyond its role as a mechanism to promote consensus. The Committees on Foreign Relations were used to gather information on the attitudes of elites throughout the nation; Robert Lovett and others used the Council as a "listening post" for the attitudes of "foreign policy constituents." Anticipated or conceivable policies were thus discussed, considered, and examined in light of the possibility of reaching a general agreement of approval.[59]

Despite critics' claims, the Council as an organization never advocated specific policies and did not devise new approaches to American foreign policy during the beginning of the Cold War. No indication could be found that Council members had pressured the administration into a foreign policy measure that ran counter to State Department officials' ideas. Individual members, however, quite often had direct channels of communication with State Department officials and participated in ad hoc committees supposedly founded to induce the administration to initiate a policy or to vocalize public sentiment. After the war, the most significant of these "citizens' committees" was the Committee for the Marshall Plan. Contrary to official declarations of these groups, however, evidence clearly shows that these committees can be more aptly termed external propaganda agencies of the State Department rather than voluntary organizations of concerned citizens. In all instances, the committees were either directly initiated by the administration or founded in close cooperation with and assisted by the State Department. To convince Congress to pass bills and appropriate funds, the myth of a "public opinion" was created, which had no reflection in actual public opinion. The achievements of these committees are excellent examples of the paternalism of elite internationalists such as the members of the Council.

The Council members based their point of reference for what they considered an adequate foreign policy and a stable international system on their perception of domestic American conditions. They were certain about the superiority of American institutions. A capitalist economy and a democratic social order were not regarded as two separate features

59. The term "foreign policy constituents" was used by a State Department official interviewed by Cohen. See his *Public's Impact*, 23.

of societal structure, but rather as the inseparable properties of a democratic system agreeing most perfectly with human nature. Council members desired economic and political international cooperation of individual nations with as little supra-national interference as possible, a point of view reflecting their perception of the cooperation existing within the United States between the different functional groups. This was their frame of reference for questions of international economic and political cooperation through the United Nations and similar organizations.

The "ideological war" between the United States and the Soviet Union led many Council members to take a myopic view of international relations, reducing virtually all aspects of foreign policy to this confrontation. Thus, arguments and political ideas advanced by members were quite often a mixture of expertise, insight, and internationally-minded analysis countered by arrogance, naiveté, and a passionate belief in the advantages of the "American way of life." They put their hopes in the newly founded United Nations Organization to provide for a stable system of defined and enforceable rules. The stability of such a system would further international trade and all countries would benefit. The United States, they demanded, should play a major role in world politics, a role that would pay tribute to the military, economic, and "moral" strength of the nation.

To make this possible, the Council on Foreign Relations provided a well-organized, yet informal, link between elites concerned with U.S. foreign relations and the administration. At the same time it served as a connection between elite and public opinion. The Council thus fulfilled an important function in a corporatist strategy to devise the foreign policy of the United States.

Appendices

Abbreviations

AAUN	American Association for the United Nations
ADA	Americans for Democratic Action, Files, State Historical Society of Wisconsin
AFL	American Federation of Labor
ASPA	Records of the Assistant Secretary of State for Public Affairs, Records Group 59, National Archives
CDA	Committee to Defend American by Aiding the Allies
CDAR	Committee to Defend American by Aiding the Allies, Files and Records, Mudd Manuscript Library
CDE	Committee for Economic Development
CEIP	Carnegie Endowment for International Peace
CEIPR	Carnegie Endowment for International Peace, Records, Baker Library, Columbia University
CFR	Council on Foreign Relations
CFRW+P	Council on Foreign Relations, War and Peace Studies — Memoranda
CIO	Congress of Industrial Organization
CMP	Committee for the Marshall Plan to Aid European Recovery
CMPR	Committee for the Marshall Plan to Aid European Recovery, Files and Minutes, Truman Library
DD	Digest of Discussion (CFR)
EPP	Dwight D. Eisenhower, Pre-Presidential Papers, Eisenhower Library
FA	*Foreign Affairs*
FFF	Fight For Freedom Inc., Archives, Mudd Manuscript Library
FPA	Foreign Policy Association
LNA	League of Nations Association
MM	Minutes of Meeting
NPC	Non-Partisan Committee for the Revision of Neutrality Legislation
PSF	President's Secretary's Files, 1945-1953, Harry S. Truman, Papers of the President of the United States, Truman Library
RCCFR	Records of Conferences, Council on Foreign Relations Archives, Harold Pratt House
RFR	Rockefeller Foundation Records
RGCFR	Records of Groups, Council on Foreign Relations Archives, Harold Pratt House

Study and Discussion Groups (Prefixes):

AE Aid to Europe
AE-M Aid to Europe, Memoranda
ARR American Russian Relations
BEA British Empire Affairs
BFP British Foreign Policy
EAAFP Economic Aspects of American Foreign Policy
EE Eastern Europe
EP Economic Policy
EPR The Economic and Political Reconstruction of Liberated Areas in Europe
FE Far East
FEA Far Eastern Affairs
IAA Inter-American Affairs
MP Marshall Plan
NME Near and Middle East
NPFP National Power and Foreign Policy
OP The Organization of Peace
OPJ Occupation Problems in Japan
PG Political Group
PofG The Problem of Germany
PMT Prosperity and Multilateral Trade
POFP Public Opinion and Foreign Policy
PSU The Power of the Soviet Union
RJ Revival of Japan
RWE Reconstruction in Western Europe
SFP Soviet Foreign Policy
USFP United States Foreign Policy
USPA U.S. Policy Toward Southeast Asia
USPC U.S. Policy Toward China
USPT U.S. Policy Towards Non-Self-Governing Territories
USR United States' Relations with Russia
WEA Western European Affairs
WEC Western European Cooperation

RMCFR Records of Meetings, Council on Foreign Relations Archives, Harold Pratt House

Important Study and Discussion Groups After 1945

Study Group on American-Russian Relations 1944-46

Chair:	William H. Schubart, 1 Wall Street
Secretary:	George S. Franklin, Jr., CFR
Members:	
Frank Altschul	40 Wall Street
Hanson Baldwin	*New York Times*
Joseph Barnes	New York *Herald Tribune*
Edwin de T. Bechtel	Carter Ledyard & Milburn, 2 Wall Street
William Benton	Assistant Secretary of State
Percy Bidwell	CFR
Edward C. Carter	Institute of Pacific Relations
John F. Chapman	Foreign Editor, Business Week
Thomas W. Childs	Lazard Frères, 44 Wall Street
John L. Curtis	National City Bank, 55 Wall Street
Norris Darell	Sullivan & Cromwell, 48 Wall Street
Arthur H. Dean	Sullivan & Cromwell, 48 Wall Street
William Diebold, Jr.	1818 H Street, Washington, D.C.
William E. Diez	CFR
Stephen Duggan	Director, Institute of International Education
Michael T. Florinsky	Dept. of Political Science, Columbia University
Peter Grimm	51 E. 42nd St.
John H. Hazard	3410 30th St. N.W., Washington, D.C.
Arthur H. Houghton	Corning Glass Company
Clarence E. Hunter	New York Trust Company
Grayson Kirk	Columbia University
Francis W. La Farge	Tricontinental Corporation
W.W. Lancaster	Sherman & Sterling & Wright
Edward C. Riley	General Manager, General Motors Overseas Operations
Geroid T. Robinson	Columbia University
W.S.S. Rodgers	President, The Texas Company
John Scott	Time-Life
Harold Smith	63 Wall Street
T. Kennedy Stevenson	Western Electric Company
Vihjalmur Stevenson	67 Morton Street
William R. Strelow	Guaranty Trust Company
Theodore Switz	Encyclopaedia Britannica Films
Maurice Wertheim	120 Broadway

(Source: RGCFR-XVID.)

Participation at Meetings of the "Study Group on American-Russian Relations," 1945

Dates	3/21	4/24	5/22	6/6	9/25	10/10	10/23	TOTAL
William H. Schubart	X	X	X	X	X	X	X	7
George S. Franklin, Jr.	X	X	X	X	X	X	X	7
Frank Altschul		X	X	X	X	X	X	6
Hanson Baldwin								0
Joseph Barnes	X							1
Edwin de T. Bechtel	X	X	X			X	X	5
William Benton		X				X		2
Percy Bidwell	X	X	X	X	X	X	X	7
(Raymond Leslie Buell)	X			X			X	3
Edward C. Carter	X			X				2
John F. Chapman	X			X		X	X	4
Thomas W. Childs	X	X	X			X		4
John L. Curtis		X	X	X	X	X	X	6
Norris Darell	—	—	—	—	—	X		1
Arthur H. Dean	X	X	X	X		X	X	6
William Diebold, Jr.			X	X				2
William E. Diez	X	X	X	X	X	X		6
Stephen Duggan	X	X	X	X	X	X	X	7
Michael T. Florinsky	X	X	X	X	X	X	X	7
Alexander Gerschenkron			X					1
Peter Grimm	—	—	—	—	—		X	1
John H. Hazard				X				1
Arthur H. Houghton	—	—	—	—	—			0
Clarence E. Hunter	X	X	X	X	X	X	X	7
Grayson Kirk					X	X	X	3
Francis W. La Farge	—	—	—	—	—	X	X	2
W.W. Lancaster	X	X						2
Edward C. Riley		X						1
Geroid T. Robinson			X					1
W.S.S. Rodgers								0
John Scott		X						1
Harold Smith	X	X	X		X	X	X	6
T. Kennedy Stevenson	X	X	X	X	X	X		6
Vihjalmur Stevenson		X	X				X	3
William R. Strelow	X	X	X	X	X	X	X	7
Theodore Switz	X	X	X	X	X			5
Maurice Wertheim	X	X		X				3
TOTAL	20	21	21	20	14	19	18	

(Source: RGCFR-XVID. "X" = attended meeting, "-" = not then member of group, " "(no entry) = did not attend meeting.)

The Economic and Political Reconstruction of Liberated Areas in Europe 1945

American members:

Frank Altschul	General American Investors Company
A.J. Barnouw	Columbia University
Percy W. Bidwell	CFR
John W. Davis	Davis, Polk, Wardwell, Sunderland & Kiendl
William E. Diez	CFR
Thomas K. Finletter	Coudert Brothers
Huntington Gilchrist	American Cynamid Company
Edward F. Johnson	Standard Oil Company of New Jersey
Eugene Meyer	*The Washington Post*
Shepard Morgan	Chase National Bank
Arthur Notman	Mining engineer and geologist
Spencer Phenix	OSS
Conyers Reed	OSS
William R. Shirer	Columbia Broadcasting System
L. M. Williams, Jr.	Freeport Sulphur Company

British members:

Harold Butler	British Minister in Washington
Maurice I. Hutton	Head of United Kingdom Food Mission to North America
Roger Makins	Advisor to British embassy
Dennis Marris	Advisor to British embassy
Colonel J. Megaw	British Joint Staff
R.J. Stopford	Economic advisor to the director of Civil Affairs, War Office

(Source: RGCFR-XVIB.)

Study Group on Economic Aspects of American Foreign Policy 1945-46

Chair:	Winfield W. Riefler, Institute for Advanced Study
Members:	
Eliot V. Bell	Superintendent of Banks, New York
Percy W. Bidwell	CFR
John Chapman	Business Week
William E. Diez	CFR
Heman Greenwood	The Carrier Corporation
Leon Henderson	Economic Consultant
Clarence Hunter	New York Trust Company
Edward F. Johnson	Standard Oil of New Jersey
J.M. Letiche	CFR
Milton Lightner	Singer Sewing Machine Company
Stacy May	McGraw-Hill
James M. Nicely	Guaranty Trust Company
Frank W. Notestein	Office of Population Research
Wallace B. Phillips	American Chamber of Commerce in London
Philip D. Reed	General Electric
Wilbert Ward	National City Bank
Leo D. Welch	Standard Oil Company of New Jersey
John H. Williams	Federal Reserve Bank of New York
Ralph Young	National Bureau of Economic Research

(Source: RGCFR-XIXA.)

Study Group on Public Opinion and Foreign Policy 1947-1948

Chair:	Lester Markel, Sunday Editor, *New York Times*
Secretary:	Arthur Altschul, *New York Times*

Research Associates:

W. Phillips Davison	Editor, *Public Opinion Quarterly*
Avery Leiserson	University of Chicago
Marvin Kriesberg	Harvard University

Members:

(Hamilton F. Armstrong	CFR)
Joseph Barnes	Foreign Editor, New York *Herald Tribune*
Edward Barrett	Foreign Editor, *Newsweek*
Hugh Beville, Jr.	Director of Research, National Broadcasting Company
David Dubinsky	President, International Ladies Garments Workers Union
(S. Everett Gleason	Harvard University)
Harold Guinzburg	President, Viking Press
Alger Hiss	President, Carnegie Endowment
Charles Jackson	Vice-President, Time, Inc.
Harold Lasswell	Yale University Law School
William Paley	President, Columbia Broadcasting Company
George N. Shuster	President, Hunter College
Shepard Stone	*New York Times*
Francis A. Truslow	President, New York Curb Exchange
James P. Warburg	*Cross Country Reports*

(Source: RGCFR-XXIIIA. Armstrong's name is only mentioned in a membership list Markel sent to Charles S. Bohlen in October 1947. In this list, Gleason's name is missing, but is mentioned in other membership lists.)

Political Group 1947-1948

Chair:	Hamilton F. Armstrong, CFR
Secretary:	Bryce Wood, Rockefeller Foundation
Rapporteur:	Lawrence Finkelstein

Members:

Hanson W. Baldwin	*New York Times*
Joseph Barnes	New York *Herald Tribune*
Benjamin V. Cohen	Winthrop House
John S. Dickey	President, Dartmouth College
William Diebold, Jr.	CFR
George F. Eliot	*New York Post*
Thomas J. Hamilton	*New York Times*
Philip C. Jessup	School of Law, Columbia University
Grayson Kirk	Columbia University
L.L. Lemnitzer	Major General, National War College
Porter McKeever	U.S. Delegation to the U.N.
Stacy May	International Basic Economy Corporation
Philip E. Mosely	Columbia University
Isidor I. Rabi	Columbia University
Charles M. Spofford	Davis, Polk, Wardwell, Sunderland & Kiendl
Arthur Sweetser	Director, U.N. Information Office, Washington
Maxwell D. Taylor	Major General, Military Academy, West Point

---

(Source: RGCFR-XXIVD.)

Participation at Meetings of the "Political Group" 1948

Date	**1/15**	**1/26**	**2/16**	**3/10**	**TOTAL**
Hamilton F. Armstrong	X	X	X	X	4
Hanson W. Baldwin	X			X	2
Joseph Barnes	X	X			2
Benjamin V. Cohen	X	X	X	X	4
John S. Dickey	X			X	2
William Diebold, Jr.	X	X	X	X	4
George F. Eliot	X	X			2
Thomas J. Hamilton	X	X			2
Philip C. Jessup		X	X	X	3
Grayson Kirk	X		X	X	3
L.L. Lemnitzer	X	X			2
Porter McKeever		X	X	X	3
Stacy May	X	X	X		3
Philip E. Mosely	X				1
Isidor I. Rabi	X	X	X	X	4
Charles M. Spofford	X	X	X		3
Arthur Sweetser	X	X	X	X	4
Maxwell D. Taylor			X	X	2
TOTAL	15	13	11	11	

(Source: RGCFR-XXIVD.)

Study Group on Aid to Europe 1949-1950

Chairman:	Dwight D. Eisenhower
Research Staff:	Howard S. Ellis, Director
	Philip W. Bell
	McGeorge Bundy
	Emile Després
	William Diebold, Jr.
	Brig. Gen. Arthur S. Nevins
	Maxwell Obst
Council Staff:	Percy Bidwell
	Walter H. Mallory
	George S. Franklin, Jr.

Members:

Hamilton F. Armstrong	CFR
Hanson Baldwin	*New York Times*
James B. Carey	CIO
William L. Clayton	Anderson, Clayton & Co., Houston, TX
Edward Mead Earle	Princeton, NJ
Graeme K. Howard	Ford International
George F. Kennan	Department of State
Grayson Kirk	Columbia University
Stacy May	International Basic Economy Corporation
Isidor I. Rabi	Department of Physics, Columbia University
Philip D. Reed	General Electric
Jacob Viner	Department of Economics, Princeton University
John H. Williams	Federal Reserve Bank
Henry M. Wriston	Brown University

(Source: RGCFR-XXXA.)

Date	3/7	5/18	9/26	10/31	11/29	12/20	1/10	1/24	2/15	3/20	4/24	TOTAL (of 11)
Armstrong	X		X	X	X	X		X				6
Baldwin		X		X	X	X	X	X		X		7
Bell			X	X	X			X	X			5
Bidwell	X	X	X	X	X	X	X	X	X	X		10
Bundy	X	X	X	X	X							5
Carey	X											1
Clayton												0
Després	X		X		X		X					4
Diebold	X	X	X	X	X	X	X	X	X			9
Dulles	X		X	X	X	X	X	X	X	X	X	10
Earle	X		X	X			X	X	X			6
Eisenhower	X	X	X	X	X	X	X		X	X	X	10
Ellis			X	X	X	X	X	X	X			7
Franklin		X	X	X	X	X	X	X	X	X	X	10
Howard	X	X		X	X			X		X		6
Kennan												0
Kirk									X	X		2
Mallory	X	X		X	X	X	X	X	X	X	X	10
May	X	X		X	X	X	X	X	X	X		9
Nevins	X		X	X	X	X	X	X	X	X	X	10
Obst			X	X	X	X	X	X	X	X		8
Rabi	X		X	X	X		X	X	X			7
Reed												0
Viner		X	X	X	X	X		X	X		X	8
Williams					X				X			2
Wriston	X	X	X	X	X			X			X	7
(Leffingwell)	X	X										(2)
(Nurske)	X	–	–	–	–	–	–	–	–	–	–	(1)
TOTAL	17	12	16	19	20	13	14	17	15	11	8	

(Source: RGCFR/XXXA. For individuals in parenthesis, no distinct evidence for group membership could be found.)

Bibliography

Archives and Manuscript Collections

Acheson, Dean G. Papers. Harry S. Truman Library, Independence, MO.

Acheson, Dean G. Private Papers. Sterling Memorial Library, Yale University, New Haven, CT.

Aldrich, Winthrop W. Papers. Baker Library, Harvard University, Cambridge, MA.

Allen, George V. Papers. Harry S. Truman Library, Independence, MO.

Altschul, Frank. Papers. Herbert H. Lehman Suite, School of International Affairs, Columbia University, New York, NY.

Americans for Democratic Action. Files. State Historical Society of Wisconsin, Madison, WI.

Anderson, Clinton P. Papers. Harry S. Truman Library, Independence, MO.

Angell, James R. Papers. Sterling Memorial Library, Yale University, New Haven, CT.

Armstrong, Hamilton F. Papers. Seeley G. Mudd Manuscript Library, Princeton University, Princeton, NJ.

Assistant Secretary of State for Public Affairs, 1945–1950. Records. Record Group 59. National Archives, Washington, D.C.

Assistant Secretary of State for Public Affairs, 1949–1953. Records. Record Group 59. National Archives, Washington, D.C.

Atlantic Union Committee. Files and Records. Library of Congress, Washington, D.C.

Ayers, Eben A. Papers. Harry S. Truman Library, Independence, MO.

Baldwin, Hanson. Papers. Sterling Memorial Library, Yale University, New Haven, CT.

Berle, Adolf A. Papers. Franklin D. Roosevelt Library, Hyde Park, NY.

Bliss, Tasker. Papers. Library of Congress, Washington, D.C.

Bohlen, Charles E. Papers. Library of Congress, Washington, D.C.

Bohlen, Charles E. Records. Record Group 59. National Archives, Washington, D.C.

Bowman, Isaiah. Papers. Milton S. Eisenhower Library, Johns Hopkins University, Baltimore, MD.

Butler, Nicholas M. Papers. Butler Library, Columbia University, New York, NY.

Carnegie Endowment for International Peace. Records. Butler Library, Columbia University, New York, NY.

Clayton, William L. Papers. Harry S. Truman Library, Independence, MO.

Clifford, Clark M. Papers. Harry S. Truman Library, Independence, MO.

Committee to Defend America by Aiding the Allies. Files and Records. Seeley G. Mudd Manuscript Library, Princeton University, Princeton, NJ.

Committee for the Marshall Plan to Aid European Recovery. Files and Minutes. Harry S. Truman Library, Independence, MO.

Connally, Tom. Papers. Library of Congress, Washington, D.C.

Council on Foreign Relations. Newspaper Clipping File. Council on Foreign Relations Archives, Harold Pratt House, New York, NY.

Council on Foreign Relations. Records of Conferences. Council on Foreign Relations Archives, Harold Pratt House, New York, NY.

Council on Foreign Relations. Records of Groups. Council on Foreign Relations Archives, Harold Pratt House, New York, NY.

Council on Foreign Relations. Records of Meetings. Council on Foreign Relations Archives, Harold Pratt House, New York, NY.

Council on Foreign Relations. War and Peace Studies — Memoranda. Council on Foreign Relations Archives, Harold Pratt House, New York, NY.

Davies, Joseph E. Papers. Library of Congress, Washington, D.C.

Davis, John W. Papers. Sterling Memorial Library, Yale University, New Haven, CT.

Davis, Norman H. Papers. Library of Congress, Washington, D.C.

Davis, William H. Papers. State Historical Society of Wisconsin, Madison, WI.

Department of State. Decimal File. Record Group 59. National Archives, Washington, D.C.

Department of State. Interdepartmental and Intradepartmental Committees. Records. Record Group 353. National Archives, Washington, D.C.

Department of State. Office Files of the Assistant Secretary for Economic Affairs and the Under Secretary for Economic Affairs (Clayton-Thorp), 1944–1948. Harry S. Truman Library, Independence, MO.

Department of State Committees, 1942–1952. Records. Record Group 59. National Archives, Washington, D.C.

Director of the Office of Public Affairs, 1945–1953. Records. Record Group 59. National Archives, Washington, D.C.

Dulles, Allen W. Papers. Seeley G. Mudd Manuscript Library, Princeton University, Princeton, NJ.

Dulles, John Foster. Papers. Seeley G. Mudd Manuscript Library, Princeton University, Princeton, NJ.

Eberstadt, Ferdinand. Papers. Seeley G. Mudd Manuscript Library, Princeton University, Princeton, NJ.

Eichelberger, Clark M. Papers. New York Public Library, New York, NY.

Eisenhower, Dwight D. Pre-Presidential Papers. Dwight D. Eisenhower Library, Abilene, KS.

Eisenhower, Dwight D. Post-Presidential Papers, 1962, Principal Files. Dwight D. Eisenhower Library, Abilene, KS.

Feis, Herbert. Papers. Library of Congress, Washington, D.C.

Fight For Freedom, Inc. Archives. Seeley G. Mudd Manuscript Library, Princeton University, Princeton, NJ.

Finletter, Thomas K. Papers. Harry S. Truman Library, Independence, MO.

Gleason, S. Everett. Papers. Harry S. Truman Library, Independence, MO.

Green, Joseph C. Papers. Seeley G. Mudd Manuscript Library, Princeton University, Princeton, NJ.

Harriman, William Averell. Papers. Library of Congress, Washington, D.C.

Hoffman, Paul G. Papers. Harry S. Truman Library, Independence, MO.

Hornbek, Stanley K. Papers. Hoover Institution on War, Revolution, and Peace, Archives, Stanford University, Stanford, CA.

House, Edward M. Papers. Sterling Memorial Library, Yale University, New Haven, CT.

Hull, Cordell. Papers. Library of Congress, Washington, D.C.

Jackson, Charles W. Files. Harry S. Truman Papers. Harry S. Truman Library, Independence, MO.

Jessup, Philip C. Papers. Library of Congress, Washington, D.C.

Jones, Joseph M. Papers. Harry S. Truman Library, Independence, MO.

Kahn, Otto H. Papers. Firestone Library, Princeton University, Princeton, NJ.

Kennan, George F. Papers. Seeley G. Mudd Manuscript Library, Princeton University, Princeton, NJ.

Kindleberger, Charles P. Papers. Harry S. Truman Library, Independence, MO.

Krug, Julius A. Papers. Library of Congress, Washington, D.C.

Lamont, Thomas W. Papers. Baker Library, Harvard University, Cambridge, MA.

Lehman, Herbert H. Papers. Herbert H. Lehman Suite, School of International Affairs, Columbia University, New York, NY.

Lippmann, Walter. Papers. Sterling Memorial Library, Yale University, New Haven, CT.

Lochner, Louis P. Papers. State Historical Society of Wisconsin, Madison, WI.

Lovett, Robert A. Diary and Daily Log Sheet. Brown Brothers, Harriman, and Co. Records. New York Historical Society, New York, NY.

McCoy, Frank R. Papers. Library of Congress, Washington, D.C.

McDonald, James G. Papers. Herbert H. Lehman Suite, School of International Affairs, Columbia University, New York, NY.

Moore, Hugh. Papers. Seeley G. Mudd Manuscript Library, Princeton University, Princeton, NJ.

Neustadt, Richard E. Papers. Harry S. Truman Library, Independence, MO.

Oaks, Raymond. Papers. State Historical Society of Wisconsin, Madison, WI.

Office of the Messrs. Rockefeller. Records. Rockefeller Archives Center, North Tarrytown, NY.

Office of the Executive Secretariat. General Records. Record Group 59. National Archives, Washington, D.C.

Page, Arthur W. Papers. State Historical Society of Wisconsin, Madison, WI.

Patterson, Robert P. Papers. Library of Congress, Washington, D.C.

Poole, DeWitt C. Papers. State Historical Society of Wisconsin, Madison, WI.

Psychological Strategy Board. Records. Harry S. Truman Library, Independence, MO.

Robinson, Geroid T. Papers. Butler Library, Columbia University, New York, NY.

Rockefeller Foundation. Records. Rockefeller Archives Center, North Tarrytown, NY.

Ross, Charles G. Papers. Harry S. Truman Library, Independence, MO.

Shaw, Albert. Papers. New York Public Library, New York, NY.

Shepardson, Whitney H. Papers. Franklin D. Roosevelt Library, Hyde Park, NY.

Sweetser, Arthur. Papers. Library of Congress, Washington, D.C.

Taft, Charles P. Papers. Library of Congress, Washington, D.C.

Truman, Harry S. Papers as President of the U.S. White House Central Files, 1945–1953. Harry S. Truman Library, Independence, MO.

Truman, Harry S. Papers of the President of the U.S. President's Secretary's Files, 1945–1953. Harry S. Truman Library, Independence, MO.

Viner, Jacob. Papers. Seeley G. Mudd Manuscript Library, Princeton University, Princeton, NJ.

Autobiographies and Published Papers

Acheson, Dean G. *Present at Creation: My Years in the State Department.* New York, 1969.

____. *Sketches From Life of Men I have Known.* New York, 1961.

Armstrong, Hamilton Fish. *Peace and Counterpeace: From Wilson to Hitler.* New York, 1971.

Berle, Beatrice B., and Travis B. Jacobs, eds. *Navigating the Rapids, 1918–1971: From the Papers of Adolf A. Berle.* New York, 1973.

Blum, John Morton, ed. *The Price of Vision: The Diary of Henry A. Wallace, 1941–1946.* Boston, 1973.

Bohlen, Charles E. *Witness to History, 1929–69.* New York, 1973.

Butler, Nicholas Murray. *Across the Busy Years.* New York, 1947.

Byrnes, James F. *All in One Lifetime.* New York, 1958.

____. *Speaking Frankly.* New York, 1947.

Campbell, Thomas M., and George C. Herring, Jr., eds. *The Diaries of Edward R. Stettinius, Jr., 1943–1946.* New York, 1975.

Churchill, Winston S. *Their Finest Hour.* Vol. 2 of *The Second World War.* London, 1949.

Clay, Lucius D. *Decision in Germany.* Garden City, NY, 1950.

Connally, Tom; as told by Alfred Steinberg. *"My Name is Tom Connally."* New York, 1954.

Dobney, Frederick J., ed. *Selected Papers of Will Clayton.* Baltimore, 1971.

Dubinsky, David, and A.H. Raskin. *David Dubinsky: A Life with Labor.* New York, 1977.

Eichelberger, Clark M. *Organizing for Peace: A Personal History of the Founding of the United Nations.* New York, 1977.

Eisenhower, Dwight D. *The Papers of Dwight David Eisenhower: Columbia University* 10–11. Baltimore, 1984. Chandler, Alfred D., and Louis Galambos, eds.

Ferrell, Robert H. ed. *The Eisenhower Diaries.* New York, 1981.

Fosdick, Raymond B. *Chronicle of a Generation: An Autobiography.* New York, 1958.

Galbraith, John K. *A Life in Our Time.* Boston, 1981.

Grew, Joseph C. *Turbulent Era: A Diplomatic Record of Forty Years, 1904–1945.* Boston, 1952.

Harriman, Averell and Elie Abel. *Special Envoy to Churchill and Stalin, 1941–1946.* New York, 1975.

Hull, Cordell. *The Memoirs of Cordell Hull.* New York, 1948.

Jones, Joseph M. *The Fifteen Weeks, (February 21—June 5, 1947).* New York, 1955.

Kennan, George F. *Memoirs, 1925–1950.* Boston, 1967.

Lamont, Thomas W. *Across World Frontiers.* New York, 1951.

Langer, William L. *In and Out of the Ivory Tower: The Autobiography of William L. Langer.* New York, 1977.

Lattimore, Owen. *Ordeal by Slander.* Boston, 1950.

May, George O. *Memoirs and Accounting Thoughts.* New York, 1962.

McLellan, David S., and David C. Acheson, eds. *Among Friends: Personal Letters of Dean Acheson.* New York, 1980.

Miller, Francis P. *Man From the Valley.* Chapel Hill, NC, 1971.

Millis, Walter, ed. *The Forrestal Diaries.* New York, 1951.

Murphy, Robert. *Diplomat Among Warriors.* Garden City, NY, 1965 (Pyramid Edition).

Nicolson, Harold. *Peacemaking 1919.* New York, 1939.

Seymore, Charles, ed. by Harold C. Whiteman, Jr. *Letters From the Paris Peace Conference.* New Haven, CT, 1965.

Shotwell, James T. *At the Paris Peace Conference.* New York, 1937.

Smith, Jean Edward, ed. *The Papers of Lucius D. Clay: Germany 1945–1949.* Bloomington, IN, 1974.

Stimson, Henry L. *On Active Service in Peace and War.* New York, 1948.

Truman, Harry S. *Memoirs, Vol. I: Years of Decision.* Garden City, NY, 1955.

____. *Memoirs, Vol. II: Years of Trial and Hope.* Garden City, NY, 1956.

Vandenberg, Arthur H., Jr., ed. *The Private Papers of Senator Vandenberg.* Boston, 1952.

White, William Allen. *The Autobiography of William Allen White.* New York, 1946.

Relevant Publications by Council Members

Aldrich, Winthrop W. "The American Heritage Program." *The Public Relations Journal* 3 (November 1947): 9–12.

____. "American Interest in European Reconstruction." Address before the 73rd Annual Convention of the American Bankers' Association, Atlantic City, NJ, 30 September 1947.

Altschul, Frank, et al. *The Political Economy of American Foreign Policy: Its Concepts, Strategy, and Limits.* New York, 1955. (Report of a Study Group sponsored by the Woodrow Wilson Foundation and the National Planning Association).

____. "Toward Building a Better America." National Planning Association, *Planning Pamphlet, No. 69* (September 1949).

Armstrong, Hamilton Fish. *The Calculated Risk.* New York, 1947.

____. "The Task — and Price — of World Leadership." *New York Times Magazine,* 29 June 1947 (reprinted by Overbrook Press, Stamford, CT).

Baldwin, Hanson W. *Power and Politics: The Price of Security in the Atomic Age.* Claremont, CA, 1950.

Bidwell, Percy W., et al. *Germany's Contribution to European Economic Life.* Paris, 1949.

Clayton, William L. "GATT, the Marshall Plan, and OECD." *Political Science Quarterly* 78 (December 1963): 493–503.

Conant, James B. "Force and Freedom." *Atlantic Monthly* 183 (January 1949): 19–22.

Douglas, Lewis W. *The Liberal Tradition: A Free People and a Free Economy.* New York, 1935.

Duggan, Stephen, and Betty Drury. *The Rescue of Science: The Story of the Emergency Committee in Aid to Displaced Foreign Scholars.* New York, 1948.

Dulles, Allen W. "Address to the Annual Meeting of the Associated Alumni of Brown University." 179th Annual Commencement, 16 June 1947.

____. *The Marshall Plan.* Edited and with an introduction by Michael Wala. Oxford/Providence, RI, 1993.

____. *The United Nations.* Foreign Policy Association, Headline Series, No. 59, New York, 1946.

____. "Alternatives for Germany." *Foreign Affairs* 25 (April 1947): 421–32.

Dulles, Allen W., and Hamilton Fish Armstrong. *Can We be Neutral?* New York, 1936.

Eliot, George F. *If Russia Strikes.* New York, 1949.

Eliot, George F., et al. "Is Universal Military Training Necessary for Our Security?" *Town Meeting Bulletin* 13 (17 July 1947).

Finletter, Thomas K. "The European Recovery Programme in Operation." *International Affairs* (London) 25 (January 1949): 1–7.

____. *Power and Policy: U.S. Foreign Policy and Military Power in the Hydrogen Age.* New York, 1954.

Galbraith, John Kenneth. "Beyond the Marshall Plan." National Planning Association, *Planning Pamphlet, No. 67* (February 1949).

____. "Recovery in Europe." National Planning Association, *Planning Pamphlet, No. 53* (November 1946).

Jessup, Philip C. *The Birth of Nations.* New York, 1974.

____. *Elihu Root.* New York, 1938.

Kirk, Grayson C. "International Politics and Policing." Memorandum No. 9, Yale Institute of International Studies. "For Private Distribution Only". New Haven, CT, 1944.

____. "Mass Aspiration and International Relations." In: *The Changing Environment of International Relations; Brookings Lectures, 1956.* Washington, D.C., 1956, 1–18.

Leffingwell, Russell C. "Managing our Economy." *The Yale Review* 34 (October 1945): 603–17.

____. "Our Fiscal and Banking Policy." *Barron's*, 13 November 1950, 27–30.

Mosely, Philip E. "Soviet-American Relations Since the War." *Annals of the American Academy of Political and Social Science* 263 (May 1949): 202–11.

Reed, Philip D. "Aid to Europe — and Economic Stability at Home." *Dun's Review* 56 (January 1948): 11–12, 42–47.

Ruml, Beardsley, and Theodore Geiger. "The Five Percent." National Planning Association, *Planning Pamphlet, No. 73* (August 1951).

Schieffelein, William J., Jr. "Today and Tomorrow." In: *150 Years Service to American Health*. New York, 1944, 68–72.

Sprout, Harold H. "Pressure Groups and Foreign Policy." *Annals of the American Academy of Political and Social Science* 179 (May 1935): 114–23.

Williams, John H. *Post War Monetary Plans and Other Essays*. New York, 1947.

____. *Trade Not Aid: A Program for World Stability*. Cambridge, MA, 1953.

Wriston, Henry M. *Diplomacy in a Democracy*. New York, 1956.

____. *Strategy for Peace*. Boston, 1944.

Publications of the Council on Foreign Relations

Foreign Affairs, 1921–1950.

Armstrong, Hamilton Fish. *Fifty Years of Foreign Affairs*. New York, 1972.

Baldwin, Hanson W. *The Price of Power*. New York, 1948.

Barber, Joseph, ed. *American Policy Toward China; a Report on Views of Leading Citizens in 23 Cities*. New York, 1950.

____. *American Policy Toward Germany*. New York, 1947.

____. *The Containment of Soviet Expansion; a Report on Views of Leading Citizens in 24 Cities*. New York, 1951.

____. *Foreign Aid and National Interest; a Report on Views of Leading Citizens in 25 Cities*. New York, 1952.

____. *The Marshall Plan as American Policy; a Report on the Views of Community Leaders in 21 Cities*. New York, 1948.

____. *Military Cooperation with Western Europe; a Report on the Views of Leading Citizens in 23 Cities*. New York, 1949.

Bidwell, Percy W., ed. *Our Foreign Policy in War and Peace: Some Regional Views*. New York, 1942.

Bundy, William P., ed. *Two Hundred Years of American Foreign Policy*. New York, 1977.

Council on Foreign Relations. *The Council on Foreign Relations: A Record of Fifteen Years, 1921–1936*. New York, 1937.

____. *The Council on Foreign Relations: A Record of Twenty-Five Years, 1921–1946*. New York, 1947.

——. *Handbook*. New York, 1919.

——. *Report of the Executive Director, 1938–1939*. New York, 1939.

____. *Report of the Executive Director, 1944–1945*. New York, n.d. (mimeograph).

____. *Report of the Executive Director, 1945–1946*. New York, n.d. (marked "Confidential for Members").

____. *Annual Report of the Executive Director, 1946–1947*. New York, 1947.

____. *Annual Report of the Executive Director, 1947–1948*. New York, 1948.

____. *Annual Report of the Executive Director, 1948–1949*. New York, 1949.

____. *Annual Report of the Executive Director, 1949–1950.* New York, 1950.

____. *Annual Report, July 1, 1991—June 30, 1992.* New York, n.d.

____. *Proceedings at the Opening of the Harold Pratt House.* New York, 1945.

____. *Publications of the Council on Foreign Relations.* New York, 1950.

____. *Report on Membership Policy and New Procedures for Admission.* N.p., n.d. [1954].

____. *The War and Peace Studies of the Council on Foreign Relations.* New York, 1946.

Dalgliesh, W. Harold. *Community Education in Foreign Affairs, a Report on Activities in 19 American Cities.* New York, 1946.

Diebold, William, Jr. *Economic Cooperation in Western Europe, 1947–1950.* New York, 1951.

____. *Trade and Payments in Western Europe: A Study of Economic Cooperation, 1947–1951.* New York, 1952.

Dunn, Frederick S. *War and the Minds of Men.* New York, 1950.

Ellis, Howard S. *The Economics of Freedom: The Progress and Future of Aid to Europe.* New York, 1950.

Goodrich, Leland M. *Korea: A Study of U.S. Policy in the United Nations.* New York, 1956.

Herter, Christian A. *Toward an Atlantic Community.* New York, 1963.

Hickman, Charles Addison. *Our Farm Program and Foreign Trade; a Conflict of National Policies.* New York, 1949.

Kirk, Grayson L. *The Study of International Relations in American Colleges and Universities.* New York, 1947.

Langer, William L., and S. Everett Gleason. *Challenge to Isolation, 1937–1940.* New York, 1952.

____. *The Undeclared War, 1940–1941.* New York, 1953.

Markel, Lester, ed. *Public Opinion and Foreign Policy.* New York, 1949.

Miller, Francis P., ed. *Some Regional Views on Our Foreign Policy.* New York, 1939 (marked "Printed for Private Distribution to Members").

Mosely, Philip E. *The Power of the Soviet Union.* New York, 1951.

Price, Hoyt, and Carl E. Schorske. *The Problem of Germany.* New York, 1947.

Reston, James B. *The Artillery of the Press: Its Influence on American Foreign Policy.* New York, 1967.

Viner, Jacob, et al. *The United States in a Multinational Economy.* New York, 1945.

Wilcox, Francis. *Congress, the Executive, and Foreign Policy.* New York, 1971.

Publicatons of the Committee for the Marshall Plan (CMP)

Committee for the Marshall Plan. . . . *about the Marshall Plan.* New York (weekly "Fact Sheet"), 1948.

____. *4 Essentials of a European Recovery Program.* New York, n.d.

____. *The Marshall Plan is Up to You.* New York, n.d.

____. *A Statement of Purpose.* New York, n.d.

Ferguson, John H. *Report of the Activities of the Committee for the Marshall Plan to Aid European Recovery.* New York, 1948.

Hiss, Alger. *What About the Marshall Plan?* New York, n.d. (reprint from *New York Times Magazine,* 16 November 1947).

Stimson, Henry L. *The Challenge to Americans.* New York, n.d. (reprint from *Foreign Affairs,* October 1947).

Publications by the U.S. Government and Other Published Documents

Carnegie Endowment for International Peace. *Minutes of Meetings, Board of Trustees, May 6, 1937; 16th Meeting, Vol. 27.* N.p., 1937.

Fight for Freedom Inc. *What is the Fight for Freedom?: The Story of the First Six Months of the Fight for Freedom Committee.* New York, n.d [1940].

Foreign Policy Association. *Annual Meeting of the Foreign Policy Association, April 28, 1926.* FPA Pamphlet, No. 40, Series of 1925–1926.

———. *Twenty-Five Years of the Foreign Policy Association.* New York, 1943.

Nelson, Anna K. *The State Department Policy Planning Staff Papers, 1947–1949.* New York, 1983.

Public Papers of the Presidents of the United States: *Harry S. Truman.* Washington, D.C., 1963.

The Public Papers and Addresses of Franklin D. Roosevelt. 1941 Volume. New York, 1950.

Royal Institute of International Affairs. *The Future of Chatham House: Report of a Planning Committee of the Council of the Royal Institute of International Affairs.* London, 1946.

U.S. Congress. House of Representatives. Committee on Foreign Affairs. *Hearings on Emergency Aid,* 80th Congr., 1st Sess.

———. *Hearings on: United States Foreign Policy for a Post-War Recovery Program.* 80th Congr., 1st Sess., Washington, D.C., 1963.

———. Committee on International Relations. *Foreign Economic Assistance Programs, Part I and II.* (Selected Executive Committee Hearings of the Committee, 1943–1950, Vols. 3 and 4, Historical Series) Washington, D.C., 1976.

———. Select Committee on Lobbying. *Lobbying, Direct and Indirect: Hearings before the House Select Committee on Lobbying Activities.* 81st Congr., 2nd Sess., Washington, D.C., 1950.

———. Special Committee on Post-War Economic Policy and Planning. *Post-War Foreign Economic Policy of the United States.* 6th Report, 79th Congr., 1st Sess., Washington, D.C., 1945.

U.S. Congress. Senate. Committee on Foreign Relations. *A Decade of American Foreign Policy.* Washington, D.C., 1949.

———. *Foreign Relief Assistance Act of 1948.* (Hearings held in Executive Session, 80th Congr., 2nd Sess., Historical Series) Washington, D.C., 1973.

———. *Hearings on the North Atlantic Treaty.* 81st Congr., 1st Sess., Washington, D.C., 1949.

———. *Hearings on the Vandenberg Resolution and the North Atlantic Treaty.* (Hearings held in Executive Session, 80th Congr., 2nd Sess., Historical Series) Washington, D.C., 1973.

———. *Hearings on United States Assistance to European Economic Recovery, Part I, II, and III.* 80th Congr., 2nd Sess., Washington, D.C., 1948.

———. *Foreign Relief Aid: 1947.* (Hearings held in Executive Session, 80th Cong., 2nd Sess., Historical Series) Washington, D.C., 1973.

U.S. Council on Economic Advisors. *The Impact of Foreign Aid Upon the Domestic Economy.* (Report submitted to the President on 21 October 1947) Washington, D.C., 1947.

U.S. Department of State. *Bulletin.* Vols. 10–20. Washington, D.C., different years.

———. *Documents on Germany, 1944–1985.* Washington, D.C., 1985.

———. *Elements in European Recovery.* Washington, D.C., 1948.

———. *Foreign Relations of the United States.* Vols. 1945–1950. Washington, D.C., different years.

____. *Peace, Freedom, and World Trade.* Address by the President on 6 March 1947. Washington, D.C., 1947.

____. *Postwar Foreign Policy Preparations, 1939–1945.* Harley Notter, ed. Washington, D.C., 1949.

____. *In Quest of Peace and Security: Selected Documents in American Foreign Policy, 1941–1951.* Washington, D.C., 1951.

____. *Register of the Department of State.* 1945–1950. Washington, D.C., different years.

____. *United States Relations with China, with Special Reference to the Period 1944–1949.* Washington, D.C., 1949.

Unpublished Dissertatons and M.A. Theses

Baskin, Myron A. "American Planning for World Organization, 1941–1945." Ph.D. diss., Clark University, 1949.

Brown, George Th. "Foreign Policy Legitimation: The Case of American Foreign Aid, 1947–1971." Ph.D. diss., University of Virginia, 1971.

Burbank, Lyman B. "Internationalism in American Thought, 1919–1929." Ph.D. diss., New York University, 1950.

Chasteen, Robert James. "American Foreign Aid and Public Opinion, 1945–1952." Ph.D. diss., University of North Carolina, 1958.

Eakins, David W. "The Development of Corporate Liberal Policy Research in the United States, 1885–1965." Ph.D. diss., University of Wisconsin - Madison, 1966.

Geiger, Clarence J. "The Marshall Plan and American Prosperity: A Study on the Economic Motivation behind the Foreign Aid Assistance Act of 1948." M.A. thesis, University of Wisconsin - Madison, 1957.

Hoffecker, Carol E. "President Truman's Explanation of his Foreign Policy to the American People." Ph.D. diss., Harvard University, 1967.

Johnson, James Herbert. "The Marshall Plan: A Case Study in American Foreign Policy Formulation and Implementation." Ph.D. diss., University of Oklahoma, 1966.

Marvel, William W. "Foreign Aid and United States Security." Ph.D. diss., Princeton University, 1951.

Minter, William M. "The Council on Foreign Relations: A Case Study in the Societal Bases of Foreign Policy Formulation." Ph.D. diss., University of Wisconsin - Madison, 1973.

Miscamble, Wilson D. "George F. Kennan, the Policy Planning Staff, and American Foreign Policy, 1947–1950." Ph.D. diss., University of Notre Dame, 1980.

Novick, Allan M. "The Origins of the Marshall Plan, April 1945 to April 1948." M.A. thesis, University of Wisconsin - Madison, 1968.

Panzella, Emmett E. "The Atlantic Union Committee: A Study of a Pressure Group in Foreign Policy." Ph.D. diss., Kent University, 1969.

Paterson, Thomas G. "The Economic Cold War: American Business and Economic Foreign Policy, 1945–1950." Ph.D. diss., University of California, Berkeley, 1968.

Pollard, Robert A. "Economic Security and the Origins of the Cold War: Strategic Aspects of U.S. Foreign Economic Policy, 1945–1950." Ph.D. diss., University of North Carolina, 1982.

Revoldt, Daryl L. "Raymond B. Fosdick: Reform, Internationalism, and the Rockefeller Foundation." Ph.D. diss., University of Akron, 1982.

Roberts, Priscilla M. "The American 'Eastern Establishment' and World War I: The Emergence of a Foreign Policy Tradition." Ph.D. diss., King's College, Cambridge, 1981.

Roche, George C., III. "Public Opinion and the China Policy of the United States, 1941–1951." Ph.D. diss., University of Colorado, 1965.

Shoup, Laurence H. "Shaping the National Interest: The Council on Foreign Relations, the State Department, and the Origins of the Postwar World, 1939–1943." Ph.D. diss., Northwestern University, 1974.

Silverman, Sheldon A. "At the Water's Edge: Arthur Vandenberg and the Foundation of American Bipartisan Foreign Policy." Ph.D. diss., University of California, Los Angeles, 1967.

Tuttle, William M., Jr. "James B. Conant, Pressure Groups, and the National Defense, 1933–1945." Ph.D. diss., University of Wisconsin - Madison, 1967.

Wright, C. Ben. "George F. Kennan, Scholar-Diplomat: 1926–1946." Ph.D. diss., University of Wisconsin - Madison, 1972.

Books and Pamphlets

Agar, Herbert. *The Price of Power: America Since 1945.* Chicago, 1957.

Alemann, Ulrich v., and Erhard Forndran, eds. *Interessenvermittlung und Politik.* Opladen, 1983.

Allen, Gary. *The C.F.R.: Conspiracy to Rule the World.* Belmont, MA, 1969. Reprint from *American Opinion,* April 1969.

____. *None Dare Call it Conspiracy.* Roosmoor, CA, 1971.

Allen, James S. *Marshall Plan — Recovery or War?* New York, 1948.

Allison, Graham T. *Essence of Decision.* Boston, 1971.

Almond, Gabriel A. *The American People and Foreign Policy.* New York, 1950.

The American Legion. *The Truth about the Foreign Policy Association.* N.p., 1960.

Americans for Democratic Action. *Toward Total Peace.* Washington, D.C., n.d.

Ambrose, Stephen E. *Eisenhower: Soldier, General of the Army, President Elect, 1890–1952.* New York, 1983.

Angermann, Erich. *Die Vereinigten Staaten von Amerika seit 1917.* Munich, 1978 (6th edition).

Arkes, Hadley. *Bureaucracy, the Marshall Plan, and National Interest.* Princeton, NJ, 1972.

Backer, John H. *Priming the German Economy: American Occupational Policies, 1945–1948.* Durham, NC, 1971.

____. *The Decision to Divide Germany: The Clash over Reparations.* Durham, NC, 1978.

Bailey, Thomas A. *A Diplomatic History of the American People.* New York, 1950 (4th edition).

Baldwin, David A. *Economic Development and American Foreign Policy, 1943–1962.* Chicago, 1966.

Balfour, Michael. *Viermächtekontrolle in Deutschland, 1945–1946.* Düsseldorf, 1959.

Ball, George W. *Diplomacy for a Crowded World.* Boston, 1976.

Baltzell, E. Digby. *The Protestant Establishment: Aristocracy and Caste in America.* New York, 1964.

Barnet, Richard J. *Roots of War: The Men and Institutions behind U.S. Foreign Policy.* New York, 1973.

Bartlett, Ruhl J. *The League to Enforce Peace.* Chapel Hill, NC, 1944.

Becker, William H., and Samuel F. Wells. *Economics and World Power: An Assessment of American Diplomacy Since 1789.* New York, 1984.

Benson, Reed, and Robert Lee. *Council for Revolution.* Reprint from *The Review of the News,* 4 February 1970.

Berman, Edward H. *The Influence of Carnegie, Ford, and Rockefeller Foundations on American Foreign Policy: The Ideology of Philanthropy.* Albany, NY, 1983.

Bernstein, Barton J., ed. *Politics and Policies of the Truman Administration.* Chicago, 1970.

Berry, Jeffrey M. *Lobbying for the People: The Political Behavior of Public Interest Groups.* Princeton, NJ, 1977.

Beyme, Klaus von. *Interessengruppen in der Demokratie.* Munich, 1980 (5th edition).

____. *Die politische Elite in der Bundesrepublik Deutschland.* Munich, 1971.

____. *Die politischen Theorien der Gegenwart.* Munich, 1986 (6th edition).

Blasier, Cole. *The Hovering Giant: U.S. Responses to Revolutionary Changes in Latin America.* Pittsburgh, PA, 1979.

Blum, John Morton. *V Was for Victory: Politics and American Culture During World War II.* New York, 1976.

Blum, Robert M. *Drawing the Line: The Origins of American Containment Policy in Asia.* New York, 1982.

Bohlen, Charles E. *The Transformation of American Foreign Policy.* New York, 1969.

Borg, Dorothy, and Waldo Heinrichs, eds. *Uncertain Years: Chinese-American Relations, 1947–1950.* New York, 1980.

Boyer, Paul. *By the Bomb's Early Light: American Thought and Culture at the Dawn of the Atomic Age.* New York, 1986.

Brähler, Reiner. *Der Marshallplan: Zur Strategie weltmarktorientierter Krisenvermeidung in der amerikanischen Westeuropapolitik 1933 bis 1952.* Köln, 1983.

Brinkmann, Heinz Ulrich. *Public Interest Groups im Politischen System der USA: Organisierbarkeit und Einflußtechniken.* Opladen, 1984.

Bruhn, Jürgen. *Schlachtfeld Europa oder Amerikas letztes Gefecht: Gewalt und Wirtschaftsimperialismus in der US-Außenpolitik seit 1840.* Berlin/Bonn, 1983.

Buchanan, Norman S., and Frederick A. Lutz. *Rebuilding the World Economy: America's Role in Foreign Trade and Investment.* New York, 1947.

Buchholz, Edwin. *Interessen, Gruppen, Interessengruppen.* Tübingen, 1970.

Burnham, James. *The Struggle For the World.* New York, 1947.

Byrnes, Robert F. *Awakening American Education to the World: The Role of Archibald Cary Coolidge, 1866–1928.* Notre Dame, IN, 1982.

Caute, David. *The Great Fear: The Anti-Communism Purge Under Truman and Eisenhower.* New York, 1978.

Chadwin, Mark Lincoln. *The Warhawks: American Interventionists Before Pearl Harbor.* New York, 1970.

Cinema Educational Guild, Inc. *Wake Up Americans.* Hollywood, March 1963.

____. *Illuminati: The Council on Foreign Relations, Exposed by Myron Fagan.* Hollywood, n.d.

Cohen, Bernard C. *The Influence of Non-Governmental Groups on Foreign Policy Making.* Boston, 1959.

——. *The Press and Foreign Policy.* Princeton, 1963.

——. *The Public's Impact on Foreign Policy.* Boston, 1973.

Cohen, Warren I. *The Chinese Connection: Roger S. Greene, Thomas W. Lamont, George E. Sokolsky and American-East Asian Relations.* New York, 1978.

——. *Empire Without Tears: America's Foreign Relations, 1921–1933.* New York, 1987.

Cole, Wayne S. *America First: The Battle Against Intervention 1940–41.* Madison, WI, 1953.

——. *Roosevelt and the Isolationists, 1932–1945.* Lincoln, NB, 1983.

Committee for International Trade Organization. *Statement of Objectives.* Washington, D.C., 1949.

Conliffe, John B. *The Foreign Economic Policy of the United States.* Yale Institute of International Studies, Memo # 11 (marked "For Private Circulation Only"). New Haven, CT, 1944.

Cook, Blanche Wiesen. *The Declassified Eisenhower: A Divided Legacy.* New York, 1981.

Courtney, Kent, and Phoebe Courtney. *America's Unelected Rulers: The Council on Foreign Relations.* New Orleans, 1962.

Courtney, Phoebe. *The CFR.* New Orleans, 1968.

——. *The CFR, Part II.* Littleton, CO, 1975.

Cousins, Norman. *The Pathology of Power.* New York, 1987.

Czempiel, E.O. *Das amerikanische Sicherheitssystem 1945–1949.* Berlin, 1966.

Dahl, Robert A. *Congress and Foreign Policy.* New York, 1950.

——. *Dilemmas of Pluralist Democracy: Autonomy vs. Control.* New Haven, CT, 1982.

——. *Who Governs?* New Haven, CT, 1961.

Davidson, Mary M. *The Secret Government of the United States.* Omaha, NB, 1962.

Dean, Vera M. *The United States and Russia.* Cambridge, MA, 1948.

DeConde, Alexander, ed. *Isolation and Security.* Durham, NC, 1957.

Divine, Robert A., ed. *Causes and Consequences of World War II.* Chicago, 1969.

——. *Foreign Policy and Presidential Elections: 1940–1960.* New York, 1974.

——. *Second Chance: The Triumph of Internationalism in America During World War II.* New York, 1971.

Doenecke, Justus D. *Not to the Swift: The Old Isolationists in the Cold War Era.* Lewisburg, PA, 1979.

Domhoff, G. William, and Hoyt B. Ballard, eds. *C. Wright Mills and the Power Elite.* Boston, 1968.

Domhoff, G. William ed. *Power Structure Research.* Beverly Hills, 1980.

Domhoff, G. William. *The Bohemian Grove and Other Retreats: A Study in Ruling-Class Cohesiveness.* New York, 1974.

——. *The Higher Circles: The Governing Class in America.* New York, 1970.

——. *The Power Elite and the State: How Policy is Made in America.* New York, 1990.

——. *The Powers that Be: Processes of Ruling-Class Domination in America.* New York, 1978.

——. *Who Rules America?* Englewood Cliffs, NJ, 1967.

——. *Who Rules America Now?* Englewood Cliffs, NJ, 1983.

Donavan, John C. *The Cold Warriors: A Policy Making Elite.* Lexington, MA, 1974.

Donavan, Robert J. *Tumultuous Years: The Presidency of Harry S. Truman, 1949–1953.* New York, 1982.

Dulles, Allen W. *The Craft of Intelligence.* New York, 1963.

——. *Secret Surrender.* New York, 1966.

Dunham, William E. *Beware of Council on Foreign Relations.* Reprint from *The Review of the News,* 9 February 1977.

Dunmore, Timothy. *Soviet Politics, 1945–1953.* London, 1983.

Dye, Thomas R. *Who is Running America?* Englewood Cliffs, NJ, 1983.

Eichelberger, Clark M. *UN: The First Twenty Years.* New York, 1955.

Epstein, Julius. *The Case Against Vera Micheles Dean and the Foreign Policy Association.* N.p., 1947 (mimeograph).

Eulau, Heinz, and Moshe M. Czudnowski. *Elite Recruitment in Democratic Polities: Comparative Studies Across Nations.* New York, 1976.

Etzioni, Amatai. *The Active Society: A Theory of Societal and Political Processes.* New York, 1968.

——. *Soziologie der Organisationen.* Munich, 1967.

Fabian, Larry L. *Andrew Carnegie's Peace Endowment: The Tycoon, the President, and their Bargain of 1910.* Washington, D.C., 1985.

Farago, Ladislav. *The Game of the Foxes: The Untold Story of German Espionage in the United States and Great Britain During World War II.* New York, 1971 (Bantam Books Edition).

Feis, Herbert. *Foreign Aid and Foreign Policy.* New York, 1964.

——. *From Trust to Terror: The Onset of the Cold War, 1945–1950.* New York, 1970.

Ferrell, Robert H. *George C. Marshall.* New York, 1966.

Fischer, David H. *Historians' Fallacies: Towards a Logic of Historical Thought.* New York, 1970.

Fraenkel, Ernst. *Das amerikanische Regierungssystem: Eine politologische Analyse.* Opladen, 1981 (4th edition).

Freidel, Frank. *Franklin D. Roosevelt: The Ordeal.* Boston, 1954.

Gaddis, John Lewis. *Russia, the Soviet Union, and the United States: An Interpretative History.* New York, 1978.

——. *Strategies of Containment: A Critical Appraisal of Postwar American National Security Policy.* New York, 1982.

——. *The United States and the Cold War, 1941–1947.* New York, 1972.

Gardner, Lloyd C. *Architects of Illusion: Men and Ideas in American Foreign Policy, 1941–1949.* Chicago, 1970.

Gelfand, Lawrence E. *The Inquiry.* New Haven, CT, 1963.

Gerschenkron, Alexander. *Economic Relations with the U.S.S.R.* New York, 1945.

Gimbel, John. *The American Occupation of Germany, 1945–1949: Politics and the Military.* Stanford, CA, 1968.

——. *The Origins of the Marshall Plan.* Stanford, CA, 1976.

Glagow, Manfred, Hrsg. *Gesellschaftssteuerung zwischen Korporatismus und Subsidarität.* Bielefeld, 1984.

Goldman, Eric F. *The Crucial Decade — and After: America, 1945–1960.* New York, 1960 (Vintage Books Edition).

Graebner, Norman A., ed. *The National Security: Its Theory and Practice, 1945–1960.* New York, 1986.

Graml, Hermann. *Die Alliierten und die Teilung Deutschlands: Konflikte und Entscheidungen, 1941–1948.* Frankfurt/Main, 1985.

Greenstein, Fred I. *The Hidden Hand Presidency: Eisenhower as Leader.* New York, 1982.

Gruchmann, Lothar. *Der Zweite Weltkrieg: Kriegführung und Politik.* Munich, 1967.

Haberl, Othmar N., and Lutz Niethammer, eds. *Der Marshall-Plan und die europäische Linke.* Frankfurt/Main, 1986.

Halberstam, David. *The Best and the Brightest.* New York, 1972.

Halle, Louis. *Cold War as History.* New York, 1967.

Halperin, Morton H. *Bureaucratic Politics and Foreign Policy.* Washington, D.C., 1974.

Harbaugh, William H. *Lawyer's Lawyer: The Life of John W. Davis.* New York, 1973.

Harbutt, Fraser J. *The Iron Curtain: Churchill, America, and the Origins of the Cold War.* New York, 1986.

Harriman, W. Averell. *America and Russia in a Changing World.* New York, 1971.

Hartman, Susan M. *Truman and the 80th Congress.* Columbia, MO, 1971.

Hazlitt, Henry. *Illusions of Point Four.* Irving on Hudson, NY, 1950.

——. *Will Dollars Save the World?* New York, 1947.

Hearden, Patrick J. *Roosevelt Confronts Hitler: America's Entry into World War II.* DeKalb, IL, 1987.

Herken, Gregg. *The Winning Weapon: The Atomic Bomb in the Cold War.* New York, 1980.

Herring, George C., Jr. *Aid to Russia, 1941–1946: Strategy, Diplomacy, the Origins of the Cold War.* New York, 1973.

Hodgson, Godfrey. *America in Our Time.* Garden City, NY, 1976.

Hogan, Michael J. *The Marshall Plan: America, Britain, and the Reconstruction of Western Europe, 1947–1952.* New York, 1987.

Horowitz, David, ed. *Corporations and the Cold War.* New York, 1969.

Hunt, Michael H. *The Making of a Special Relationship: The United States and China to 1914.* New York, 1983.

Ireland, Timothy P. *Creating the Entangling Alliance: The Origins of the North Atlantic Treaty Organization.* Westport, CT, 1981.

Iriye, Akira and Yonosuke Nagai, eds. *The Origins of the Cold War in Asia.* New York, 1977.

Isaacson, Walter, and Evan Thomas. *The Wise Men: Six Friends and the World they Made; Acheson, Bohlen, Harriman, Kennan, Lovett, McCloy.* New York, 1986.

Janis, Irving L. *Victims of Groupthink: A Psychological Study of Foreign-Policy Decisions and Fiascoes.* Boston, 1972.

Johnson, Arthur M. *Winthrop W. Aldrich: Lawyer, Banker, Diplomat.* Boston, 1968.

Johnson, Walter. *The Battle Against Isolation.* Chicago, 1944.

Josephson. Emmanuel M. *Rockefeller "Internationalist": The Man Who Misrules the World.* New York, 1952.

Josephson, Harold. *James T. Shotwell and the Rise of Internationalism in America.* Cranburry, NJ, 1975.

Kahn, David. *Hitler's Spies: German Military Intelligence in World War II.* New York, 1978.

Kahn, Helmut W. *Der Kalte Krieg: Spaltung und Wahn der Stärke, 1945–1955.* Köln, 1986.

Kaplan, Lawrence S. *A Community of Interests: NATO and the Military Assistance Program, 1948–1951.* Washington, D.C., 1980.

Kellogg, Paul U. *Ten Years of the Foreign Policy Association.* New York, 1929.

Kelso, William A. *American Democratic Theory: Pluralism and its Critics.* Westport, CT, 1978.

Kennan, George F. *American Diplomacy, 1900–1950.* Chicago, 1951.

Key, V.O. *Politics, Parties, & Pressure Groups.* New York, 1964.

King-Hall, Stephen. *Chatham House: A Brief Account of the Origins, Purposes, and Methods of the Royal Institute of International Affairs.* London, 1937.

Kirkendall, Richard S. *The Truman Period as a Research Field.* Columbia, MO, 1967.

Kolko, Gabriel. *The Roots of American Foreign Policy: An Analysis of Power and Purpose.* Boston, 1969.

——. *The Politics of War: The World and United States Foreign Policy, 1943–1945.* New York, 1968.

Kolko, Joyce, and Gabriel Kolko. *The Limits of Power: The World and United States Foreign Policy, 1945–1954.* New York, 1972.

Kuehl, Warren F., ed. *Biographical Dictionary of Internationalists.* Westport, CT, 1983.

Kuklick, Bruce. *American Policy and the Division of Germany: The Clash with Russia over Reparations.* Ithaca, NY, 1972.

Kuniholm, Bruce R. *The Origins of the Cold War in the Near East: Great Power Conflict and Diplomacy in Iran, Turkey, and Greece.* Princeton, NJ, 1980.

Kutler, Stanley I. *The American Inquisition: Justice and Injustice in the Cold War.* New York, 1982.

Lader, Lawrence. *Breeding Ourselves to Death.* New York, 1971.

LaFeber, Walter. *America, Russia, and the Cold War, 1945–1966.* New York, 1967.

Larson, Deborah W. *Origins of Containment: A Psychological Explanation.* Princeton, NJ, 1985.

Lattimore, Owen. *Solution in Asia.* Boston, 1945.

Leigh, Michael. *Mobilizing Consent: Public Opinion and Foreign Policy, 1937–1947.* Westport, CT, 1976.

Levering, Ralph B. *American Opinion and the Russian Alliance, 1939–1945.* Chapel Hill, NC, 1976.

____. *The Cold War, 1945–1972.* Arlington Heights, IL, 1982.

____. *The Public and American Foreign Policy, 1918–1978.* New York, 1978.

Levin, N. Gordon. *Woodrow Wilson and World Politics: America's Response to War and Revolution.* New York, 1968.

Lippmann, Walter. *The Cold War: A Study in U.S. Foreign Policy.* New York, 1972.

____. *Essays in Public Philosophy.* Boston, 1955.

____. *U.S. Foreign Policy: Shield of the Republic.* New York, 1943.

____. *U.S. War Aims.* Boston, 1944.

Lipset, Seymour M. *Political Man: The Social Bases of Politics.* Garden City, NY, 1960.

Luce, Henry R. *The American Century.* New York, 1941.

Lundestad, Geir. *America, Scandinavia, and the Cold War, 1945–1949.* New York, 1980.

____. *The American Non-Policy Towards Eastern Europe, 1943–1947.* Oslo, 1975.

Lyon, Peter. *Eisenhower: Portrait of the Hero.* Boston, 1974.

McAuliffe, Mary Sperling. *Crisis on the Left: Cold War Politics and American Liberals, 1947–1954.* Amherst, MA, 1978.

McCormick. Thomas C.T., ed. *Problems of the Postwar World.* New York, 1945.

McManus, John F. *The Insiders.* Belmont, MA, 1983 (filmscript).

McQuaid, Kim. *Big Business and Presidential Power: From FDR to Reagan.* New York, 1982.

Maier, Charles S., and Stanley Hoffman, eds. *The Marshall Plan: A Retrospective.* Boulder, CO, 1984.

Maney, Patrick J. *"Young Bob" La Follette: A Biography of Robert M. La Follette, Jr., 1895–1953.* Columbia, MO, 1978.

Marchetti, Victor, and John D. Marks. *The CIA and the Culture of Intelligence.* New York, 1980 (Dell Book Edition).

Mastny, Vojtech. *Russia's Road to the Cold War: Diplomacy, Warfare, and the Politics of Communism, 1941–1945.* New York, 1979.

May, Ernest R. *American Imperialism: A Speculative Essay.* New York, 1968.

____. *"Lessons" of the Past: The Use and Misuse of History in American Foreign Policy.* New York, 1973.

May, Gary. *China Scapegoat: The Diplomatic Ordeal of John Carter Vincent.* New York, 1979.

Mee, Charles L. *The Marshall Plan: The Launching of the Pax Americana.* New York, 1984.

Melanson, Richard A., and David Mayers, eds. *Reevaluating Eisenhower: American Foreign Policy in the Fifties.* Urbana, IL, 1987.

Merli, Frank, and Theodore A. Wilson, eds. *Makers of American Diplomacy.* New York, 1974.

Milbrath, Lester W. *The Washington Lobbyists.* Chicago, 1963.

Mills, C. Wright. *The Power Elite.* New York, 1959.

Morison, Elting E. *Turmoil and Tradition: A Study of the Life and Times of Henry L. Stimson.* Boston, 1960.

Morison, Samuel Eliot. *The Battle of the Atlantic.* 1. Boston, 1950.

Mosley, Leonard. *Dulles: A Biography of Eleanor, Allen, and John Foster Dulles and Their Family Network.* New York, 1978.

Mosely, Philip E. *The Kremlin and World Politics.* New York, 1969.

Neustadt, Richard E. *Presidential Power: The Politics of Leadership.* New York, 1960.

Nevins, Allan. *Herbert H. Lehman and His Era.* New York, 1963.

Ninkovich, Frank A. *Germany and the United States: The Transformation of the German Question Since 1945.* Boston, 1988.

Nübel, Otto. *Die amerikanische Reparationspolitik gegenüber Deutschland, 1941–1945.* Frankfurt/Main, 1980.

Oye, Kenneth A., et al., eds. *Eagle Entangled: U.S. Foreign Policy in a Complex World.* New York, 1979.

Painter, David S. *Oil and the American Century: The Political Economy of U.S. Foreign Oil Policy, 1941–1954.* Baltimore, 1986.

Paterson, Thomas G. *On Every Front: The Making of the Cold War.* New York, 1979.

———. *Soviet-American Confrontation: Postwar Reconstruction and the Origins of the Cold War.* Baltimore, 1973.

Paterson, Thomas G., ed. *Major Problems in American Foreign Policy: Volume II, Since 1914.* (Lexington, MA, 1978.

Pike, Fredrik B., and Thomas Stritch, eds. *The New Corporatism.* South Bend, IN, 1974.

Pogue, Forrest C. *George C. Marshall: Statesman, 1945–1959.* New York, 1987.

Polenberg, Richard. *War and Society: The United States, 1941–1945.* Philadelphia, 1972.

Pollard, Robert A. *Economic Security and the Origins of the Cold War, 1945–1950.* New York, 1985.

Prange, Gordon W. *At Dawn We Slept: The Untold Story of Pearl Harbor.* New York, 1981.

Pratt, Julius W. *Cordell Hull.* New York, 1964.

Presthus, Robert. *Elites in the Policy Process.* Cambridge, MA, 1974.

Prewitt, Kenneth, and Alan Stone. *The Ruling Elites: Elite Theory, Power and American Democracy.* New York, 1973.

Price, Harry B. *The Marshall Plan and Its Meaning.* Ithaca, NY, 1955.

Radosh, Ronald. *American Labor and United States Foreign Policy.* New York, 1969.

Reid, Escott. *Time of Fear and Hope: The Making of the North Atlantic Treaty, 1947–1949.* Toronto, 1977.

Reischauer, Edwin O. *The United States and Japan.* Cambridge, MA, 1950.

Resis, Albert. *Stalin, the Politburo, and the Onset of the Cold War.* Pittsburgh, 1988.

Rivera, Joseph H., ed. *The Psychological Dimension of Foreign Policy.* Columbus, OH, 1968.

Robertson, Pat. *The New World Order.* Dallas, TX, 1992.

Rodgers, William. *Think: A Biography of the Watsons and IBM.* London, 1970.

Rodosh, Ronald. *American Labor and United States Foreign Policy.* New York, 1969.

Rose, Arnold M. *The Power Structure: Political Process in American Society.* New York, 1967.

Rosenau, James N., ed. *Domestic Sources of Foreign Policy.* New York, 1967.

Rosenau, James N. *National Leadership and Foreign Policy: A Case Study in the Mobilization of Public Support.* Princeton, NJ, 1963.

———. *Public Opinion and Foreign Policy.* New York, 1961.

———. *The Scientific Study of Foreign Policy.* New York and London, 1980.

Rubin, Barry. *Secrets of State: The State Department and the Struggle Over U.S. Foreign Policy.* New York, 1985.

Russel, Ruth B. *A History of the United Nations Charter: The Role of the United States, 1940–1945*. Washington, D.C., 1958.

Russett, Bruce M., and Elizabeth C. Hanson. *Interest and Ideology: The Foreign Policy Beliefs of American Businessmen*. San Francisco, 1975.

Sapin, Burton M. *The Making of United States Foreign Policy*. New York, 1966.

Seagrave, Sterling. *The Soong Dynasty*. New York, 1985.

Schaller, Michael. *The American Occupation of Japan: The Origins of the Cold War in Asia*. New York, 1985.

____. *Douglas MacArthur: The Far Eastern General*. New York, 1988.

Schlafly, Phyllis, and Chester Ward. *Kissinger on the Couch*. New Rochelle, NY, 1975.

Schlesinger, Arthur M., Jr. *A Thousand Days*. Boston, 1965.

____. *Vital Center: The Politics of Freedom*. Boston, 1949.

Schonberger, Howard B. *Aftermath of War: Americans and the Remaking of Japan, 1945–1952*. Kent, OH, 1989.

Schriftgiesser, Karl. *Business and Public Policy: The Role of the Committee for Economic Development, 1942–1967*. Englewood Cliffs, NJ, 1967.

____. *Business Comes of Age: The Story of the Committee on Economic Development and Its Impact Upon the Economic Policies of the United States, 1940–1960*. New York, 1960.

Schulzinger, Robert D. *The Making of the Diplomatic Mind: The Training, Outlook and Style of United States Foreign Service Officers, 1908–1931*. Middletown, CT, 1975.

____. *The Wise Men of Foreign Affairs: The History of the Council on Foreign Relations*. New York, 1984.

Schweigler, Gebhard. *Politikwissenschaft und Außenpolitik in den USA: Am Beispiel der europäisch-deutschen Beziehungen*. Munich, 1977.

Shea, Robert, and Robert A. Wilson. *Illuminatus!: The Eye in the Pyramid*. New York, 1975.

Shell, Kurt L. *Der amerikanische Konservativismus*. Stuttgart, 1986.

Shepardson, Whitney H. *Early History of the Council on Foreign Relations*. Stamford, CT, 1960.

Sherwin, Martin G. *A World Destroyed: The Atomic Bomb and the Grand Alliance*. New York, 1977.

Sherwood, Robert E. *Roosevelt and Hopkins: An Intimate History*. New York, 1948.

Shirer, William L. *The Rise and Fall of the Third Reich*. New York, 1960.

Shoup, Laurence H., and William Minter. *Imperial Brain Trust: The Council on Foreign Relations and United States Foreign Policy*. New York, 1977.

Shulman, Marshall D. *Expansion and Coexistence*. New York, 1974.

Silk, Leonard, and Mark Silk. *The American Establishment*. New York, 1980.

Smith, R. Harris. *OSS: The Secret History of America's First Central Intelligence Agency*. Berkeley and Los Angeles, CA, 1972.

Smoot, Dan. *The Invisible Government*. Dallas, TX, 1962.

Spanier, John. *American Foreign Policy Since World War II*. New York, 1971 (4th Edition).

Spector, Ronald H. *Eagle Against the Sun: The American War With Japan*. New York, 1984.

Stanley, David T., et al. *Men Who Govern: A Biographical Profile of Federal Political Executives*. Washington, D.C., 1967.

Starobin, Joseph. *Should Americans Back the Marshall Plan?* New York, 1948.

Steele, A. T. *The American People and China*. New York, 1966.

Steel, Ronald. *Pax Americana*. New York, 1967.

____. *Walter Lippmann and the American Century*. New York, 1980.

Steffani, Winfried. *Pluralistische Demokratie: Studien zur Theorie und Praxis.* Opladen, 1980.

Stein, Harold, ed. *Public Administration and Policy Development: A Case Book.* New York, 1952.

———. *American Civil-Military Decisions: A Book of Case Studies.* Birmingham, AL, 1963.

Stephanson, Anders. *Kennan and the Art of Foreign Policy.* Cambridge, MA, 1989.

Stiller, Jesse H. *George S. Messersmith: Diplomat of Democracy.* Chapel Hill, 1987.

Streit, Clarence K. *Union Now.* New York, 1939.

Stueck, William W., Jr., *The Road to Confrontation: American Policy Toward China and Korea, 1947–1950.* Chapel Hill, NC, 1981.

Survey Research Center — University of Michigan, Ann Arbor, Michigan. *Public Attitudes Toward American Foreign Policy.* 2 Vols. Ann Arbor, MI, May 1947.

Taubman, William. *Stalin's American Policy: From Entente to Détente to Cold War.* New York, 1982.

Thomas, John N. *The Institute of Pacific Relations.* Seattle, WA, 1974.

Toynbee, Arnold J. *A Study of History.* New York, 1935–1961.

Truman, David B. *The Governmental Process.* New York, 1951.

Tucker, Nancy Bernkopf. *Patterns in the Dust: Chinese-American Relations and the Recognition Controversy, 1949–1950.* New York, 1983.

Walker, Samuel J. *Henry A. Wallace and American Foreign Policy.* Westport, CT, 1976.

Walworth, Arthur. *Wilson and His Peacemakers: American Diplomacy at the Peace Conference, 1919.* New York, 1986.

Warburg, James P. *Put Yourself in Marshall's Place.* New York, 1948.

Ware, Edith E., ed. *The Study of International Relations in the United States.* New York, 1945.

Weinstein, James. *The Corporate Ideal in the Liberal State: 1900–1918.* Boston, 1968.

Weinstone, William. *The Case Against David Dubinsky.* New York, 1946.

Welles, Sumner. *Seven Decisions that Shaped History.* New York, 1951.

Wersich, Bernd Rüdiger. *Zeitgenössischer Rechtsextremismus in den Vereinigten Staaten.* Munich, 1978.

Westerfield, H. Bradford. *Foreign Policy and Party Politics: Pearl Harbor to Korea.* New Haven, CT, 1955.

Wexler, Immanuel. *The Marshall Plan Revisited: The European Recovery Program in Economic Perspective.* Westport, CT, 1983.

Wilkins, Mira. *The Maturing of Multinational Enterprise: American Business Abroad from 1914 to 1970.* Cambridge, MA, 1974.

Williams, William A. *The Tragedy of American Diplomacy.* New York, 1962.

Willkie, Wendell. *One World.* New York, 1943.

Wittner, Lawrence. *Rebels Against War: The American Peace Movement, 1941–1960.* New York, 1969.

———. *Cold War America.* New York, 1974.

Wooton, Graham. *Interest Groups.* Englewood Cliffs, NJ, 1970.

Yergin, Daniel. *Shattered Peace: The Origins of the Cold War and the National Security State.* Boston, 1977.

Zeitlin, Maurice, ed. *American Society, Inc.* Chicago, IL, 1970.

Scholarly and Newspaper Articles

"A Brief History of Thirty-Five Years of Service Toward Developing International Understanding." *International Conciliation* 417: 17–39.

"A Round Table: Explaining the History of American Foreign Relations." *Journal of American History* 77 (June 1990): 93–180

Accinelli, Robert D. "Militant Internationalists: The League of Nations Association, the Peace Movement, and U.S. Foreign Policy, 1934–38." *Diplomatic History* 4 (Winter 1980): 19–38.

____. "Pro-U.N. Internationalists and the Early Cold War: The American Association for the United Nations and U.S. Foreign Policy, 1947–52." *Diplomatic History* 9 (Fall 1985): 347–62.

Adler, Kenneth, and Davis Bobrow. "Interest and Influence in Foreign Affairs." *Public Opinion Quarterly* 20.1 (1956): 89–101.

Alger, Chadwick F. "The External Bureaucracy in United States Foreign Affairs." *Administrative Science Quarterly* (June 1962): 50–78.

Anderson, Sheldon. "Poland and the Marshall Plan, 1947–1949." *Diplomatic History* 15 (Fall 1991): 473–94.

Barnes, Trevor. "The Secret Cold War: The CIA and American Foreign Policy in Europe, 1946–1956." Part I, *Historical Journal* 24.2 (1981): 399–415; Part II, *Historical Journal* 25.3 (1982): 649–70.

Beichman, Arnold. "Council on Foreign Relations." *Christian Science Monitor*, 1 September 1961, sec. II: 1.

Billington, Ray Allen. "Origins of Middle Western Isolationism." *Political Science Quarterly* 60 (March 1945): 44–64.

Blaisdell, Donald C. "Pressure Groups, Foreign Policies, and International Politics." *Annals of the American Academy of Political and Social Science* 319 (September 1958): 149–57.

Bonilla, Frank. "When's Petition Pressure?" *Public Opinion Quarterly* 20.1 (1956): 39–48.

Borger, Catherine. "National Organizations and International Policy." *International Conciliation* 409: 223.

Brown, John H. "The Disappearing Russian Embassy Archives, 1922–49." *Prologue* 14 (Spring 1982): 5–13.

Burdette, Franklin L. "Influence of Non-Congressional Pressure on Foreign Policy." *Annals of the American Academy of Political and Social Science* 289 (September 1953): 92–99.

Byrnes, Robert F. "Encouraging American Interest in World Affairs in the 1920's: The Council on Foreign Relations and *Foreign Affairs*." In: *Ostmitteleuropa: Berichte und Forschungen.* Ulrich Haustein, Georg W. Strobel and Gerhard Wagner, eds., 385–402. Stuttgart, 1981.

Campbell, John Franklin. "The Death Rattle of the Eastern Establishment." *New York*, 20 September 1971, 47–51.

Caspary, William R. "U.S. Public Opinion During the Onset of the Cold War." *Peace Research Society (International) Papers.* 9 (Cambridge Conference 1968): 25–46.

Cohen, Warren I. "The History of American-East Asian Relations: Cutting Edge of the Historical Profession." *Diplomatic History* 9 (Spring 1985): 101–12.

Cripps, Thomas. "Movies, Race and World War II: *Tennessee Johnson* as an Anticipation of the Strategies of the Civil Rights Movement." *Prologue* 14 (Summer 1983): 49–67.

Divine, Robert A. "The Cold War and the Election of 1948." *Journal of American History* 59 (June 1972): 90–110.

Dockrill, M.L. "Historical Note: The Foreign Office and the 'Proposed Institute of International Affairs 1919.'" *International Affairs* (London) 56 (Fall 1980): 665–72.

Domhoff, G. William. "Social Clubs, Policy-Planning Groups, and Corporations: A Network Study of Ruling-Class Cohesiveness." *The Insurgent Sociologist* 5 (Special issue, Spring 1975): 173–84.

Dye, Thomas R., et al. "Concentration, Specialization, and Interlocking Among Institutional Elites." *Social Science Quarterly* 54 (March 1973): 8–29.

Dye, Thomas R. "Oligarchic Tendencies in National Policy-Making: The Role of Private Policy-Planning Organizations." *The Journal of Politics* 40 (May 1978): 309–31.

Erdmann, Andrew P.N. "Mining the Corporatist Synthesis: Gold in American Foreign Economic Policy, 1931–1936." *Diplomatic History* 17 (Spring 1993): 171–200.

Femia, Joseph V. "Elites, Participation, and the Democratic Creed." *Political Studies* 27 (March 1979): 1–20.

Ferrell, Robert H. "The Peace Movement." In: *Isolation and Security.* Alexander DeConde, ed., 82–106. Durham, NC, 1957.

Gable, Richard W. "Political Interest Groups as Policy Shapers." *Annals of the American Academy of Political and Social Science* 319 (September 1958): 84–93.

Gaddis, John Lewis. "Containment: A Reassessment." *Foreign Affairs* 55 (July 1977): 873–87.

———. "The Corporatist Synthesis: A Skeptical View." *Diplomatic History* 10 (Fall 1986): 357–62.

———. "The Emerging Post-Revisionist Synthesis on the Origins of the Cold War." *Diplomatic History* 7 (Summer 1983): 171–90.

Gelber, H. G. "Der Morgenthau-Plan." *Vierteljahrshefte für Zeitgeschichte* 13 (1965): 372–405.

Gershman, Carl. "The Rise and Fall of the New Foreign Policy Establishment." *Commentary* 70 (July 1980): 13–24.

Gimbel, John. "Byrnes' Rede und die amerikanische Nachkriegspolitik in Deutschland." *Vierteljahrshefte für Zeitgeschichte* 20 (1972): 39–62.

Hawley, Ellis W. "The Discovery and Study of a 'Corporate Liberalism.'" *Business History Review* 52 (Fall 1978): 309–20.

Helbich, Wolfgang. "American Liberals in the League of Nations Controversy." *Public Opinion Quarterly* 31.4 (1967): 568–96.

Herring, George C., Jr. "Lend-Lease to Russia and the Origins of the Cold War, 1944–1945." *Journal of American History* 56 (June 1969): 97–105.

Hitchens, Harold. "Influences on the Congressional Decision to Pass the Marshall Plan." *The Western Political Quarterly* 21.1 (1968): 51–68.

Hodgson, Godfrey. "The Establishment." *Foreign Policy* 10 (Spring 1973): 3–40.

Hogan, Michael J. "Corporatism: A Positive Appraisal." *Diplomatic History* 10 (Fall 1986): 363–72.

———. "Corporatism." *Journal of American History* 77 (June 1990): 153–68.

———. "Revival and Reform: America's Twentieth-Century Search for a New Economic Order Abroad." *Diplomatic History* 8 (Fall 1984): 287–310.

Horowitz, David, and David Kolodney. "The Foundations (Charity Begins at Home)." *Ramparts* 7 (April 1968): 38–48.

Howard, Toni. "Berlin Circuit: MG's Guided Tour for Congressmen." *Newsweek*, 13 October 1947, 20.

Huck, Susan M. L. "The CFR in the Armed Forces: Lost Valor." *American Opinion* 20 (October 1977): 1–14.

———. "Vietnam in El Salvador." *The Review of the News* 19 (30 March 1983): 49–60.

Hyland, William G. "Foreign Affairs at 70." *Foreign Affairs* 71 (Fall 1992): 171–93.

Jackson, Scott. "Prologue to the Marshall Plan: The Origins of the American Commitment for a European Recovery Program." *Journal of American History* 65 (March 1979): 1043–68.

Jakab, Elisabeth. "The Council on Foreign Relations." *Book Forum* 3.4 (1978): 418–72.

Jones, Howard, and Randall B. Woods. "Origins of the Cold War in Europe and the Near East: Recent Historiography and the National Security Imperative." *Diplomatic History* 17 (Spring 1993): 251–76.

Judis, John B. "Twilight of the Gods: The Rise and Fall of the American Establishment." *Wilson Quarterly* 15 (Autumn 1991): 43–55.

Kennan, George F. "Sources of Soviet Conduct." *Foreign Affairs* 25 (July 1947): 566–82.

Kimball, Warren F. "Response to John Lewis Gaddis, 'The Emerging Post-Revisionist Synthesis on the Origins of the Cold War,'" *Diplomatic History* 7 (Summer 1983): 198–200.

Kindleberger, Charles P. "The Marshall Plan and the Cold War." *International Journal* 23 (Summer 1968): 369–82.

Kirchwey, Freda. "Marketing the Plan." *The Nation*, 28 June 1947, 758–59.

Kraft, Joseph. "School for Statesmen." *Harper's*, July 1958, 64–68.

LaFeber, Walter. "'Ah, If We Had Studied It More Carefully:' The Fortunes of American Diplomatic History." *Prologue* 11 (Summer 1979): 121–31.

Lee, Robert W. "Confirming the 'Liberal' Establishment." *American Opinion* 24 (March 1981): 27–32.

Linz, Susan J. "Foreign Aid and Soviet Postwar Recovery," *Journal of Economic History* 45 (December 1985): 947–54.

Lukas, J. Anthony. "The Council on Foreign Relations — Is it a Club? Seminar? Presidium? 'Invisible Government'?" *New York Times Magazine*, 21 November 1971, 34, 123–132, 142.

Lundestad, Geir. "Empire by Invitation? The United States and Western Europe, 1945—1952." Paper at the Salzburg conference "Reconstruction and the Restoration of Democracy: U.S.-European Relations, 1945–1952," 16 to 17 April 1983.

McCormick, Thomas J. "Corporatism: A Reply to Rossi." *Radical History Review* 33 (1985): 53–59.

____. "Drift or Mastery? A Corporate Synthesis for American Diplomatic History." *Reviews in American History* 20 (December 1982): 318–30.

____. "Toward a New Diplomatic History: Social History, Revisionism, and the Corporatist Synthesis." Colloquium Paper, 22 June 1981, Woodrow Wilson International Center for Scholars.

McLean, David. "American Nationalism, the China Myth, and the Truman Doctrine: The Origins of Accommodation with Peking, 1949–50." *Diplomatic History* 10 (Winter 1986): 25–42.

Maier, Charles. "The Two Postwar Eras and the Conditions for Stability in Twentieth-Century Western Europe." *American Historical Review* 86 (April 1981): 327–67.

____. "Marking Time: The Historiography of International Relations." In: *The Past Before Us: Contemporary Historical Writing in the United States.* Michael Kammen, ed., 355–87. Ithaca, NY, 1980.

Mallalieu, William C. "The Origins of the Marshall Plan: A Study in Policy Formation and National Leadership." *Political Science Quarterly* 73 (December 1958): 481–504.

Messer, Robert L. "Paths Not Taken: The United States Department of State and Alternatives to Containment, 1945–1946." *Diplomatic History* 1 (Fall 1977): 297–319.

Masland, John W. "The 'Peace' Groups Join Battle." *Public Opinion Quarterly* 4.4 (1940): 664–73.

____. "Pressure Groups and American Foreign Policy." *Public Opinion Quarterly* 6.1 (1942): 115–22.

Miller, Helen Hill. "Congress and European Recovery." *Virginia Quarterly Review* 25 (1949): 48–59.

Miller, James E. "Taking Off the Gloves: The United States and the Italian Election of 1948." *Diplomatic History* 7 (Winter 1983): 35–55.

Morgan, Roger. "'To Advance the Science of International Politics ...:' Chatham House's Early Research." *International Affairs* (London) 55 (April 1979): 240–51.

Nagorski, Zygmunt. "A Member of the CFR Talks Back." *National Review* 29 (9 December 1977): 1416–19.

Neuman, William L. "How to Merchandise Foreign Policy: I. British Loan and Greek Turkish Aid." *American Perspective* 3 (October 1949): 183–93.

———. "How to Merchandise Foreign Policy: II. From ERP to MAP." *American Perspective* 3 (September 1949): 235–50.

O'Connor, Raymond G. "Thomas A. Bailey: His Impact." *Diplomatic History* 9 (Fall 1985): 303–309

Oldendick, Robert W., and Barbara Ann Bardes. "Mass and Elite Foreign Policy Opinions." *Public Opinion Quarterly* 46.3 (1982): 368–62.

Oliver, Revilo P. "To See the Invisible." *American Opinion* 5 (October 1962): 43–61.

"The Origins of the Cold War: A Symposium." *Diplomatic History* 17 (Spring 1993): 251–310.

Ovinnikov, R. "U.S. Foreign Policy 'General Staff.'" *International Affairs* (Moscow), November 1979, 62–71.

Pach, Chester J., Jr. "The Containment of Military Aid to Latin America, 1944–1949." *Diplomatic History* 6 (Summer 1982): 225–43.

Pasmovsky, Eugene, and Carl Gilbert. "Bilderberg: The Cold War International." In: "Extension of Remarks: Hon. John R. Raick of Louisiana, 15 September 1971." *Congressional Record* 117: 32051–60.

Paterson, Thomas G. "The Quest for Peace and Prosperity: International Trade, Communism, and the Marshall Plan." In: *Politics and Policies of the Truman Administration.* Barton J. Bernstein, ed., 78–112. Chicago, 1970.

———. "Foreign Aid under Wraps: The Point Four Program." *Wisconsin Magazine of History* 56 (Winter 1972/73): 119–26.

Quade, Quentin L. "The Truman Administration and the Separation of Powers: The Case of the Marshall Plan." *The Review of Politics* 27 (January 1965): 58–77.

Resis, Albert. "The Churchill-Stalin 'Percentages' Agreement on the Balkans, Moscow, October 1944." *American Historical Review* 83 (April 1978): 368–87.

Reston, James. "The Gentlemen from the Tenth Street." *New York Times,* 20 October 1970.

Roberts, Priscilla M. "The American 'Eastern Establishment' and Foreign Affairs: A Challenge to Historians." Part I, SHAFR *Newsletter* 14 (December 1983): 9–28; Part II, SHAFR *Newsletter* 15 (March 1984): 8–19.

Rosenberg, David A. "American Atomic Strategy and the Hydrogen Bomb Decision." *Journal of American History* 66 (June 1979): 62–87.

Rovere, Richard H. "The American Establishment." *Esquire,* May 1962, 106–108, 155–58.

———. "Notes on the Establishment in America." *The American Scholar* 30 (Fall 1961): 489–95.

———. "Postscript: A 1978 Commentary." *The Wilson Quarterly* 2 (Summer 1978): 182–84.

Sanford, William F. "The Marshall Plan: Origins and Implementations." U.S. Department of State *Bulletin* 82 (June 1982): 17–33.

Schaller, Michael. "MacArthur's Japan: The View From Washington." *Diplomatic History* 10 (Winter 1986): 1–23.

____. "Securing the Great Crescent: Occupied Japan and the Origins of Containment in Southeast Asia." *Journal of American History* 69 (September 1982): 392–414.

Schmitter, Philippe C. "Still the Century of Corporatism?" In: *The New Corporatism.* South Bend, IN, 1974.

Schulzinger, Robert D. "Whatever Happened to the Council on Foreign Relations?" *Diplomatic History* 5 (Winter 1981): 277–90.

Seabury, Paul. "George Kennan vs. Mr. 'X'." *New Republic*, 16 December 1981, 17–20.

Shepard, Susan. "Foreign Policy Think Tanks: A Critical Guide." *Book Forum* 5.4 (1979): 462–96.

Shoup, Laurence H., and William Minter, "The Council on Foreign Relations and American Policy in Southeast Asia," *The Insurgent Sociologist* 7 (Winter 1977): 19–30

Siracusa, John L. "Will the Real Author of the Cold War Please Stand Up?" SHAFR *Newsletter* 13 (September 1982): 9–11.

____. "Will the Real Author of Containment Please Stand up: The Strange Case of George Kennan and Frank Roberts." SHAFR *Newsletter* 22 (September 1991): 1–27.

Smith, Richard M. "Arm Twister, Stylist, Gentleman — Ham Armstrong." *Newsweek*, 2 October 1972, 40.

"The Soviet Side of the Cold War: A Symposium." *Diplomatic History* 15 (Fall 1991): 523–63.

Stang, Alan. "The Reagan Administration and the CFR." *American Opinion* 25 (April 1982): 17–22.

Stimson, Henry L. "The Decision to Use the Atomic Bomb." *Harper's*, February 1947, 97–107.

Stromberg, Roland N. "American Business Goes to War." In: *The Shaping of American Diplomacy*, Vol. 2. William A. Williams, ed., 789–797. Chicago, 1956.

"Symposium: Responses to Charles S. Maier, 'Marking Time: The Historiography of International Relations.'" *Diplomatic History* 5 (Fall 1981): 353–82.

Turner, Henry A. "How Pressure Groups Operate." *Annals of the American Academy of Political and Social Science* 319 (September 1958): 63–72.

Wala, Michael. "Advocating Belligerency: Organized Internationalism 1939–1941." *Amerikastudien/American Studies* 38 (Spring 1993): 49–59.

____. "Dwight D. Eisenhower at the Council on Foreign Relations." *Reexamining the Eisenhower Presidency*, Shirley A. Warshaw, ed., 1–15. Westport, CT, 1993.

____. "Selling the Marshall Plan at Home: The Committee for the Marshall Plan to Aid European Recovery." *Diplomatic History* 10 (Summer 1986): 247–65.

____. "Selling War and Selling Peace: The Non-Partisan Committee for Peace, the Committee to Defend America and the Committee for the Marshall Plan." *Amerikastudien/American Studies* 30 (1985): 91–105.

Walker, J. Samuel. "The Decision to Use the Bomb: A Historiographical Update." *Diplomatic History* 14 (Winter 1990): 97–114.

____. "Historians and the Cold War Origins: The New Consensus." In: *American Foreign Relations: A Historiographical Review.* Gerald K. Haines and J. Samuel Walker, eds., 207–236. Westport, CT, 1981.

Wallace, Henry A. "My Alternative for the Marshall Plan." *New Republic*, 12 June 1948, 13–14.

Westin, Alan F. "The John Birch Society: Fundamentalism on the Right." In: *Pressure Groups in American Politics.* H.R. Mahood, ed., 205–24. New York, 1967. Reprint from *Commentary* 32 (August 1961): 93–104.

Widenor, William C. "American Planning for the United Nations: Have We Been Asking the Right Questions?" *Diplomatic History* 6 (Summer 1982): 245–65.

____. "The Role of Electoral Politics in American Foreign Policy Formation: Are Historians Meeting the Conceptual Challenge?" SHAFR *Newsletter* 16 (December 1985): 3–29.

Wilson, Theodore A., and Richard D. McKinzie. "The Food Crusade of 1947." *Prologue* 3 (Winter 1971): 136–52.

Wittkopf, Eugene R., and Michael A. Maggiotto. "Elites and Masses: A Comparative Analysis of Attitudes Toward America's World Role." *Journal of Politics* 45 (May 1983): 303–34.

Wright, C. Ben. "Mr. 'X' Containment." *Slavic Review* 25 (March 1976): 1–31.

Wrigley, Gladys M. "Isaiah Bowman." *Geographical Review* 41 (January 1951): 7–65.

"Writing the History of U.S. Foreign Relations: A Symposium." *Diplomatic History* 14 (Fall 1990): 553–605.

Young, Kimball. "Content Analysis of the Treatment of the Marshall Plan in Certain Representative American Newspapers." *The Journal of Social Psychology* 33 (1951): 164–81.

Magazines and Newspapers

- *Business Week*, 1945–1950
- *The Christian Century*, 1940
- *Commercial and Financial Chronicle*, 1945-1950
- *Foreign Affairs*, 1922—1993
- *New York Times*, 1939–1941, 1945–1950
- *Newsweek*, 1945–1950
- *Time*, 1945–1950
- *U.S. News*, 1945–1950
- *Wall Street Journal*, 1945–1950
- *Washington Post*, 1945–1950

Oral Histories, Interviews and Correspondence

Bissell, Richard M., Jr., to Michael Wala, 5 February 1992.

Bohlen, Charles E.; John F. Dulles Oral History Collection, Mudd Manuscript Library, Princeton, NJ (in the following abbreviated as "OH-ML").

Brundage, Percival F.; OH-ML.

Clay, Lucius D.; OH-ML

Diebold, William, Jr., to Michael Wala, various letters.

Diebold, William, Jr., Interviews: 17 September 1985; 20 September 1988; 23 August 1990; 2 October 1990, 16 October 1990.

Dulles, Allen W.; OH-ML.

Geiger, Theodore, to Michael Wala, 8 January 1992.

Kennan, George F., to Michael Wala, 24 October 1986; 19 December 1991.

Kindleberger, Charles P; Oral History Interviews, Harry S. Truman Library, Independence, MO (in the following abbreviated as "OH-TL").

Kindleberger, Charles P., to Michael Wala, 1 October 1985.

Kirk, Grayson, to Michael Wala, 1 October 1990; 17 December 1991.

Lindsay, Franklin, to Michael Wala, 15 December 1991.

Lovett, Robert M.; OH-TL.

Russell, Francis H.; OH-TL.

Thorp, Willard L.; OH-TL.

Stein, Harold, Interview; Harry B. Price Interview Project, Truman Library.

Wriston, Henry B.; Columbia University Oral History Interview, Butler Library, Columbia University, New York.

INDEX